TEACH YOURSELF...

VISUAL C++ 4.0

TEACH YOURSELF...
VISUAL C++ 4.0

David A. Holzgang

A Subsidiary of
Henry Holt and Co., Inc.

Trademarks

Throughout this book, trademarked names are used. Rather than put a trademark symbol after every occurrence of a trademarked name, we used the names in an editorial fashion only, and to the benefit of the trademark owner, with no intention of infringement of the trademark. Where such designations appear in this book, they have been printed with initial caps.

Associate Publisher: Paul Farrell

Managing Editor: Cary Sullivan

Development Editor: Jono Hardjowirogo

Copy Edit Manager: Shari Chappell

Technical Editor: Jim Cohn

Copy Editor: Karen Tongish

Production Editor: Joe McPartland

CONTENTS

Chapter 5: Drawing in Documents........................... 115

Chapter 6: Understanding Object-Oriented Programming and Microsoft Foundation Classes......................... 169

CHAPTER 1

INTRODUCTION

This chapter presents an overview describes the contents, and provides an introduction to how to use the book. The chapter begins by explaining a little about Visual C++ and its working environment. Then it describes how this book is organized and gives a short summary of the contents of each chapter.

WHAT IS VISUAL C++ 4.0?

The latest version of Visual C++ is a major advance in programming tools for developing Windows programs. It is a high-performance, highly integrated development environment that allows you to create, build, and debug Windows applications faster and easier than ever before. In addition, it is now a fully functional vehicle for cross-platform development. In itself, it builds on two important concepts. First, the Visual C++ environment itself runs in Windows, so you have a full set of Windows-based tools to help you create and manage projects and applications in Windows. Second, it uses the now-famous "visual" user interface to help you handle these new tools.

PREVIEW OF THE VISUAL C++ 4.0 ENVIRONMENT

The core of the Visual C++ environment is built around three elements: the C/C++ compiler and linker; the Developer Studio; and the Microsoft Foundation Class Library. Each of these makes a vital contribution to the success of Visual C++ as a comprehensive development environment.

Developer Studio

The Developer Studio is at the center of the Visual C++ development environment. It includes a code editor that has several excellent features, such as automatic tabbing—once you tab in to place code, the next line automatically starts at the same point; this is invaluable for indenting code. It provides complete project management, allowing you to link a variety of code modules into one project, which is then handled as a unit for building your application. It contains a integrated resource editor, which allows you to create and edit all types of Windows resources, and an integrated debugger that allows you to run your application in a controlled fashion, viewing and changing data and setting breaks within your code. The latest version even allows "just-in-time" debugging, which can switch into the debugger just when an error occurs.

The Developer Studio also incorporates Microsoft's special helper tools, AppWizard and ClassWizard. These tools allow you to create and customize an application based on the Microsoft Foundation Class Library very easily. You use them to select modules from the Microsoft Foundation Class Library for your initial skeleton application and then to add new functions and classes to the skeleton. As you will see in the exercises in this book, this facility is a major benefit that helps you get the complete range of support you need without being overwhelmed by the complexity of the Microsoft Foundation Class Library.

Microsoft Foundation Class Library (MFC)

In and of itself, the programming environment provided by Visual C++ 4.0 would be a good reason to learn and using Visual C++. However, there is—believe it or not—a much better and more compelling reason: access to the Microsoft Foundation Class Library (MFC).

The MFC enables you to write Windows applications using C++ easily and quickly, compared to any other method of development that I know. The class library consists of a number of C++ classes that represent an "application framework." The classes are designed to be used together to create a working skeleton application that provides much of the user interface and functionality that users expect in a Windows application. Because the framework application uses C++ classes, it is easy for you to extend the functionality of the skeleton application by simply overriding the appropriate classes with new ones that only need to provide the new functions that you want.

The Visual C++ environment is directly linked into the MFC by the two wizards that are built into the Developer Studio: AppWizard and ClassWizard. These tools allow you to select and customize your skeleton application and add new processing capabilities that are directly tied into the current code base easily and, most importantly, safely. As you will see later in the book as you work with these tools, the wizards are an important component in getting the most out of the MFC.

BOOK PURPOSE AND ORGANIZATION

The overall purpose of this book is to teach you—or more accurately, to help you teach yourself—basic Windows application programming. For this task, it uses the Visual C++ development environment and the Microsoft Foundation Class Library to allow you to create and enhance a simple sample application.

This book is not intended to be a substitute for a complete tutorial on Windows programming. There are a lot of issues to address when you are working on development of a Windows application. In this book, you will use the MFC, which generally shields you from much of the complexity inherent in Windows application programming—that is, after all, what it was developed for. However, if you are going to develop a professional-quality application for Windows, you should be aware of and understand many of these areas. Even though the MFC shields you from them, you will find that understanding pays dividends as you do your development.

The problem here is that only so much can be covered in a single book. For that reason, this book focuses on using the Visual C++ environment and the MFC. Windows programming issues are discussed in relation to these and not in general terms. As a result, you will learn Windows programming basics in a practical fashion; for the detailed theory, you need to delve deeper in other sources. The Books OnLine library that comes with your Visual C++ has several references that will help you learn more.

What this book does have is lots of example code with detailed explanations both of how to generate and edit the code and of what the code does. As you work the examples, you will see how a typical Windows application is put together, how it uses C++ classes and inheritance, and how the MFC have constructed it to allow you to add your own code to make it do whatever task you have in mind.

Objectives

This broad objective—to help you teach yourself Windows programming—is clearly too expansive to help actually organize and guide selection of material for a book like this. Therefore, four more specific objectives have been preeminent in helping design and orient this book.

The first objective is to make it easy for you to use the Developer Studio and the other Visual C++ tools. The intention here is that by the end of the book you should be able to work on any size or type of project in the Developer Studio with ease. This means that you should not have to use reference materials to look up anything other than, say, setting certain compiler or linker options, or other topics that are not a regular part of working with Visual C++.

The second objective is to show you how to use the MFC. Since the MFC forms the basis for most work within the Developer Studio, you want to be quite familiar with how to access and use it, taking advantage of tools, such as AppWizard and ClassWizard, that allow you to integrate it into your application.

The third objective is related to the second but is somewhat different. When you are finished with this book, you should be familiar with the basic classes that form the backbone of the MFC. The complete MFC spans an enormous range of classes and functions. A real mastery of this broad and powerful combination will require some time for you to acquire, and it will entail working with several Windows applications. However, in the space of this book, I do believe that you can become familiar with the classes that make up an integral part of all Windows applications, and that will most likely appear in any application that you create.

Finally, this book is designed to help you learn about the organization and structure of a typical Windows application. The MFC will build such an application for you with a few clicks of the mouse; but you need to understand how it is constructed and why it is organized in a specific manner. Otherwise, like a pilot who only knows how to work the autopilot, you risk getting into a situation where your application does not function properly, but you don't know why it doesn't work and you don't know how to fix it.

Obviously, these specific objectives are so closely related and intertwined that each supports and makes use of the others. Like any good text, this book does not distinguish each objective but instead tries to teach each of them together. In this way, you will learn Visual C++, the MFC, and Windows programming in a unified way.

Requirements

What do you need to get the most out of this book? Requirements fall into two categories: physical and mental—or "hardware" and "software," if you prefer. Let's start with the physical requirements. You need to have an operating copy of Visual C++. If you haven't yet installed it on your system, that's all right, since you will read here about some of the installation considerations. If you have installed, that's fine as well. You can simply skip to learning about the Developer Studio and the first exercises. Everything else that you need is here in this book, or on the Visual C++ CD-ROM, or is a normal part of the Windows environment.

On the mental side, you need to have at least some familiarity with the C language. You need basic programming knowledge, and you need to be able to read and understand C code. Finally, you also need a reasonable familiarity with Window NT operations: you need to understand how to find files, for example, and how to access Help when you need it.

Except for the C language, this book covers all the rest of the information essential to creating and modifying a standard Windows application. It doesn't get off into the more advanced realms of creating DLLs or Visual Controls but sticks to the basic work you need to do to create a typical Windows application and its user interface.

This book doesn't teach C++, but it does explain the most essential C++ concepts. In that way, if you don't know C++, you should still be able to work through the examples and understand the code. However, C++ is a rich and varied language; I strongly recommend that you work through a good tutorial on the language before trying to do much programming with Visual C++ and the MFC. (A recommendation would be *Teach yourself... C++, 3rd Edition*, Al Stevens, MIS:Press.) Many C++ concepts are at the core of how the MFC work and handle items, and a good understanding of C++ will help you as you are working in the MFC.

Organization

This book is organized as a series of lectures and exercises. The intention is that you will be able to immediately work with each new concept and function as you learn about it. To help you see the progressive nature of Windows development, one application is used as an example throughout the book. This will help you understand how real Windows applications are built and how to grow a complete and sophisticated application from the ground up.

There is a method here. The development of this application grows naturally out of an increasing understanding and ability to use the Visual C++ tools and the MFC. Many developers will tell you, and quite rightly, that you should thoroughly understand how your application will work before starting coding; however, the reality is that most of us, even professional developers like myself, have only a general notion about what we want when we start. Even with a detailed design, you will often find that you need to go into an area or in a direction that you didn't expect when you started. The process that you will follow here mimics, as best I could, the actual process of creating a simple Windows application.

The good news in all this is that by using the MFC and Visual C++, you have more flexibility than ever before to modify and adjust your application as you work. The exercises here will show you how you can use these tools to make changing and maintaining your application easier and safer.

Notation

This book uses what has become fairly standard typographic conventions to help you identify specific items:

`int i = x + y;`	Text that is in a monospaced font is code or a code fragment such as a function name, a variable name, or a defined constant.
<u>F</u>ile	When a single letter is underlined in the text, this represents the access key for the named item. This is primarily done to help you match the text to your display screen; you should never use these keys for access without verifying them on screen.
Class object	When one or more words are italicized in the text, they represent a term that is being defined for the first time.

This book also has several icons that designate text of special significance. These icons are as follows:

N O T E

This icon represents a note to you. Information in the note is of special interest or importance.

WARNING

This warning icon alerts you to a specific problem or danger you might encounter when working.

C++

The C++ icon marks out definitions and discussions of C++ terms and concepts. If you are familiar with C++, you may wish to skip the text in these icons, since it's likely to be information you already know. Because some readers may not be as familiar with C++ as others, I have tried to fill in any specific C++ concepts that are essential to understanding or using the code in the examples.

SHORTCUT

The shortcut icon gives you quick and easy ways to do some of the tasks that are presented in a longer fashion in the main text.

Chapter Summaries

Here is a brief overview of what lies ahead in this book. These chapters take you progressively from installing Visual C++ through building a complete, if basic, working Windows application using Visual C++ and the Microsoft Foundation Class Library.

- Chapter 1: Introduction. This is the chapter you are reading. It presents the overview of the book, describes the book contents, and provides an introduction to how to use the book.

- Chapter 2: Installing Visual C++. This chapter discusses installation issues such as amount of material to install, installation options, and installation requirements. It also gives a short example of how to test whether you have correctly installed Visual C++.

- Chapter 3: Using the Developer Studio. The Developer Studio is the heart of Visual C++. Before you can do any meaningful work, you must become familiar with the Developer Studio tools, settings, and options. This chapter teaches you how to set up a project and how to access the tools in the Developer Studio.

- Chapter 4: Using AppWizard. This chapter discusses AppWizard, which is the basis for creating MFC-based applications in Visual C++. This chapter also presents the standard Windows program development cycle and shows how AppWizard fits into and shortens this cycle. You will be lead through the series of steps necessary to generate a skeleton application with AppWizard.

- Chapter 5: Drawing in Documents. This chapter introduces the basics of drawing in a Windows application. It also introduces the ClassWizard, which is class generator and manager for MFC classes. In this chapter, you will add basic message processing for mouse messages and Windows messages to the demonstration application.

- Chapter 6: Understanding Object-Oriented Programming and Microsoft Foundation Classes. At this point, almost halfway through the book, you have had a good introduction into the Visual C++ environment. Before proceeding to enhance the demonstration application and make further use of the Visual C++ Wizards, you must be given a short introduction to object-oriented programming and the Microsoft Foundation Class Library. This chapter covers the basic principles of object-oriented programming on a practical level, discussing issues such as class hierarchy, keywords, and inheritance. You also learn about the MFC application framework. You will see the overall structure of the MFC and how you can use it to enhance the demonstration application.

- Chapter 7: Views and Documents. The basis of most Visual C++ programming is centered around views and documents. This chapter describes how views and documents interact and how you can modify each layer to get the desired functionality. As an example, you will add scrolling to the demonstration application.

- Chapter 8: Exceptions and Debugging. Debugging is a fact of life for any programmer. Visual C++ provides outstanding tools for avoiding errors in the first place and finding any that slip through. This chapter discusses in detail how to debug and trace problems in a Visual C++ application using the demonstration application.

- Chapter 9: Using Resources. Visual C++ comes with an integrated resource editor and interface to resource handling. In earlier versions of Visual C++ (through version 1.51), this was a separate but integrated application called App Studio. In Visual C++ 4.0, it is completely integrated into the Developer Studio, in this chapter you will learn how to add resources to the project file by creating them in the resource editor. It also discusses and illustrates the major basic types of resources.

- Chapter 10: Controls and Messages. This chapter shows how to use resource controls in your application and how to link them to messages to get your application to respond correctly. As an example, you add dialog-box processing to the demonstration application.

- Chapter 11: Measurement and Presentation. This chapter discusses the tools provided by Visual C++ and the Application Framework for providing device-independent drawing. You will add classes to the demonstration application to change measurement systems to a device-independent mode. The chapter also covers adding new printing functions that rely on device-independent measurement.

- Chapter 12: Enhancing Your Application. This chapter covers a variety of enhancements that you will want to make to most applications. It shows how to save and retrieve persistent information for your application. It shows you how to create a split window so that you can view more than one section of a document in a window. And it shows how to use the new Component Gallery to add new functionality, such as a status bar display, to your application.

CHAPTER 2

INSTALLING VISUAL C++

This chapter covers installation issues such as amount of material to install, installation options, and installation requirements. It will also give a short example of how to test whether you have correctly installed Visual C++.

Important topics in this chapter include:

- contents of the Visual C++ distribution CD-ROMs
- hardware and software requirements to install Visual C++ versions
- installation procedures for Visual C++ 4.0
- installation options for Visual C++ components
- customization and removal procedures for Visual C++
- testing Visual C++ installation

CONTENTS

Visual C++ 4.0 comes on two CD-ROM disks that contain the materials to install all the Visual C++ components. One disk contains the Visual C++ 4.0 components, and the other contains Visual C++ 1.52.

Why Visual C++ 1.52?

Actually, this is a bit of a trick question. You have to use Visual C++ 1.52 for developing 16-bit applications; and you cannot install Visual C++ 4.0 if you are not running a 32-bit operating system such as Windows NT or Windows 95. So you need Visual C++ 1.52 when you are not currently running a 32-bit operating system—in other words, if you're still running Windows 3.1 or Windows for Workgroups 3.11—or if you want to develop 16-bit native applications to run under these operating systems.

Visual C++ 4.0 is a development environment that is designed to create 32-bit applications that will run under Window NT 3.5 or later and the Windows 95 operating systems. As such, it is itself a 32-bit application. If you are not running Windows NT 3.5 or Windows 95 you will not be able to install Visual C++ 4.0. In that case, you will have to install Visual C++ 1.52, which is a 16-bit version of the development environment.

Although you cannot install Visual C++ 4.0 under a 16-bit operating system such as Windows 3.1, you can install Visual C++ 1.52 under Windows NT 3.5. If you do so, you will run it in the Windows-compatibility mode (WOW). You may choose to do this for two reasons. First, if you are developing 16-bit applications, either alone or in conjunction with 32-bit applications, you must do so in Visual C++ 1.52; this is the only development environment that will produce 16-bit applications. Second, you may choose to use Windows NT as a development platform because it is more robust and secure than Windows 3.1 or other 16-bit operating systems. The major drawback to this approach is the large amounts of disk space required for each environment.

As you read this chapter, therefore, keep in mind that the Visual C++ 4.0 options and tools will be available only if you are running a 32-bit operating system.

N O T E

These days, everyone seems to be running a 32-bit operating system, such as Windows NT or Windows 95. Because of this, I have restricted my screen shots and other descriptions to Windows NT. This is a very common development platform, and in my experience, one that is both stable and forgiving. In any case, all of the description provided here for both installation and customization is based on running in Windows NT 3.51. If you are running Windows 95, the procedure will be the same, although the displays may look slightly different.

Starting the Visual C++ 4.0 Installation

To begin installation of the 4.0 version of Visual C++, run the program SETUP.EXE located in the root directory of the Visual C++ 4.0 CD-ROM drive. This displays the initial Master Setup dialog box shown in Figure 2.1.

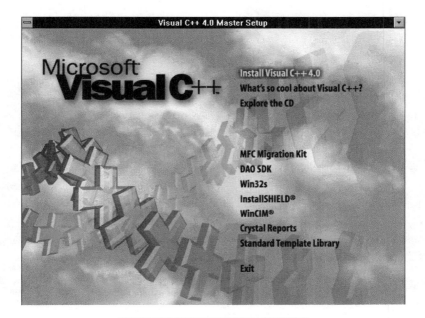

FIGURE 2.1 THE MASTER SETUP DIALOG BOX.

As you can see, in addition to allowing you to install Visual C++ 4.0, this dialog box gives you access to many additional features and applications included on the CD.

Although many of these additional features, such as the Crystal Reports generator, Win32s, the Standard Template Library, and CompuServe facilities (WinCIM) are valuable and interesting, they are not the focus of this book. We will not discuss them any further here or cover how to use or install them. If you want to use these, check the on-line documentation that comes on the Visual C++ CD for further information.

REQUIREMENTS

The requirements for installation of Visual C++ from the CD vary, depending on two things: the operating system that you are running, and the options that you choose at installation time. As you might expect, the requirements for running Visual C++ 4.0 are more exacting than those for Visual C++ 1.52.

Visual C++ 4.0

These are the minimum requirements to install Visual C++ 4.0 on your system.

- An IBM personal computer or 100% compatible running a 80486 or better processor (Pentium recommended)
- A VGA or better display system (SVGA recommended)
- 16 MB of available memory (20 MB recommended)
- A CD-ROM drive compatible with your operating system
- Microsoft mouse or compatible pointing device
- Microsoft Windows NT 3.51 or later, or Windows 95
- A hard disk drive with sufficient room to install the options that you choose. You must have 15 MB of hard disk space for the installation that uses the least amount of the disk

The amounts of memory given here are Microsoft's minimum and recommended amounts. For the combination of Visual C++ and Windows NT, they are, in my experience, not adequate for any actual work. For acceptable performance, you will require at least a 486 processor running at a high speed (100 mhz) and you should seriously consider adding additional memory. 32 MB of memory and a Pentium processor are a good development system. The speed difference in compiling and linking is very substantial. In this case, take the minimums given here as what Microsoft has been able to squeeze the system into, not as any useful configuration. If you are going to do any productive work in Visual C++, you will need at least Microsoft's "recommended" system, but a more substantial system will serve you even better.

The disk requirement for installation of Visual C++ 4.0 are as follows:

- Typical installation: 82441 KB
- Minimum installation: 46758 KB
- CD-ROM installation: 16204 KB
- Custom installation per item selected:
    - Microsoft Developer Studio: 18240 KB
    - Microsoft Visual C++ Build Tools: 12384 KB

- OLE Controls: 4240 KB
- Run-time Libraries: 21104 KB(recommended set)
- Microsoft Foundation Classes: 52544 KB (recommended set)
- Database Options: 1808 KB(recommended set)
- Tools: 5744 KB(recommended set)
- Books Online: 0 KB(recommended set)

For the entries listed here with a recommended set, you can choose other installation options that may increase or decrease the space requirements. In particular, the recommendation is to keep all of the Books Online data on the CD. The full Books Online installation takes 91824 KB on your hard drive.

Remember that these are the amounts required for the Visual C++ package that I have; they may change in later releases. Also note that installation requires about 20488 KB on your system drive in addition to the space listed here. (The numbers here assume that you will be installing Visual C++ on a different drive or partition from your system drive.) However, these numbers should give you some idea of the amount of space required for you to use Visual C++ on your system.

Note that much of this material, such as the Books Online files may not be directly relevant to your everyday work. If you are short of working disk space— and who isn't?—you can choose to follow the recommendation and leave some or all of this material on the CD and access it only from there. This will take longer when you want to access the material and will require that you have the CD in your drive, but it will save disk space. The Typical Installation process does exactly this, leaving most of the help files to be accessed from the CD. The CD-ROM installation takes this to the extreme, leaving most of the tools, compilers, and libraries on the CD as well as the samples and help files. Only the Visual C++ Development Environment and a few other essential items are on the hard disk. All other materials are accessed from the CD drive. In that case, having the CD on line at all times during use of Visual C++ is essential. The minimum installation is a compromise position, since it installs the Development Environment, the MFC files, and basic tools and libraries for 32-bit development onto your hard disk and leaves the compiler on the CD as well as the samples and help files. As in the CD-ROM installation case, having the CD on-line at all times during use of Visual C++ is essential with this installation option.

WARNING

Whenever you leave the sample files on CD, you should be prepared to move some or all of these files to a working directory on your hard disk if you want to use the samples. Remember that a CD is a read-only device; for that reason, if you try to load a sample project from the CD, you will receive a warning that you cannot save any changes. The best way around this is to create a directory structure on your hard disk—using File Manager, for example—that mimics the structure on the CD. Then you can simply copy the files that you want to use—and only those files—to the hard disk when you are working with the sample code.

There is one additional point. If you are developing 32-bit applications, that you wish to run on 16-bit machines or operating systems, you will need to have either a separate computer or a dual-boot setup (where you can, at your option, boot from either Windows NT or Windows 3.1) and you will have to install Win32s on the 16-bit system. The best arrangement for this is to have a separate computer and to install the Win32s libraries on that computer. To do this, you either need to have a CD-ROM drive on that computer, or you need access to a compatible CD-ROM drive on your network. These DLLs require Microsoft Windows 3.1 or Windows for Workgroups 3.1 or later and MS-DOS 5.0 or later.

Visual C++ 1.52

These are the minimum requirements to install Visual C++ 1.52 on your system:

- An IBM personal computer or 100% compatible running a 80386 or better processor

- A VGA or better display system

- 4 MB of available memory (8 MB recommended): if you are running Windows NT, you will require at least 16 MB

- A CD-ROM drive compatible with your operating system

- Microsoft Windows 3.1 running in enhanced mode; Windows for Workgroups 3.1 or later, or Windows NT (Visual C++ provides command-line access to some utilities and functions, but Windows is required for the installation process.)

- A hard disk drive with sufficient room to install the options you choose; 13 MB of hard disk space is required for the minimum installation.

The amount of memory given here is Microsoft's minimum and recommended amounts. They are, in my experience, absolute bare-bones minimums. For acceptable performance, you will require at least 16 MB of memory. The speed difference in compiling and linking is very substantial. Also, if you have only a limited amount of disk space, you should look into setting up a permanent Windows swap file. Lack of working space for Windows can also slow down your performance significantly. I have seen several serious complaints in network forums about the performance of Visual C++; all have been traced to inadequate system resources. So take these minimums as exactly that: the absolute least that you must have to run—not work productively—in Visual C++ 1.52.

The disk requirements for installation of Visual C++ 1.52 are as follows:

- Typical installation: 72688 KB
- Minimum installation: 12400 KB
- Custom installation, per item selected:
  - MS Visual Workbench: 4864 KB
  - MS C/C++ Compiler: 6032 KB
  - Run-time Libraries: 6832 KB(recommended set)
  - Microsoft Foundation Classes: 26112 KB(recommended set)
  - Tools: 4080 KB(recommended set)
  - Online Help Files: 8560 KB(recommended set)
  - Sample Source Code: 30960 KB(recommended set)
  - MFC OLE: 2240 KB(recommended set)
  - MFC Database (ODBC): 2304 KB(recommended set)

For the entries listed here with a recommended set, you can choose other installation options that may increase or decrease the space requirements. Note in particular that you may wish to use different options for the Tools and MFC OLE if you are developing OLE Custom Controls.

Remember that these are the amounts required for the Visual C++ package that I have; they may change in later releases. Also, the amount of space required may change slightly if you split the files up over more than one volume. However, these numbers should give you some idea of the amount of space required for you to use Visual C++ on your system.

Note that much of this material, such as the Help file and Sample Source code may not be directly relevant to your everyday work. If you are short of working disk space, you can leave some or all of this material on the CD and access it only from there. This will take longer when you want to access the material and it will require that you have the CD in your drive, but, it will save disk space. The Typical Installation process does exactly this, leaving most of the help files to be accessed from the CD. The minimum installation takes it to the extreme, leaving most of the tools, compilers, and libraries on the CD as well as the samples and help files. In that case, having the CD on-line at all times during use of Visual C++ is essential. However, if you choose either of these options, see the Warning given earlier in this chapter.

INSTALLATION FOR VISUAL C++ 4.0

You begin your installation of Visual C++ 4.0 under Windows NT 3.51 by running SETUP.EXE from the CD. This will bring up the Master Setup dialog box shown earlier in Figure 2.1.

Once you are in the Master Setup dialog box, select **Install Visual C++ 4.0** from the list. Each of the dialog boxes that follow has a standard navigation mechanism that uses buttons along the bottom of the box. All are self-explanatory. The setup first displays a Welcome dialog box, followed by the License and Registration dialog boxes. To proceed past the Registration dialog box, you will need the CD registration key. This is printed on a yellow sticker on the back of your CD case. Don't lose the CD case! You will need the registration key any time you wish to install or reinstall Visual C++. Once you have filled in the Registration information, including the key, the setup application will display the Installation Options dialog box shown in Figure 2.2.

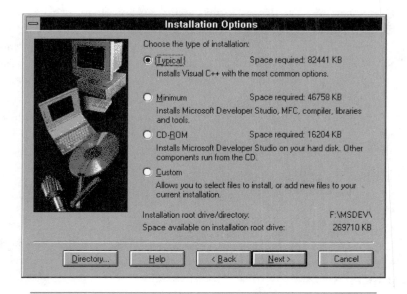

FIGURE 2.2 THE INSTALLATION OPTIONS DIALOG BOX ALLOWS YOU TO CHOOSE THE
COMPONENTS OF VISUAL C++ THAT YOU WANT TO INSTALL.

The bottom of the dialog box shows the default root directory that will be used
for installation of all your Visual C++ 2.0 files and the total space available on
that drive. If you want to alter this, press the **Directory...** button. Figure 2.3
shows you the Change Directory dialog which will be displayed.

FIGURE 2.3 THE CHANGE DIRECTORY DIALOG BOX ALLOWS YOU TO SPECIFY A NEW ROOT
DIRECTORY FOR INSTALLATION.

Visual C++ is set up so that most functions access information using a relative path structure. For this reason, you can install Visual C++ 4.0 anywhere on your disk by simply changing the placement of the root directory used for installation. The rest of the subdirectories will remain the same. Note also that some files will be placed in your Windows system directory. As it is a fixed directory, you cannot alter this.

At this point, you may choose any of the four installation options described earlier:

- Typical installation
- Minimum installation
- CD-ROM installation
- Custom installation

Typical Installation

Typical installation performs a standard, default installation with the following components installed to your hard disk:

- Microsoft Developer Studio
- Microsoft Visual C++ Build Tools
- OLE Controls
- Static and Shared Run-time Libraries
- Static and Shared Microsoft Foundation Class Libraries
- Selected Database Drivers
- Tracer and Spy Tools
- Index files for Books Online

Within these main components, the Setup program selects the most common and useful options. If you have enough disk space—a big "if"—this installation option may be good for you.

Minimum Installation

As an alternative, you should consider the minimum installation, which installs the following components on your hard disk:

- Microsoft Developer Studio
- Microsoft Visual C++ Build Tools
- Microsoft Foundation Classes
- Tools

If you are not going to be developing applications that access database information, this is a good choice. It is about half the size of the typical installation, with very little loss of speed in processing, since most commonly used tools and features are all loaded on your hard disk. If you choose this option, you will have to access all of the help files and the sample code files only from the CD, but this is a small price to pay for a large savings in disk space.

Custom Installation Options

You can use the custom installation to select what sets of components or subcomponents you want to install. Figure 2.4 shows the Custom Installation dialog box.

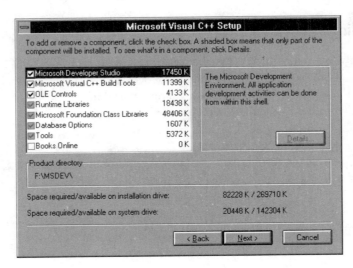

FIGURE 2.4 THE CUSTOM INSTALLATION DIALOG BOX ALLOWS YOU TO SELECT THE EXACT SET OF COMPONENTS YOU WANT TO INSTALL.

Checkboxes next to the component names indicate which components will be installed. Components with a black check in a white box will be installed in their entirety. Components with a dark gray check in a gray box will have some subcomponents of the component installed but not all. Components with no check will not be installed.

Several of the main components have subcomponent or associated information selections. When you select one of these items, the Details button on the right of the dialog box becomes active. By pressing the button, you can select specific subordinate items to the indicated main component.

The bottom of the Custom Installation dialog box displays how much room the current set of selected items will require on your disk and how much room you have on your disk. As you can see in Figure 2.4, the default selections in custom installation total exactly 82288 KB. Not surprisingly, this is very close to the amount of space required for a typical installation—in other words, the default set of custom installation selections is identical to the typical installation.

This completes the various custom installation options that you can select. You can easily move through this dialog box and alter the components that you want installed. However, I recommend that you use the typical installation if you have the room, or the minimum installation otherwise. Later, if you find you need additional libraries or tools you can add them by reinstalling Visual C++.

Reinstalling Visual C++

You can always return to the installation program by running SETUP from the CD-ROM. When you begin the installation process, be sure to choose the custom installation. Otherwise, you will spend time reinstalling portions of the system that you have already installed, which is a waste of time.

In the custom installation, select only the options you want to install. Remember that further customizations are possible for each of the individual options, so check them to ensure that you are installing only the portions of Visual C++ that you did not install previously.

RESULTS

Once you have installed Visual C++, you should run a short test to be sure that all the installed components work together correctly. You can use the following process to verify that the Visual C++ installation has functioned correctly before you proceed to the next chapter.

The best way to do this is to load, build, and run the simplest sample program, called Hello. Here is how to do this for Visual C++ 4.0.

For Visual C++ 4.0, the Hello project and source files are located in the path `msdev\samples\mfc\general\hello`. If you did not install the sample code files to your hard disk, use the File Manager to create a temporary directory for these files now and move all of the files in the hello subdirectory into your new directory. For convenience, I created a new SAMPLES\HELLO subdirectory for this under the MSDEV directory on my hard disk, but, you can use any location that seems good to you. Then:

1. Launch the Visual C++ application from your desktop.

2. Once the application is open, be sure that no files and no projects are loaded.

3. Open the file `hello.mdp` by choosing the command **Open Workspace** from the File menu. Note that you cannot use this file directly from the CD, since you will be building a new executable file that needs to be written to the project directory.

4. Select **Build** from the Build menu. This builds the executable version of the file.

5. When the build process has completed successfully, select **Execute** from the Build menu to run the Hello application. You should see a window that looks something like Figure 2.5.

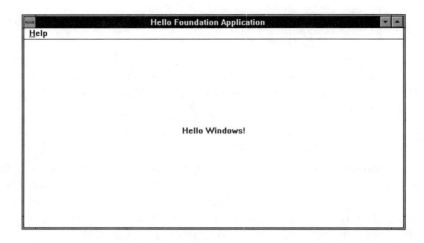

FIGURE 2.5 THE HELLO APPLICATION DISPLAYS A SIMPLE WINDOW WITH A TEXT MESSAGE.

The successful completion of this test ensures that you have installed the complete Visual C++ 2.0 system correctly and that it works as you would expect.

SUMMARY

In this chapter you have seen how to install Visual C++. It discussed the differences between Visual C++ 4.0 and Visual C++ 1.52 and how to install each version on your system. The chapter also discussed how to understand and set the installation options for each system. Finally, it showed you how to perform a quick test to ensure that the installation was successful. Now you are ready to work with the Visual C++ environment and create your first projects.

CHAPTER 3

USING THE DEVELOPER STUDIO

The Developer Studio is the heart of Visual C++. Before you can do any meaningful work, you must become familiar with the Developer Studio tools and options. This chapter will help you understand some of the Developer Studio's controls and features and allow you to use them comfortably.

Important features in this chapter are:

- how to arrange your display
- menu selections and controls
- setting options for your workbench
- how to create and control a project

DISPLAY

Let's begin our look at the Developer Studio by looking at the display itself. Figure 3.1 shows the basic default display of the Developer Studio environment when you have a project loaded and a file open for editing.

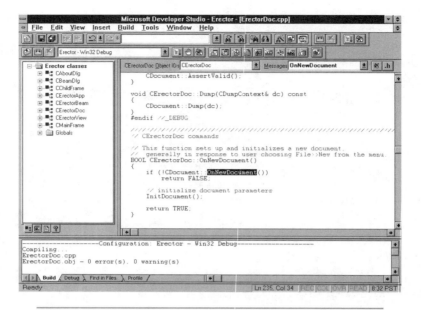

FIGURE 3.1 A TYPICAL DEVELOPER STUDIO DISPLAY WHEN WORKING ON A PROJECT.

The display consists of the following items, from the top of the display down and from left to right:

- The standard Windows title bar with the usual control boxes. This shows the name of the current project, if one is open.

- The Menu bar

- The Standard toolbar

- The Project toolbar

- On the leftside of the main display is the Project Workspace pane. It displays various types of information about the open project and the InfoViewer hierarchy of help information.

- On the right of the main display is the Source Editor pane. It displays files open for editing and any other Developer Studio windows that you activate or are activated for you.

- Beneath the top two panes is the Output pane. It displays a variety of output information from the build and debug processing, as selected by the tabs at the bottom of the pane.
- The Status bar

NOTE The Microsoft documentation is not entirely consistent when dealing with various display elements of the Developer Studio. In particular, the sections of the main window are variously referred to as *panes* or *docking windows*. I have chosen to use *pane* for any subsection of the main display. The idea here is that the entire display is one *window*, while the various segments of it are *panes*. This seems to me to be consistent and quite understandable.

The main display area of Developer Studio is divided into three panes: the Project Workspace pane, the Source Editor pane, and the Output pane. In addition, you can choose a variety of other displays while working in various stages of your project. Most of these panes share common characteristics, primarily that they are docking panes. A *docking pane* is a section of the display that can be placed against one side of the main window and will form itself to the window's size. This process is called *docking* the pane. If you wish, you can change the pane from docking mode to standard mode. In standard mode, the selected pane displays as a normal document.

You will read about several of these items in the remainder of this chapter. You will focus on the major controls and menu items that are unusual or unique to an integrated development environment, such as the Developer Studio.

Several of these items, such as the Debug and Browse menus and their related toolbars and panes, are particularly important, but they are understandable only in the appropriate context—that is, when running or debugging an application that you are developing. For that reason, complete discussion of these items will be left to the appropriate place later in the book.

Arranging and Displaying Windows

One useful feature of the Developer Studio editor is its ability to display multiple files. If you have several files open, the Window menu offers three ways to display files: on top of one another, so that only one file is displayed at one time, tiled, or cascaded. The most common display is to allow only one file to show in the edit pane at one time. The top file will then fill the pane. If you have more than one file open, you can use the Window menu to select a file name, which moves that file to the front.

Files displayed in a cascaded manner show each file window offset from the one behind it by just enough room so that you can see the title of the previous window. In this way, you can see the titles of all the windows at once, but you can work only on the window that is in front. You can rearrange the windows either by clicking on the window that you want—since you can see the title bar of each window, there is always at least that one part that you can click on—or you can use the Window menu.

If you want to work simultaneously in more than one window, you can tile the windows. Figure 3.2 shows two windows tiled horizontally and displayed full screen so you can see the contents of both windows at once.

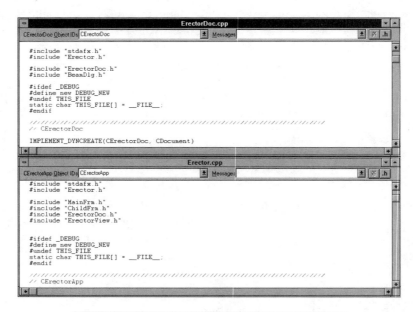

FIGURE 3.2 YOU CAN TILE WINDOWS AS WELL AS CASCADE THEM.

You can choose to tile the windows either horizontally (one on top of the other), as shown in Figure 3.2, or vertically (side by side). Tiled windows are particularly useful when you are comparing text in one file to another, or when you want to copy code from one file to another.

Notice also that each document window has its own control box. This allows you to minimize windows if you need extra room for display. Windows that are minimized do not participate in the tiling or cascading effect, so you can adjust your display for maximum utility. For example, if several files are open and you wish to tile two of them for comparison, you can minimize the other windows and then tile the remaining two to see only the files you want to work with.

Customizing Developer Studio

There is a trick, however, to getting your files displayed both full screen and tiled as shown in Figure 3.2. To get the tiling effect, you must select **Tile Horizontally** from the Window menu, and to get full-screen display, you must select **Full Screen** from the View menu. However, if you tile the edit pane before going to full screen, the two files are not expanded to fill the screen, and, if you try to go to full screen before tiling, you can't access the Window menu.

The solution to this dilemma is to use the customization procedures of the Developer Studio to assign keys to the Window menu tiling options. To do this, select **Customize...** from the Tools menu to display the Customize dialog box. In the dialog box, select the **Keyboard** tab. The result should look like Figure 3.3.

FIGURE 3.3 THE KEYBOARD TAB OF THE CUSTOMIZE DIALOG BOX ALLOWS YOU TO ADD KEYBOARD SHORTCUTS FOR MANY COMMON ACTIONS.

From this dialog box, you can add or change keyboard shortcuts for many common actions that you take in Developer Studio. The tasks are organized by type of editor and category within each editor. When you select a specific item from the Editor and Categories lists, the Commands list shows all the actions that you can map to the keyboard.

In this case, you want to add a keyboard command for the Main editor in the Window category. Commands list will display a list of Window commands, arranged alphabetically. Scroll down the Commands list to Window Tile Horizontally. Now position the cursor in the Press new shortcut key box and press the key combination you want to assign to this action—I used **Alt+Shift+H**—and then press the **Assign** button. That's all there is to it.

You may want to add some other keyboard shortcuts while you're here. In addition to Window Tile Horizontally, I have assigned shortcuts to Window Tile Vertically and View Full Screen. This allows me to do all my editing in full-screen mode with full control of tiling, without ever going back to the normal Developer Studio display until I'm done with my work in the editor.

Dismiss the dialog box by pressing the **Close** button at the bottom. When you return to the standard Developer Studio display, notice that the menu item Tile Horizontally in the Window menu now shows the new keyboard shortcut that you have assigned to it.

This dialog box also allows you to remove existing keyboard shortcuts from menu items and actions. You can completely control what keys are assigned to what actions. In this way, you can make your work most productive for your normal work habits and save yourself a lot of time and motion. You can also use the other two tabs in this dialog box to further customize your work. The Tools tab allows you to add and delete items in the Tools menu and control the parameters passed to the auxiliary tool applications listed there. You will read more about this in Chapter 8 on debugging. The Toolbar tab allows you to customize the buttons shown in the various toolbars, which you will read about later in this chapter.

Setting Developer Studio Options

The Developer Studio has powerful options that you can use to control how your personal workspace looks and operates. Using these options, you can organize your working environment to suit yourself and make you a more productive programmer. As you work with Developer Studio, you will find some things that are repetitive or that do not work well for you. When that happens, you should look at the variety of options that you control and see about reorganizing your working environment to eliminate them. This section of the chapter covers you some of the many optional controls and settings that you can modify to customize your work.

You access all the options settings by selecting **Options...** from the Tools menu. This displays the Options dialog box with a series of tabs. Figures 3.4 and 3.5 show you the displays for two of these tabs: Workspace and Directories. Each tab controls different elements of the Developer Studio and each one has a direct impact on how you work. To find out what the features of each tab are, simply select that tab and press the **Help** button. This displays the Help information for that tab, with a full description of what each selection does.

For the most part, my experience is that the default settings are quite acceptable, but you can change any of them at any time and they will then be saved and remain in effect for any other work that you do in Developer Studio. My recommendation is to work with the default settings for a while and see how you progress. After you have some experience, you can make any changes that seem appropriate.

Most of these option tabs set features that are easily understood from their description and the help information. However, there are two tabs where the Help description may not give you all the information you need. They are the **Workspace** tab and the **Directories** tab, which are discussed in the following sections.

Workspace Options

As you might expect, the Workspace tab allows you to control how features of Developer Studio are displayed in your project workspace. Figure 3.4 shows you the Workspace tab of the Options dialog box.

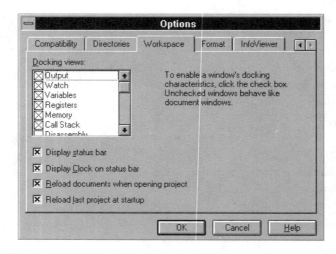

FIGURE 3.4 THE WORKSPACE TAB IN THE OPTIONS DIALOG BOX ALLOWS YOU TO CONTROL HOW PANES ARE DISPLAYED.

The checkboxes at the bottom of the dialog box are fairly simple and easily understood. However, the difference between docking and non-docking (or document) panes, controlled by checking or unchecking the Document views list, may not be clear to you. Notice from the Document views list that almost all of the panes in Developer Studio are capable of being docked, and most are docked by default.

Panes that are checked in the Document views list have docking characteristics. For example, the Output pane is checked in the list, meaning that the Output pane has docking characteristics enabled by default. This means that the pane can be placed on one edge of your workspace display and will conform itself to the display. Figure 3.5 shows the Output window docked in its default position at the bottom of the project workspace display.

Docking panes can be moved and docked at any side of the display. They can also be "torn off" from the edge of the display and turned into free-floating panes, as shown in Figure 3.6.

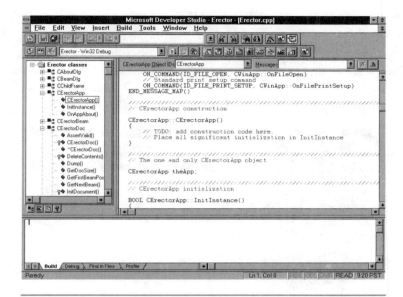

FIGURE 3.5 THE OUTPUT PANE IS DOCKED AT THE BOTTOM OF THE DISPLAY BY DEFAULT.

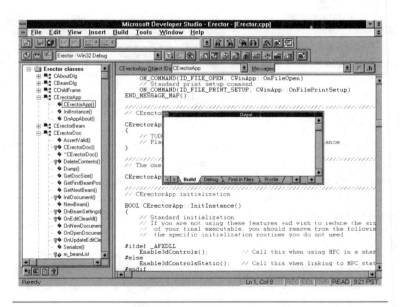

FIGURE 3.6 A PANE WITH DOCKING CHARACTERISTICS CAN ALSO BE DISPLAYED UNDOCKED.

You can tell that this is a dockable pane by its small title bar and thin frame. To redock the pane, simply move it to the side of your display where you want it to dock. It will automatically reshape itself to fit the frame.

If you remove the docking characteristics of the Output pane by unchecking the box in the Workspace Options dialog box, the Output window will display like a standard document window. Figure 3.7 shows how this looks.

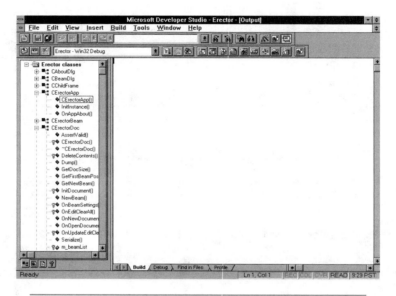

FIGURE 3.7 WITHOUT THE DOCKING CHARACTERISTIC ENABLED, PANES LOOK LIKE STANDARD DOCUMENT WINDOWS.

Overall, I think you get the best use of your display by using these panes in docked mode, which is the default. However, if you have a different display size or resolution or have other display issues, you may find that one of the other display options is more suitable. The point here is that you have complete control over all these features in Developer Studio.

Directories Options

You can also set where Developer Studio searches for files when building your project in the Directories tab. The Directories Option dialog box is shown in Figure 3.8.

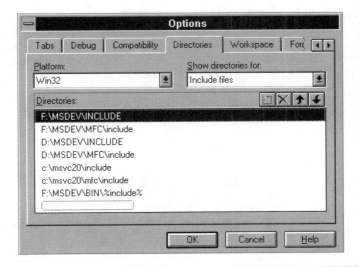

FIGURE 3.8 THE DIRECTORIES TAB ALLOWS YOU TO SET SEARCH PATHS FOR YOUR PROJECTS.

You can use this dialog box to set a series of directories that the Developer Studio will search for files. You can set the search paths separately for Include, Executable, Library, and Source files, by choosing the type of file from the Show directories for list. You can also set directories for each development platform you have installed in Visual C++. For example, if you have the Macintosh cross-development edition installed, you can choose either Win32 or Macintosh targets from the Platform list.

The main point that I want to make about the Option dialog box, however, is what isn't here. If you set it with a project open, you may think that these settings are specific to your project, but that would be incorrect. These settings are for the Developer Studio in general, and are not specific to the currently open project. That means if you have some special files—for example, some special Include files—that you need to include in a project, when you add that path to the Include directories, the path will be included for all your projects. I mention this because this type of change can cause problems in other unrelated projects if you use common names or symbols. The redefinition may cause some errors in compilation that are hard to understand and debug. Therefore, if you make changes to this list, be sure to keep good project notes or, better yet, use symbols and names that are unique to each project.

Organizing the Toolbars

The various toolbars are an optional part of the standard Developer Studio display. The toolbars provide alternative access to many common functions. You have complete control over the Developer Studio's toolbars, including the ability to modify any toolbar and to create new, customized toolbars.

The Developer Studio has eight standard toolbars. You control the display and modify these toolbars by selecting **Toolbars...** from the View menu. This displays the Toolbars dialog box shown in Figure 3.9.

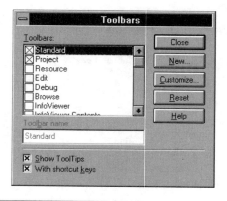

FIGURE 3.9 THE TOOLBAR DIALOG BOX GIVES YOU THE ABILITY TO CONTROL AND CUSTOMIZE YOUR TOOLBAR DISPLAY.

As you can see in Figure 3.9, there are eight toolbars, two of which, Standard and Project, are displayed by default. Actually, this is a bit misleading, as other toolbars are displayed by default at the appropriate times. For example, the Debug toolbar is displayed when you are in debugging mode. The Standard toolbar is the top toolbar in the Developer Studio window, while the Project toolbar is the one underneath it. You display a toolbar by checking the box next to its name, and you hide a toolbar by unchecking the box.

You can customize any of the toolbars simply by pressing the **Customize** button in the Toolbar dialog box. This automatically takes you to the Customize dialog box that you saw in Figure 3.3 with the Toolbar tab selected. From there, you can add, move, or delete buttons from any visible toolbar. Note that the toolbar you want to edit must be visible, so you should use the Toolbar dialog box to display the toolbar before entering the Customize dialog box.

You can also create new toolbars by using the New button. This allows you to name a new toolbar and add your own selection of buttons to it. You can also combine toolbars. For example, you may create a new toolbar and add it to the end of the Standard toolbar.

The Toolbar dialog box also allows you to control whether Tool Tips are displayed and whether shortcut keys are displayed with the tips. Tool Tips are the small notes that appear under your cursor when you place the cursor on a toolbar button. They are extremely useful, since many of the icons on the toolbar buttons may not make the function of the button immediately obvious if you aren't already familiar with it. Note, however, that similar information (minus the key shortcut) is displayed in the message area of the Status Bar at the bottom of your window if you have the Status Bar displayed.

As you can see by running the cursor over the buttons, most of these buttons have keyboard equivalents. Whether you choose to use the Toolbar or the keyboard is mostly a function of your preferred style of programming. Personally, I find using the keyboard more useful, but you should experiment and see what works best for you. There are, however, two functions that I think work best from the toolbars: setting the target application mode and Find in Files. In both cases, the menu selections are hard to get to and are much less easy to use than the toolbar. I strongly recommend that you have these two buttons available while you are programming.

I have customized my standard toolbar to remove common editing functions, such as Cut and Paste, and to include setting the target application, running the application in Debug mode, and compiling the current file. In this way, I only have to display a single toolbar to have all the functions I want available. I find these useful functions to perform from the toolbar. As you work with Developer Studio, you will find which toolbars and buttons work best for you. The important point here is to remember that you have complete control over both the content and the display of the toolbars.

The Status Bar Display

The Status bar, which is displayed along the bottom of your Developer Studio window by default, provides valuable information about the current state of the Developer Studio and your files. You can control the display of the Status bar and whether the clock is displayed, from the Workspace tab of the Options dialog box shown earlier in Figure 3.4.

The Status bar has several panes that display information about the current status of the project. The exact number of panes displayed depends on what you're doing and whether you have customized the Status bar display. When using the editor, the default panes display the following information, from left to right:

- The Help message pane displays a short help message about the selected function or a message that tells you about actions or errors that have happened.

- The Cursor Location pane shows the number of the line and of the column where you have set the insertion point. Lines and columns are numbered from 1. If you have selected a range, the number shown is the number of the line and/or column after the last selected line.

- The Macro Recorder pane displays REC if you are recording keystrokes for a macro. You enable macro recording by selecting **Record Keystrokes** from the Tools menu.

- The Column Select pane displays COL if you are in column selection mode. The column selection mode allows you to select columns, rather than lines, of text. To enter the column select mode, hold down the **Alt** key and click at the top-left corner of the text you want to select. Release the **Alt** key but continue holding the left mouse button down and drag the cursor to the bottom right corner of the text. The resulting rectangular block of text will be selected. This is the column select mode.

- The Overtype pane displays OVR if the Developer Studio editor is in overtype mode. The pane is dimmed if the editor is in insert mode (the default). You toggle this setting by pressing the **Insert** key on the keyboard.

- The Read Only pane displays READ if the current file is a read-only file. It is dimmed if the file can be edited and saved in the normal way.

- The Clock pane displays the current time if you have the clock display activated in the Workspace tab of the Options dialog box.

The line and column numbers are particularly useful when you are inserting items into your code, as they allow you to move directly to given lines, to ensure that code blocks line up, and so on.

MENU BAR

The Menu bar gives you access to all the functions in the Developer Studio. There are very few functions that are not directly accessible from the menu selections.

Here is a brief review of all of the menu selections in the Developer Studio. Many are standard commands with which you are already familiar. Some, such as the Browse and Debug menus, cover features you will read about and work with in detail later in the book. Later in this chapter, you will read in detail about handling and using Projects and the Project menu. The discussion of the menu items here is intended only as a brief overview and reference, not a comprehensive discussion.

 Many menu selections can be accessed by keyboard shortcuts. These are shown in the figures and are not discussed further in the text.

N O T E

File Menu

The File menu is shown in Figure 3.10.

```
                          Microsoft D
File   Edit   View   Insert   Build   Tools
New...                          Ctrl+N
Open...                         Ctrl+O
Close
Open Workspace...
Close Workspace
Save                           Ctrl+S
Save As...                     F12
Save All
Find in Files...
Page Setup...
Print...                       Ctrl+P
1 ErectorDoc.cpp
2 F:\MSDEV\...\ErectorDoc.cpp
3 F:\MSDEV\...\ErectorView.cpp
4 F:\MSDEV\...\Erector.rc
5 Erector
6 F:\MSDEV\...\Erector
7 F:\MSDEV\Projects\Test\Test
8 E:\TEMP\Erector\Erector
Exit
```

FIGURE 3.10 THE FILE MENU.

The File menu has the following commands:

- **New...** displays the New dialog box which allows you to create a new version of any one of several types of files.

- **Open...** displays the Open File dialog box which allows you to select a file to be opened for editing. The opened file becomes the current (front-most) file displayed in the Developer Studio.

- **Close** closes the current file you are working on. If you are not working on any file, or if your cursor is not positioned in a file that can be closed, this entry is dimmed.

- **Open Workspace...** displays the Open File dialog box, which allows you to select a workspace file (.MDP) to be opened. This closes any project workspace currently open and opens the selected project, which becomes the current project in the Developer Studio.

- **Close Workspace** closes the current project workspace. If you are not working on a project, this entry is dimmed.

- **Save** saves the current file. This entry is available only if the current file has been changed.

- **Save As...** displays the Save As dialog box, which allows you to save the current file under an new name.

- **Save All** saves all changed files that are currently open.

- **Find in Files...** displays the Find in Files dialog box which allows you to search for text in a set of files or folders. This a powerful and sophisticated searching tool, similar to the UNIX `grep` command, that allows you to find items across many files.

- **Page Setup...** displays the Page Setup dialog box, which allows you to set margins for your page and add header and footer text.

- **Print...** displays the Print dialog box, which allows you to print the current file, using the currently selected printer and print settings. If you have selected a block of text, the dialog box allows you to print only the selection.

- The next section of the File menu displays the last four files that you have opened. You may select any one of them to immediately open that file and make it the current file. Essentially, this is a quick way to access recently used files, instead of going through the Open File dialog box.

- The next section of the File menu displays the last four projects you have opened. You may select any one to immediately open that project and make it the current project workspace. Essentially, this is a quick way to access recently used projects, instead of going through the Open Workspace dialog box.

- **Exit** closes all open files and exits the Developer Studio. If any open files have changes and are not saved, it prompts you to save them.

Edit Menu

The Edit menu is shown in Figure 3.11.

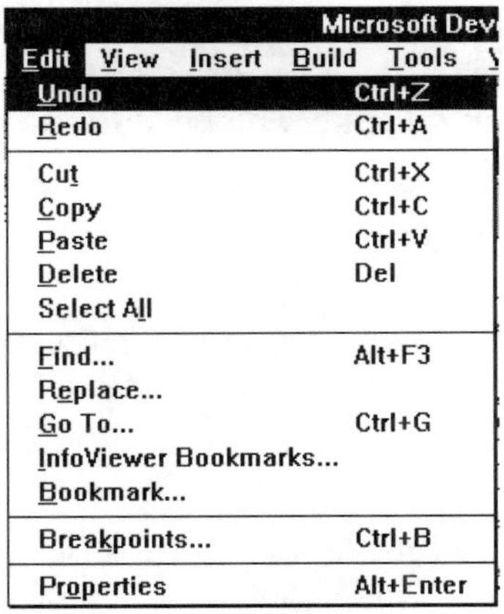

FIGURE 3.11 THE EDIT MENU.

The Edit menu has the following commands:

- **Undo** reverses the last action that you took in the editor. You can undo a series of actions; the exact number depends on the size of the Undo buffer set in the Editor Options dialog box. (See Options below.)

- **Redo** reverses the last undo that you did, in effect, restoring the previous action.

- **Cut** deletes the selected text and places it on the clipboard.

- **Copy** copies the selected text to the clipboard.

- **Paste** pastes the contents of the clipboard into the current file at the current insertion point, optionally replacing any selected text.

- **Delete** deletes the selected text. The text is lost and not placed on the clipboard, but you may undo the action using the **Undo** command.

- **Select All** selects all of the text in the currently active file.

- **Find...** displays the Find dialog box, which allows you to search the active file in either direction for a given string. If you select a text string in your current file, that string is automatically displayed as the default string to be found.

- **Replace...** displays the Replace dialog box, which allows you to find a given string in the current file and replace it with another string. The last string used in a Find operation is automatically displayed as the string to find, unless you have selected a text string in your current file, in which case that string is the default string used for the Find.

- **Go To...** displays the Go To dialog box, which allows you to go directly to any one of a number of items, such as line numbers, bookmarks, error tags, and so on.

- **InfoViewer Bookmarks...** displays the list of InfoViewer bookmarks. You can create bookmarks when reading InfoViewer material, which will automatically be placed in this list. This allows you to return to this information directly.

- **Bookmark...** displays the Bookmark dialog, which displays the list of current bookmarks in your project and allows you to create, delete, and move to a bookmark in your project.

- **Breakpoints...** displays the Breakpoints dialog box, which allows you to set or remove a breakpoint anywhere in your code. The dialog box allows you to set, disable, or remove different types of breakpoint at any location. The default location is the current insertion point.

- **Properties** displays the Properties dialog box for the selected file or item. The information in the Properties dialog box varies by what you have selected. For example, if you select a currently active text file, the Properties dialog box will tell you the complete path and file name, file size, date last modified, and other useful information for that file.

View Menu

The View menu is shown in Figure 3.12.

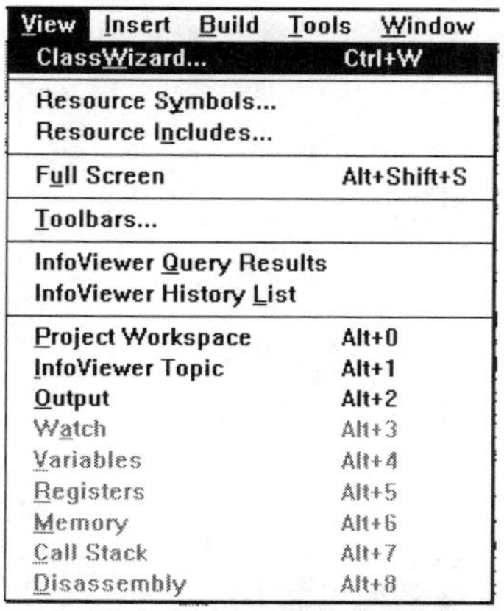

FIGURE 3.12 THE VIEW MENU.

The View menu controls what you see on the display. It has the following commands:

- **ClassWizard** takes you to the ClassWizard, which allows you to manage your classes. You will see in later chapters how to use this powerful and important feature.

- **Resource Symbols...** displays the Resource Symbols dialog box, which displays all the symbols currently defined for your project in the resource file, with the assigned value and whether the resource is in use within the project.

- **Resource Includes...** displays the Resource Includes dialog box, which shows you the header files that are included in your resource files.

- **Full Screen** toggles the edit pane to full screen display. (Note that the keyboard shortcut shown here is the one I added, as you read earlier.)

- **Toolbars...** displays the Toolbars dialog box (shown in Figure 3.9) to display or hide selected toolbars as discussed earlier.

- **InfoViewer Query Results** shows the results of the last InfoViewer query that you made.

- **InfoViewer History List** shows the last 50 InfoViewer topics that you have viewed.

- The next section of the View menu displays all the panes of the Developer Studio. You can select any available pane here to display it, if it's not already displayed, and move to it. Panes that are not currently available, such as the Debug pane when you're not running your application, are dimmed.

Insert Menu

The Insert menu is shown in Figure 3.13.

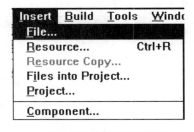

FIGURE 3.13 THE INSERT MENU.

The Insert menu allows you to insert items into your project. It has the following commands:

- **File...** allows you to select and insert an existing file into your currently active file at the current insertion point.

- **Resource...** allows you to insert a new resource into your project. You will see how to use this in Chapter 8.

- **Resource Copy...** inserts a copy of the selected resource into your application. You must change the resource language or add a condition to insert a copy of an existing resource in your project.

- **Files into Project...** displays the Insert Files into Project dialog box. This allows you to add new files to your project, which will then be included in the project's next build.

- **Project...** allows you to insert an existing project into your current project as a unit.

- **Component...** allows you to select a component from the Component Gallery to insert into your project. You will see how to use this valuable tool in Chapter 12.

Build Menu

The Build menu is shown in Figure 3.14.

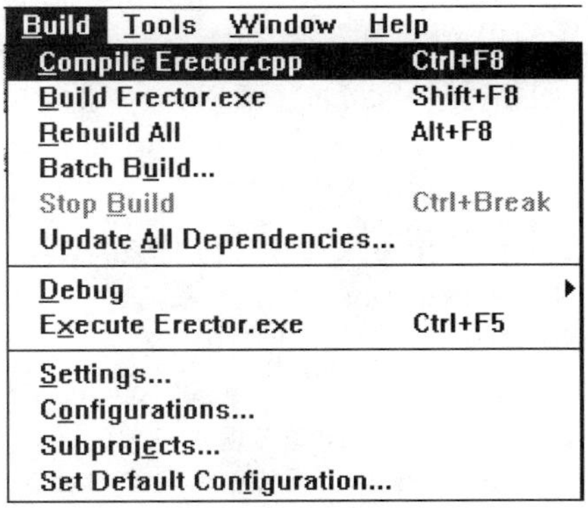

```
Build   Tools   Window   Help
  Compile Erector.cpp        Ctrl+F8
  Build Erector.exe          Shift+F8
  Rebuild All                Alt+F8
  Batch Build...
  Stop Build                 Ctrl+Break
  Update All Dependencies...

  Debug                               ▶
  Execute Erector.exe        Ctrl+F5

  Settings...
  Configurations...
  Subprojects...
  Set Default Configuration...
```

FIGURE 3.14 THE BUILD MENU.

The Build menu has the following commands:

- **Compile** *file* compiles the current file. The current file name is displayed to the right of the command.

- **Build** *application* builds the application represented by the current project. The name of the executable file that will be generated is displayed next to the command. Build compiles or links only modules that have been updated since the last time the application was created; if the application is up-to-date, you will see a dialog box telling you that the application is ready to run.

- **Rebuild All** builds all components of the current project into the executable file whose name is displayed next to the command. It ignores whether the files have been changed.

- **Batch Build...** displays the Batch Build dialog box, which with allows you to build selected target versions of your application, either building only the out-of-date components or all components. This feature allows you to build both debug and release versions of a project, or to build versions for multiple platforms simultaneously.

- **Stop Build** stops a build process. Note that the keyboard shortcut for this command and for Build are identical. If you are not in the build process, the *B* will start the build; if you are in it, the *B* stops the process.

- **Update All Dependencies...** scans all the files in your project for dependencies and relinks the dependent files in the project.

- **Debug** starts the current application using the debugger. If the current application is not up-to-date, it presents the same warning dialog box as selecting the Execute command.

- **Execute *application*** executes the application file whose name is displayed to the right of the command. If you select this command and the executable file is not up-to-date—that is, there are some later changes to the source files that are not included in the current version of the application—you will see a warning dialog box that allows you to either continue executing the current version of the file or to rebuild the executable file.

- **Settings...** displays the Project Settings dialog box, which allows you to set a variety of important variables for your project.

- **Configurations...** displays the Configurations dialog box, which allows you to create, delete, and manage projects and configurations to the current project workspace.

- **Subprojects...** displays the Subprojects dialog box, which allows you to create, delete, and manage subprojects of your main project. A subproject is a logically separate set of code that is included into your project as a unit. When you have subprojects, the subprojects are compiled and built before the project is compiled and built.

- **Set Default Configuration...** displays the Default Project Configuration dialog box, which allows you to select one of your current configurations as the configuration that you are currently working with. This is the configuration of your project that will be built and executed when you use the other entries in this menu. For example, this is where you change from the Debug to the Release version of your project.

Each of the last four options controls certain aspects of your project. They will be discussed in more detail as you work the examples throughout the book.

Tools Menu

The Tools menu is shown in Figure 3.15.

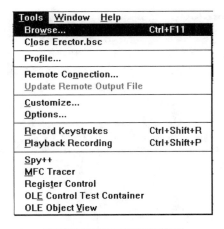

FIGURE 3.15 THE TOOLS MENU.

The Tools menu has the following commands:

- **Browse...** displays the Browse dialog box, which allows you to search your project for a specific term and move directly to it. You will learn about the Browser functions and how to use them in Chapter 4.

- **Close *browse file*** closes the current browse file. The current browse file name is displayed to the right of the command.

- **Profile...** displays the Profile dialog box, which allows you to run the profiler to see how your application uses Windows resources. To make this menu choice active, you must build your application with profiling enabled.

- **Remote Connection...** displays the Remote Connection dialog box, which allows you to set and control remote execution and debugging for your application.
- **Update Remote Output File** copies the current version of the executable application to the remote server for remote execution and debugging.
- **Customize...** displays the Customize dialog box, which you read about using this dialog earlier in this chapter.
- **Options...** displays the Options dialog box, which you read about earlier in this chapter.
- **Record Keystrokes** records a series of keystrokes as a macro for later repetition.
- **Playback Recording** plays back (re-executes) a series of keyboard commands recorded earlier with the **Record Keystrokes** command.
- The remainder of the Tools menu lists the tools that are available in the Developer Studio. These are other applications that you can run directly from this menu. The actual number of entries will depend on what you have installed with Visual C++ and what version of Visual C++ you are using. You can also add tools, such as your own editor program, to the Tools menu by using the Tools tab in the Customize dialog box.

Window Menu

The Window menu is shown in Figure 3.16

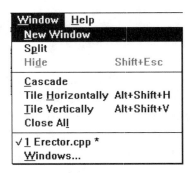

FIGURE 3.16 THE WINDOW MENU.

The Window menu has the following commands:

- **New Window** displays the currently active file in a new window.
- **Split** enables a cross-hair cursor which allows you to split the current editor pane into as many as four sections, each of which can be scrolled separately. This menu item is active (that is, not dimmed) if the cursor is positioned in a pane that can be split.
- **Hide** hides the currently selected pane, if it is dockable. This item is only active (that is, not dimmed) if the cursor is positioned in a pane that can be hidden.
- **Cascade** displays all the open windows so that their title bars are offset by the width and height of the title bar. This allows you to see the titles of all the windows, while the current window is displayed in front.
- **Tile Horizontally** displays all the open windows so that each one gets an equal amount of display room vertically, with each file taking up the full horizontal width of the display. This allows you to see equal amounts of the contents of each window.
- **Tile Vertically** displays all the open windows so that each one gets an equal amount of display room horizontally, with each file taking up the full vertical height of the display. This allows you to see equal amounts of the contents of each window.
- **Close All** closes all open windows. If any windows contain changed text, you are prompted to save them.
- The Window menu ends with a display of all the currently open windows. You may select any one of them to bring that window to the front and make it the current window. The windows are listed in the order that they were opened. The last item on the menu is **Windows...**, which displays a list of all open windows. This is identical to the list above the **Windows...** selection, unless there are more than nine files open, in which case only the first nine files are shown in the menu and the complete list is shown in the windows dialog list.

Help Menu

The Help menu is shown in Figure 3.17.

FIGURE 3.17 THE HELP MENU.

Each of these items allows you to access the help files or information indicated. The last item displays the About dialog box, which is similar to the one displayed when you start Visual C++. It also displays the serial number of your Visual C++ installation, in case you need to call for support.

PROJECT WORKSPACE STRUCTURE

The project workspace is the heart of your Visual C++ application. The project workspace controls which files are included in the application and governs how they are combined to build the finished application. It also stores the type of application that you are creating and the settings for the compiler, linker, and so on that are associated with your current application. In short, the project workspace is the control center that manages your application.

Project workspaces help you in several ways. First of all, by defining all the related elements that go into your application, they allow the Developer Studio to keep track of all these elements. This allows, for example, the facility to compile and link only those modules that have changed since the last time you built your project. The project also stores all the compiler and linker settings for your application, so you don't have reset them every time you reload your project. For a large and complex application, both of these features save time and frustration.

Elements of the project workspace

A project workspace consists of a project subdirectory on your hard disc, which contains at least two required files: the project makefile, which has the file extension of .MAK; and the project workspace file, which has the extension .MDP. The project directory is the root directory for all work that you will do with your project. It usually also contains the source files for your top-level project, but you can add files from any accessible location to a project workspace.

The makefile file defines the rules that must be followed by the compiler and linker to build your application. For example, it lists all the files that are involved in creation of your final application, including libraries, resource files, and included headers. The file generated by the Developer Studio is also compatible with the stand-alone NMAKE facility used in earlier versions of Microsoft's development environment. The project workspace file, however, is used only by the Developer Studio and controls things such as the arrangement of panes and windows in your workspace, the currently open files, breakpoint status and locations, and so on.

A project workspace will contain two essential elements: at least one project and a configuration. A *configuration* is a collection of settings for a project that define what platform the application will run on and the tool settings for building that version of the application. For example, a configuration might specify that the application is to be targeted for a Macintosh platform and that the application is to be built with the debug settings enabled. A *project* is a set of source files that define your code, along with an associated configuration that defines the type of application to build. A project workspace may contain multiple projects, and projects may themselves contain sub-projects. Every project workspace contains one *top-level* project on which all other projects and sub-projects depend.

NOTE

All this nomenclature is a little confusing at this point, I know. This stuff is mostly designed for groups of developers who are working together on large, complex applications. For example, you might be creating a game application that uses a library of animation routines (which are also created using MFC and Developer Studio) and is targeted for both Macintosh and Windows platforms. In such cases, all these distinctions are relevant, and quite useful. However, for your work in this book, we will be using only a single, top-level project in the project workspace, and we will keep all our files in the project directory. So if this all seems a bit confusing, don't worry—it won't be on the test.

Creating and Maintaining a Project

Generally, you will not have to create a separate project for your application. When you use AppWizard and the MFC to generate a skeleton application, it also automatically generates the appropriate project files, as you will see in subsequent chapters. When AppWizard generates a project workspace for your application, it automatically generates two configurations: one that includes debugging information, called the *Debug* configuration, and one that does not, called the *Release* configuration. Generally, the Debug configuration will be larger and slower to execute than the release version. You can also optimize the release version—but not the debug version—for speed, memory, and other features.

Once you have created a project workspace, you can add additional source files, configurations, projects and subprojects. Each of these elements is added from the Insert menu, which you read about earlier.

How you go about building your project workspace and adding projects to it depends on the type of project you are creating. Developer Studio supports nine different types of projects:

- MFC AppWizard (.EXE): a full MFC application developed using AppWizard

- MFC AppWizard (.DLL): a dynamic link library developed using AppWizard and MFC

- OLE Control Wizard (.OCX): an OLE control developed using MFC

- Application (.EXE): a standard Windows application developed using the Windows API or MFC (but not using AppWizard)

- Dynamic Link Library (.DLL): a standard Windows dynamic link library developed using the Windows API.

- Console Application (.EXE): an application that uses the console API in Windows for character-mode input and output.

- Static Library (.LIB): a standard library that is created in your project and linked to your application.

- Makefile (.MAK): a command-line program or a makefile that you can use to create and manage projects.

- Custom AppWizard (.AWX): a custom modification to the MFC AppWizard. You can use this as a custom starter for subsequent applications.

If you select one of the AppWizard types or the OLE Control Wizard or Custom AppWizard types, Visual C++ will create the necessary starter source files for you. However, if you select one of the other types, you must create or import all the necessary source files and related files for your project. In any case, the Developer Studio will create the project workspace files and directory for you if this is a new top-level project in a new project workspace.

That's all you need to know at this point about creating a new project work-space. As you will see in the next chapter, creating a skeleton application, using AppWizard and the Microsoft Foundation Class Library, is very easy, since these tools automatically generate all the necessary starter files for a complete skeleton application.

SUMMARY

In this chapter, you have learned about the Developer Studio environment. This has presented you with a brief look at how you can do all your development work in the Developer Studio. Microsoft has gone to a lot of trouble to make this an excellent, integrated development environment. For the remainder of the book as you work the examples, you will be using the Developer Studio for all your tasks. As you will see, it actually makes creating and managing the files necessary for a Windows application fairly easy.

CHAPTER 4

USING APPWIZARD

This chapter will discuss how to use the AppWizard to create and maintain Windows applications. It will also discuss the standard Windows development cycle and present how AppWizard fits into and shortens this cycle. You will work through the standard series of steps necessary to generate a skeleton Windows application in AppWizard. This skeleton will be the basis for many of the examples in the following chapters as you add features and functionality. Important topics include:

- How Windows programs work
- Using Windows messages in your application
- Creating an application with AppWizard
- Using the InfoViewer to view your application

WINDOWS PROGRAMMING

Windows programming is not like most other programming. If you have written programs for other environments, it is very likely that you will find Windows programming confusing at first. Windows programs use a graphic interface to respond to commands from the user. These two important features—a graphic interface and acting on command—are what make Windows applications fundamentally different from typical DOS applications. Although these are obviously desirable features, a programmer can spend months getting these aspects of a program to work correctly before actually getting on with the fundamental work that the program is intended to accomplish. Fortunately, the Visual C++ environment provides powerful tools and techniques that provide shortcuts to creating a program with these necessary Windows features. In this chapter, you will see how to create a fully functional basic Windows application using a few keystrokes and the AppWizard feature that is included in your Visual C++ package.

How Windows Programs Work

Windows programs have two special elements that make them easier to use and more understandable for the user. First, all Windows programs use a standard window display to show users what they are doing and to allow users to control the program. Second, Windows programs are constructed to respond to commands from the user. These two features together make Windows applications much easier and more natural for most users, but they make writing Windows programs more difficult for programmers.

Naturally, as a Windows user, you are familiar with these features in Windows from a user's perspective. In this section and the next, you will begin to see what this looks like from the programmer's side and how all this functionality is added to a program. I think you'll quickly appreciate how much ingenuity and effort has to go into generating an application that correctly uses the Windows environment.

The Windows Graphic User Interface (GUI)

The most obvious element of a Windows application is the window or windows, which are used to display information and communicate with the user. These windows all share a standard look and generally have a standard set of features that are an important element in creating the Windows "look and feel." In turn, this standard appearance gives Windows users the ability to perform many tasks in an easy and familiar way, and it makes the Windows environment familiar and comfortable across multiple applications.

The entire appearance of the Windows screen, including the windows, icons, and the display of current applications is called the Windows *graphic user interface*, commonly abbreviated GUI. When an application wishes to run under Windows, it needs to preserve and implement its part of the GUI to allow the user to understand and work with it in a standard way. This means, in general, that the application must support all the standard Windows GUI features, including menus, application switching, and windows movement and resizing, to the degree that they are appropriate for the application. For most applications, all the Windows GUI features need to be available. If you don't supply these features, your application will have a much steeper learning curve than typical Windows applications, and you will have unhappy and frustrated users. For these reasons, you need to support the Windows GUI in any Windows application you develop.

Every Windows application that conforms to the Windows standards provides certain features. Let's review the standard features for windows in an application as specified in the Windows user manual. First, every running application has a primary *application window* that displays the name of the application and the primary application *menu bar*. In addition, an application may support having multiple documents open at once—for example, most office applications that run in Windows allow you to work on several documents at once. This is called a *multiple document interface*, or MDI, and each document that is open is displayed in one or more *document windows*. Some applications, such as the Write and Notepad accessories that come with Windows, only allow you to have one document open at a time. This is called the *single document interface*, or SDI. In such applications, there is no separate document window; the application displays the current document in the application window. You can tell document windows from the application window by the menu bar; only the application window has a menu bar. In addition, the application window will display the name of the application, while the document window, if present, displays the name of the document. For SDI applications, the application window displays both the name of the application and the name of the document.

Every window in a Windows application has certain common features, but not all windows use every feature. Here is a brief list of the common features you are expected to provide in a window:

- Standard window corners and border that allow the user to resize the window.
- Control-menu box in the upper-left corner of the window
- Title bar, across the top of the window, containing the appropriate information: the name of the application or document, depending on the type of window
- Menu bar across the top of the application window
- Minimize and maximize buttons in the upper-right corner of the window
- Horizontal and vertical scroll bars if the display area is larger than the window

Every window in an application doesn't necessarily need to have all of these features, but most windows do have them, and you need to support most of these features if you are going to create a genuine Windows application.

Windows User-Driven Commands

Another important part of Windows applications, which may be less obvious to the user, is the fact that you can interrupt a Windows application at almost any point and tell it to do something, often even if it is in the middle of some other task. In any case, accepting and responding to commands from the user are important features of Windows applications.

Actually, this requirement grows naturally out of the GUI presentation. One of the more important features of the Windows GUI is that the user has effective control of the application or tasks being performed. Unlike many DOS applications, Windows applications generally allow the user to work in a natural manner, even stopping the application or switching to another task in the middle of ordinary processing. The user chooses the currently active application in the Windows environment by bringing its window to the front of all other windows on the display. The front window is called the *active* window; it displays visual clues, such as color and highlighting, to show that it is active.

Once an application is active, the user tells it what to do by interacting with the elements displayed in the windows: menu items, control boxes, and so on. In this way, the user can work in a natural and simple fashion with the application. All of this is part of the standard Windows interface.

Behind the scenes, however, there is a somewhat different—and more complex—picture. The Windows system environment provides many of the features that you see in a standard Windows application. For example, it knows how to draw a window on the screen and how to color that window to show that it is active. However, it is up to the individual application to take over once it becomes active. The application must understand when it is active and when it is not, and it must cooperate with the Windows system to implement the various features that are required in each case.

In a similar fashion, the application can tell Windows when to implement certain features, and Windows will correctly change the GUI to show the result. For example, all standard Windows applications display a menu bar. Typically, one of these is the Edit menu, which includes commands to cut, copy, paste, and so on. If an application cannot perform these operations at a given moment, it will dim, or *disable*, these commands in the menu to show the user that they are not available. To do this, the application simply sends Windows a command telling it to disable the specific menu items. Windows knows what *disable* means for menu items and will correctly select the text from the menu and make it dimmer by displaying it in gray rather than black. In this way, the application and Windows have cooperated to make the GUI work correctly.

Understanding Windows Communications

The most challenging part of programming for Windows applications is the requirement to allow the user to control the application virtually at all times. To do this, the application uses the elements of the GUI, such as menus, to display to the user the current commands and functions that are available. When the user selects a command from those available, the application responds to that command in some appropriate manner. This is quite different from batch applications, such as most DOS programs, which process data on command until they have finished and only then allow the user to give a new command or start a new function.

As you know, a Windows application typically displays a menu bar across the top of its window that gives a series of command groups. When the user chooses one of these groups, the application displays a list of commands available in that category. If the user selects one of these commands, the application performs the requested action immediately. In this way, the user has direct control over what the application does at each step.

Let's consider the simple example of opening a file within an application. In a DOS program, you usually have to enter the file name when you start the program or—for a more "user-friendly" application—enter it at a prompt. In Windows, on the other hand, you may at almost any time select **Open** from the File menu. This triggers the application to display a file dialog box, asking you to select a file to be opened. This dialog normally allows you to move around the system storage to find the desired file. You don't need to remember the file's name or where it's located on your disk; you need to know only how to get there and recognize the file when you find it. In addition, a typical Windows application will screen out all files that do not belong to the application, so you see only the application's files in the display. In all these ways, the entire process works with you to make finding the file easy.

Now think about what the application had to do to make all this work. First, it must be ready at any time to handle a command from the menu. It must display the desired dialog box. Within that dialog box, it must display the correct set of files and allow you to move to other parts of the disk, displaying the correct files at each step. Finally, when you select the file you want in the dialog box, the application has to retrieve the necessary location information for that file from the dialog box and then get the file, finally returning to process the selected file. As you think about that, think about how much code it represents. This is all code that is essential to being a Windows application, and yet it has moved you no closer to actually processing the file than the few lines of code in the DOS counterpart that simply reads a console string. This is part of the reason why Windows applications are so hard to develop.

Windows 95 adds a further wrinkle to the user interface. With the advent of Windows 95, your application is expected to provide the user with context-sensitive menus that display when the *right* mouse button is clicked inside a document. For example, in a word-processing application, clicking the right mouse button within a document might pop up a menu displaying editing commands, such as **Cut**, **Copy**, and **Paste**, along with a file **Save** or **Save As** command, a **Print** command, and a **Help** command that automatically displays some context-related help information. As you can see, these commands would normally be presented in two or more menu items. Allowing the user to access such common commands directly from within a document is a nice way to make the user more productive. So adding Windows 95 support to your application now requires even more programming for the user interface.

Messages and Windows

When a user selects a menu item or asks for some other action, that request must be transmitted to the application by the Windows environment. Windows does this by sending *messages* to the application. Every time the user takes some action, selects a command item, or presses a key on the keyboard, Windows sends an appropriate message to the application that allows you to respond to the user correctly. Windows has more than 120 such messages, ranging from basic messages that tell you a key was pressed or the mouse was moved to complex and unusual messages that tell you that the Windows initialization file has changed or that Windows is compacting memory. In a similar way, your application can send messages to the Windows environment to tell Windows about actions your application has taken or to request action or information from Windows. You will learn more about processing Windows messages in the following chapters, especially Chapter 6 in the section "Using Messages in Windows."

NOTE

Here, and throughout the book, I will use standard C notation for numbers, strings, and characters. All of these standard formats are also used in C++, which is based on C. For reference, here is the standard notation:

- *Decimal integers* are written as simple numbers: 10, -21, 99, and so on.
- *Hexadecimal integers* are written with a prefix of 0x: 0x1F, 0xA2, 0x0000, and so on.
- *Octal integers* are written with a prefix of 0: 017, 077, 0377, and so on.
- *Real* or *floating-point numbers* are written like decimal integers but contain a decimal point, an exponent, or end with an F or f suffix: 1.2, 3.1414E2, 0.123, 12F, and so on. Note that 0.123 is not octal, even though it begins with a zero, because it contains a decimal point.

In this scheme, you can see that the numbers 255, 0xFF, and 0377 all represent the same integer.

In addition, you can adjust the type and storage requirements of your integers when you create them by using the following notation:

- A suffix of L or l makes an integer long: 12L, 0x1Fl, 0377L, and so on.
- A suffix of U or u makes an integer unsigned: 12U, 0x1fu, 0377u, and so on.

Finally, C supports single characters and arrays of characters, or strings. These are written as follows:

- A single character is written between single quotes: 'a', '1', '$', and so on. Note that this generates a single integer value between 0x00 and 0xFF, which normally may be signed or unsigned depending on the compiler you are using. In Visual C++, the default is to generate signed characters.
- An array of characters, or a string, is written between double quotes: "abcd", "a1b2", "$12.95", and so on. A standard C character string is an array of character codes terminated by a value of 0x00. Remember that this means that the string "abcd" will actually contain five codes: the codes for 'a', 'b', 'c', and 'd', followed by the 0x00 terminator.

Types of Windows Messages

All these messages are sent to your application in a standard format. Windows messages are numbers between 0x0000 and 0xFFFF. Each Windows message consists of three parts: a message number, a word parameter, and a long parameter. Message numbers are identified by predefined message name constants, which are standard for all Windows applications. These names begin with two or three letters that indicate the origin of the message, followed by an underscore and a name that is suggestive of the nature or meaning of the message. Since these are predefined constants, they are written in all capital letters—this is a standard convention for writing predefined constants in most C programs and is followed throughout Windows, Visual C++, and this book. For example, the message that your application receives is WM_MOUSEMOVE. The *WM* indicates that this is a *Windows Message*, and the MOUSEMOVE tells you that this message is caused by movement of the mouse. Table 4.1 lists all the types of Windows messages (that is, the two- or three-letter codes that begin each type of message).

TABLE 4.1 THE TYPES OF WINDOWS MESSAGES

BM_	Button message. Sent by your application to a button in a dialog window. Buttons may be standard buttons or radio buttons. Figure 4.1 shows an example of standard buttons.
BN_	Button Notification message. Sent from a dialog window button to your application to tell you that the button has been activated in some way.
CB_	Combo-Box message. Sent by your application to a combo-box item in a dialog window. A *combo-box* is an alternative method for displaying lists of information; it has a name or title displayed as text, along with a list box. Generally, the list box will be displayed only when requested by the user. For example, the List Files of Type box at the bottom of the Open File dialog box in Figure 4.1 is a combo-box.
CBN_	Combo-Box Notification message. Sent from a combo-box item to your application.
EM_	Edit Control message. Sent by your application to an edit text window in a dialog window. An *edit text window* is the por-

tion of a dialog window where you can enter text information. For example, the File Name box in the Open File dialog box shown in Figure 4.1 is an edit text window.

EN_   Edit Control Notification message. Sent from an edit text box in a dialog window to your application.

LB_   List Box message. Sent by your application to a list box item in a dialog window. A *list box*, as the name implies, is where you display lists of items in your dialog window. For example, the list of files in the current directory shown in the Open File dialog box in Figure 4.1 is displayed in a list box.

LBN_   List Box Notification message. Sent from a list box to your application. This type of message is only sent if the list box was created with the LB_NOTIFY style.

WM_   Windows message. Messages that can be sent from Windows to your application or from your application to Windows. Although some messages are sent from the application to Windows, most of the messages go from Windows to the application.

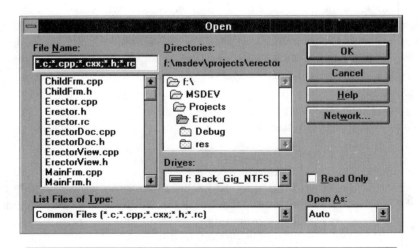

FIGURE 4.1 THE OPEN FILE DIALOG BOX CONTAINS EXAMPLES OF MOST OF THE STANDARD
WINDOWS ELEMENTS THAT GENERATE MESSAGES.

As you can see, most of the message identifiers have to do with handling and controlling information from dialog boxes. This does not reflect practical Windows programming, however; in Windows programming, as in so many things, 80% of the messages come from a few simple actions: keyboard entries, using the mouse, and changes in the working window. Nevertheless, I wanted to show you all the prefixes in one place, so you have some idea of the variety and complexity of Windows messages. The good news is that you can avoid worrying about most of these messages by using Visual C++ and Microsoft Foundation Classes (MFC) as a basis for your Windows application.

In addition to the message number, each Windows message comes with two parameters: a word parameter, denoted by wParam, and a long parameter, denoted by lParam. The two parameters, wParam and lParam, contain information that varies according to the message number. In general, these two parameters provide the necessary information to process the message. In addition, the lParam parameter may carry two items of information: one in the high-order portion of the long value and the other in the low-order portion. These two items can be extracted from the lParam using the standard Windows macros HIWORD and LOWORD, respectively.

Let's look at two simple examples to see how this might work. For example, when your application receives the message WM_MENUSELECT, the wParam value will indicate the number of the menu item selects, while the lParam value will tell you additional information about the specific menu item, such as whether it is checked, whether it contains a pop-up menu, and so on. In this case, the lParam only contains a single value. As another example, suppose your application receives the message WM_MOUSEMOVE. In that message, the wParam value tells you what keys (if any) were being held down while the mouse moved. The lParam value contains two numbers, which give you the x coordinate of the cursor in the lower-order portions of the value, and the y coordinate in the high-order portion.

N O T E This is a good time to introduce the standard Windows naming conventions. Whenever you read any Windows documentation, Windows code, articles about programming in Windows, or most books about Windows programming (including this one), you will quickly notice that the names of Windows objects look a little strange, with names such as the wParam and lParam values mentioned earlier, or even stranger items, such as lpszFileName and lpNewItem. These are names using the Hungarian naming conventions—so called, I am told, after Charles Simonyi, one of the early and legendary programmers at Microsoft. These naming conventions were defined in his doctoral dissertation as a part of a complete meta-programming schema.

The complete convention is quite elegant and detailed, but you don't need to know all that. All you really need to know is the basic method for reading and creating these names. The basic method is to use a lowercase letter or a short series of lowercase letters to indicate the data type of the variable being named. Then the rest of the name uses upper and lowercase letters for the descriptive portion of the name. So each variable name consists of two parts: a first part, in lowercase, that shows the type of data for the variable and a second part, in combined upper and lowercase, that names the variable.

Table 4.2 lists the lowercase letters that are used as conventions in Windows and what they mean.

TABLE 4.2 HUNGARIAN NAMING CONVENTIONS

Prefix	Data Type	Description
b	BOOL	A Boolean value (int)
c	int	Count variable
ch	char	8-bit character (may be signed or unsigned, see earlier note)
cx, cy	short	Used as count values for length of an object
dw	DWORD	32-bit unsigned integer; a double word
fn	function	
h	HANDLE	A 16-bit pointer to a Windows object
l	LONG	32-bit signed integer
lp	FAR*	32-bit pointer
lpfn	void*	32-bit pointer to a function
lpsz	LPSTR	32-bit pointer to character string

TABLE 4.2 HUNGARIAN NAMING CONVENTIONS (CONTINUED)

Prefix	Data Type	Description
n	short or int	Signed or unsigned integer; size depends on operating system
p	*	Pointer (length determined by the compiler)
s	char[]	String
sz	STR	String with a 0x00 termination byte (a standard C string)
w	WORD	16-bit unsigned value

Table 4.2 lists the basic data types, but there are also some additional conventions. If the variable is a member of a class, the name will be further prefixed with m_ to show that it is a class variable. If the variable refers to a class type or a structure, an abbreviated form of the class or structure name is used as the lowercase introduction to the name.

I know this all sounds strange and fairly complex, but in practice you'll find it to be fairly simple and easy to work with. Here are some live examples, with an explanation, to give you an idea of how this works:

- pszPathName   The pointer to a C string (ends with 0x00) that gives you the path name for the current document.
- m_szPathName   The actual string value of the path name when you store it as a class variable in your application.
- nPenWidth   An integer value for the width of the current pen.
- rectBounding   A RECTANGLE structure that gives the bounding region of the current window.
- strPathName   A CString object that holds the path name for the current document.

The last one needs a little more explanation than the others. CString is a class defined in the Microsoft Foundation Classes. As the class name implies, it allows you to handle standard C strings in a simple and elegant manner. In this case, instead of keeping the path name as a simple string, the name has been stored as a member of this String class. Later, in Chapter 6, you will read about these classes and how they work. Then, in Chapter 7, you will work with CStrings (and other MFC classes) and see how they make your programming easier and safer.

These conventions are not only used by Microsoft. They have been adopted and used by a wide spectrum of Windows and non-Windows programmers because these conventions are so clearly successful in aiding programmers to avoid common mistakes and to help them understand what types of data they are using. For example, one of the common problems in C programming is remembering whether a particular value is a pointer to a value or the value itself. The Hungarian naming conventions easily solve that problem, as the value will have a name like `szFileName`, while the pointer to the name will have a name like `pszFileName`. In this way you can immediately tell that one of these is a pointer and the other is the actual string. As you work through the examples in this book, I will occasionally point out how these naming conventions help you make the correct programming choices.

All this no doubt sounds a little complex right now—and it is. As I said at the beginning of this chapter, programming in Windows is both different and somewhat more complicated than standard DOS batch programming. Here are the essential points that you need to take away from this discussion:

- Windows and your application communicate by using messages.
- These messages have standard names that are used in all Windows applications.
- The messages have additional information attached to them that allows your application to take the necessary action to respond to the message.

CREATING A WINDOWS PROGRAM WITH APPWIZARD

After all this discussion, you may feel somewhat intimidated—but don't be. The AppWizard that is built into Visual C++ is designed to help you automatically generate a skeleton application that contains most of the user-interface code and some of the Windows message handling that you need in your application. In fact, you can generate a fully functional application that works and does all of the standard Windows actions—such as resizing, moving, and closing the application window; opening multiple documents; creating, displaying, and understanding menu items; and so on—without ever worrying about Windows messages or how this all works. This section shows how to set the options in AppWizard to create such a basic Windows application.

Using AppWizard to Create ErectorSet

Theory is fine, but practice is best. The easiest way to see how to use AppWizard—and, parenthetically, the best way to appreciate what it does for you—is to use it to create a simple, basic Windows application.

To do this, start the Visual C++ Developer Studio in the standard way. Make sure that you don't have any current workspace loaded by checking the File menu. Most entries in the menu should be grayed out—in particular, the **Close Workspace** entry should be gray and the **Open Workspace** command should be active (dark). To begin your new project select **New** from the File menu. This displays the New dialog box with a short list of the various types of new items you might want to add to your project. Since you want to create a new project, select **Project Workspace** from the New dialog box and click **OK**. This brings up the New Project Workspace dialog box shown in Figure 4.2.

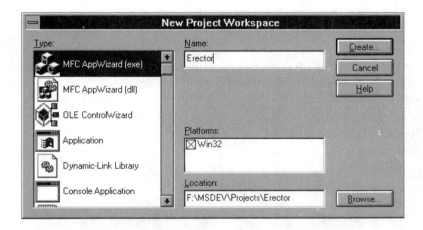

FIGURE 4.2 THE NEW PROJECT WORKSPACE DIALOG BOX IS WHERE YOU START TO BUILD YOUR PROJECT.

The New Project Workspace dialog box displays icons for nine types of projects. For now, simply choose the default, which is the MFC AppWizard (.exe) icon. This allows you to create a project to build a standard Windows application. The other icons allow you to configure your project to create a variety of other useful types of executable output, such as a dynamic link library (DLL), OLE controls, and so on. Later in this chapter, you will read about each of these different types of projects, but generally you will want to create an MFC application.

This dialog box also shows the current platform or platforms that you have installed for your Developer Studio and the location where the new project will be installed.

The default platform is Win32, which is always installed with Visual C++. If you have installed other platforms, such as Macintosh, they will show up here as well. For now, simply select **Win32**.

Use the **Browse** button, if necessary, to navigate to the \MSDEV\Projects directory, as shown in the Location text box in Figure 4.2. (This assumes that you have used the standard directory names. If you didn't, or if you wish to place your project somewhere else, move to the location where you want to place your project either by using the **Browse** button or by typing the path into the Location text box.) This is the path where your new project will be created. The project files will be placed in a new subdirectory that is created under the path that you have selected in the Location box.

Enter **Erector** as the project name. This will automatically create a new subdirectory under the path you selected in Location that will hold all your ErectorSet code. Note that the Location display is now updated to show you the new subdirectory. When everything is set the way you want, press **Create**.

Setting Up Options and Classes

Pressing **Create** begins the process of setting up your new MFC application, which proceeds in a series of steps. The first step displays the MFC AppWizard— Step 1 dialog box shown in Figure 4.3.

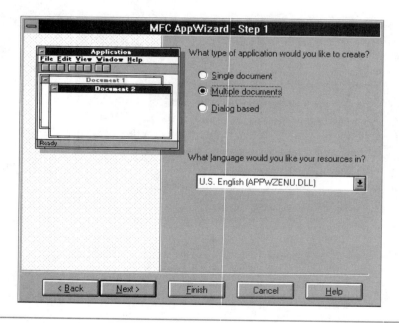

FIGURE 4.3 THE STEP 1 DIALOG BOX BEGINS THE PROCESS OF CREATING YOUR MFC APPLICATION.

As you see in Figure 4.3, the dialog box asks two important questions: What type of application would you like to create? and What language would you like your resources in? Each of the dialog boxes for the steps in creating your application use questions such as these to help you organize your application's features and requirements.

The dialog box also displays a series of buttons along the bottom, which allow you to move through the steps in creating and application. All the creation dialogs use these buttons. Most are quite clear: **Back** moves you to the previous step; **Next** moves you to the next step; **Finish** fills in any remaining choices with default values and moves you directly to the last step, which displays the completed application choices; **Cancel** terminates the creation process; and **Help** brings up context-specific help for the current step.

For now, you won't change any of the default selections here. (I'm assuming, if you're reading this book, that you prefer your text in English.) However, I want you to notice particularly the first question and its related radio buttons. The default button is marked **Multiple documents**. These buttons control whether your application allows multiple documents or supports only a single document: in other words, whether it is an MDI or an SDI application, as you read earlier. The third choice, a Dialog-based application, is used in special circumstances, but we won't discuss it here. After you review these options, click **Next** to move to the next step.

This brings up the Step 2 dialog box, shown in Figure 4.4.

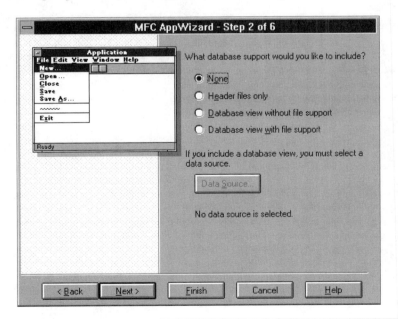

FIGURE 4.4 THE STEP 2 DIALOG BOX ALLOWS YOU TO INCLUDE DATABASE SUPPORT IN YOUR NEW APPLICATION.

This dialog box allows you to include database support in your application. For ErectorSet, you won't be using database support, so the default choice of **None** is fine. Click **Next** to display the Step 3 dialog box, shown in Figure 4.5.

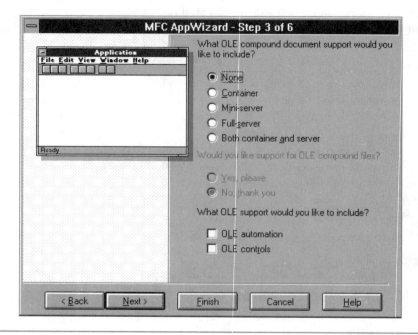

FIGURE 4.5 THE STEP 3 DIALOG BOX ALLOWS YOU TO INCLUDE OLE SUPPORT IN YOUR NEW APPLICATION.

The Step 3 dialog box allows you to include several types of OLE support in your application. For this version of ErectorSet, you won't be using OLE support, so the default choice of **None** is fine. Click **Next** to display the Step 4 dialog box, shown in Figure 4.6.

The Step 4 dialog box has three questions, but it actually covers a number of items. The primary issue is a selection of optional features that you can add to your application. These are listed as a series of checkboxes under the first question: What features would you like to include? Generally, you should include most of these features. Table 4.3 lists these options and what each one controls.

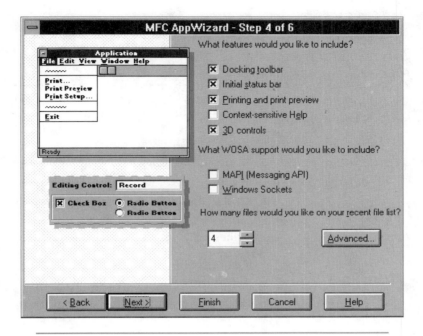

FIGURE 4.6 THE STEP 4 DIALOG BOX ALLOWS YOU TO CHOOSE A SET OF FEATURES TO SUPPORT IN YOUR NEW APPLICATION.

TABLE 4.3 THE OPTIONS THAT YOU CAN SET WHEN YOU CREATE AN APPLICATION WITH APPWIZARD

Option	Function
Docking toolbar	Determines whether the toolbar created by MFC for your application is movable and dockable or not. Default is checked.
Initial status bar	Determines whether your application will initially display and use the status bar. Checking this also adds menu commands for displaying or hiding both the toolbar and status bar. Default is checked.

TABLE **4.3** THE OPTIONS THAT YOU CAN SET WHEN YOU CREATE AN APPLICATION
WITH APPWIZARD (CONTINUED)

Option	Function
Printing and Print Preview	Determines whether your application handles these two features and adds them to the menu if checked. Default is checked.
Context Sensitive Help	Determines whether your application provides context-sensitive Windows help features and text. Default is unchecked. (You will learn about adding Windows Help features in Chapter 13.)
3D Controls	Determines whether the visual interface (buttons, window frames, and so on) used by your application have shading, giving them a three-dimensional appearance. This is the standard Windows "look and feel." Default is to add the shading.

The next question enables you to add communication support to your application. You can add support for MAPI (Microsoft's messaging program interface), which allows e-mail creation, transmission, and handling, and support for Windows sockets, which provides an interface for various communications protocols, such as TCP/IP and AppleTalk. The default is not to add support for any communications, and that's what you want now.

NOTE   This question asks what WOSA support you want to add to your application. This is a bit misleading, since WOSA (Windows Open Systems Architecture) includes some parts of database support, which you selected in Step 2. This question covers the remaining parts of WOSA, which deal with networking and communications.

The last selection allows you to set how many files will be displayed in the most recently used (MRU) file list in your application. The default is 4, which corresponds to what most Windows applications provide and is perfectly satisfactory for most users. You should change this value only if you have some clear reason to do so.

Now press the **Advanced** button to display the Advanced Options dialog box. This dialog box has two tabs: Document Template Settings and Window Styles. The Document Template Settings tab display is shown in Figure 4.7.

FIGURE 4.7 THE DOCUMENT TEMPLATE SETTINGS TAB OF THE ADVANCED OPTIONS DIALOG BOX ALLOWS YOU TO SET IMPORTANT DOCUMENT INFORMATION FOR YOUR APPLICATION.

This tab allows you to define several important variables for the files that will be created and used by your application. In this portion of the dialog box you can make a lot of changes; in addition, you have to fill in the File extension edit box yourself to set it correctly. Generally, the default values are fine; but you should make it a practice to review all these settings. Since they are generated automatically, you need to review them to make sure that the automatic truncation method that generates them hasn't made them difficult to use. The Doc type name is a good example of this. This is the name you will see at the top of the document window, and it is the default name of all the documents generated by your application. In this case, AppWizard has truncated **Erector** at six characters, the maximum for the document name, since the application will append a number to this name to create the document names. However, this doesn't look like a good name broken off as it is; change the Doc type name to **Build**. Then enter **set** in the File extensions edit text box. I also edited the Main frame caption and Filter name text boxes to make them somewhat more readable. The result looks like Figure 4.7, which shows the dialog box after the changes.

These settings mean that the documents generated by the ErectorSet application will be called **Build1.set**, **Build2.set**, and so on, and your application will automatically screen out files that do not have the file extension **.set**. (Of course, you can override this behavior in your application code.)

The other tab, Window Styles, sets the styles that the application will use when it generates windows. This tab is shown in Figure 4.8.

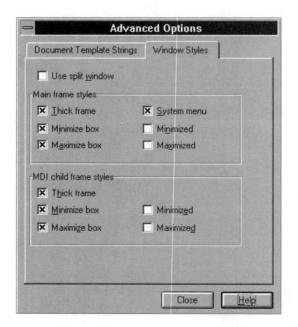

FIGURE 4.8 THE WINDOW STYLES TAB OF THE ADVANCED OPTIONS DIALOG BOX ALLOWS YOU TO DETERMINE HOW YOUR APPLICATION WINDOWS WILL LOOK.

You should leave most of these set to their default values, which represent standard Windows behavior. Table 4.4 lists the style checkboxes and what each one means.

TABLE **4.4** WINDOW STYLES FOR CREATING MFC APPLICATIONS WITH APPWIZARD

Style	Meaning
Thick Frame	Provides a thick frame around the window, which allows the window to be resized and provides room for a window title. Default is checked.
Minimize box	Provides a standard minimize button on the window. Default is checked.
Maximize box	Provides a standard maximize button on the window. Default is checked.
System Menu	Specifies that the main frame window will include a control menu box in the upper-left corner. This is a standard Windows feature which allows the user to display the System menu to resize, move, or close the application, and to switch applications. (This style option only applies to the main frame window.) Default is checked.
Minimized	Determines whether the application's windows will automatically be minimized (displayed as an icon) on opening. Default is unchecked.
Maximized	Determines whether the application's windows will automatically be maximized on opening. Default is unchecked.

This dialog tab also has a Use split window checkbox. Checking this box generates an application that supports split windows, which allow a user to divide a window into horizontal and vertical sections, called *panes*, which can be moved over a single document independently of one another. The default for this is unchecked, and for now you should leave it unchecked. Later, in Chapter 12, you will see how to use the code generated by this option to support multiple panes in your windows.

When you have finished your selections in this dialog box, click on the **Close** button to return to the Step 4 dialog box. When you get there, click on **Next** to move to the next step and display the Step 5 dialog box shown in Figure 4.9.

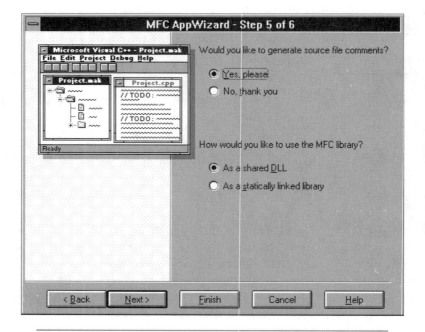

FIGURE 4.9 THE STEP 5 DIALOG BOX ALLOWS YOU TO GENERATE COMMENTS AND SET HOW TO USE MFC IN YOUR NEW APPLICATION.

This dialog box asks two questions about your application. The first is would you like to generate source file comments? The default is to generate the comments. Generally, I recommend strongly that you chose to have the source code generated for your application containing comments showing where to add specific functionality. (I'm a big believer in comments in code, as you will see later in this chapter.)

The second question is how would you like to use the MFC library? This is a little more complex. If your application will be using only MFC and C++, you should choose the default option of using MFC as a shared DLL. When you do this, your application can share the MFC DLL code with any other MFC application that is running at the same time, using less memory and resources. This is the most "Windows friendly" way of adding the MFC code to your application. However, if your application has any non-C++ code, has non-MFC C++ code, or is targeted for any other platforms, include MFC as a static library.

Now click the **Next** button to move to the final step, Step 6. This displays the Step 6 dialog box shown in Figure 4.10.

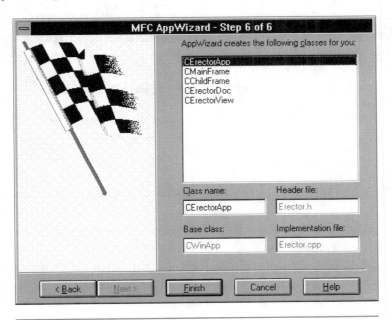

FIGURE 4.10 THE STEP 6 DIALOG BOX ALLOWS YOU TO EDIT THE CLASS ATTRIBUTES AND FILE NAMES FOR YOUR APPLICATION.

As you can see in Figure 4.10, the dialog box has already filled in a lot of information based on the name of the project that you entered earlier.

The dialog box shows five classes: CErectorApp, CMainFrame, CChildFrame, CErectorDoc, and CErectorView. For now, don't worry about what each one does, just work with the names as provided.

N O T E

Here are some more naming conventions that are commonly used in C++ programming. As a matter of convention, all classes in C++ are given names that begin with the uppercase letter *C*, followed by a descriptive name in both upper and lowercase. In this way, you can easily and immediately tell that something is a C++ class name, rather than a variable or function.

Each of these entries is a class. A *class* is a collection of C++ objects, including a user-defined data structure, member functions, also called *methods*, member data, and possibly custom operators. Classes are the basis for C++ programming; indeed, they are fundamental to object-oriented programming in any form. A class definition must follow a specific and fairly rigid structure to work correctly. Visual C++ automatically creates these classes and sets up the correct structure and linkage for you. As you work with the examples provided in this book, you will learn more about C++ and classes. In particular, Chapter 6 discusses classes in some detail.

C++

If you are not already familiar with C++ (or some other object-oriented programming language), at this point there are three things that you need to know about classes:

1. Classes contain the functions (also called *methods*) that you create to implement various tasks in your applications.

2. Classes are organized in a *class hierarchy*. The classes or classes at the top of the hierarchy are called *base classes* and the classes that are beneath a base class are called *derived classes*.

3. A derived class *inherits* all of the functions that are in the classes above it in the hierarchy.

Object-oriented programming has many important features, but inheritance is the most useful and the most powerful. Essentially, *inheritance* means that a derived class immediately has access to all the functions of every class above it in the hierarchy. This feature is extremely important in understanding and using the MFC.

The bottom of the dialog box that you see in Figure 4.10 shows you the Class name and other information for the selected class, CErectorApp. The Class name text box is the only item that you can change; the other items are fixed by AppWizard. In this case, you don't need to change the class name.

Now select the CErectorDoc class from the list of application classes. As you select a new class, the display items at the bottom of the dialog box also change to match the selected class. Note that the header file and implementation file names are now available for you to change. For ErectorSet, leave them as their default values.

The `CMainFrame` and `CChildFrame` classes have the same type of display as `CErectorDoc`, and, like that class, they don't require any changes.

N O T E

Since you must be working in Windows 95 or Windows NT 3.51, which support long file names, AppWizard will generate long file names for your header and implementation files. However, if you are running on a shared volume using the FAT format, you may wish to change these names. By default, long file names are truncated at six characters by the operating system and files that have identical names for the first six characters (as the file names here do) are made unique by adding a "twiddle" character, ~, and a number to the name. (You can see the generated name in the File Manager display for your application files when they have been generated. The DOS name is displayed in capitals to the right of the long file name.)

If you want file names to fit into the DOS eight-character plus extension format, the name of your application—in this case, *erector*—must be shortened to five characters for use in the file names. Five characters is the maximum because you need to add a three-character suffix to the base name to generate the complete file name. So, for the document class, the file name would be the base value *erect* plus the suffix *doc* and the file extension, which will be either *.cpp* to indicate that this is an implementation file containing C++ code or *.h* to indicate that this is a header file.

Finally, select the `CErectorView` class from the list of application classes. For this class, the Base Class list box becomes active. If you click on the box or press the down arrow next to it, it will display a possible list of classes from which you can derive your View class. The default is to derive your View class from the standard CView class in MFC. This gives you basic view processing, which you will read about in Chapter 5. The other selections add additional features to your View class, over and above the basic features supplied by CView. For now, simply scroll down and select `CScrollView` as the base class for the `CErectorView` class. This means that your new class will have the scrolling capabilities provided by the MFC class CScrollView. (The standard CView class does not support scroll bars.)

You have now completed your selections for the ErectorSet application. Press the **Finish** button. AppWizard now displays the New Project Information dialog box that you see in Figure 4.11.

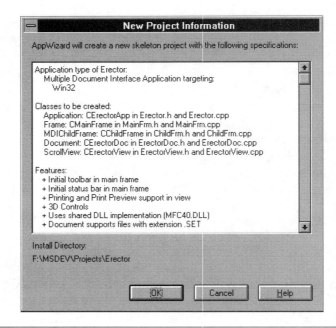

FIGURE 4.11 THE NEW PROJECT INFORMATION DIALOG BOX SHOWS THE SETTINGS AND FEATURES THAT WILL BE USED TO GENERATE THE SKELETON ERECTORSET APPLICATION.

As you can see, this dialog box summarizes all the options and the class information for your application. Read through this dialog box and check that everything is set the way you want. If it is, press the **OK** button to generate your skeleton application.

AppWizard now creates the files that will generate your application and places them in the directory that you selected. It then returns you to the Developer Studio, where it automatically opens the project workspace file, Erector.mdp. Your screen should now look like Figure 4.12.

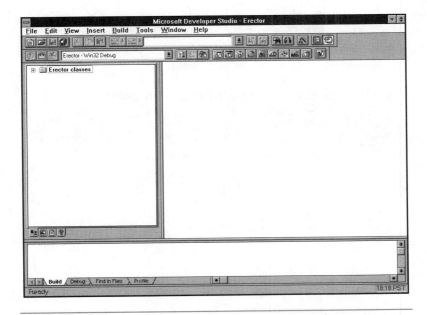

FIGURE 4.12 WHEN YOU RETURN TO THE DEVELOPER STUDIO, YOUR WINDOW SHOULD SHOW
THAT THE NEW WORKSPACE IS LOADED.

When the project is loaded, the Developer Studio also scans the project to establish the links between all the elements of your new application. In fact, the project is now ready to be compiled for the first time.

To do this, choose **Build Erector.exe** from the Build menu or press **Shift+F8**. This will compile and link all of the elements that you have created so far into your skeleton application, ERECTOR.EXE. When you do this, the Developer Studio displays a series of messages in the lower output pane showing you what it is doing and what progress has been made on your application. If there were any errors in the compilation or linking of your application, they will show up here. Since at this point the entire application consists of MFC code, there won't be any errors.

Since this is the first time all of the code has been compiled, this build generally takes longer than any subsequent ones. When you're done, your Developer

Studio output pane should look something like Figure 4.13. (I've expanded the screen here to show all the messages. By default, your output pane will be docked at the bottom of your Developer Studio workspace, and it won't look quite like this, but all the same messages should be there.)

FIGURE 4.13 THE DEVELOPER STUDIO OUTPUT WINDOW SHOWS YOU THE COMPLETE STORY OF YOUR BUILD.

A Quick Checklist for Creating an Application

One thing that you will notice in using Visual C++ —I certainly have—is that you may forget from one time to the next exactly what steps you need to take to make a new project file and to build an application. This is natural enough, since most of the time, you are working on application enhancements or maintenance and not on creating new applications. To help you get through the process quickly, here is a checklist of the steps to creating an new project and application:

1. Make sure you aren't in any project and that you don't have a workspace loaded. You do this by checking the File menu.

2. Select **New** from the File menu.

3. Select **Project Workspace** from the list in the New dialog box.

4. Fill in the name of your project. Remember that this name will be the basis for a variety of names in the project, including (normally) the subdirectory for the project files.

5. Move through the steps in creating the project, making appropriate selections for your new application.

6. In Step 5, use the Advanced Options to set the document class file extension and names.

7. In Step 6, check the classes for valid names. Also be sure to derive your View class from the correct base class.

8. Check the application settings in the New Application Information dialog box.

9. Press **OK** to assemble the files for your skeleton application from the MFC.

10. Select **Build** (**Shift+F8**) from the Build menu to compile and link the skeleton application.

Reviewing ErectorSet

With these few keystrokes and selections, you've gotten a marvelous start on building a true Windows application. AppWizard has plundered the Foundation Classes to create exactly the type of application you requested. Moreover, the application already has many of the functions and features your users expect to see in a true Windows application. Now that you've created and built it, let's review ErectorSet to see what you have "straight out of the box," as it were.

Examining the Generated Files

Let's start by looking at some of the information that AppWizard has generated for you. If you look at your new subdirectory with File Manager or some other file browser, you will see that you now have 19 files in the new subdirectory that AppWizard created for you. In addition, the subdirectory has two additional subdirectories of its own: RES and Debug. The RES directory, which contains four more files, contains all the resources for your application. Initially, these consist of two icons—one for your application and one for your documents—a toolbar bitmap, and a resource file. The Debug directory contains the object and other output files that have been generated when your application was compiled and linked, along with the actual application file, Erector.exe.

Of the files that AppWizard created, only 16 have any direct relation to your work; the remainder are specific files for use by AppWizard, ClassWizard, and the Developer Studio that you will never need to edit or concern yourself with, although they are important to you. In particular, AppWizard creates a special file called ReadMe.txt that tells you what each of the useful files it generated for you contains.

You can open the ReadMe.txt file from the Developer Studio. Select **Open** from the File menu (or press **Ctrl+O**) to get the standard Open File dialog box. Make sure that you are in your application subdirectory. Type **ReadMe.txt** into the File Name edit text box. If you prefer, you can change the List Files of Type selection to **All Files** (*.*). This will list all the files in your application subdirectory; you can then select the **ReadMe.txt** file from the list. In either case, press **OK** to see the text file in the standard Edit window. Figure 4.14 shows you the ReadMe display for the ERECTOR application that you just built, displayed in full-screen mode. (To view your file in full-screen mode, select **Full Screen** from the View menu; to return to your normal display, press **Esc**.)

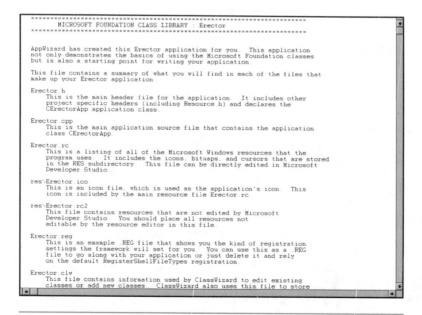

FIGURE 4.14 THE README FILE TELLS YOU EVERY FILE THAT APPWIZARD GENERATED FOR YOU AND WHAT IT CONTAINS.

At least the first time you create an application, you should read through this ReadMe file to see what AppWizard has created for you.

C++

As you look at the generated files, you will notice that you have both code files (with the extension .cpp) and header files (with the extension .h) for most of your files. This is a standard C++ convention.

C++ requires a substantial number of definitions. Every class must have a series of class definitions, including both member variables and prototypes for the class functions, or methods. By convention, all this information is placed in a class header file. Then the actual code for the functions is placed in a separate code file. In this way, the definitions—which generally don't change as much as the code—are safely out of the way as you work. Since this is a convention, it isn't required that you use these two separate files; if you want, you can both define the class and the function code in one file. In fact, many tutorials on C++ do just this, to simplify viewing these two essential items of information and to make working with the simple tutorial files easier for the student.

For real-life applications, however, the two-file arrangement works very well. This is the method used by Visual C++ and AppWizard when creating your skeleton application, and you should continue it in your own work. As you work through the examples in this book, you will see how efficient this structure is.

Running the Skeleton Application

The best way to see what AppWizard has done for you is to actually run the application. Go to the Project menu and select **Execute ERECTOR.EXE** (or press **Ctrl+F5**) and see what you get. You should see something very much like Figure 4.15.

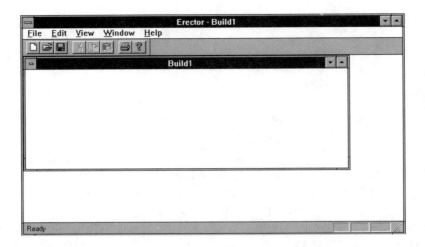

FIGURE 4.15 THIS IS THE SKELETON ERECTORSET APPLICATION IN ACTION.

Look at what you have here. To start with, you have a working Windows application—no small accomplishment. It has both an application window—the window with the menu bar—and a blank document window, titled Build1, within your application window. Note that this is the name that you supplied to AppWizard in the CErectorDoc class dialog box during the generation process.

Your application is already fairly smart; for example, it supports multiple documents. If you choose **New** from the File menu, you will get a new document window titled Build2. You can switch from one document window to the next or rearrange the document windows by using the Window menu selections. This is all done for you by the skeleton application code. Also, you can move, resize, maximize, and minimize the application or the document windows by using the standard Windows methods, both with the mouse and with keys. You can use the Control-menu box to perform all the standard Windows functions for your application. Except for the fact that it can't actually do anything yet, your application behaves just like any other Windows application.

You really need to take a moment and appreciate what AppWizard has done for you here. Using the MFC, AppWizard has created a complete, functional Windows application to your specifications. If you had ever worked with

Windows programming before the Foundation Classes, as I have, you would jump up and cheer, believe me. This is a great start to a full-fledged, professional-quality application.

CODE NAVIGATION IN DEVELOPER STUDIO

Once you have created such a complex application, you need to be able to move around it to see what it does and how it works. The Project Workspace docking window in the Developer Studio allows you to look at all your generated class information and to see how the various elements are connected. It also provides access to other useful information and can be switched to display reference documentation contents.

The Project Workspace provides several different ways to view the application that you have created. You can view it as a hierarchy of classes (ClassView), you can view it as a list of files (FileView), and you can view it as a list of resources (ResourceView). The default view is to display the classes and functions in a class hierarchy display.

When you are writing C++ programs, a browser that displays class information is almost a necessity. Even in ordinary C programs, there are often many functions and subroutines. Commercial and corporate developers often use compiled libraries of functions to allow them to provide specific functions such as serial or network communications within their applications quickly and efficiently. C++, with its many layers of hierarchical classes, presents an even more complex web of relationships. The ClassView display shows you graphically how the classes and functions in your application relate and allows you to jump directly to any given function or class definition.

The InfoViewer goes beyond simply viewing code. It also integrates all of the on-line documentation that you have in the Developer Studio: general references, tutorials and sample code, error information, and more. In earlier versions of Visual C++, this information was also generally available within one or two mouse-clicks, but it required a separate Help application and switching between the Help display and your code. Now, all this information is available in one place and in a very convenient and accessible format.

ClassView Pane and Viewing Options

The ClassView pane is displayed to the left of the Developer Studio display, shown in Figure 4.16.

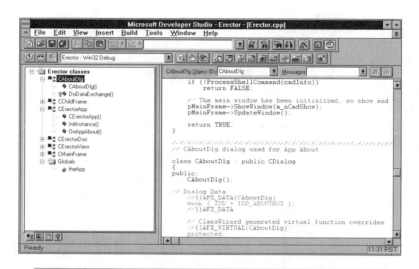

FIGURE 4.16 THE CLASSVIEW PANE IS THE DOCKING PANE TO THE LEFT SIDE OF YOUR DEVELOPER STUDIO DISPLAY.

The display in Figure 4.16 shows you the ErectorSet application opened up to display a variety of class and function information. In the next section, you will see what each symbol in this display means and how you can use it to navigate around your code.

The ClassView pane is a standard, docking tool window. You can control its display by moving the mouse cursor to any empty area in the pane and clicking the right mouse button. This displays a short pop-up menu that gives you a set of options for handing the pane. In particular, the menu allows you to hide the pane and change it from a docked pane to a floating pane. Many of the Developer Studio tools use this type of display, and you will see more about this as you work with Developer Studio, especially as you begin adding to and debugging the ErectorSet code. For now, leave the InfoView pane in its default location to the left of the Developer Studio display.

Viewing Code

You may have noticed when you started the Developer Studio, that this pane displayed the contents of the Visual C++ documentation. Now it displays the code that you have generated for ErectorSet. The set of four icon buttons at the bottom control what information you see in the pane and how it is organized. This is your control center for handling both your code and the Visual C++ and Developer Studio documents.

Viewing Classes and Functions

The default ClassView pane display is to show you the classes and functions that you have created in your application. This display is represented by the first icon button at the bottom of the pane, which shows a miniature class and function display.

If you look again at Figure 4.16, you will see several interesting pieces of information about ErectorSet in the ClassView pane. To begin with, the display is arranged in a hierarchy, showing you each of the current classes. The square button to the left of the class name shows either a plus sign, indicating that there is additional information that can be displayed under that level, or a minus sign, indicating that the level is fully expanded and all available information is displayed. To expand any level showing a plus, simply click on the box; to contract a level showing a minus, click on the box again.

The display under each class shows you several things about the class. First, it shows you all the functions for the class, listed in alphabetical order. These are represented by small purple rectangles, tilted to the left (in case you don't have a color display.) Any member variables for the class are displayed using small blue rectangles, tilted to the right. Global variables for the application are also displayed with this symbol under the separate heading of "Globals," as shown in Figure 4.16.

Next to each function or variable icon may be displayed two other icons: a small key, indicating that the function or variable is *protected*, or a lock, indicating that the item is *private*. No icon displayed indicates that the item is *public*.

C++

There are three types of class members (data, variables, and functions) in C++: private, protected, and public. Each allows a specific access range where other classes can see and use the member:

- *Private* means that the member can be accessed only by other members of this class.

- *Protected* means that the member can be accessed by other members of this class or the members of any class derived from this class.

- *Public* means that the member is publicly visible and can be accessed by any other class.

To move directly to a function, simply double-click on the function name in the ClassView pane. The Developer Studio immediately opens the file containing that function, moves to the function definition, and displays the result in the text editor pane on the right of your display.

If you click on the class definition, rather than on a function, the text editor displays the class header (.h) file instead of the code. This is a very quick way to move to the header if you need to make some changes there. In the same way, clicking on a member variable will display the definition of that variable, whether it's in the code file or in the header file.

Viewing Files

Usually, using the class view is the best and fastest way around your code. Mostly, you want to go to a specific class and/or function and don't really care exactly what file the code is in. However, sometimes it's best or easiest to look at a specific file. You can do that quite easily, by selecting the File View icon at the bottom of the pane: that's the third button from the left, which shows a picture of a listing. Clicking on it changes the display to show all the files in the project, as shown in Figure 4.17.

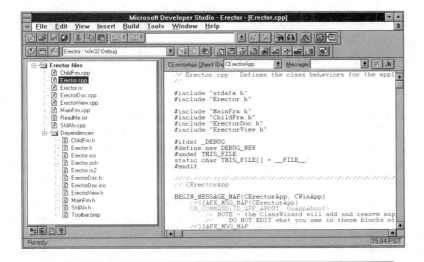

FIGURE 4.17 THE FILEVIEW PANE CAN SHOW YOU A DISPLAY ORGANIZED BY FILE NAME.

This display shows you all the code files, sorted by name. The Dependencies box shows all the dependent files that are referenced in the code files listed. As with the class display, the listings can be expanded if the box to the left shows a plus (+) and contracted if it shows a minus (-). Double-clicking on any one of the files immediately displays that file in the text editor pane to the right.

As you can see, this is less satisfactory for moving around your code than the class view for two reasons. First, when you open a file, as opposed to a class, the display opens at the top of the file. If you're looking for a specific function or data item in that file, you may have to scroll a long way until you get to it. Second, you may have more than one class in a file. For example, the class CAboutDialog, which controls and displays the About dialog box in the application, is part of the file erector.cpp—something you might not guess without prior knowledge—so looking for it might entail opening and scrolling through several files. With the class view, you move directly to your desired location, regardless of what file it's in and where it's located in the file.

However, there are times when the file view is the one you want. For example, when adding header comments and so on, you generally want to add to each file, not each function. Since that's what you'll do in the next section, leave your display in the FileView mode for now.

Adding Comments to the Generated Code

One of the best ways to become familiar with your generated code is to actually work with it. In the subsequent chapters, you will be adding code to all the working parts of your skeleton application. As a beginning, let's add some header comments so that you can see what the code looks like and become familiar with some of the most important items of generated code.

Like most professional programmers, I like to add comments to my code that will refresh my memory when I have to come back to rework or correct it. To do that, I use comments at the beginning of each code file that tells when the last change was done to the code, what the change was, and who did it. For this book, of course, I'm going to be making all the changes myself—which is how most small projects would be handled—so that all the changes will have my initials. On a larger project, with several programmers, such a list is invaluable, since it allows each person who works with the file to see what the previous changes were and who made them.

Since you are just starting this project, now is the best time to insert these headers on the major application files. Listing 4.1 shows you the beginning of the file Erector.cpp, which is the main application file.

Listing 4.1

```
// Erector.cpp : Defines the class behaviors for the application.
//

#include "stdafx.h"
#include "Erector.h"

#include "MainFrm.h"
#include "ChildFrm.h"
#include "ErectorDoc.h"
#include "ErectorView.h"
```

```
#ifdef _DEBUG
#define new DEBUG_NEW
#undef THIS_FILE
static char THIS_FILE[] = __FILE__;
#endif


/////////////////////////////////////////////////////////////////////////////
// CErectorApp
```

Listing 4.2 shows the same block of code after I added some heading comments to it.

Listing 4.2

```
/////////////////////////////////////////////////////////////////////////////
// Erector.cpp : Defines the class behaviors for the application.
//
//
// Created by AppWizard 11 December 1995 11:39:42
// Modifications:
/////////////////////////////////////////////////////////////////////////////

#include "stdafx.h"
#include "Erector.h"

#include "MainFrm.h"
#include "ChildFrm.h"
#include "ErectorDoc.h"
#include "ErectorView.h"


#ifdef _DEBUG
#define new DEBUG_NEW
#undef THIS_FILE
static char THIS_FILE[] = __FILE__;
#endif
```

```
////////////////////////////////////////////////////////////////////////////
// CErectorApp
```

C++

If you are not familiar with C++ notation, this may look a little strange to you. In C, as you probably know, comments are bracketed by the character strings /* to start the comment and */ to end it. In C, a comment between these two strings may cover several lines, or it may be inserted inside working code. Only the information *between* the two delimiter strings is considered a comment.

C++ also accepts such comments—generally, C++ is completely compatible with C in such matters—but it also has another type of comment, which begins with the string // and continues to the end of a line. Each method has certain advantages. C-style comments can be used, for example, to bracket lines of code to remove the entire block from the functioning program without losing the code itself; the single-line comment allows you to insert a comment on any line without accidentally affecting other lines, for example. In any case, since C++ supports both types of comments, you can use either one.

In the code in this book, I will use C++ comments unless C-style comments work better or are essential to what I want to do. You may use either—or none, if you prefer.

I would not tell you that such careful annotation is essential to good programming; I will tell you that it is something that I and all good programmers of my acquaintance do. (There is a certain amount of paranoia in a good programmer.) I do recommend, for the duration of this book and its exercises, that you adopt the habit of making similar notes in your code. As you read along, you will see that I have done this repeatedly. In the long run, you will find that such careful habits will make you a better programmer.

If you want to follow along, you should add these comment lines to your erector.cpp file, changing the date and time of creation to the correct values for your work. Then you can add the same comments to each major application file. AppWizard has already generated the one line describing the file contents that differs in each file; you should add the additional comments shown in Listing 4.2 to these other files as well:

- Erector.h
- ErectorDoc.cpp
- ErectorDoc.h
- ErectorView.cpp
- ErectorView.h

At this point, all you are doing is changing this beginning comment in each file to stand out a bit, adding the date and time that this file was created by AppWizard and leaving a space for notation of any modifications. The whole operation won't take more than a few minutes using **Copy** and **Paste**, but it will give you the basis for a complete log of your changes as you proceed.

N O T E   You will notice that you're not adding comments to all the files in the project. In particular, you're not commenting any of the MainFrm, ChildFrm, or StdAfx files. That's because you will generally not have to modify these files for the exercises in this book, so it isn't necessary to add header comments to them. If you do work on these files later, you can easily add comments to them as you need to.

Viewing Documentation

The InfoViewer also allows you to move to the Visual C++ documentation easily. Previously, you needed to use the Help menu to access most of this information and you had to launch a separate Help application. Now you can still use Help if that's the best way, or you can move directly to what you want, saving several clicks in the Help menu, if you have a good idea of what you're looking for.

Viewing General Documentation

To view the Visual C++ documentation library contents, click on the help information icon button at the bottom of the pane—it's the last on the right, with the question mark on it. This changes the InfoView display from your application to the InfoView Visual C++ documentation contents, as shown in Figure 4.18.

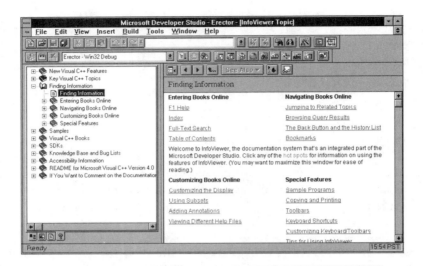

FIGURE **4.18** THE INFOVIEW PANE CAN ALSO SHOW YOU THE CONTENTS OF YOUR VISUAL C++ DOCUMENTATION.

As before, plus and minus signs show you which texts are fully displayed and which are only titles. Navigate among the topics to find the entry that you want. To display to any one of the topics, simply double-click on it. This will display the full text in the text editor pane. For ease of viewing, you should expand this to full screen by selecting **Full Screen** from the View menu.

SHORTCUT

I find the full-screen view the easiest to work in when I'm editing code. If you do, too, you may wish to set up a key combination on your keyboard that toggles from the full screen to the standard work-space display and back. To do this, choose **Customize** from the Tools menu to display the Customize dialog box, and then select the **Keyboard** tab. Now select **Text** from the Editor drop-down list, **View** in the Categories list, and scroll down to **ViewFullScreen** in the commands list. Place your cursor in the **Press new shortcut key** box and press a key combination that suits you—I use **Alt+Shift+S** (for screen), which isn't used for anything else. With this set, you can toggle from full-screen display and back by simply pressing the shortcut key combination that you have set.

You can also use InfoViewer's search mechanism to find references to specific items. This is especially useful when you are looking something up but are not sure what book or topic may contain the exact information that you want.

To use the search feature, simply bring any topic up in the display pane. Move the mouse cursor to any inactive area of the pane and press the right mouse button. Select **Search** from the pop-up menu to display the InfoViewer Search dialog box shown in Figure 4.19.

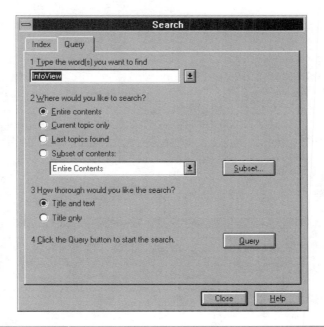

FIGURE **4.19** THE INFOVIEWER'S SEARCH DIALOG BOX ALLOWS YOU TO SEARCH FOR SPECIFIC TEXT IN THE DOCUMENTATION.

The **Query** tab is the one to select to make a general search through the documentation. You can enter any text that you want in the query text box at the top of the dialog box. Notice that it also saves the last several queries for you, so if you want to repeat a search, you don't have to type the text all over again. The search can go through all the text or titles in the documentation, or you may restrict it to a specific subset, using the radio buttons and the Subject of contents edit text box.

Pressing the **Query** button starts the search. When complete, the Search function presents you with a list of all of the entries found that match whatever you requested. You can then examine them one at a time to find what you want.

The other tab, Index, presents you with an index of items in the documentation. You can select one of these and go directly to that part of the documentation.

Jumping to Code-Specific Documentation

However, there is a faster way to find specific information in the documentation. Besides using the contents and the search features, you can use the **F1** key to move directly to a specific function or topic if you have it selected and highlighted in your code.

For example, switch the InfoView pane back to the ClassView and double-click on the function InitInstance in CErectorApp. This will bring up the class display at the desired function. Within the InitInstance function, you will see a line of code that calls the function LoadStdProfileSettings. This isn't one of your functions—as you can see in the InfoView display, since the function isn't listed there—so it must be one of the MFC functions. To see its description, use the mouse to highlight the function name as shown in Figure 4.20 and press **F1**.

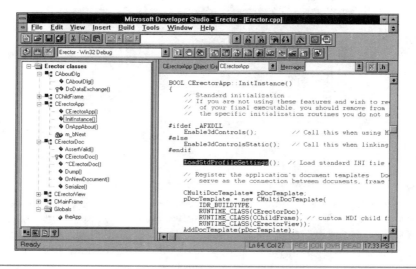

FIGURE 4.20 YOU CAN SELECT A SPECIFIC FUNCTION CALL IN YOUR CODE AND USE THE **F1** KEY TO JUMP DIRECTLY TO THE APPROPRIATE DOCUMENTATION.

This automatically starts the Help function and, after a little searching, brings up the display shown in Figure 4.21.

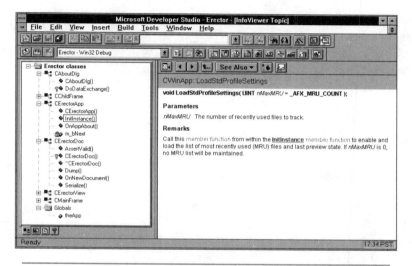

FIGURE 4.21 THE F1 SEARCH FOR YOUR SELECTED TEXT GOES DIRECTLY TO THE FUNCTION INFORMATION IN THE DOCUMENTATION.

This quickly displays all the information you need on the selected function and shows what class it belongs to as well.

CODE NAVIGATION USING BROWSE

In addition to InfoViewer, the Developer Studio has a more extensive Browse function, which is accessed by choosing **Browse** from the Tools menu. This feature allows you to look at all your generated class information and to see how the various elements are connected, including MFC classes as well.

This is a very nice feature and, in earlier versions of Visual C++, was essential because it was the only effective way to navigate around your project. However, with the advent of InfoViewer, this is no longer the case. Most of the time, InfoViewer gives you all the flexibility and visibility that you need to move around your application, no matter how complex it becomes. For this reason, you may decide not to use the Browse function, which has substantial overhead, at all and to stick to the Project Workspace pane for all your work.

The Browser does a few things that are not incorporated in the InfoViewer function which sometimes make it the more desirable tool for working with your application code. First, it shows the classes and functions in a complete class hierarchy, including the MFC base classes, and it allows you to move to the base classes as well as to your own code. Naturally, you should never be modifying the MFC base classes, but it is often useful to look in detail at the MFC code if you have a sticky problem or need some guidance on how to do some special task. Second, the Browser shows you all functions and relationships in your code, including ones generated by MFC macros, which are hidden by the InfoViewer. Again, you should never change these directly—that's what ClassWizard is for—but you may need to know that they're there.

Building the Browser Database File

There are several ways to get into the Browser. As you work through these exercises, you will use several of the ones that I find most useful. First, however, let's look at the basic requirements for using the Browser.

The first requirement of using the Browser is that you have built your application and created a Browser database. The Browser database has the same name as your project, with the extension .bsc; so, for ErectorSet, the Browser database is named Erector.bsc. The Browser function uses this database to find all the references in your code and to display the correct linkages for your application.

Building the Browser database is an optional feature of the compiler. Because adding the Browser database and adding browse information to the workspace takes both time and disk space, and because InfoViewer does such a great job of handling most viewing requirements, building the database is *not* the default option, so you will need to make changes to your build settings to generate the browse database. To do so take the following step:

1. Choose **Settings** from the Build menu to display the Project Settings dialog box. From there, select the **C/C++** tab to display the C/C++ Compiler Options, and then select **General** from the Category list. The display changes to show the General Category setting options, as shown in Figure 4.22.

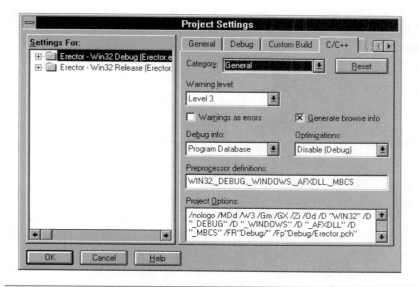

FIGURE 4.22 THE GENERAL CATEGORY OF THE C/C++ COMPILER OPTIONS ALLOWS YOU TO ENABLE
OR DISABLE CREATING THE BROWSER DATABASE FOR YOUR PROJECT.

The setting shown in Figure 4.22 is the one that you want to use. This selects **Generate browse info**, to tell the compiler to collect the necessary symbols to create the Browser database file.

2. Choose **Rebuild All** from the Build menu (or press **Alt+F8**) to rebuild the project with the browse information and create the Browser database. Note that the last line of the information in the Output window will tell you that the build process has created a browser database for your project.

   Once this is competed, you can proceed to browse your files using the Browser.

SHORTCUT

Although you can reset and rebuild the project like this, you will generally find it easier and faster to simply select **Browse** from the Tools menu. If the Browser database doesn't exist, you will see a dialog box that tells you that and asks if you want to change the workspace Build settings, rebuild the project, create the database, and automatically open the Browser for you. Simply click **Yes** and the and the entire process is handled for you.

N O T E

All of the Browser functions are available using the pop-up menus that are available by clicking the right mouse button in the appropriate location in your InfoView or text editor pane. However, all of the menu items that perform browse functions require the Browser database, just as the main menu selections or keyboard shortcuts do, so you must still build the database as described here before using them.

Browser Windows and Viewing Options

Once you have your Browser database, you can select **Browse** from the Tools menu (**Ctrl+F11**) to open the browser database. Browse is disabled (dimmed) if no project workspace is currently open. If the Browser database is already open—because you did some earlier search that required it—the Tools menu will show **Close Erector.bsc** (or whatever your project's Browser database file is named), which you can select to close the file and save memory while you are working.

When you open the Browser, you will see the Browse dialog box shown in Figure 4.23.

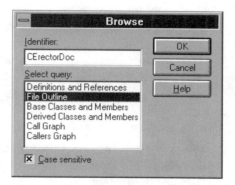

FIGURE 4.23 THE BROWSE DIALOG BOX ALLOWS YOU TO SELECT THE TYPE OF QUERY THAT YOU WANT TO DIS-
PLAY.

The key to the Browser windows is the Select Query list box. This gives you the
choice of six browse types:

- Definitions and References. The default. This displays the definition and
  all references to the name that you type into the Identifier text box.

- File Outline. This display requires you to select a file in the project window or that you enter a fully qualified file name in the Identifier text box.
  It displays all the functions and classes that are in the selected file by
  default.

- Base Classes and Members. This display requires that you enter a class
  name in the Symbol text box. It displays all the classes from which the
  selected class is derived.

- Derived Classes and Members. This display requires that you enter a class
  name in the Identifier text box. It displays all the classes that are derived
  from the selected class.

- Call Graph. This display requires that you enter a function name in the
  Identifier text box. It displays all the functions that are called by the selected function.

- Callers Graph. This display requires that you enter a function name in
  the Identifier text box. It displays all the functions that call the selected
  function.

As you can see, there are logically four groups of Browser queries: definitions and references for any type of object, file displays, functions displays, and class displays. For both functions and classes, you can display up or down the chain by using the appropriate type of query. These are useful and powerful tools, and you will see how they work in detail in the remainder of this section.

Viewing Files

One of the more useful tools of the Browse function is the ability to see all the functions and classes that are defined in any file. This is particularly useful when you are working in a large project and have a number of functions in a class. This is similar to the ClassView of the InfoViewer, but it is restricted to the functions and classes defined in a single file rather than the entire project. On the other hand, it displays functions that are hidden in the ClassView display.

Using the File Outline view, you can see all the classes defined in a file, all the functions for these classes, and even the data members and macros defined in the file. Figure 4.24 shows you the File Outline display for the file ErectorDoc.cpp.

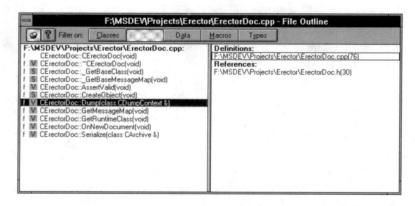

FIGURE 4.24 THE FILE OUTLINE DISPLAY IS A GREAT HELP IN SEEING ALL THE FUNCTIONS AND DATA IN A FILE AT ONCE.

This window is divided into two panes. The left pane displays the functions and classes in the selected file, using the filter settings that you have chosen by setting the filter buttons along the top of the display. The right pane displays the definition and references for the item selected in the left pane.

The filter buttons—Classes, Functions, Data, Macros, and Types—allow you to control what is displayed in the left pane. The default display shows you all the functions and classes that are in the file.

The initial in front of the entries in the left pane tell you what type of filter the given entry responds to. For example, the entry highlighted in Figure 14.15 (CErectorDoc::Dump) has an *f* in front of it, showing that it is a function. A *V* or *S* after the filter type tells you whether the function has been defined with the virtual or static attributes. Table 4.5 lists the abbreviations you may find in the Browse window.

TABLE 4.5 ABBREVIATIONS USED IN THE BROWSE WINDOW

Abbreviation	Meaning
c	class
d	data
f	function
m	macro
t	nonclass type
V	Virtual function or data member
S	Static function or data member

To see the definition or references for any item listed in the left pane, simply click once on the item to select it. The definition and references are displayed in the right pane. To jump directly to the item in your code, double-click on it. (Note that this will automatically close your Browse window as well, unless you click on the pin icon in the upper left-hand corner of the dialog box to "pin" it.)

Viewing Classes

One of the most important functions of the Browser is its ability to show the relationships among the various classes in your application and their relationships with the MFC base classes. To see how this works, begin by entering the class name **CErectorDoc** into the Identifier text box and selecting **Base Classes and Members** from the Select Query list. Then press **OK** to see the display shown in Figure 4.25.

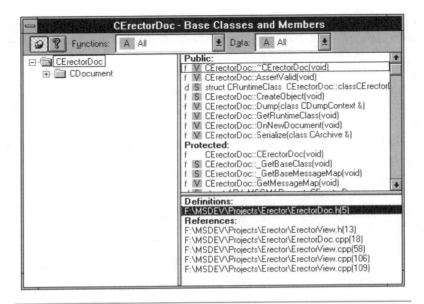

FIGURE 4.25 THIS BASE CLASSES AND MEMBERS DISPLAY SHOWS YOU THE CLASSES FROM WHICH
CERECTORDOC WAS DERIVED.

On the left of the display, you see the hierarchy of classes that generated the
CErectorDoc class. CErectorDoc is directly derived from CDocument. Notice that
CErectorDoc is represented by empty folders with a minus in front, while
CDocument has a closed folder with a plus in front, indicating that CDocument
is itself derived from classes that are not displayed. To see the next level up, simply double-click on the box next to CDocument. This is a great visual way to see
the relationship of your class to the complete MFC class structure.

The two panes on the right side of the dialog box show you additional valuable information about the selected node, or class. The top pane shows you all
the functions that are defined in the class. The bottom pane shows you where
the class is defined and where it is referenced throughout your application. In
both cases, simply double-clicking on a selection in one of these panes takes you
back to the editor at that specific location.

The corresponding Derived Classes and Members display works in the same
way, but it shows all the classes in your application that are derived from the
given class. The basic display is the same as the Base Classes and Members, but
the direction of the display is different.

SHORTCUT

You can also access the same displays of Base classes (or Derived classes) by selecting a class in the ClassView and pressing the right mouse button. This displays a pop-up menu that includes **Base Classes...** and **Derived Classes...** items. Selecting either of these brings up the same display that you saw earlier.

Because classes are the heart of your MFC Windows application, you will find that this class display feature of the Browser is exceptionally useful. The entire MFC structure is a little overwhelming at first. By using the Browser on your selected classes, you can easily see how your code fits into the whole picture without being overcome by all the complexity or becoming lost in the complete MFC hierarchy.

Viewing Functions

The Class Browser can also be used to determine the relationships among the various functions in your application. The **Call Graph** and **Caller Graph** selections allow you to see how your functions are related and, more importantly, they allow you to see where functions are referenced in your project, something that isn't displayed in the InfoViewer.

To see an example of this, select **Call Graph** as the Select Query entry in the Browser dialog box and enter the name **CErectorDoc::** into the Identifier text box.

WARNING

Note that this name is slightly different from the one you entered to view the CErectorDoc class. There you simply entered **CErectorDoc**; now you are entering the name with two colons behind it. One is the class name (without the colons), and the other is the beginning of a function name (with the colons). This can be annoying if you get the name wrong; indeed, it can be most disconcerting. However, if you make this error, the Browser puts up a dialog box that tells you it can't find the requested symbol as a function.

You get this even though CErectorDoc is the beginning, in standard C++ parlance, of every function name in that class. You will get the error dialog box even if you append the * character, which is supposed to allow you to match multiple names. The only way to display all the functions in the class from the Call or Caller Graph Browse dialog box is to append the required two colons to the class name.

Now press the **OK** button. This presents you with the Resolve Ambiguity selection dialog box shown in Figure 4.26.

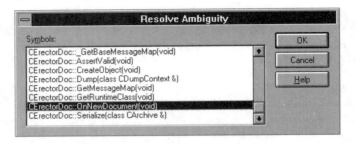

FIGURE **4.26** IF YOU ARE LOOKING AT FUNCTIONS IN THE BROWSER AND ENTER A NAME IN THE IDENTIFIER TEXT BOX THAT MATCHES MORE THAN ONE FUNCTION, THE BROWSER DISPLAYS THIS DIALOG BOX TO ALLOW YOU TO RESOLVE THE AMBIGUOUS REFERENCE.

This window displays all of the functions in the class CErectorDoc and allows you to select the specific function that you want to examine. Note that this list shows several more functions than the equivalent display in the ClassView pane. The additional functions, like _GetBaseClass or GetMessageMap, are embedded in macros that are used in the class, and as such are not directly available to you. So both displays are correct, each in a different context.

As an example, select **CErectorDoc::OnNewDocument(void)** from the scrolling list, as shown in Figure 4.26, and press **OK**. The Browser window now displays the Call Graph for the selected function, as shown in Figure 4.27.

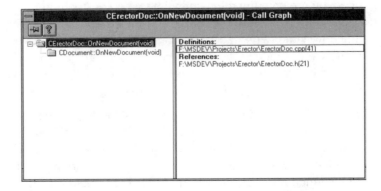

FIGURE **4.27** THE CALL GRAPH DISPLAY SHOWS ALL THE FUNCTIONS THAT ARE CALLED BY A GIVEN FUNCTION.

This window displays the function that you have selected—in this case, OnNewDocument—and all functions that are called from this function. As you can see in Figure 4.27, the one function that OnNewDocument calls is the OnNewDocument function in its base class, CDocument. As before, the right-hand side of the Browser window shows you the location of the definition and all references to the selected function.

The Caller Graph display is exactly the same as the Call Graph display, except that it shows you all the functions that call the selected function instead of all the functions that are called by the function. In both cases, this gives you useful information about the relationships between your functions.

Viewing Definitions and References

Finding the definition or references for a function or class works best from your ClassView pane; access to general symbol names works best from your editor pane. Although you can open the Browser and type in a symbol name, as you read earlier, you must get the name and syntax exactly correct to display anything. For this reason, it is generally easiest and most useful to select a name from one of these panes.

As an example, use the ClassView pane to select the function OnNewDocument in the class CErectorDoc. Next press **F11** to display the definition of this function or press **Shift+F11** to display the first reference for this function in your project in the text editor window. This is the fastest and best way to perform this maneuver.

As an alternative, you can double-click on the function in the ClassView pane, which automatically opens and displays the selected function in the text editor window.

This is also the same function you examined in the previous section. Just to tie this all together, you can also reach the same place in your code by using the Browser in each of the two ways that you just read about:

NOTE

- You can open the Browser for your application and use either of the Class Graph displays. Enter **CErectorDoc** in the Identifier text box as the class to be displayed, then choose the OnNewDocument function from the top-right pane of the display. Double-click on the function name to go directly to the function definition.

- You can open the Browser for your application and use either the Call Graph or Caller Graph displays. Enter **CErectorDoc::OnNewDocument** in the Identifier text box. This displays the definition of OnNewDocument in the right-hand pane. Double-click on the reference address to go directly to the function definition.

However you get there, select the name of the function: OnNewDocument. Now press **Shift+F11** or select **Go To** from the Edit menu and then select **Reference** from the Go to what list in the dialog box and click the **GoTo** button. Figure 4.28 shows you the Go To dialog box when you have selected OnNewDocument.

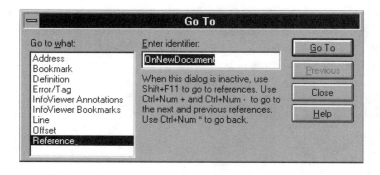

FIGURE 4.28 THE EDIT MENU'S GO TO FUNCTION ALLOWS YOU TO SELECT AN ITEM AND GO TO IT IN A VARIETY OF WAYS.

In this case, the name that you have selected here is not unique; the base class also has an OnNewDocument function. Because of this, the Browser will present you with a Resolve Ambiguity dialog box, similar to the one you saw earlier in Figure 4.16, to prompt you to select the item that you want.

When you select the desired reference and click **OK**, the Browser will automatically open the file containing the first reference to your selected function and move to the correct line. In this case, select **CErectorDoc::OnNewDocument(void)** from the dialog list. When you click **OK**, the Browser opens the file ErectorDoc.h and displays the line that is the prototype of the OnNewDocument function. Selecting the name in the InfoView pane saves these steps since the name is automatically fully qualified, so the Browser can move directly to the reference (or definition, as the case might be) without any further work on your part.

If you want to see if there are more references, you can press **Ctrl** and the + sign on the number pad keyboard (or click **Next** in the Go To dialog box if you used the Edit menu to get here). This move to the next reference in the list, if any. If there are no further references, the display simply remains the same. To move back down the chain of references, simply press **Ctrl** and the - sign on the number pad (or click **Previous** in the Go To dialog box if you used the Edit menu to get here). Finally, to return to the original position where you began the search, you can press **Ctrl** and the * on the number pad keyboard.

To go to the definition of the selected name, use the same techniques but press **F11**. Once you have made your selection, you can use the same key combinations to navigate the definition chain.

N O T E

All of these Browser functions have menu selections, which are available through the Edit menu's Go To function. However, you will find it easier and faster to use the shortcut keys. The Browser structure and selection mechanism makes them extremely easy to use. In fact, in the editor pane, you don't even have to select the name that you want to examine. All you have to do is place the cursor anywhere in the name and then press the appropriate key; the Browser automatically examines the word under the cursor and looks it up.

There are two things to watch out for when you use this selection feature. The first one you have seen already, when you simply selected the function name for browsing. Namely, if the name is not unique, the Browser will have to prompt you for the specific item you want. This really isn't much of a problem, but you can avoid it by selecting the function or class name from the InfoView pane instead of the editor pane. The second thing to watch out for is that you must place the cursor inside or at the beginning of the name that you want to look up; if it is at the end of the name, the Browser will try to look up (), which, naturally, isn't a valid name.

You aren't limited to looking up functions in this way. You can look up any symbol name that is defined in your application. Remember that you can always return to the starting point of your queries by pressing **Ctrl** and the * on the number pad.

SHORTCUT You can also find definitions and references for items that you have selected in your editor pane, as described earlier, by pressing the right mouse button after you have made your selection. This displays the editor pop-up menu, which includes **Go To Definition Of...** and **Go To Reference To...** selections, with the selected item name appended, on the menu. Personally, I still find the keyboard method easier, but you may prefer the mouse/menu approach.

SUMMARY

In this chapter, you have begun to create a complete, working Windows application. The chapter began with a short overview of what makes Windows applications different from other applications and how Windows communicates with your application. Then you used AppWizard to create the skeleton application for ErectorSet. As you saw, this is actually a pretty complete application that can open multiple documents and handle commands from the user to move, resize, minimize and do all the other user interface things that you normally expect from a Windows application. Finally, you saw how to look at your code using the InfoViewer function and the Browser. With the InfoViewer, you can look at class definitions, and you can also look at a specific functions and follow references to any symbol defined in your application. With the Browser, you can examine the class hierarchy in detail and see specifically where your functions and variables are referenced. In the next chapter, you will see how use the ClassWizard to enhance your skeleton to begin to do some actual processing.

CHAPTER 5

DRAWING IN DOCUMENTS

In this chapter, you will learn how to add basic message processing for mouse messages and Windows messages to an application, and how to use these messages for drawing in your application. To simplify this process, Visual C++ uses the ClassWizard to help you develop and maintain processing for a wide range of standard Windows messages. You will work through a series of steps that allows you to add processing for basic mouse movement and menu selection items to your skeleton application. In addition, you will learn how to save and restore your files easily and quickly using MFC's serialization processing. Important topics include:

- Handling Windows drawing messages
- Handling Windows mouse movement messages
- Adding functions to your application with ClassWizard
- Saving and opening saved documents using the MFC Serialization class

ADDING FUNCTIONS TO A CLASS

Now that you have a basic skeleton of a Windows application, you need to add real functionality to it. You do that by adding new functions to the classes that AppWizard has generated for you and by adding new classes that implement various functions. Because most Windows applications need to process the same or very similar messages, Visual C++ includes a ClassWizard that will help you create and maintain standard message processing for your application.

The most basic functions that every application needs to have are functions that create and display documents that are specific to that application. ErectorSet is a simple drawing application: it is intended to draw erector beams in a document window. In this section of the chapter, you will see how to add drawing functions to the ErectorSet application and how to use ClassWizard to handle mouse and menu information to create your drawing.

Drawing in the ErectorSet Document

When you create your skeleton application, you get a document class and code to handle one or more documents in your application. As you saw in Chapter 4, your skeleton application will open and display one or more document windows whenever you select **New** from the File menu. Up to this point, however, your document doesn't have anything in it to display. You see only an empty window when you display a document in the skeleton application. Your skeleton application can't save documents, either, since there isn't (as yet) any information in a document to save, and it can't retrieve documents, since there aren't any documents created for it to retrieve.

You must draw in the document window to have a display. In the case of the ErectorSet application, what you want to see in the document are a series of erector beams. Each document will consist of a series of beams. These need to be created, displayed, and stored in your document.

Defining the Document Contents

Each document, then, will consist of one or more beams, which are simply rectangles. You want to create and display these rectangles in your document window. The rectangles will be created with the mouse by clicking and dragging. Since each beam will be a rectangle, you can use the MFC class CRect to define and manipulate beam size and position, and since each Erector document will consist of a series of beams, it makes sense to handle these beams as a *class*, which you can call CErectorBeam.

Here are the steps that you need to take to create, display, and manage the beams:

1. Create a CErectorBeam class.
2. Keep a list of all the beams that make up the display for a document in the document.
3. Capture information from the mouse to define the location of the beam.
4. Draw the beams on the screen to display them.

Note that you need to take this last step when the beam is created and anytime the screen needs to be redrawn. This will happen whenever the window showing the document is moved and when anything is moved over it or off of it.

Because the CErectorBeam class is directly associated with the documents, the code defining and managing the beam class will be added to the files that contain the code for defining and managing your documents: ErectorDoc.h and ErectorDoc.cpp. If the class were more complex or not so closely tied to the document class, then you might choose to place the code into two separate class files, one a header (.h) file for the class definitions and the other a code (.cpp) file for the functions.

Since there may be many beams in a document, it makes sense to keep these beam objects in a list. MFC provides a series of *collection classes* that allow you to store and retrieve groups of MFC objects. MFC supports collection classes that are lists, arrays, and maps (more commonly called *dictionaries*) of objects. In this case, you will use the simplest form of collection class, a list. So each document will need to keep a list of the beams as a class data member. In the next sections, you will see how to add this type of functionality to your document class.

Expanding the Document Class

Before you add beam information to your document, you need to take two steps to expand your document class:

1. Add a function that handles opening new documents to your CErectorDoc class. You will do this using the WizardBar, which makes this type of addition both fast and easy.

2. Set up a method to define a collection of beam objects in the CErectorDoc class. This requires a small change to your standard header file, StdAfx.h.

Let's take each of these items in turn. Here is how you can add the new code for processing existing documents to your CErectorDoc class.

First, switch into the File view in your InfoView pane and double-click the ErectorDoc.cpp file to display it in the editor pane. Next, move to the editor pane and click the right mouse button to display the pop-up menu. If the Toolbar entry is not checked, select it from the pop-up menu. This displays the WizardBar toolbar at the top of the editor pane, as shown in Figure 5.1. (If the Toolbar entry was checked, the WizardBar is already displayed at the top of the pane.)

FIGURE 5.1 THE WIZARDBAR IS DISPLAYED AT THE TOP OF YOUR EDITOR PANE WHEN EDITING AN APPLICATION FILE.

The WizardBar has two drop-down lists and two buttons. The first list shows you the Object ID of all the items in the project that can send messages to the class—menu items, dialog box controls, and so on. The first item in the list is the class name itself. The second list shows you all the Messages that can be handled by the selected object. The first button allows you to remove processing for a selected message from the class. the second opens the class header (.h) file. All of these features are primarily associated with the ClassWizard, which is a special feature of Visual C++ and the Developer Studio. You will learn in detail how to use the Class Wizard in a later section when you add mouse movement handling to ErectorSet.

For now, you simply want to add handling for opening an existing document to your CErectorDoc class. To do this, make sure that **CErectorDoc** is selected in the Object IDs list, and then drop down the Messages list and scroll to the message OnOpenDocument. This is the message CErectorDoc will get when an existing document is opened. At this point, your screen should look like Figure 5.2.

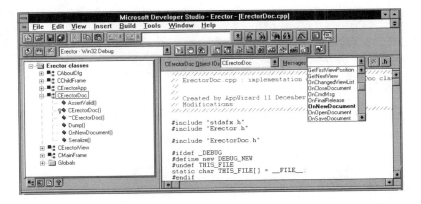

FIGURE 5.2 SCROLL DOWN THE MESSAGES LIST IN THE WIZARDBAR TO DISPLAY THE
ONOPENDOCUMENT MESSAGE.

Notice that the OnNewDocument message, immediately above OnOpenDocument is displayed in bold. This indicates that it is already handled in your code. Now select **OnOpenDocument**. The Developer Studio displays a dialog box asking if you want to add code to handle this message; press **Yes**. This automatically allows your class to process this message and adds the skeleton code for handling the message to the bottom of the code file. The editor window also automatically moves to display the added code.

That's all there is to adding this new functionality to your document class. Of course, at this point, your class doesn't actually do anything with any of these messages; you'll add that processing when you add the new CErectorBeam class.

Next, you need to prepare your project to use the MFC collection classes. As you read earlier, you will use a list class—one of the collection classes—to store the beams for a document. Since not all applications need collection classes, MFC does not add these functions to a standard project. (Although why they are not an option during project creation, like database support, is beyond me! I suppose that will come in version 4.1, or something like that.) Since these additional classes are not presently part of your project, you need to add them by including the required header file in your project. These classes are defined in the file afxtempl.h which is part of the MFC. There are several ways to include these classes in your project, but the best way is to add the necessary #include statement to the StdAfx.h file. Listing 5.1 shows you the new code added to the StdAfx.h file, with the added line highlighted in bold.

Listing 5.1

```
// stdafx.h : include file for standard system include files,
//  or project specific include files that are used frequently, but
//      are changed infrequently
//

#define VC_EXTRALEAN        // Exclude rarely-used stuff from Windows headers

#include <afxwin.h>         // MFC core and standard components
#include <afxext.h>         // MFC extensions
#include <afxtempl.h>       // MFC templates
#ifndef _AFX_NO_AFXCMN_SUPPORT
#include <afxcmn.h>         // MFC support for Windows 95 Common Controls
#endif // _AFX_NO_AFXCMN_SUPPORT
```

There are several reasons for adding the #include here. The StdAfx.h file defines the precompiled header for your project. That means that the data in that file gets built only one time, and after that is used as a unit, sort of like including a library. This speeds up compilation and linking and ensures that these headers will always be available throughout your project. Also, you won't be actually changing the afxtempl.h entries; you simply need to be able to access them correctly. This makes them a natural candidate for inclusion in the standard, precompiled header, since once you have loaded them, you don't need to reload or access them further. If you included the header in your CErectorDoc header, for example, then the header would be compiled each time you recompiled the document class, which is extra overhead that you don't need.

Note that, although you have made some changes to your project files, you are not recompiling these files or rebuilding the project at this time. You still have more code to add to your document handling to create and process the beams. The correct time to rebuild your project is after you have added all of the code that you need.

With these two changes made to your project, you are ready to add some processing code to build and display the beams in your document.

Building the CErectorBeam Class

One of the primary tenets of object-oriented programming is that each object should have enough internal data to allow it to perform the appropriate functions. In the case of a beam object, the primary function is to display itself. To do that, a beam needs to have a position and a color for the display. Ultimately, you intend to allow the user to control the display characteristics of the rectangle, such as color and border; therefore, although you could make these a internal constant of the beams, you choose to set them for each beam when you create it. In that case, each beam needs to have three pieces:

- A rectangle
- A color
- A border

A CRect class in the MFC provides all of the necessary definitions and functions for creating and managing rectangles. (If you think about it, rectangles occur in graphics programming in an enormous number of situations, so this make a lot of sense.) The color of an object in a window is provided by the Windows COLOR-REF data structure. Finally, the border of a graphic object displayed in a window is provided by a graphic pen. For this exercise, the pen will always be black, and the only element of the pen that you will be able to change is the pen width. This is stored in your code as an unsigned integer, UINT. You also need to add the color and pen width to the document class as well. This will be the current brush width and color settings. Keeping them in the document class means that each document will have its own default settings for these items, which will be set in all new beams as they are created.

There is one more catch, however. Once you have inserted the class data members to support the pen width and brush color into to the CErectorDoc class, you need to initialize them. One of the basic tenets of object-oriented programming is that data members should always be correctly initialized with default values when a new object of the given class is created. Therefore, you need to add initialization code to your CErectorDoc class to make sure that both the color and the width are initialized.

One approach to initialization is to place the necessary code into the constructor for the class. For document-based data, however, you also have another alternative, which you will use here: you can put the initialization code with the code that creates a new document or opens an old one. Then you can send the initialization values that you want when you create the new class object. The document class now has two functions that perform these tasks: OnOpenDocument and OnNewDocument. You can override them to provide the necessary initialization code for the color and width. Since the code is identical in both cases, it makes sense to consolidate this into a single auxiliary function, InitDocument, which is called from both of the initialization functions.

Adding Class Definitions and Interface Code

As you read earlier, you will add the necessary CErectorBeam code to the files ErectorDoc.h and ErectorDoc.cpp. In addition, you need to add some new code to ErectorDoc.cpp to link to the new CErectorBeam class. The ErectorDoc.h file contains the class definition for CErectorDoc; you will add the additional definitions to support the CErectorBeam class to this file. Listing 5.2 shows you the complete new version of ErectorDoc.h, with the added code shown in bold type.

Listing 5.2

```
//////////////////////////////////////////////////////////////////////
// ErectorDoc.h : interface of the CErectorDoc class
//
//
// Created by AppWizard 11 December 1995 11:39:42
// Modifications:
//    12 Dec 95   DH    Add OnOpenDocument to generated code,
//    along with new common InitDocument().
//    12 Dec 95   DH    Add CErectorBeam class to generated code:
//    initialization; serialization; contents
//////////////////////////////////////////////////////////////////////

// Forward declaration of the data structure class, CErectorBeam
class CErectorBeam;
```

```
class CErectorDoc : public CDocument
{
protected: // create from serialization only
    CErectorDoc();
    DECLARE_DYNCREATE(CErectorDoc)


// Attributes
protected:
    CTypedPtrList<CObList, CErectorBeam*> m_beamList; // each list element
is a beam object

    // We track the beam color or pattern and outline width
    //    at the document level for all views. This allows
    //    the user to choose a new beam style for all the views
    //    together, rather than one at a time.
    COLORREF    m_crBrushColor;       // the brush color
    UINT        m_nPenWidth;          // the border width

public:


// Operations
public:
    CErectorBeam*    NewBeam();


// Overrides
    // ClassWizard generated virtual function overrides
    //{{AFX_VIRTUAL(CErectorDoc)
    public:
    virtual BOOL OnNewDocument();
    virtual void Serialize(CArchive& ar);
    virtual BOOL OnOpenDocument(LPCTSTR lpszPathName);
    //}}AFX_VIRTUAL


// Implementation
public:
    virtual ~CErectorDoc();
```

```
#ifdef _DEBUG
     virtual void AssertValid() const;
     virtual void Dump(CDumpContext& dc) const;
#endif

protected:
     void InitDocument();

// Generated message map functions
protected:
     //{{AFX_MSG(CErectorDoc)
          // NOTE - the ClassWizard will add and remove member functions
here.
          //     DO NOT EDIT what you see in these blocks of generated code
!
     //}}AFX_MSG
     DECLARE_MESSAGE_MAP()
};


/////////////////////////////////////////////////////////////////////////
// class CErectorBeam
//
// A beam defines the size and characteristics of a rectangle
//    that is filled to make a beam element of the drawing.
// An erector document may have multiple beams.
//

class CErectorBeam : public CObject
{
public:
     CErectorBeam(UINT nPenWidth, COLORREF crBrushColor);

protected:
     CErectorBeam();                         // required for serialization
     DECLARE_SERIAL(CErectorBeam)
```

```
// Attributes
protected:
        CRect       m_rectBeam;         // the beam rectangle
        CPoint          m_ptStart;      // the beam starting point
        COLORREF    m_crBrushColor;     // the color for the rectangle
        UINT        m_nPenWidth;        // the rectangle border size


public:
        virtual ~CErectorBeam();
        // This is both prototype and inline definition
        CRect* GetCurrentBeam() { return &m_rectBeam; };


// Operations
public:
        void BeginBeam(CPoint pt);
        void EndBeam(CPoint pt);
        BOOL DrawBeam(CDC* pDC);


// Helper Functions
public:
        virtual void Serialize(CArchive& ar);


};
```

///

N O T E   This is a complete listing because the changes are quite extensive and because this is the first time that you are working with the actual working code of the application. The first time you see any section of code, you will have a complete display, as you do here. Subsequent listings of the same file will show only the code that needs to be added or changed along with a few lines on either side of the new code for placement. This is basically a space-saving maneuver; note that you can always look at the code at our web site (http:)if you have any questions about how the added code should look or where it should be placed.

Let's review this new code. Here is a brief explanation, from the top down, of the new code that you have added to `ErectorDoc.h`:

1. At the beginning, you add two short comment lines as shown here, giving the date, your initials, and a brief summary of what changes were done. (In this case, the comment covers all the changes in this chapter, so this won't need to be revised again.)

2. A forward declaration of the new CErectorBeam class. You need this so that the C++ compiler knows that CErectorBeam is a new class when it comes to the declaration of the object list, `m_beamList`, which is defined as a collection of beam pointers, and for the function, `NewBeam`, which returns a pointer to a beam. If you didn't have this, the compiler would generate an error at these points because it would not know what type of object a CErectorBeam pointer pointed to.

3. A series of protected data members for the class. These are:

   - `m_beamList`, the class member where the document class stores the list of beams that makes up the document. `m_beamList` is a CTypedPtrList, which is a list class built from a template. As the code is set up, each member of this list must be a pointer to a CErectorBeam object.

This code uses a *template* to create an instance of the class CTypedPtrList that will hold the CErectorBeam pointers and saves this list as `m_beamList`. *Template classes* are special types of C++ classes that are built using a type argument that you supply. Template classes are used to create a class that can perform similar functions on many types of data without sacrificing type safety. MFC uses template classes to implement its collection classes.

In this case, you are creating an instance of a list class that is derived from CObList and holds pointers of the type CErectorBeam. To create the new class instance, you give the class name, CTypedPtrList, and two parameters: the base class of the list, CObList, and the type of the pointers themselves, CErectorBeam*. This new class is then assigned to the member variable, `m_beamList`.

Templates are a new feature of the C++ language, and this implementation gives you some significant improvements over the old methods of handling such items. In earlier versions of MFC, you would have created an instance of the CObList class to hold your ErectorBeam pointers. This works fine, but it is subject to a possible error in that you could accidentally add any type of class pointer to the list. If you did that, when you went to draw the document, you would generate a bad error, and one that you would have some difficulty in tracing. The new template-based class won't let you add anything but ErectorBeam pointers to your list. That's a big advantage for producing solid, reliable code.

- `m_crBrushColor` is the color reference for the brush that is used to fill each new beam.
- `m_nPenWidth` is the width of the pen that draws the border of each beam.

4. A new function, `NewBeam`, is called to define a new beam in the document. It returns a pointer to the new beam object.

5. A new function, `InitDocument`, is used to initialize the class data members as discussed earlier.

6. The definition of the new class, CErectorBeam. The class definition begins with a short set of comments about what the class is and what it does. Next is the actual class definition, which states that this class is derived from the CObject class. The class begins with two constructor functions and a destructor function. These functions are:

- `CErectorBeam()` is the public constructor function for CErectorBeam. The function takes two arguments, as you read earlier: a pen width and a brush color.
- `CErectorBeam()` is the protected constructor function. It is distinguished from the public constructor in that it takes no arguments and is required by the MFC serialization code.
- The `DECLARE_SERIAL` macro is also placed here. This allows the CErectorBeam class to use the MFC serialization functions for saving and restoring beam objects.
- `~CErectorBeam()` is the public destructor function for CErectorBeam.

> **C++**
>
> Every C++ class must have two functions: a constructor and a destructor. A constructor function is called automatically when a new object of this class is needed.

Next come a series of protected member variables:

- `m_crBrushColor` holds the brush color for this beam.
- `m_nPenWidth` holds the pen width used for drawing the border of this beam.
- `m_rectBeam` holds the rectangle object that forms the beam.
- `m_ptStart` holds the starting point for the beam.

Finally, there are the prototypes for all the working functions in the class:

- `GetCurrentBeam()` is an inline function that allows you to get the current beam.
- `BeginBeam()` is called with the point where the beam begins.
- `EndBeam()` is called with the point where the beam ends.
- `DrawBeam()` is called with a pointer to the window where the beam is to be drawn.
- `Serialize()` allows the MFC classes to save and restore beam objects. You will see how this works later in the chapter. The reference is simply inserted here for now.

Adding Functional code

This doesn't add any actual processing code to ErectorSet, however. Up to this point, all the code that you have added has been in the header portion of the document and beam classes. This is essential, because it defines the functions and data that make up the classes, but the actual work is done in the code part. What you need to do now is add the functional code to the file `ErectorDoc.cpp`.

As before, Listing 5.3 shows the complete code listing for `ErectorDoc.cpp` with the changes and new code shown in bold. This listing also shows the code that was added earlier to open existing documents. Note, however, that the functional code for most of the CErectorBeam class is still simply stubbed in; you will add that code after you add code to get and use the mouse messages in the next section of this chapter.

Listing 5.3

```
///////////////////////////////////////////////////////////////////////
// ErectorDoc.cpp : implementation of the CErectorDoc class
//
//
// Created by AppWizard 11 December 1995 11:39:42
// Modifications:
//    12 Dec 95  DH    Add OnOpenDocument to generated code,
//                          along with new common InitDocument().
//    12 Dec 95  DH    Add CErectorBeam class to generated code:
//                          initialization; serialization; contents.
///////////////////////////////////////////////////////////////////////


#include "stdafx.h"
#include "Erector.h"

#include "ErectorDoc.h"

#ifdef _DEBUG
#define new DEBUG_NEW
#undef THIS_FILE
static char THIS_FILE[] = __FILE__;
#endif


///////////////////////////////////////////////////////////////////////
// CErectorDoc

IMPLEMENT_DYNCREATE(CErectorDoc, CDocument)

BEGIN_MESSAGE_MAP(CErectorDoc, CDocument)
```

```
        //{{AFX_MSG_MAP(CErectorDoc)
                // NOTE - the ClassWizard will add and remove mapping macros
here.
                //      DO NOT EDIT what you see in these blocks of generated
code!
        //}}AFX_MSG_MAP
END_MESSAGE_MAP()


/////////////////////////////////////////////////////////////////////////////
// CErectorDoc construction/destruction

CErectorDoc::CErectorDoc()
{
    // TODO: add one-time construction code here

}


CErectorDoc::~CErectorDoc()
{
}



// This function uses current pen width to create a pen object
//    and a brush for drawing. This must be done whenever
//    a document is created Uses the CPen class.
void CErectorDoc::InitDocument()
{
    // the default pen is 2 pixels wide
    m_nPenWidth = 2;
    // the default brush is solid 50% gray
    m_crBrushColor = RGB( 128, 128, 128 );


    return;
}


/////////////////////////////////////////////////////////////////////////////
```

```
// CErectorDoc data management

// This function creates a new beam object
//    and initializes it with the document default settings
//    for pen width and brush color.
CErectorBeam* CErectorDoc::NewBeam()
{
    // create a new beam object using our pre-set width and color
    CErectorBeam* pBeam = new CErectorBeam( m_nPenWidth, m_crBrushColor );
    // insert the beam into the list of beam objects
    m_beamList.AddTail( pBeam );
    // and mark the document as modified to avoid accidental close without
save
    SetModifiedFlag();
    return pBeam;
}


/////////////////////////////////////////////////////////////////////////
// CErectorDoc serialization

void CErectorDoc::Serialize(CArchive& ar)
{
    if (ar.IsStoring())
    {
        // TODO: add storing code here
    }
    else
    {
        // TODO: add loading code here
    }
}


/////////////////////////////////////////////////////////////////////////
// CErectorDoc diagnostics

#ifdef _DEBUG
```

```
void CErectorDoc::AssertValid() const
{
    CDocument::AssertValid();
}


void CErectorDoc::Dump(CDumpContext& dc) const
{
    CDocument::Dump(dc);
}
#endif //_DEBUG


/////////////////////////////////////////////////////////////////////////////
// CErectorDoc commands

// This function sets up and initializes a new document,
//    generally in response to user choosing File>>New from the menu.
BOOL CErectorDoc::OnNewDocument()
{
    if (!CDocument::OnNewDocument())
        return FALSE;

    // initialize document parameters
    InitDocument();

    return TRUE;
}



// This function opens and initializes an existing document,
//    generally in response to user choosing File>>Open from the menu.
BOOL CErectorDoc::OnOpenDocument(LPCTSTR lpszPathName)
{
    if (!CDocument::OnOpenDocument(lpszPathName))
        return FALSE;
```

```
    // initialize document parameters
    InitDocument();

    return TRUE;
}


///////////////////////////////////////////////////////////////////////
// CErectorDoc end



///////////////////////////////////////////////////////////////////////
// CErectorBeam

IMPLEMENT_SERIAL(CErectorBeam, CObject, 0)


///////////////////////////////////////////////////////////////////////
// CErectorBeam construction/destruction

// This is an empty constructor required by serialization.
//    It is defined as protected in the header file.
CErectorBeam::CErectorBeam()
{
    // This empty constructor is used by serialization only
}



// This is the standard public constructor.
//    When you invoke this, it initializes the class variables
//    to the requested pen width and brush color, and clears out
//    the rectangle by setting all coordinates to 0.
CErectorBeam::CErectorBeam(UINT nPenWidth, COLORREF crBrushColor)
{
    m_nPenWidth = nPenWidth;
    m_crBrushColor = crBrushColor;
    m_rectBeam.SetRectEmpty();
```

```
}


    // This is the standard public destructor.
    CErectorBeam::~CErectorBeam()
    {
    }


    /////////////////////////////////////////////////////////////////////////
    // CErectorBeam data management

    // This function adds the first mouse location to the beam.
    //    TODO: This is a stub. Fill in the code after handling mouse movement.
    void CErectorBeam::BeginBeam(CPoint pt)
    {

        return;

    }



    // This function finishes a beam by calculating the rectangle
    //    required for the beam, using the starting and ending points.
    //    TODO: This is a stub. Fill in the code after handling mouse movement.
    void CErectorBeam::EndBeam(CPoint pt)
    {

        return;

    }


    /////////////////////////////////////////////////////////////////////////
    // CErectorBeam drawing

    // This function draws a beam by drawing the beam rectangle.
    //    It requires a Windows device context (DC) to draw in.
    //    TODO: This is a stub. Fill in the code after handling mouse movement.
    BOOL CErectorBeam::DrawBeam(CDC* pDC)
    {
```

```
        return TRUE;
}


/////////////////////////////////////////////////////////////////////
// CErectorBeam serialization

void CErectorBeam::Serialize(CArchive& ar)
{
        if (ar.IsStoring())
        {
                // TODO: add storing code here
        }
        else
        {
                // TODO: add loading code here
        }
}
```

As before, you can see that I have added comments to every section of code that has been added here. In particular, there are comments inserted at the start of every function. I use these comments as a memory aid, so that I can recall what a function is supposed to do without reading the code in detail. This can be extremely helpful when you return to a section of code after some time. Many programmers use such notes as an important part of their standard practice. On the other hand, such notes are a positive hindrance if you don't keep them current with the code itself. Nothing is worse than an out-of-date comment, as it really confuses the next person to handle the code. First of all, that requires reading the code in detail, which is exactly what you set out to avoid. Then it raises the question of what is correct—the code or the comment? If you adopt this practice, be sure to keep your comments up to date, or they won't be of any use at all.

For all the functions in this book, I have included header comments like the ones shown here. From now on, you can simply take these as a given; I won't mention them again. It's up to you whether you want to put them into your own code or not.

One additional point: I have also moved the OnNewDocument function to the same part of the file as the OnOpenDocument function. To my mind, these are related functions and should be kept together, but because one was built with the application and the other was added by ClassWizard, they don't show up together. Keeping them together isn't necessary, of course; the compiler doesn't care what order they are in as long as they're there. I'm just a fuss-budget about this, and you don't have to move your function if you don't want to. I note this here only so you'll understand why my code is in a different order than yours.

With that out of the way, here is a short review of the functional code that has been added to ErectorDoc.cpp:

- OnNewDocument() adds a call to the new auxiliary function, InitDocument, which sets the values for the class member data items as discussed earlier.

- OnOpenDocument() is basically identical to the code in the OnNewDocument function and performs the same function when you open an existing document.

- InitDocument() initializes the two class member variables for pen width and brush color. Each of these variables is initialized with a fixed default value: 2 pixels for the pen width and 50% gray for the brush color.

N O T E   Here is how you determine colors for windows. The RGB macro allows you to set individual values for each of the three primary display colors: red, green, and blue, and it returns a COLORREF structure that you use to initialize various Windows functions. Each color takes a value, a single number between 0 and 255, with 0 being the darkest setting of the color and 255 being the lightest setting—that is, none of the selected color is included. So, a value of (0, 0, 0) is black, while (255, 255, 255) is white. In this instance, you are setting the colors to (128, 128, 128) which is a 50% gray, or dark gray as it is sometimes called.

- NewBeam() creates a new beam object by creating a new instance of the CErectorBeam class. When it calls the CErectorBeam constructor function, it also passes the pen width and brush color from the member variables. Once created, the beam object is added to the list of beams for this document by calling the `AddTail` member function of the CObList class instance, `m_beamList`. (Remember that you defined this class variable in `ErectorDoc.h` as a holder for the list of beam objects.) Finally, the function calls the `SetModifiedFlag` function to mark that the document has been modified. This flag prevents the document from being closed without being saved; more precisely, the flag causes a standard dialog box to appear if you try to close the document, asking if you want to save the modified document before closing.

C++

You may be wondering where the `m_beamList` came from. After all, you didn't create it anywhere in the code, as you just did with CErectorBeam.

This is an interesting and important point in C++. When you declare a member variable in C++ that is itself a class, the constructor for your class will automatically call the *default constructor* for the member's class to create a new member of that class, which is then stored in your class as the member variable. That means you automatically have an object stored in the member variable from the moment that you create a new instance of your class. This is extremely important, as it guarantees that you never have to worry about referencing an uninitialized class variable, which could be disastrous.

WARNING

The automatic construction of class objects is a wonderful tool. There is, however, one point of caution. Note that the constructor called for the member variable's class is the default constructor. If a member variable has more than one constructor, or if there are specific initial values that you need to pass to the constructor, you must add code to your class constructor that calls the constructor for the variable's class rather than using the default.

I know that sounds confusing. Let's use this as a concrete example. Here, you have defined a member variable, `m_beamList`, as an instance of CTypedPtrList. When the application creates a new document, it calls your document constructor function, `CErectorDoc::CErectorDoc`. At present, this function (at the top of your CErectorDoc code) does nothing; the only thing in the function is a comment to add one-time construction code if required. When your document is created, the C++ constructor mechanism will automatically create a CTypedPtrList instance from the template classes defined in afxtempl.h, using the template information provided in your header file, and then will store it in your document class as m_beamList.

After the functions for CErectorDoc, there is a whole new section of functions for CErectorBeam. For now, most of these are simply stubs, but here is a review of the functions that are currently in place:

- CErectorBeam::CErectorBeam() is the empty constructor function; that is, a constructor function that takes (and requires) no arguments.

- CErectorBeam::CErectorBeam(...) is the standard constructor function, which requires arguments for pen width and brush color. It stores these arguments in the appropriate class member variables, thereby initializing them. It also initializes the class member m_rectBeam by setting it to the empty rectangle using the CRect function SetRectEmpty.

- CErectorBeam::~CErectorBeam() is the destructor function. It takes (and requires) no arguments. The actual destruction of the class is done automatically; this function is used only if you have data members that you have allocated yourself which must be destroyed when this class is destroyed.

- BeginBeam(), EndBeam(), and DrawBeam() will capture the mouse coordinates and drawing the resulting beam. You will fill in these stub functions after you add the mouse message processing in the next section.

- Serialize() saves and restores the beam information using the MFC serialization processing. You will see how to add the required code for this process later in this chapter.

At this point, I would suggest that you rebuild the project. Although this new code hasn't added any functionality to ErectorSet, you have entered a lot of data. If you rebuild the project now, you will have an easier time finding any small coding errors—the traditional missing semicolon, for example—that may have crept into your code. If you have a problem, try switching to the File view and compiling first StdAfx.cpp and then ErectorDoc.cpp. Doing the compiles in two steps will help isolate any errors. At the end, switch back into Class view and your screen should look something like Figure 5.3, which shows the new class CErectorBeam.

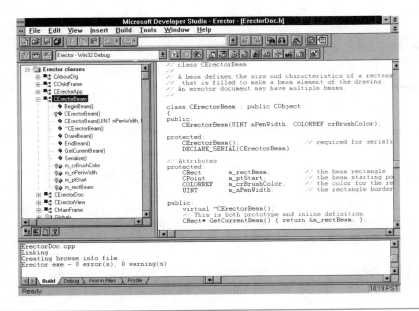

FIGURE 5.3 YOU MAY WISH TO REBUILD YOUR PROJECT NOW TO CATCH ANY INADVERTENT CODING ERRORS.

SHORTCUT

You will notice, in Figure 5.3, that I have docked my Output pane across the bottom of the Developer Studio display. This is more useful, in my opinion, than the default display, which displaced your text editor, for two reasons. First, it allows you to see the output without losing sight of the current text, which is a major help when making changes and corrections. Second, by making the pane wider, you can read the full text of any error messages more easily.

Adding Mouse Message Handling

To create the beams for a document, you need to draw the beam with the mouse. To draw a beam, you will move the mouse to the position where you want the beam to start, click the left mouse button, and then drag the mouse to where you want the beam to end. The rectangular region that you have selected with the mouse will become the beam that is created, stored, and displayed in your document.

NOTE

There are three types of standard mouse actions:

- *Clicking* means pressing and releasing one of the mouse buttons.
- *Double-clicking* means pressing and releasing one of the mouse buttons two times in quick succession.
- *Dragging* means moving the mouse while you hold down one of the mouse buttons.

Most mice used with Windows have two buttons: a left button and a right button, and Windows sends separate left-and right-button messages. However, Windows is set up to handle a mouse with one, two, or three buttons. If your mouse has only one button, all messages from the mouse are left-button messages. If a mouse has three buttons, there are left-, middle-, and right-button messages. All of your code here will handle only left-button messages, but you can easily generalize it to handle middle- or right-button messages.

To start with, you need to capture the mouse movements so that you can save the beginning and ending points and use these to define a beam. Windows sends a message to your application for every mouse action: movement, left and right button down, left and right button up, and so on. Each action that the mouse takes is called a *mouse event*. The trick is to capture these event messages and use them for your processing.

In a traditional Windows application, you would define a procedure to handle your window and use a case statement within that to identify and process the mouse messages. Luckily, with MFC and Visual C++, processing mouse messages is a lot simpler. Visual C++ provides another processing wizard, called ClassWizard, that will help you handle these messages almost automatically.

Mouse messages are processed in a window—that is, Windows sends the message that a mouse event happened to the application that owns the window that the mouse is in when the event happens. Because of this, the natural place to record and handle mouse messages is in your window-processing code. MFC applications handle their windows in the view. For ErectorSet, this is the code in the CErectorView class, which is contained in the files `ErectView.cpp` and `ErectView.h`.

In the next chapter, you will learn all about views and their relationship to documents. For now, however, all you need to know is that the view represents the window in your application where you see your document and this is where you need to add the code to handle mouse messages.

There are two steps in the process of handling the mouse. First, you use ClassWizard to add the necessary message reception code to your application. This adds new functions as skeletons to your view code and inserts the necessary code into the application to capture the mouse message and route it to the new function. Then you add the message processing code to the skeleton function to deal with the message in any way that you require.

Using ClassWizard to Handle a Basic Message

Begin by closing any open files, using **Close All** from the Window menu. (This isn't strictly necessary, but I like to do it to minimize clutter.) Next, choose **ClassWizard** from the View menu or press **Ctrl+W**. This brings up the ClassWizard dialog box shown in Figure 5.4.

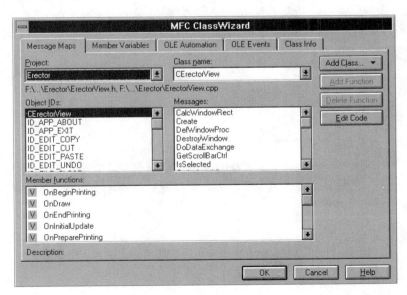

FIGURE 5.4 THE CLASSWIZARD DIALOG BOX ALLOWS YOU TO ADD MESSAGE HANDLING CODE TO YOUR MFC APPLICATION AUTOMATICALLY.

This dialog box is the entry point to ClassWizard, and it allows you to add classes to handle messages and to add functions to existing classes to handle messages. Here, you simply want to handle messages in an existing class: CErectorView.

Make sure that CErectorView is selected in the Class name drop-down list and that it is also selected in the Object IDs scrolling list box. Once these are set, the Messages scrolling list will show you a list of Windows messages that are appropriate for the selected class and object. In this case, these are the messages that are appropriate to a window, as shown in Figure 5.4. Scroll down the list to the message WM_LBUTTONDOWN. As you can guess, this is the message sent when the left button is clicked on the mouse. Select this message and press the **Add Function** button. This adds a new function, `OnLButtonDown` as a member function to the CErectorView class. At this point, the dialog box should look like Figure 5.5.

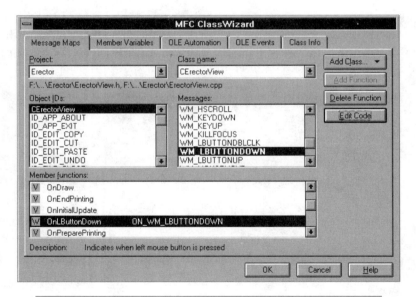

FIGURE 5.5 AFTER YOU ADD THE FUNCTION TO YOUR SELECTED CLASS, THE MEMBER FUNCTION LIST SHOWS THE NAME OF THE NEW FUNCTION AND THE MESSAGE THAT IT HANDLES.

This lists the name of the new member function that has been added to the class, and shows the MFC message that this function processes. This may seem a bit strange until you understand what has happened. Your application has received a message from Windows, WM_LBUTTONDOWN, that tells it that the mouse's left button has been pressed in a window that belongs to ErectorSet. The MFC classes provide code that determine which window the mouse click was in— remember that you may have several documents open in the ErectorSet application. So the MFC code determines which view needs to receive this mouse message and sends an ON_WM_LBUTTONDOWN message to that view. In this way, the Windows message is transformed from an application message to a corresponding message to the specific view that is displaying the affected document.

Adding Processing Code for Message Handling

Although ClassWizard has added the message handling mechanics to ErectorSet, you still need to actually do something once you get the message. To do that, you add code to the skeleton of the function that ClassWizard has created for you. Press the **Edit Code** button, and the ClassWizard automatically opens a new editor pane positioned at the point where you need to enter the code, as shown in Figure 5.6.

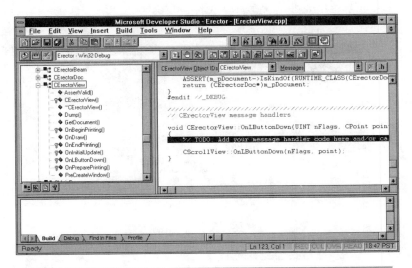

FIGURE 5.6 YOU CAN GO DIRECTLY FROM THE CLASSWIZARD TO THE EXACT PLACE IN THE CODE WHERE YOU NEED TO ENTER THE PROCESSING FOR THE NEW FUNCTION.

Open this window up to the full size of your screen and notice what ClassWizard has done. It has added a skeleton function for handling a press of the left mouse button. The skeleton function has a place for your code—marked by the TODO comment that is highlighted in Figure 5.3—and then calls the default mouse handler function in CView. It has also added message handling code to your application that will automatically call this function in the view when the left mouse button is pressed. Now you have to add the code to capture and use this information.

Looking at the parameters for the function, you see that you have an unsigned integer (UINT) called `nFlags` and a CPoint object called `point`. These parameters tell you the state and position of the mouse when the left mouse button was pressed.

There is an easy way to find out what function parameters, like `nFlags` and `point`, mean:

1. Select the function name, `OnLButtonDown`, in the text editor window.

2. Press **F1** to automatically enter the documentation at the correct function. Figure 5.7 shows you the reference that is displayed.

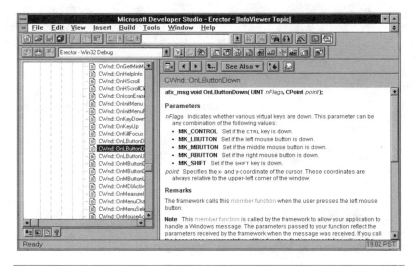

FIGURE 5.7 YOU CAN USE THE AUTOMATIC HELP TO FIND OUT WHAT FUNCTION VALUES MEAN.

As you see, this shows you that `OnLButtonDown` is defined in the CWnd class, and it tells you what each parameter means and how to use it.

The nFlags value tells you what keys and buttons were pressed at the time the left button was down. For your application here, this information isn't necessary. The point tells you the location of the mouse when the button was clicked; this is important because this is the starting position of the beam that you want to draw.

Here are the three steps that you need to take when your view is notified that the user pressed the left mouse button:

1. Create a new beam in the document.
2. Store the point where the mouse was clicked as the starting point of the new beam.
3. Notify Windows that you want to track the mouse.

This last requirement is a bit obscure. Normally, Windows only notifies you when the mouse takes some action in your view. That's why you are notified when the user presses the mouse button. However, under normal circumstances, the user might move the mouse across your view window simply in passing, on the way to select a menu, say, or to click on another application's or document's window. In that case, you don't want to be notified that the mouse is there; you only want to know if the mouse actually does something in your view. Now, however, things have changed. You want to know where the mouse goes so that you can keep track of where the beam ends. For this reason, you need to set the mouse capture to ensure that Windows sends all mouse messages to your view, no matter where the mouse goes—even if it goes outside the edge of the current view window. If you don't set this, the message generated when the button is released will be lost.

Listing 5.4 shows the code that you need to add for this. Note that you remove both the TODO comment and the code that calls the inherited function OnLButtonDown in CView.

Listing 5.4

```
////////////////////////////////////////////////////////////////////////
// CErectorView message handlers

// This function handles LeftMouseButton down messages.
//    NOTE that this does _not_ call inherited behavior.
void CErectorView::OnLButtonDown(UINT /* nFlags */, CPoint point)
```

```
    {
            // When the mouse button is down, the user may be starting a new beam,
            //    or selecting or de-selecting an existing beam.
            //    However, for now just create a new beam.
            //    TODO: Add beam selection feature.
            m_pBeamCur = GetDocument()->NewBeam();

            // Insert our point as the starting point of the new beam.
            m_pBeamCur->BeginBeam( point );

            SetCapture();          // Establish mouse capture.

            return;
    }
```

Let's look at what this code does. You use a class member variable, m_pBeamCur, to hold a pointer to the new beam that you get from CDocument's NewBeam function. Once the beam is created, you store the starting point in the beam, using the beam's BeginBeam function. Finally, you invoke the SetCapture function for this window to ensure that you get the mouse-up message.

There are two important points to note in this code. First, you need to have a class variable, m_pBeamCur, which is the beam being constructed. This is not yet been defined. Second, you need to comment out or remove the nFlags parameter. If you don't, the compiler will generate a warning message that nFlags is defined but not used in your function. As a matter of good coding practice, you should remove all warning messages from your code if possible. This will give you the cleanest code, and it will pay off in the long run. I prefer to simply comment out the nFlags variable name, rather than remove it, so that I can easily restore it if required at some later time. This is a matter of personal preference, however, and you can remove it if that suits your programming style.

Adding Additional Message Processing

Next you need to do the same thing for handling the WM_LBUTTONUP message. This will tell you where to end the beam so that you can draw it. Once again, use the ClassWizard to add handling for WM_LBUTTONUP to the

CErectorView class. When you're done, your ClassWizard dialog box should look like Figure 5.8.

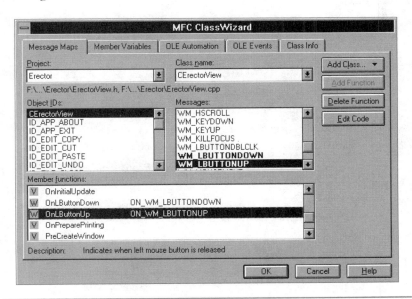

FIGURE 5.8 THE CLASSWIZARD SHOWS YOU BOTH OF YOUR NEW MESSAGE HANDLING FUNCTIONS.

SHORTCUT

Although it's important to know how to use the Class Wizard, the easiest way to add new message-handling code to your class is to use the WizardBar, as you did earlier to add the OnOpenDocument processing to CErectorDoc. To use the WizardBar, just be sure that it is displayed at the top of your editor pane. Check that CErectorView is the Object ID and scroll the Messages list down to WM_LBUTTONUP. As before, the Developer Studio tells you that there is no code currently in place to handle this message and asks if you want to add it. Click **Yes** to add the new function and move directly to it in your editor pane, where you can add your new code.

As before, you can use the **Edit Code** button to go directly to the new skeleton function. Listing 5.5 shows you the code to add here.

Listing 5.5

```
// This function handles LeftMouseButton up messages.
//    NOTE that this does _not_ call inherited behavior.
void CErectorView::OnLButtonUp(UINT /* nFlags */, CPoint point)
{
    // Mouse button up is notable only if the user is currently drawing
    //    a new beam by dragging the mouse.
    //    In that case, we need to capture the mouse position.
    if ( GetCapture() != this )
        return;              // If this view didn't capture the mouse,
                             //    the user isn't drawing in our window.


    // End the current beam.
    m_pBeamCur->EndBeam( point );


    // Now draw the beam.
    //    First, set the device context to this view...
    CClientDC dc( this );
    //    TODO: Add error handling in case we can't get a DC.
    CDC* pDC = (CDC*)&dc;
    //    then ask beam to draw itself.
    m_pBeamCur->DrawBeam( pDC );


    ReleaseCapture();       // Release the mouse capture established earlier


    return;
}
```

This appears to be somewhat more complex than starting the beam, but in fact the function still does only three things:

1. Captures the end point for the beam
2. Asks the beam object to draw itself
3. Notifies Windows that you don't need to track the mouse any longer

This time, I suspect that it's the second point that sounds a little strange if you haven't done object-oriented programming before. The normal expectation for a program would be to get the required information from the beam and then draw it. However, that's not the way to handle a class object. Instead, the view tells the object that it wants the object to display itself in the view now. It's up to the object itself—in this case, the beam—to draw itself in the view.

Let's review the code. First, check the origin of the button-up message. The GetCapture function returns a pointer to the window that currently has the mouse capture. If that isn't the view, exit now because you don't want to process this message. If it is, store the ending point in the current beam, which is stored in the class variable m_pBeamCur by calling its EndBeam function.

The next part is a bit more complex. Remember that the beam needs to know where to draw itself; in particular, it needs to know what window it should draw into. For it to know that, you must pass it a Windows device-context. The *device-context*, abbreviated DC, is a Windows data structure that describes all of the information required in a window: the pens and brushes available, the currently selected font and color, the drawing modes and background color for the window, and so on. In particular, it specifies the clipping region, which is the precise area of the window that is available for drawing.

There are two ways to look at the area available in a window. The most common is to divide the window's area into two parts: one that contains durable window display objects, such as the borders, title bar, scroll bars, and so on, and a second, called the *client area*, which is the blank space inside all of the other parts of the window. Generally, when you are drawing into your view window, you want to draw only in the client area. To draw the beam, you need a device-context that points to the client area of the view window.

MFC provides just such a function. This is the CClientDC class. When you create a object of this class, you give it a pointer to the window whose client area will be the target for the device-context. It returns a member of the class CClientDC, which is the device-context for the client area of the target window.

The client area, like all windows, has an imposed coordinate system that you use when drawing text or graphics into the window. Figure 5.9 shows you the client area of a window and the standard windows coordinates that you use.

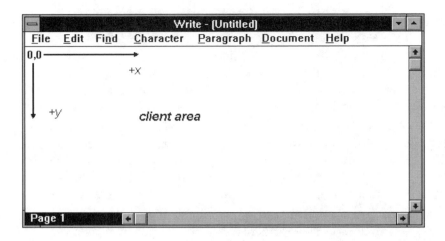

FIGURE 5.9 YOU USE STANDARD WINDOW COORDINATES TO DRAW INTO THE CLIENT AREA OF YOUR WINDOW.

Notice that the window coordinate system has its origin at the top, left corner of the client area, with the x coordinates increasing to the right and the y coordinates increasing downward. This means that greater values of x move your drawing to the right and greater values of y move it down. Each unit in this coordinate system represents one device pixel. For now, you will use this standard coordinate system, called MM_TEXT, for your drawing. Later in the book you will see how to separate the coordinates that you use for drawing from the device pixels to get device independence.

So here you first create a CClientDC object for this view window. With that, you call the `DrawBeam` function of the current beam, which should draw the beam into the client area of the view window. Once this is done, tell Windows that you no longer need to track the mouse by executing the `ReleaseCapture` function.

N O T E

As you can see in Listing 5.5, there is a TODO comment that notes that a fully functional application would have to check here for an error, specifically, an error if Windows could not return the requested device-context. Windows has only five common display contexts available at any time, and all Windows applications compete for these. It might happen that the call to create CClientDC would fail. If so, the Class Library Reference tells you that CClientDC will throw a

Resource Exception. (You will learn about exceptions and exception handling in Chapter 8.) The important point here is that this can fail and a professional-quality application would have code here to handle this problem. At this early stage, I have not included any code like that, as it would simply obscure the basic coding issues that we want to discuss. However, when you are working like this, it's good practice to note the changes that will ultimately be required to make your final application robust.

This is all the message processing that you need to do in CErectorView for now. However, before we move on to fill in the required drawing code in CErectorBeam, you need to do one more thing: add the new class member.

This actually requires adding only a single line of code to the CErectorView header (.h) file, but the easiest way to do it is to use the Developer Studio's special class editing feature. Move the mouse cursor to the Class view and select **CErectorView**. Then press the right mouse button to display the pop-up menu and select **Add Variable...** from the list. This displays the Add Member Variable dialog box.

Enter **CErectorBeam*** as the variable Type, and **m_pBeamCur** as the variable Declaration and select the **Protected** radio button, as shown in Figure 5.10.

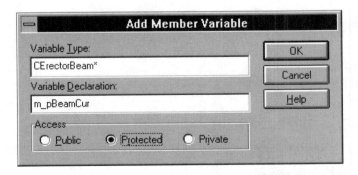

FIGURE 5.10 THE ADD MEMBER VARIABLE ALLOWS YOU TO EASILY ADD THE NEW m_pBeamCur
VARIABLE TO CERECTORVIEW.

Press **OK** to enter this variable into your class. Listing 5.6 shows you the new line added to your header file.

Listing 5.6

```
protected:
        CErectorBeam* m_pBeamCur;
```

This simply defines the member variable m_pBeamCur as a pointer to a CErectorBeam object.

Creating the Beam Object

Next, you need to fill in the code in CErectorBeam that uses the information from the view to create the beam. You called the functions `BeginBeam` and `EndBeam` in the view code to actually do the work of recording a new beam. Notice that the new beam was created by a call to the document's `NewBeam` function, but the coordinates of the beam, which determine its size, are stored by these two functions within the beam class.

Creating the Beam Rectangle

Listing 5.7 shows the code that needs to be added to the existing stubs to handle recording the mouse information to determine the size and position of the beam.

Listing 5.7

```
//////////////////////////////////////////////////////////////////////
// CErectorBeam data management

// This function adds the first mouse location to the beam.
//     The coordinates are stored in the class member variable.
void CErectorBeam::BeginBeam(CPoint ptStart)
{
        m_ptStart = ptStart;
        return;
}



// This function finishes a beam by calculating the rectangle
```

```
//   required for the beam, using the starting and ending points.
void CErectorBeam::EndBeam(CPoint ptStop)
{
    // TODO: Add error checking code here to ensure that
    //   ptStart and ptStop are not too close to one another.

    // Set top and bottom
    if ( ptStop.y < m_ptStart.y )
    {
        m_rectBeam.top = ptStop.y;
        m_rectBeam.bottom = m_ptStart.y;
    }
    else
    {
        m_rectBeam.top = ptStart.y;
        m_rectBeam.bottom = m_ptStop.y;
    }


    // Set left and right
    if ( ptStop.x < m_ptStart.x )
    {
        m_rectBeam.left = ptStop.x;
        m_rectBeam.right = m_ptStart.x;
    }
    else
    {
        m_rectBeam.left = ptStart.x;
        m_rectBeam.right = m_ptStop.x;
    }


    return;
}
```

You need to modify two functions here. For the first one, BeginBeam, the code is quite simple: you just store the beginning point in the class member variable that you defined earlier (see Listing 5.2). The EndBeam code, however, is a little more complex, and that requires some explanation.

The beam dimensions are stored in a CRect object, which represents a rectangle. The rectangle is stored as a pair of points: the top-left point and the bottom-right point. (If you think about it, these two points fully describe a rectangle, since the other two corners—the top-right and bottom-left—can be determined from the two points that are already given.) By the nature of the coordinate system, then, the *x* coordinate of the left point must be less than the *x* coordinate of the right point, and the *y* coordinate of the top point must be less than the *y* coordinate of the bottom one.

Checking for a Valid Rectangle

The catch is that you need to determine the top-left and bottom-right points from the coordinates of the mouse. Since the user may draw the beam in any direction—top to bottom, bottom to top, left to right, right to left—you must ensure that you store the coordinate values in the correct sequence to define valid top-left and bottom-right corners for the rectangle.

WARNING

What will happen if you don't check the coordinates and simply store them? Well, just about the worst thing that could happen. You won't get an error or any other warning message; you simply won't get a valid rectangle. If you store the coordinates incorrectly, there will be no display when you try to draw the rectangle. And that's about the worst outcome, from a programmer's view, because you could spend a lot of time trying to figure out why what appears to be working code isn't producing the result that you expected.

The code in Listing 5.6 does the tests that you need. It takes the values for *x* and *y* from the starting point that you saved in the class member variable m_ptStart and compares them with the coordinates of the current, ending point. Then it stores the correct values as the top, bottom, left, and right coordinates for the rectangle. It's easy enough, as long as you remember to do it.

You will also notice that there is a TODO comment at the beginning of this code that reminds you to add code to check that the beam rectangle is formed by points that are not too close together. To display the rectangle, the width and height of the rectangle must be less than 32,767 and greater than 2. The larger size isn't much of a problem, since these coordinates are derived from the mouse movements, and it's highly unlikely that the user can draw a rectangle on screen that is larger than 32,767 in any direction (most screens are between 640 by 480 pixels and 1024 by 768 pixels). However, the lower limit is a concern, since it might represent the user simply clicking on two points very close together. Such a small rectangle will not display—this is similar to the problem of a rectangle where the coordinates are not set up correctly. The point here is that you don't want to store a beam that can't be displayed correctly.

Drawing the Beam Object

Once you have your beam, you still need to display it in the document. Notice that the beam is not automatically visible, just because you have captured and processed the mouse movements. You also need to display the resulting rectangle in your document window. To do this, you need to add drawing code to your CErectorBeam class as the function DrawBeam. Listing 5.8 shows you the drawing code that you need to display the beam.

Listing 5.8

```
// insert after CErectorBeam::EndBeam...


/////////////////////////////////////////////////////////////////////////
// CErectorBeam drawing

// This function draws a beam by drawing the beam rectangle.
//    It requires a Windows device context (DC) to draw in.
BOOL CErectorBeam::DrawBeam(CDC* pDC)
{
    CPen penStroke;
    CBrush brushFill;

    // Create the pen and brush values for this beam using
    //    initialized values of width and color.
    if( !penStroke.CreatePen( PS_SOLID, m_nPenWidth, RGB(0, 0, 0)) )
        return FALSE;
```

```
if( !brushFill.CreateSolidBrush( m_crBrushColor ) )
    return FALSE;


// Save the old pen and brush values and set the new ones into the DC
CPen* pOldPen = pDC->SelectObject( &penStroke );
CBrush* pOldBrush = pDC->SelectObject( &brushFill );


// Draw the beam
pDC->Rectangle( m_rectBeam );


// Restore the old brush and pen
pDC->SelectObject( pOldBrush );
pDC->SelectObject( pOldPen );


return TRUE;
}
```

Drawing an Individual Beam

This function begins by defining a pen and brush for use in drawing the beam rectangle. Then each of the objects is initialized. The pen is set to a solid black line of the desired width; the brush is simply initialized to the desired color. Each function is set in an `if` statement because they may fail. If either one fails, the function ends, since you can't draw the beam without them.

The function returns `FALSE` if it fails so that the calling function can tell that the beam will not display correctly and take some action if required or appropriate. Note that the calling function, `OnLButtonUp`, does not, in fact, check to see if the `DrawBeam` function worked correctly. In a complete implementation of this application you might wish to insert a debug assertion here to test whether the beam drawing function ever fails.

Next, the function sets the new pen and brush and saves their old versions. This is essential, since you don't know what else may be happening. You should always save and restore items like the pen and brush settings when you work with them. In this way, you don't have to worry about destroying some setting that won't show up as a problem until some subsequent point in processing when it may be very hard to determine what happened. Note that the

`SelectObject` function in the device-context automatically returns a pointer to the old version of whatever object you are setting, so you can easily save the old version.

The drawing itself is almost an anticlimax. You simply call the `Rectangle` function, with the beam rectangle `m_rectBeam` as an argument. This function displays the given rectangle as a filled outline in the current device-context, using the current settings for the pen to draw the border of the rectangle, and using the current brush to fill the rectangle.

Once the rectangle has been displayed, you simply restore the original pen and brush settings and return. And that's all there is to drawing the beam.

Drawing All the Beams in a Document

However, drawing the one beam that you have just created isn't sufficient to draw your document. You also need to be able to display all of the beams in the document. There are many circumstances where you may have to redisplay an entire document by drawing all of the beams: when your document window is moved, for example, or when a document is opened from a file. (You'll see in the next section how to save and read documents from a disk file.)

To completely display a document, you need to do two things. First, you need to add code to the document view that asks all of the beams that currently make up the document to display themselves. Then you need to add code to the document that provides access to the beams in some order. The beams, of course, already know how to display themselves, since you have added the `DrawBeam` code to CErectorBeam.

Your view already has a skeleton drawing function in it, which is provided by AppWizard. All you have to do is add the required code to your CErectorView class to ask the document to draw all the beam; and add code to your CErectorDoc class to retrieve the list beams and ask each of them to draw itself.

The view processing is quite simple, as shown in Listing 5.9.

Listing 5.9

```
/////////////////////////////////////////////////////////////////////////
// CErectorView drawing

void CErectorView::OnDraw(CDC* pDC)
{
```

```
CErectorDoc* pDoc = GetDocument();
ASSERT_VALID(pDoc);

// The document now requests each individual beam draw itself
//    by called CErectorBeam::DrawBeam()
for( POSITION pos = pDoc->GetFirstBeamPosition(); pos != NULL; )
{
    CErectorBeam* pBeam = pDoc->GetNextBeam( pos );
    pBeam->DrawBeam( pDC );
}


return;
}
```

The OnDraw function shown here is fairly straightforward. The function gets the position of the first beam by invoking a new CErectorDoc auxiliary function, GetFirstBeamPosition. Then it iterates over the list of beams, and gets a pointer to every beam in the list in succession by invoking another new CErectorDoc function, GetNextBeam. Once it gets the beam, it calls the beam's DrawBeam function to ask the beam to draw itself. The loop terminates when the position of the next beam is NULL, which indicates that the list is finished.

The only confusing point about this code is the termination of the loop. To understand this, you need to look at both the code in the for loop and the code in the function GetNextBeam. Let's start with the for loop. The usual for loop looks like this:

```
for( i=0; i < 20; i++)
```

and has three sections: initialization, termination test, and increment function. When you look at the loop here, you notice that there is an initialization, and a termination test, but no increment function. This means that the increment of pos, which is being tested to terminate the loop, comes inside the loop itself. Since there is no obvious place where pos is incremented, you need to look at the support functions in CErectorDoc.

To see how this works, let's examine the two new functions in CErectorDoc: GetFirstBeamPosition and GetNextBeam.

You can add these functions to the CErectorDoc class by using the pop-up menu in the Class View pane. To do that, change to the Class View and select the pop-up menu item Add Function... by selecting the CErectorDoc class folder and clicking the right mouse button. This displays the Add Member Function dialog box, shown in Figure 5.11 with the data for DrawAll filled in.

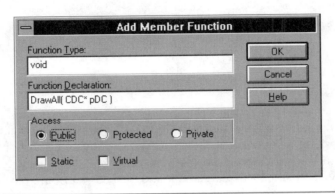

FIGURE 5.11: THE ADD MEMBER FUNCTION DIALOG ALLOWS YOU TO EASILY ADD NEW FUNCTIONS TO YOUR CLASSES.

To create each function use the dialog three times with the entries given in Table 5.1. (Figure 5.11 shows you the first set filled in).

Function Type	Function Declaration	Access
void	DrawAll(CDC* pDC)	Public
POSITION	GetFirstBeamPosition()	Public
CErectorBeam*	GetNextBeam(POSITION& pos)	Public

With the functions defined, add the required processing code and comments as shown in Listing 5.10.

Listing 5.10

```
// This function returns the position of the first beam in the list
POSITION CErectorDoc::GetFirstBeamPosition()
{
```

```
        return m_beamList.GetHeadPosition();
    }



    // This function retrieves from the list the beam at the given position
    //    and updates the POSITION to point to the next beam in the list.
    CErectorBeam* CErectorDoc::GetNextBeam( POSITION& pos)
    {
        return m_beamList.GetNext( pos );
    }
```

GetFirstBeamPosition, as its name implies, gets the position of the first beam in the list by calling the CObList function GetHeadPosition. Notice that this returns the beam position, not the beam itself. The second function, GetNextBeam, gets a pointer to the beam at a given position, by using the CObList function GetNext. GetNext takes a position as an argument and, besides returning a pointer to the beam at that position, updates the position to point to the next element in the list. This is the key to the loop processing that you saw earlier in CErectorView. Since the position variable, pos, is being updated by GetNextBeam each time the loop executes, it will eventually be a NULL value when there is no next element in the list, which is what you are testing for in the loop.

C++

This is a good point to discuss some of the design complexities that are inherent in using C++. There is a joke that goes: if you give the same problem to four C programmers, you will get four different sets of code; if you give the same problem to four C++ programmers, you will get four different designs.

Here you could approach this drawing code in one of two ways: first, by having the view ask the document to draw the beams and then having the document ask the beams to draw themselves; and second, by having the view ask the beams to draw themselves directly, as you see here. I have chosen the second approach. This seems to me to keep the view processing in one place: CErectorView. In this way, the view controls how the data is displayed in the window. In particular, you might have multiple views for a single document. Suppose that you might wish to display our beam documents in two ways—say, one is a drawing of a set of beams and the other displays the beam dimensions and weight in an ordered list. In that case, either you could have the views iterate the beam list themselves and order the display the way they want, or you would have to provide two functions in the document to support the two different views. (Note that, no matter how you design this, the beam class would have to have new functions to display the beam data in the correct manner.)

The first method also has benefits and drawbacks. For example, you might well choose to create a new function in CErectorDoc to handle the drawing. That would encapsulate the processing of the beams more completely in the document. There is, after all, no reason why the view should have to know what elements make up a document; for example, the document might contain several types of elements, say nuts and bolts, as well as beams. In the second approach, the view needs to know all of the elements in the document, whereas in the first, it simply asks the document to display whatever elements make up the document. However, this seeming simplicity is offset by the fact that the document needs to understand and manipulate the device context for graphics. As it turns out, in future exercises you will be working more intensively with the device context, so there is a real benefit to be had by concentrating all device-context operation in the view. That's why you see the second approach used here. However, both approaches are correct, and either one might be chosen.

Note that the function prototypes have automatically been added to your header file, as shown in Listing 5.11.

Listing 5.11

```
class CErectorDoc : public CDocument
{
protected: // create from serialization only
     CErectorDoc();
     DECLARE_DYNCREATE(CErectorDoc)


// Attributes
protected:
```

```
// each list element is a beam object
CTypedPtrList<CObList, CErectorBeam*> m_beamList;

// We track the beam color or pattern and outline width
//    at the document level for all views. This allows
//    the user to choose a new beam style for all the views
//    together, rather than one at a time.
COLORREF    m_crBrushColor;        // the brush color
UINT        m_nPenWidth;           // the border width

public:
    POSITION GetFirstBeamPosition();

    CErectorBeam* GetNextBeam( POSITION& pos );
```

With this code, you now have all the functions necessary to draw and display beams in your document. The beams are created by clicking and dragging a mouse across the document view window. In the next section, you will see how to use the MFC serialization functions to save and restore these documents so that you can reuse them.

SAVING AND RESTORING

Next to actually displaying the drawing in the document window, you need to be able to save your document to a file and read it back when a user wants to reopen it. The MFC have generalized this process and encapsulated it into a class, CArchive, that performs *serialization*. The process of serialization saves your document to an external file in a binary format that depends on the type of information that you want to store. It also allows you to read the saved information back into your application and display it, just as it looked on the initial display. This ability to save and restore documents is one of the major time- and effort-saving features that you get when you use the MFC.

In this section of the chapter, you will see how to perform serialization for your documents. Once you have implemented serialization, you will be able to save and open existing documents in your application.

The Serialization Process

Serialization is the process of storing all types of objects and variables in a permanent binary format. Normally, this is done by writing the objects in this format as a file to disk storage. Once that is done, you can retrieve the file and restore the serialized data.

For our purposes, you can serialize any document that ErectorSet produces. Each document can be saved to a file that, by default, has the same name as the document window—of course, you can save the document and give it a different name if you want. Once you have saved the document, you can open it from the File menu and read it back into ErectorSet, where it will display just as it was when you saved it.

You serialize a document in two steps. First, serialize any specific information that you need to save for each document. So far, there isn't any special information in the CErectorDoc that you need to save, since the beams themselves will save and restore items like their color and so on. However, as an example, if your document allowed the user to set a default color, you would serialize that. Next, you have to serialize each beam that makes up the document by calling the Serialize function for the list of beams that makes up the document. For a CObList item, the Serialize function simply calls the Serialize function of each item in the list—in this case, the Serialize function in the class CErectorBeam.

When you created the CErectorBeam class, you did three things to make it able to be serialized:

1. You used the DECLARE_SERIAL macro in the class definition in the header for CErectorBeam. (Remember that this is included in the file ErectorDoc.h.) The DECLARE_SERIAL macro takes a single argument, which is the name of the class to be serialized.

2. You used the IMPLEMENT_SERIAL macro at the beginning of the CErectorBeam functional definitions. The IMPLEMENT_SERIAL macro takes three arguments: the name of the class to be serialized, the name of the base class, and a UINT version, or *schema* number, that is used to ensure that your application can identify the version of the application that created the file that is being read. By default, the MFC will display an error dialog box if you attempt to read a file with a schema number dif-

ferent than the current number in your application. (You will see how to use this number in a later chapter.)

3. You defined a `Serialize` function in your class to read and write the necessary class variables. Up to now, this function is simply a stub that does nothing.

These three steps must be taken for every class to be serialized make the class serializable. For classes generated by AppWizard, these steps are done automatically; you need only to add them for new classes that you create, like CErectorBeam.

Serialization works in both directions. That is, you can both save and restore data using the serialization functions. Obviously, there is a difference: in one case you are writing the data and in the other you are reading it. To handle this difference, CArchive has a function `IsStoring`, which tells the serialization function whether you need to read or write your serialization data. As you would expect, `IsStoring` returns the Boolean `TRUE` if the data is being written and `FALSE` if it's being read.

Adding Serialization to ErectorSet

You can easily add serialization to your ErectorSet application. With the code you have already stubbed in, you simply have to add a few lines of code to have a fully functional save and restore for your documents.

To begin with, Listing 5.12 shows you the revised code to add to the Serialize function in CErectorDoc.

Listing 5.12

```
///////////////////////////////////////////////////////////////////////
// CErectorDoc serialization

// This function saves and restores the document to an external file
//    using the class CArchive.
void CErectorDoc::Serialize(CArchive& ar)
{
    if (ar.IsStoring())
    {
```

```
            // TODO: add storing code here
    }
    else
    {
            // TODO: add loading code here
    }

    // now ask our data members to serialize themselves
    m_beamList.Serialize( ar );
}
```

This is really quite simple. All you do is ask the object list to serialize itself. As you read earlier, the object list simply passes this request on to each object in the list in turn. So that leads us to Listing 5.13, which is the code you need to put into CErectorBeam to serialize a beam.

Listing 5.13

```
///////////////////////////////////////////////////////////////////////
// CErectorBeam serialization

// This function saves and restores the beam information
//     using the class CArchive.
void CErectorBeam::Serialize(CArchive& ar)
{
    if (ar.IsStoring())
    {
            ar << (WORD)m_nPenWidth;
            ar << m_crBrushColor;
            ar << m_rectBeam;
    }
    else
    {
            WORD w;
            ar >> w;
            m_nPenWidth = w;
            ar >> m_crBrushColor;
```

```
        ar >> m_rectBeam;
   }
}
```

This is only a little more complicated than the code in CErectorDoc. There are three elements that you need to know for each beam: its pen width, its color, and the rectangle that makes up the beam. So, those are the three items that you save (or restore).

To store the items, you simply use the << operator. In the same way, you restore the data by using the >> operator. Both of these operators are overloaded in the CArchive class to allow you to serialize any one of a range of data types.

C++

Overloading is a the process of allowing an operator to perform different actions, depending on the type of the operands that it encounters. Let's look at a brief example. Suppose that you define a Date class, which might consist of a structure that holds a month, day, and year value. A Date object might be written as Date(9,15,1994) to indicate 15th of September, 1994. Then you can define overloaded + and - operators that will add and subtract these dates correctly. The idea is that you can write something like Date(2,28,1995) + 1 and get a result of Date(3,1,1995), while Date(3,1,1996) - 1 gives you Date(2,29,1996), and so on. Normally, the plus and minus operators would require simple numbers, but by overloading them, you can use them in a natural way with items that are not simple numbers. This is one of the major advances in C++.

The only point to note here is that you must cast the pen width, which is stored internally as a UINT as a WORD data type. If you review the << and >> operators in CArchive, you will see that they do not support a UINT data type; however, they do support WORD. The bottom line is that CArchive understands how to convert a WORD to a serialized data item, while it doesn't understand UINT.

Once you have completed this code, your documents can be saved and restored in a normal way, using the standard **Save** and **Open** command from the File menu, as you would expect. Once again, MFC provides you with a significant benefit at a small price in coding and testing.

TESTING THE APPLICATION

At this point you have completed the job of adding basic functions for drawing beams in your ErectorSet code. You've added quite a bit of code here, so now you should choose **Build Erector.exe** again from the Build menu. This will recompile all of the modules that you have changed and re-link them to rebuild the executable code. Figure 5.12 shows you how the ErectorSet application looks when you've drawn a few beams.

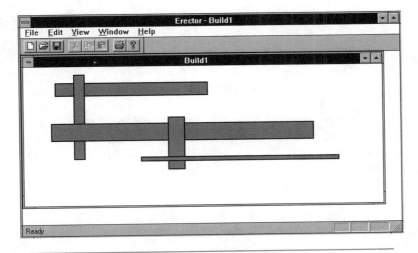

FIGURE 5.12 THE ERECTORSET APPLICATION NOW ALLOWS YOU TO CREATE AND DISPLAY BEAMS IN A DOCUMENT WINDOW.

For testing, you should do several things. Draw a few beams. Save the document. Without closing that document, open a new document and draw some beams in that. Then close both documents. Notice that the application prompts you to save the second document, which you haven't saved, but not the first one, which you have. Once you have closed the documents, open the first document that you saved. The beams will reappear just as you had them originally, showing that the save and restore functions that you added are working.

SUMMARY

In this chapter, you have added code to the skeleton application, which was generated by AppWizard in the last chapter, to handle the basic drawing function. You learned how to capture mouse movements and link Windows messages regarding mouse movements to your application code using ClassWizard. You also learned how to add save and restore functionality to your application by using the MFC serialization process. At this point, you have a functioning application.

This version of the program does all the basic things that you want: it draws beams, saves documents, and reads documents back into the application. However, there are several things that you notice are missing immediately. The most obvious, I think, is that you don't get any visual feedback on the beam that you are drawing. Most Windows applications that support drawing show you what you are drawing on screen, so you have a direct image of what you're doing. The natural expectation here is that the user would see a dotted rectangle while drawing the beam to have a clear picture of where the beam was going to be. A second point, perhaps less obvious but no less important, is that there isn't any way to erase the document. In the next chapter, you will see how to add these functions to the application.

CHAPTER 6

UNDERSTANDING OBJECT-ORIENTED PROGRAMMING AND MICROSOFT FOUNDATION CLASSES

At this point, you have a good introduction to the Visual C++ environment. Before proceeding to enhance the demonstration application and making further use of the Visual C++ development environment, you should have a short introduction to object-oriented programming. This chapter will cover the basic principles of object-oriented programming on a practical level, discussing issues such as class hierarchy, keywords, and inheritance.

The Microsoft Foundation Classes (MFC), which are an integral part of developing the examples in this book, are inextricably tied to the concepts and practices of object-oriented programming. Therefore, in addition to knowing something about object-oriented programming, you need to understand some things about the Microsoft Foundation Classes. This chapter will discuss the MFC Application Framework. It will present an overview of the basic classes and how they are intended to be used. This is a short overview to introduce the MFC classes so that you won't necessarily have to return to the MFC documentation for review.

Important topics in this chapter include:

- Benefits of object-oriented programming
- Understanding and working with classes
- Processing messages in your application
- How the Microsoft Foundation Classes are organized
- Using the basic MFC class structure

OBJECT-ORIENTED PROGRAMMING

The terms *object* and *object-oriented* have become so widely—and wildly—used that you would be forgiven for thinking that they are simply the latest programming buzzwords withour any real meaning or justification. Certainly a lot of the time that I hear these words in connection with one or another product or service, I wonder if there is any relationship between what is being sold and the reality of object-oriented programming.

Nevertheless, behind all the hype, there is a solid foundation of practical programming techniques described by the term *object-oriented programming*, or OOP. This section of the chapter discusses why you should be interested in OOP and why the ideas behind it have resulted in a significant productivity boost for programmers like us.

Why Object-Oriented Programming

Object-oriented programming is part of a long process of improving programmer productivity that has moved from standard programming to structured programming to OOP. For years, all professional programmers have reused code. A very common approach to a new programming assignment is to copy an existing program and modify it to solve the new problem. This approach has both distinct benefits and problems. The major benefit is that you start with a body of working code. This is particularly useful in areas like Windows programming, where applications inevitably require the same basic code for things like handling windows, menus, and other common elements. However, there are also drawbacks, most notably that every time you change your code, you risk introducing a new bug. As programmers grew in experience and knowledge, the problems of dealing with reuse of traditional procedural code were addressed by following specific rules, called *structured programming*, for creating blocks of code. This was an improvement, because it made code easier to understand and easier to debug, but it still did not accomplish the ultimate goals of allowing you to add to existing code easily and reliably. Object-oriented programming was created to solve this problem. By establishing certain coding features and practices that are enforced by the compiler, it allows the computer to help you keep blocks of code in a standard format so that you can easily reuse code without creating additional problems.

What this tells you is that OOP is more about program organization than coding techniques. Naturally, there are certain rules and requirements, which are inevitable when you want to use the computer to help create and enforce structure. But the coding techniques used in OOP generally, and in C++ in particular, are a small part of the process. How you organize your data into classes is a much more important part of OOP programming than the details of how it's coded. The basic difference between OOP and traditional program organization is that OOP looks at a programming problem as a collection of data, with associated routines to manage the data, rather than as a collection of processes or functions.

Overall, there are two major advantages to using object-oriented programming and MFC for your Windows applications:

- Your application will take less time to develop and will be more robust. The time for development will be shorter because you can use software components, provided by the MFC, to build your user interface. The application will be more robust because you can isolate changes to a few classes.

- Your application will be easier to maintain and easier to upgrade. You will localize changes to single classes when you need to add enhancements or make fixes.

Each of the key advantages of OOP grows out of the specific nature of the object-oriented design and coding process. All of the benefits mentioned here are, to some extent, intertwined. For example, you get the ability to reuse code easily because your code is done in independent blocks. Nevertheless, I have tried here to point out three compelling reasons why you should become familiar with OOP in general and the MFC in particular.

Matching the Application to User Requirements

Object-oriented programming is focused on delivering functionality to the user of the code, rather than on how the code works. The entire basis of OOP, in fact, the defining *object* in *object-oriented*, is a unit that combines both data and functionality together. When you are working in OOP, you think first about what data is required, rather than on what needs to happen to the data. The nature of OOP allows you to design classes of data that (hopefully) more closely match user requirements. The intention is that the process of decomposing the problem into data types will match the physical or logical entities in the system being modeled.

OOP also allows you to design and implement much more quickly than more traditional methods. Because the design is closely linked to the physical or logical structures being used and because the code can be implemented in a series of classes and methods, you can often get clear and immediate feedback on your design. OOP also allows easy modification of code, so you can refine the implementation without causing major problems.

Reuse of Code

Object-oriented programming allows you to reuse code with a minimum of problems. As proof of this, simply look at how you are using the MFC to create your ErectorSet application. In effect, you are reusing literally thousands of lines of code that have been created by Microsoft and stored in the MFC. The process of reusing this code doesn't require that you investigate or explore any specific lines of the classes provided. All you need to do is to use AppWizard to select the features that you want in your application, and then either add code to the provided application, document, and view classes, or subclass them to add more or different functionality. This flexibility is built into OOP.

Visual C++ 4.0 carries this ability to reuse code even further by adding a Component Gallery to the Developer Studio. The Component Gallery includes a series of useful features that you can add to your project at any time. And by following a few simple rules, you can add your own modules to the Component Gallery for you or someone else to reuse easily in the future. You will see how to use the Component Gallery in Chapter 12.

Code Independence

Creating code in an object-oriented environment allows you to handle code blocks as independent units, without worrying about the internal structures and features of the code blocks themselves. Each block of code represents a class, which is essentially self-contained. As you use the classes, you are able to adapt their behavior by creating subclasses.

Each class has external access through its public methods. By limiting access to the public members, you keep the code within the class separate from all the other code in your application. In this way, OOP allows, in fact encourages, you to maintain your code in independent units that are easy to access and therefore easy to use and reuse.

Features of Object-Oriented Programming

Certain specific features make object-oriented programming different from other forms of programming. Most texts agree that four features are essential to make a language suitable for object-oriented programming:

- Abstract data types
- Inheritance
- Encapsulation
- Polymorphism

Let's look at each of these features, so you can see how OOP differs from more conventional types of programming. I have also included the concept of *overloading*, which is similar in some ways to polymorphism and is also an important feature of C++, although it generally isn't counted as a defining characteristic of OOP.

Abstract Data Types

We are all familiar with data types in programming. Some types are strictly physical—like bits and bytes, which always have a precise physical size and meaning—while some are a bit more conceptual—like integers, which always represent an integer number but may be different sizes and have a different organization on different computer systems. Object-oriented programming takes this one more level, and allows you to package any type of data as a single, reusable unit—the *object* in *object-oriented*. To do this, all data objects of a single type, or *class*, must be gathered together. So a class represents an *abstract data type*, while any object represents a specific instance of some class.

CErectorBeam is a good example of this. The class itself represents an idea, or abstraction, of how beams work in the ErectorSet application. Beams are constructed by mouse movements. They have certain physical properties such as color, they can display themselves on a device, and so on. Every time you need a beam in your document, you create another beam object, an instance of the class CErectorBeam, to be one of the beams for a specific document. So CErectorBeam is an abstract type of data that can be used in your application; specifically, it is a type of data that is used to create images of rectangles on the screen.

Probably the most difficult part of object-oriented programming is organizing and understanding the objects that make up your application. Defining the objects that make up your application and setting up the relationship between them is a new task for most programmers. The novelty of this approach makes it harder initially than designing a traditional application. Don't be discouraged. With experience and effort, you will find that designing around data classes in much easier and more efficient than the traditional methods that are familiar to you now.

Inheritance

As you have already seen in the exercises so far, a new class of objects can be derived from an old one. This process is called class *inheritance* because the new class inherits the characteristics of the original class. The new class is called a *derived class* of the original class, and the original class is called the *base class* of the new class.

N O T E   In some books on object-oriented programming, the base class is called the *superclass*, and the derived class is called the *subclass*. I personally don't care for this terminology, which seems to be harder to understand and remember—not to mention the sociological connotations. The whole *super* and *sub* idea implies an up and down orientation in the class hierarchy, which is certainly open to some misunderstanding—when was the last time you thought of the roots of a tree as being above the leaves? On the other hand, the *base* and *derived* terminology seems to me to be quite clear and understandable in any circumstance. Nevertheless, I mention this here so you can translate what you've learned in this book into another reference's language.

Most classes inherit from only one base class. This is called *single inheritance*. However, it is possible to derive a class from two base classes. This is called, naturally enough, *multiple inheritance*. You use multiple inheritance when you need a new class that inherits behavior from each of two distinct and unrelated classes. This is a very powerful technique but one that requires a lot of thought for correct and effective use. Multiple inheritance is an advanced technique that isn't often necessary in ordinary programming, and you won't find any examples of it in this book. Single inheritance, however, is the foundation of MFC programming, and you will use it repeatedly.

Encapsulation

Once you have determined the type of object in a class, you need to define its components, how it is represented, and how it is accessed. One of the most powerful and important points of OOP is that the access to a class is strictly regulated. The user of a class does not need to know details of how the class is organized internally; all access to the class data is through a series of external function calls, or *methods*. The process of binding class organization so that it is not directly accessible to the user is called *encapsulation*.

Encapsulation has three important features:

1. It provides a clear boundary that defines and protects all of an object's internal structure.

2. It defines an interface that describes and controls how other users work with an object.

3. It provides a protected, internal implementation of the object's behavior and structure. This implementation is not generally accessible outside the scope of the class itself.

From this list you can see that two distinct types of data and functions are used in class: *public* information, which is available to users of the class, and *private* information, which is strictly kept within the class itself. In C++, these two types of data and procedures are marked by using the keywords `public` and `private` in the definitions.

This division into public and private areas is nice, logical, and above all unambiguous: either something is public or it is private—there is no in-between state. As so often happens in real life, however, there is a need for a state in between public and private. Because a class can inherit behavior and information from a base class, there is a need for a type of information that is available to derived classes but not to other users of the class. This is the *protected* data type. It is much more restricted than public information, which is available to any user of the class, but less restricted than private information, which is available only within the class itself.

CErectorBeam is a good example. Listing 6.1 shows a part of the header file for CErectorBeam.

Listing 6.1

```
//////////////////////////////////////////////////////////////////////////
// class CErectorBeam
//
// A beam defines the size and characteristics of a rectangle
//     that is filled to make a beam element of the drawing.
// An erector document may have multiple beams.
//

class CErectorBeam : public CObject
{
public:
        CErectorBeam(UINT nPenWidth, COLORREF crBrushColor);

protected:
        CErectorBeam();                    // required for serialization
        DECLARE_SERIAL(CErectorBeam)

// Attributes
protected:
        CRect      m_rectBeam;         // the beam rectangle
        CPoint     m_ptStart;          // the beam starting point
        COLORREF   m_crBrushColor      // the color for the beam
        UINT       m_nPenWidth;        // the rectangle border size

public:
        virtual ~CErectorBeam();
        // This is both prototype and inline definition
        CRect* GetCurrentBeam() { return &m_rectBeam; };
```

```
// Operations
public:
        void BeginBeam(CPoint pt);
        void EndBeam(CPoint pt);
        BOOL DrawBeam(CDC* pDC);


// Helper Functions
public:
        virtual void Serialize(CArchive& ar);


};
```

`/////////////////////////////////////////////////////////////////////////`

As you can see in Listing 6.1, the data describing the beam—m_crBrushColor, m_nPenWidth, m_rectBeam, and m_ptStart—are all protected data. What this means is that, if you derived a new class from CErectorBeam, the new class would be able to reference these items just as CErectorBeam functions can, by simply using their names. However, no outside class can access this information. For example, CErectorView and CErectorDoc cannot use any of this information directly.

However, it isn't necessary or even desirable to make this information private. If you were to derive a new class from CErectorBeam, you would want to be able to test and use this data as a part of your normal programming. You can do that only if the data is protected and not private. You should reserve the private label for data that you would never want to share outside of the given class and would never want to use directly in a derived class.

If you want to make information available outside the class itself (or its direct descendants), you must use a function to access the desired data. For example, suppose you want to get the beam's rectangle for processing. To do this, you must use the supplied function, GetCurrentBeam, which provides a pointer to m_rectBeam. This is typically how you access protected or private data from outside the class itself.

Overloading and Polymorphism

These two features of OOP are, in my opinion, complementary. Of the two, polymorphism is a defining feature of OOP, but wherever you have polymorphism, you also have overloading, so I am presenting them here as a pair of related concepts.

The idea of *polymorphism* is that subclasses can have different functions that respond to the same message as a base class, but they can perform different functions. A good example of this is the OnDraw function in CErectorView. This function provides a specific action that happens when a view needs to be drawn. However, the exact nature of the drawing action can't be determined until you know the type of view that needs to be drawn. Let's suppose, for a moment, that you had another type of view that displayed only text. In that view, the drawing process would be quite different than it is in CErectorView. As the message gets passed down the class hierarchy, CWnd and CView—which are base classes for all document views—don't know exactly what action to take until they look at the type of the view that needs to be drawn. OOP allows you to ignore determining the action taken in response to a message until the type of object is available. In other words, the behavior of your application changes depending on the type of object that receives the drawing message.

The process of *overloading* is similar in many ways. This is the process of defining operators that implement common behavior for a class in a special way. The CRect class that you use for the beams has some good examples of this. Using CRect objects, you can define operations like + and - on a CRect object. Therefore, a line of code like this is perfectly acceptable:

```
rectTemp = (CRect) rectTemp + (CPoint) ptOffset;
```

This code moves the rectangle, rectTemp, by the distance specified by the values in the point object, ptOffset. That's pretty straightforward, but it isn't what + does when you use it normally. A rectangle isn't actually a simple number, so + and - aren't C operators, and you couldn't write that line of code in C. In C++, however, you can overload the + operator, so that the compiler knows that this type of + must call the + operator defined in the CRect class. In this way, you can use common operators for complex functions in a natural way, simply by overloading them in the class definitions.

There is a difference in these two features. They are similar, in that the action taken each time depends on the type of the operands for the function or operator being used. They differ, however, in one important respect. In the case of polymorphism, you can't know what action will be required to respond to a message until you run the program. The object of the message—in this example, the type of view—is determined as you are executing. In the case of overloading, because you know when you compile the program what the objects involved will be, the compiler can adapt the operator to the type of the objects at compile time, rather than at run time. Nevertheless, I think you can see why I think of these two features together—they are indeed similar but not the same.

Classes and Hierarchy

Classes are arranged in a hierarchy based on derivation; that is, a class that is derived from another class is considered inferior in the hierarchy to its base class. A common metaphor for this is an inverted tree, where the base class is at the top and the derived classes are arranged beneath it in a widening pyramid. However, this can be a bit confusing, and it really doesn't provide much insight into how classes are used. I like to take the view that classes are built, like the floors of a house, on top of one another. The base class becomes the basement, and the derived classes are like rooms and floors above it. This obviously turns the "lower" and "upper" notions of inferior and superior classes on their head, so I usually ignore that metaphor: in my world, it's superior to be closer to the basement. However, either approach to class visualization is fine, as long as you're clear about how this works.

The Browser in the Developer Studio displays classes in two directions: up and down the hierarchy. Each of these displays helps you navigate your classes and also gives you an insight into how you can visualize these relationships. The first display looks up the hierarchy, as shown in Figure 6.1. This view is provided by selecting the CErectorApp class in the Class view and then choosing the **Base Classes...** pop-up menu item for the display.

This display shows all the classes that are superior to the selected class—the class name that you select in the Class view. In this view of the class hierarchy, the current class sits on top of all its base classes. Figure 6.1 shows that CErectorApp inherits from (moving up the hierarchy): CWinApp, CWinThread, CCmdTarget, and finally CObject. This is a very useful picture, because it shows the classes from which your class inherits behavior. If you are looking for a specific function, for example, this picture shows you all the classes where you should look for that function.

NOTE

This is one of the trickiest parts of using a class structure: where can you find the function that implements the behavior that you need? There isn't (unfortunately) any quick and easy way to see all the functions that your class has inherited—and it might not be useful, even if you could, because there are so many. However, this Base Class display is a good place to start. Begin by looking up the functions provided by the class immediately above your class. If you select the class in the pane on the left, the top pane on the right shows you the names of all the functions in that class. If you see the function that you need, you can look up how to use it in the *Class Library Reference*. If the function you want isn't there, move to the next class up the chain, and so on. This will give you a simple and secure method for finding all the functions that you can use in your current class.

The other display provided by the Browser is the view down the hierarchy from a given class. This view is provided by choosing **Browse** from the Tools menu and entering **CCmdTarget** as the identifier in the Browse dialog box and selecting **Derived Classes and Members** in the Select query list. Figure 6.2 shows the resulting display for the CCmdTarget class. (Figure 6.2 doesn't use one of the ErectorSet classes as an example because none of them have any derived classes, so there wouldn't be much to see.)

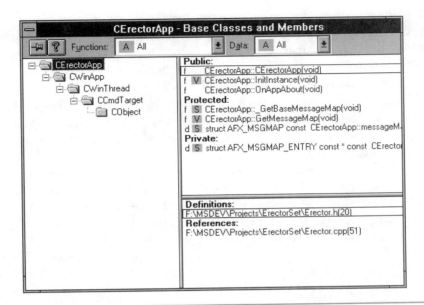

FIGURE 6.1 THE **BASE CLASSES...** DISPLAY IN THE BROWSER SHOWS YOU THE VIEW UP THE CLASS HIERARCHY.

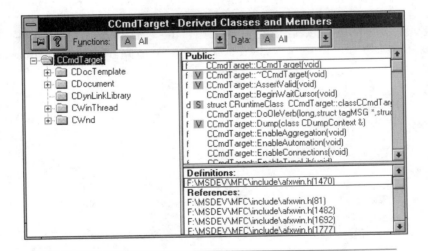

FIGURE 6.2 THE DERIVED CLASSES AND MEMBERS DISPLAY SHOWS YOU THE VIEW FROM THE SELECTED CLASS DOWN THE HIERARCHY.

In this view, the selected class is again at the top of the display, while all its derived classes are shown below it. Figure 6.2 shows that CCmdTarget is the base class for CWnd, CWinThread, CDynLinkLibrary, CDocument, and CDocTemplate. In addition, each of these classes except CDynLinkLibrary have other classes beneath them that also inherit from CCmdTarget.

A class inherits behavior from all the classes superior to it in the hierarchy. When you are working in a class, you have access to all the functions and data that are not marked `private` in the classes above you in the hierarchy. Your class automatically inherits all these functions. Look at the CErectorApp as an example. Suppose the user selects **Open** from the File menu. Your application must respond to this action by displaying a file dialog box that allows the user to select a file to open. However, there is no code like that in CErectorApp, and there is no reference to anything about opening files. Instead, all that is handled by CWinApp, in the functions that it provides. Your application object, CErectorApp, inherits all this behavior without any direct effort on your part and without a single line of code being added to it. It comes automatically from being derived from CWinApp.

Also, any function that you define can use the functions inherited from your base classes. You simply call them, just as you would call a function in your own class. This makes the whole process very easy and simple. Whenever you see function calls in a class that aren't in the class header (.h) file and have no external reference, you can be sure that these are calls to inherited functions. Listing 6.2 shows you a short code segment from CErectorDoc that illustrates this point.

Listing 6.2

```
//////////////////////////////////////////////////////////////////////
// CErectorDoc data management


// This function creates a new beam object
//      and initializes it with the document default settings
//      for pen width and brush color.
CErectorBeam* CErectorDoc::NewBeam()
```

```
{
        // Create a new beam object using our pre-set width and color
        CErectorBeam* pBeam = new CErectorBeam( m_nPenWidth, m_nBeamColor );
        // insert the beam into the list of beam objects
        m_beamList.AddTail( pBeam );
        // and mark the document as modified
        //      to avoid accidental close without save.
        SetModifiedFlag();
        return pBeam;
}
```

This is the function, NewBeam, in CErectorDoc. As you see, the next-to-last line of the function calls another function, SetModifiedFlag, that is not defined in CErectorDoc. In fact, this function is defined in the MFC CDocument class.

SHORTCUT

There are several ways to find the definition and uses of functions that are inherited in your code: use the printed *Class Reference* manual, if you have it; select the desired class from the *Class Library Reference* manual displayed in InfoViewer if you have the CD documentation on-line; or use the Developer Studio Help facilities. However, the fastest method is as follows:

1. Highlight the name of the function that you want to look up, not including the parameter list. A simple double-click on the function name will do the job.

2. Press **F1**. This will either display the desired information or display the Select Reference dialog box with the highlighted word automatically displayed as the keyword for the search. Figure 6.3 shows how this would look.

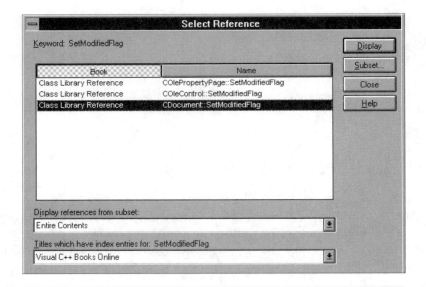

FIGURE 6.3 THE SELECT REFERENCE DIALOG BOX WILL TAKE YOU DIRECTLY TO THE REFERENCE
FOR AN UNKNOWN FUNCTION THAT IS DEFINED IN ONE OF YOUR BASE CLASSES.

If the item that you're looking for is discussed in more than one place,
you may have to select the correct Reference file from the list shown
in the dialog. In this case, SetModifiedFlag appears in the Class
Library Reference in three classes: COlePropertyPage, COleControl,
and CDocument. Since your document is derived from CDocument,
select CDocument from this list.

3. Press **Display**. The search takes you directly to the information
   about this function in the selected class. Figure 6.4 shows the display for SetModifiedFlag as an example.

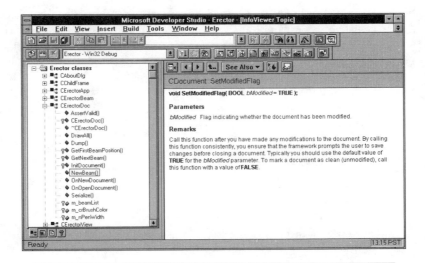

FIGURE 6.4 ALL THE REFERENCE INFORMATION ABOUT INHERITED FUNCTIONS IS AT YOUR
FINGERTIPS USING THE **F1** HELP KEY.

However you look up this information, you will find that the class reference information tells you both the class where the function is defined and how to use the function. This can be a great help.

There are obviously two cases where you need to modify behavior in a class. First, there may be an existing function that you inherit where you need to do something different—either replacing the existing behavior or adding to it. You do this by overriding an existing function in the base class(es). Second, you may need to add new functions to your class. You do that by including new code and new message processing in your class.

If you need to override an inherited function, you have to declare it in your header file and then override it in your class by providing a new function with the same name and parameters as the inherited function. In this way, the function defined in your class will be called before any inherited function. Now you can add new processing code to the function. If you want to use the inherited behavior, you simply call the function in your base class. Listing 6.3 shows you how to call the same function in a base class from within your own function.

Listing 6.3

```
// This function sets up and initializes a new document,
//     generally in response to user choosing File>>New from the menu.
BOOL CErectorDoc::OnNewDocument()
{
        if (!CDocument::OnNewDocument())
            return FALSE;

        // initialize document parameters
        InitDocument();

        return TRUE;
}
```

This is the OnNewDocument function in your CErectorDoc class. This function overrides the same function in CDocument. However, it wants to execute the OnNewDocument function in CDocument before it adds its own processing for new documents. The highlighted code in Listing 6.3 shows how this is done. Place the name of the base class whose function you want to execute in front of the function name and followed by two colons. This tells the compiler to use the function in the named class rather than any other version of the function. This is always how you refer to a specific class variable or function in C++.

Each class also has its own functions, which it passes on to the classes below it in the hierarchy. For example, the function NewBeam from the CErectorDoc class, which you saw in Figure 6.2, is a new function—that is, it does not exist in any base class for CErectorDoc. However, if you were to derive a new class from CErectorDoc, then NewBeam would automatically be inherited by that class, and it would be available within the class.

Functions and Messages

The class hierarchy is designed to handle events in a regular and orderly fashion. As you can already see, the basis for this is a notification system. When a certain task—that is, function—is requested, the C++ system dispatches the request for action to the selected class. So far, this is just like function calls in C or any other programming language. If the function is defined in the specific class, the job is over. Unless the function specifically requests action from its base class or classes, as you saw in Listing 6.3, the function definition in the class overrides any other function definition.

Where things differ from other, non–object-oriented languages, is what happens if the desired function is not found in the selected class. In that case, the function request passes up the chain of classes until the function is found or the chain of classes is exhausted. The first class to respond to the request is the class that will handle it, just as though the code were in the initial selected class. If the chain of classes is exhausted without finding the function, you get an error, just as you would if you tried to execute a function that doesn't exist in any other language.

Most C++ programmers simply use the term *call* for any instance when you invoke a public member function of a class, even though this implies invoking the entire chain of classes and so is not just a simple function call. Wherever you read about calling a function or method in this book, you must understand that this means invoking the calling chain for the class hierarchy, not just for the single class mentioned. Note that a program calls, or invokes, a public method just like you call any function in C, including if necessary parameter values for the method's use. The extra work of routing the calls through the hierarchy is done by the C++ language.

N O T E   The natural analogy for this type of request handling and processing is to call them *messages,* and that is one standard terminology used in OOP books and references. However, since Windows uses the term *messages* for commands routed to your application from the user interface, I have avoided using *message* in any other way in this book to avoid confusion.

You may also remember that public member functions can be called *methods.* Many OOP books and documents use both terms and talk about sending messages to methods. If you read one of these books, you can now translate that so it matches what you have learned here.

Windows Messages

In addition to processing function calls, the application must also handle requests for action from Windows. These Windows *messages* are requests that are generated by clicking a mouse button or selecting a menu item. The Windows operating system gets these messages, decides what application is responsible for the message, and passes the message on to the application for processing. Of course, some messages are handled by Windows itself, without any application being involved. For example, if you move the Program Manager window, Windows will handle all of the necessary display functions without involving another application. However, when the user clicks the left mouse button in an ErectorSet document window, for example, Windows sends a mouse-down message, WM_LBUTTONDOWN, to the ErectorSet application.

The ErectorSet application processes all Windows messages that relate to it: that is, all messages generated in any of its windows or generated by selecting it in the Program Manager. In this case, the mouse-down message is passed to ErectorSet as a Windows message. Then the ErectorSet application forwards that message to the view class that is derived from the window where the mouse was pressed. The message map in the view turns that command into a function call to OnLButtonDown.

So you see that two things are being done here: sending the Windows message, WM_LBUTTONDOWN, and generating the MFC function call, OnLButtonDown. The important point is to realize that there are, in fact, two types of information being processed; one from Windows informing the application (and ultimately the view of what has happened) and one generated by the application for internal use and processing.

N O T E

There is one small additional complication to all of this in actual code. In fact, the application uses Windows to send the message to the correct window. Here's how the full process works:

- The application registers its window class with the Windows operating system when it begins.

- The application marks windows as it creates them as members of a window class.

- The application gets the next message for it out of a message queue maintained by Windows.

- The application then returns the message to Windows and asks Windows to dispatch the message to the correct window.

The net result is just what you read before. The only difference is that the message gets passed back through Windows again before being finally translated into a class message. This additional detail is only important if you're tracing program execution, and it explains why you have to use breakpoints in your code rather than trying to step though the entire program.

Commands and the Message Map

How your application handles routing these messages to the correct functions is an important part of this entire process. This is where the handling of messages and functions all ties together.

An entire class of objects in your user interface, such as menu items, buttons, and so on, can generate commands. In the same way, many parts of your application can receive and process commands. These objects are called *command targets* and they all derive from the CCmdTarget class in the MFC. Each object derived from CCmdTarget contains a message map and message handler functions.

A *message map* is a table that connects command IDs with the names of message-handler functions. Each command target has its own message map that defines what messages it can handle and that points to the correct functions within the target that can handle individual messages. One of the most important parts of constructing a Windows application is writing these message-handler functions.

Normally, you will use the Class Wizard to construct and maintain the message maps for your classes. This process allows you to concentrate on the handler functions and not worry too much about connecting controls and other message-generating objects in the user interface with the handlers. The message maps in your application code will be bracketed by the BEGIN_MESSAGE_MAP and END_MESSAGE_MAP macros. This code is generated by the Class Wizard, which also maintains portions of the message map code between these two macros as well. For most purposes, you can simply let Class Wizard do the work for you.

As you might expect by now, command messages reach their handler functions in a manner similar to how the class hierarchy handles processing function calls. In fact, the entire process is designed to mirror the class handling of function calls. Messages are routed through a standard, hierarchical sequence of command target objects until the message is handled. If a message is not handled by any subordinate targets, the command is returned to the application object for default handling.

The important point to understand here is that this process, although similar in many respects to the class hierarchy and class function call routing, is entirely separate from it. Command messages are created, handled, and routed by code within the MFC, not by using C++ class routing. For this reason you need to keep both the message map and the class hierarchy synchronized if you need to change the derivation of a class after you have generated your application.

Adding ClearAll Processing to ErectorSet

Let's use a practical example to see how to add a new message to your application and how to process that message in your code. One thing that ErectorSet doesn't have at the moment is any way to delete beams once you have drawn them. For now, let's add a menu item that allows you to delete all of the beams that you have already drawn in the document.

To do this, you will add a new menu selection, **Clear All**, to the Edit menu. When the user selects this, all of the beams currently in the document will be erased. Simple enough.

Here are the steps that you need to take to add Clear All processing to ErectorSet:

1. Add the **Clear All** entry to the Edit menu and assign it a message ID using the Developer Studio's built-in resource editor.

2. Use the ClassWizard to add Clear All functionality to your CErectorDoc class.

3. Create the required code in the new CErectorDoc functions to delete the beams and redisplay the document.

NOTE Menus are a type of resource used in your Windows application. A variety of resources are used in Windows applications. The Developer Studio provides a built-in resource editor that allows you to create and modify resources for your application. For now, you will simply modify the existing resources. In Chapter 9, you will learn more about all types of resources, including how to create new resources and add them to your application.

Using the Resource View to Modify a Menu

First make sure that you are in the ErectorSet project workspace and close any edit windows that you may have open. This makes the process a bit easier to follow.

Start the process by selecting the Resource view in the InfoView pane. This opens the resource file for your project, `Erector.rc`, and displays the resources that are currently defined for your project. Click next to the Menu folder to display the Menu resources. At this point, your screen should look like Figure 6.5.

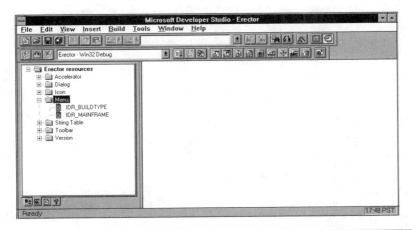

FIGURE 6.5 THE RESOURCE VIEW ALLOWS YOU TO EDIT THE RESOURCES FOR THE ERECTORSET APPLICATION.

Notice that there is an IDR_BUILDTYPE selection as one of the menu resources. Remember that 'Build' was the identification for your documents, as you read earlier. This is the resource ID for the menu that is displayed when a document is open in your application.

Double-click on **IDR_BUILDTYPE** or select **Open** from the pop-up menu. This displays your document menu items in the editor pane, which has now become the resource editor. Select the **Edit** item in that display. At the bottom of the display of Edit, you will see a blank rectangle; double-click on that rectangle, or select it and choose **Properties** from the Edit menu (**Alt+Enter**). At this point, your screen should look like Figure 6.6.

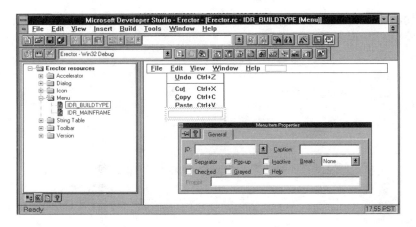

FIGURE 6.6 THE RESOURCE EDITOR DISPLAYS THE SELECTED MENU WITH SPACES WHERE YOU CAN ADD NEW ITEMS.

The blank rectangle at the end of the Edit menu—and the rectangle after the Help menu item—are places where you can add new items to the menu. In this case, you want to add a menu item that says **Clear All** with a separator bar in front of it; to do this, you need to set the menu item properties, which you can do in the dialog box that you have displayed at the bottom of the screen.

Start by checking the **Separator** box. This will place a single line separator bar across the menu. When you have done that, a new blank rectangle appears beneath the bar. Move down and select that rectangle and double-click or choose **Properties** again. Now you are ready to enter the menu item.

The ID scrolling list in the dialog box presents a series of message IDs that you can use. These cover most common menu items. Scroll down until you see the item `ID_EDIT_CLEAR_ALL`. As you might suspect, this is the standard message ID for a Clear All menu selection. Move your mouse cursor to the Caption text box. Notice that the Prompt text line automatically fills in for you. This is the information line that will be displayed in the status bar at the bottom of your application's window when the user chooses this Edit menu item.

However, you still need to put in the menu label itself. You type this in the Caption edit text box in the dialog box. In this case, type the following, just as shown here (note that there is a single blank space between *r* and *&*):

```
Clear &All\tDel
```

As you type, the menu item appears in the blank rectangle. Figure 6.7 shows the result.

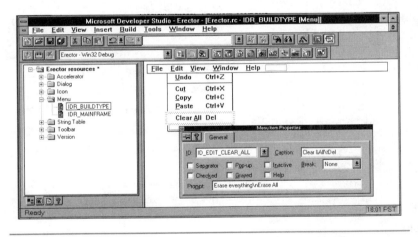

FIGURE 6.7 THE CAPTION THAT YOU ENTER IN THE PROPERTIES DIALOG BOX APPEARS IMMEDIATELY IN ITS DISPLAY FORMAT IN THE MENU DISPLAY.

As you see, the *&* and the *\t* don't appear on the menu item itself. You place the *&* character before the letter of the menu selection that you want to be the access character for that selection—in this case, pressing **A** on the keyboard will select **Clear All** from the Edit menu. The *\t* is a tab character, and moves the label text after the tab out to a fixed tab position. The *Del* stands for the **Delete** key on the keyboard. This is called an *accelerator key*, meaning a key that the user can press to execute this selection without displaying the menu at all. You will learn how to add code to tie the accelerator key to the menu item in Chapter 9. For now, you can just include it here for future use.

Let's just review what you have done here. You have created a new menu item and given it a command message ID number, which is represented by the label ID_EDIT_CLEAR_ALL. When this menu item is selected, Windows will send this message ID to your application to notify you that the user selected the **Clear All** command. Now your application must add code within the class hierarchy to handle this message when it comes.

Using ClassWizard to Bind a Menu Command

At this point, you now need to map the Windows message ID to a function. This is exactly where ClassWizard comes in: it specializes in tying messages to functions. Because this transition is so common, you can go directly to ClassWizard. Simply press **Ctrl+W**, select **ClassWizard** from the View menu, or press the **ClassWizard** button on the toolbar. This takes you directly to the ClassWizard dialog box that you've seen before. Notice that much of the information is already filled in for you; in particular, the **Message Maps** tab is selected, the **ID_EDIT_CLEAR_ALL** item is selected in the Object IDs list, and the **CErectorView** class is selected in the Class name list.

The first thing that you must do in ClassWizard is select the class where you will place the code to implement **Clear All**. This raises a problem, because the **Clear All** command performs two functions:

1. It clears the view of all visible objects.
2. It deletes the current list of objects from the document.

Based on this, you have two options. First, you can put the code in CErectorView—as ClassWizard is suggesting—because clearing the display is important, and the view should have the opportunity to control its display functions. This would be the obvious option if you think of item 1 as the most important item of this list. Second, you can place the code in the CErectorDoc class. This would be the obvious option if you think that the deletion of the beams is most important.

In this case, I think that all of this should be centralized in the document. To do this, select **CErectorDoc** from the Class name list in the ClassWizard dialog box, as shown in Figure 6.8.

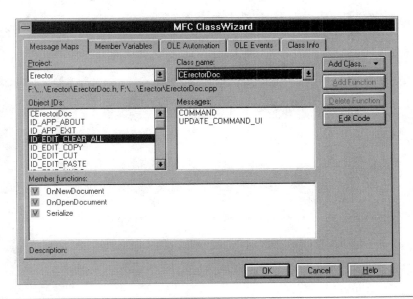

FIGURE 6.8 YOU CAN CHOOSE ANY ONE OF YOUR CLASSES FOR ADDITION OF A MESSAGE PROCESSING FUNC-
TION.

Notice that there are two messages listed in the ClassWizard dialog box for this message ID: COMMAND and UPDATE_COMMAND_UI. These are always the two messages for all commands. The first one performs the actual command processing, while the second one allows you to update the menu display if you want. For now, you will just implement the command portion. After that's complete, you will add the user-interface update code.

Select the **COMMAND** message and double-click on it, or select it and press the **Add Function** button. This prompts you with the Add Member Function dialog box, which provides the name of the new function. For this function, ClassWizard suggests the name OnEditClearAll, which is fine. Click **OK** to accept it. Now your ClassWizard dialog box should look like Figure 6.9.

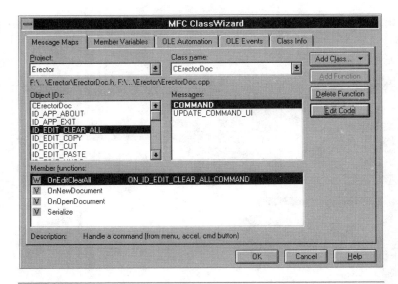

FIGURE 6.9 YOU ADD A MEMBER FUNCTION IN YOUR SELECTED CLASS FOR EACH MESSAGE THAT YOU WANT TO PROCESS.

Adding the Functional Code

Now you're ready to add the code that actually produces the desired action. Press the **Edit Code** button in the ClassWizard dialog box to go directly to the new function that has been added to the end of your `ErectorDoc.cpp` file. At the same time, the necessary functional prototype has been added to your header file. Figure 6.10 shows you what the new skeleton function looks like.

NOTE The MFC use the convention of prefixing message handler functions with the word *On*. If you generate these handlers with the ClassWizard, as you have here, then you will automatically get the correct parameters and return values for the specific handler function that you request. Note that the default message handler for all WM_ messages are documented in the CWnd class. Of course, as always, the easiest way to find out about a specific default WM_ function is to use the Help Search. However, the messages that begin ID_ , such as the ID_EDIT_CLEAR_ALL message being processed here, are not Windows messages. They are handled by the framework application itself and exist only in the class where you place the handler function.

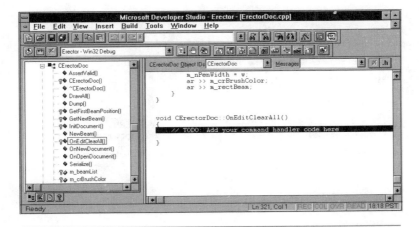

FIGURE 6.10 THE CLASSWIZARD AUTOMATICALLY CREATES A SKELETON FUNCTION FOR YOUR MESSAGE HANDLING.

However, ClassWizard automatically places this at the end of the ErectorDoc.cpp file, after your CErectorBeam class, since it can't know where else to place the code. However, you don't really want the code there; it would be much better if placed up with the other CErectorDoc code, earlier in the file. Listing 6.4 shows you the new code in place in your CErectorDoc class, along with some auxiliary code and comments.

Listing 6.4

```
///////////////////////////////////////////////////////////////////////////
// ErectorDoc.cpp : implementation of the CErectorDoc class
//
//
// Created by AppWizard 11 December 1995 11:39:42
// Modifiications:
//   12 Dec 95   DH    Add OnOpenDocument to generated code,
//                         along with new common InitDocument().
//   12 Dec 95   DH    Add CErectorBeam class to generated code:
//                         initialization; serialization; contents.
//   15 Dec 95   DH    Add menu item Edit>>Clear All with new function,
//                         OnEditClearAll, and function DeleteContents.
///////////////////////////////////////////////////////////////////////////
```

```
//   ...after CErectorDoc::InitDocument()...


// This function clears the current drawing in response to
//  the Edit>>Clear All or any equivalent user action.
void CErectorDoc::OnEditClearAll()
{
    DeleteContents();                // delete the beam list data
    SetModifiedFlag( TRUE );         // mark the document as dirty
    UpdateAllViews( NULL );          // re-draw all the views
}



//   ...after CErectorDoc::GetNextBeam...



// This function provides a way to destroy the document's data
//  when you wish to save the document itself. The function iterates
//  through the data list and deletes the beam objects. It also
//  clears the pointers to the beam in the beam list.
void CErectorDoc::DeleteContents()
{
    while( !m_beamList.IsEmpty() )
    {
        delete m_beamList.RemoveHead();
    }


    return;
}
```

The first part of this code is the OnEditClearAll function. This does three things: it deletes the contents of the document by calling a new function, DeleteContents; it sets the modification flag to note that the document has changed by calling the inherited SetModifiedFlag function; and it sends a message to all views that they need to redraw themselves by calling the inherited UpdateAllViews.

You also add the code for the new protected function, DeleteContents, as shown in Listing 6.4. You can do this most easily by changing to the Class View, selecting the CErectorDoc class, using the pop-up menu selection **Add Function...** (as you did in Chapter 5 to add the DrawAll function), and then moving the generated code as you did for OnEditClearAll.

DeleteContents is actually a function that is defined in CDocument to do nothing; in effect, you are overriding that function here. It is provided in CDocument because this is a common function to implement; for SDI applications, it's essential, because you can only have a single document. For an MDI application, like ErectorSet, it isn't as crucial since you can delete documents and open new ones without any complications. Naturally, when you close a document, the contents of the document are deleted unless you save them to a file. DeleteContents simply removes the top item in the list of beams until the list is empty. Note that it does this in two steps. First, it removes the top item in the list using the RemoveHead function. This removes the beam object at the top of the list and returns a pointer to it. To delete the beam itself, the function calls the C++ delete operator, which removes a C++ object from memory and cleans up afterward.

There is one last point to note. Since you added two new functions, the header file has been changed as well. Listing 6.5 shows the new header file, which I have rearranged slightly.

Listing 6.5

```
/////////////////////////////////////////////////////////////////////////////
// ErectorDoc.h : interface of the CErectorDoc class
//
//
// Created by AppWizard 11 December 1995 11:39:42
// Modifiications:
//   12 Dec 95   DH    Add OnOpenDocument to generated code,
//                         along with new common InitDocument().
//   12 Dec 95   DH    Add CErectorBeam class to generated code:
//                         initialization; serialization; contents
//   15 Dec 95   DH    Add menu item Edit>>Clear All with new function,
//                         OnEditClearAll, and function, DeleteContents.
/////////////////////////////////////////////////////////////////////////////
```

```
// Forward declaration of the data structure class, CErectorBeam
class CErectorBeam;


class CErectorDoc : public CDocument
{
protected: // create from serialization only
    CErectorDoc();
    DECLARE_DYNCREATE(CErectorDoc)

// Attributes
protected:
    CTypedPtrList<CObList, CErectorBeam*> m_beamList; // each list element
is a beam object

    // We track the beam color or pattern and outline width
    //    at the document level for all views. This allows
    //    the user to choose a new beam style for all the views
    //    together, rather than one at a time.
    COLORREF    m_crBrushColor          // the brush color
    UINT        m_nPenWidth;            // the border width

// Operations
public:
    CErectorBeam* NewBeam();
    POSITION GetFirstBeamPosition();
    CErectorBeam* GetNextBeam( POSITION& pos);

// Overrides
    // ClassWizard generated virtual function overrides
    //{{AFX_VIRTUAL(CErectorDoc)
    public:
    virtual BOOL OnNewDocument();
    virtual void Serialize(CArchive& ar);
    virtual BOOL OnOpenDocument(LPCTSTR lpszPathName);
    //}}AFX_VIRTUAL
```

```
// Implementation
public:
    virtual ~CErectorDoc();
#ifdef _DEBUG
    virtual void AssertValid() const;
    virtual void Dump(CDumpContext& dc) const;
#endif

protected:
    void InitDocument();
    void DeleteContents();

// Generated message map functions
protected:
    //{{AFX_MSG(CErectorDoc)
    afx_msg void OnEditClearAll();
    //}}AFX_MSG
    DECLARE_MESSAGE_MAP()
};
```

Notice that you don't need to add prototypes for either function. The ClassWizard has already added `OnEditClearAll` to your header file in the generated message map functions list which it handles, and the Developer Studio has automatically added.

Now clean up your project by choosing **Save All** from the File menu and then **Close All** from the Window menu. You're finished working with both your code and your resources for the time being.

Updating the Menu Display

This provides the functional working for deleting the contents of an ErectorSet document. However, there is one more task that you, as a good programmer, should undertake. As presently implemented, you could delete the contents of an empty ErectorSet document. Although this wouldn't cause any problems in the application because your `DeleteContents` function tests whether there are any beams before trying to delete them, it isn't good practice. Instead, you should *dim* the **Clear All** item in the Edit menu until there is at least one beam in a document. This is what the other message ID that you saw in ClassWizard,

UPDATE_COMMAND_UI, is intended to do. The message ID UPDATE_COM-MAND_UI stands for (in the usual programmer's shorthand) "update command user interface." Now let's return to that message ID in ClassWizard and add the required code to enable and disable the **Clear All** menu item.

From the Class view, select the CErectorDoc class and choose the **ClassWizard** command from the View menu (or press **Ctrl+W**). This takes you back into the ClassWizard dialog box, right where you left off in Figure 6.9. This time, click on the UPDATE_COMMAND_UI message. The ClassWizard prompts you with the name of the new function, OnUpdateEditClearAll, which is certainly descriptive, if a bit long. Accept this name by pressing **OK** and choose **Edit Code** to go to the skeleton code in your ErectorDoc.cpp file. As before, the skeleton code is added to the bottom of the file. Cut it and paste it right after the OnEditClearAll function. The complete code for the OnUpdateEditClearAll function is shown in Listing 6.6.

Listing 6.6

```
// This function updates the user interface to allow the user
//   to select the Edit menu item, Clear All.
void CErectorDoc::OnUpdateEditClearAll(CCmdUI* pCmdUI)
{
    // If the document is not empty (i.e., has at least one beam)
    //    enable Edit>>Clear All; otherwise, disable it.
    pCmdUI->Enable( !m_beamList.IsEmpty() );


}
```

This is very simple code. The function, OnUpdateClearAll, is called with a parameter that is a CCmdUI object. The CCmdUI class is a special class that is only used in this context: updating a menu, dialog box, or other user-interface item. When a menu is first displayed, or when it is activated by being selected for example, the class framework searches for and calls the update handler for the menu item, and passes it a CCmdUI class object. This class implements a series of functions that allow you to change the display status of the user interface item(s) being referenced.

In this case, you use the CCmdUI class function Enable to enable (darken) or disable (dim) the **Clear All** item in the Edit menu. The Enable function takes a Boolean value: if the Boolean is TRUE, the menu item is enabled; if it is FALSE, the menu item is disabled—simple enough. To determine whether you want the menu item enabled or disabled, call the IsEmpty function of the CObList class. As you would expect from its name, this function returns TRUE if the list is empty and FALSE if it isn't. The code here simply reverses the Boolean value returned by IsEmpty and uses it to set the menu.

NOTE I'd like you to notice in this one line of code how our naming conventions have helped create the correct code. You can tell from the name that pCmdUI is a pointer to a UI object, so you have to use -> to access its member function, Enable. On the other hand, you also know that m_beamList is the actual object itself, so you use . to access its member function, IsEmpty. Without the naming conventions to guide you, you wouldn't know, off hand, which method to use in which case, and you couldn't tell immediately, as you can here, that the code is correct.

Thanks to the Developer Studio, that's all that there is to adding a new menu item and making it work. However, don't rebuild ErectorSet to test this just yet. In the next section, you will add some more useful feedback information to the application. Once that's in, you can rebuild the application and see how it works.

MFC APPLICATION FRAMEWORK

As you have seen in the preceding chapters, the Microsoft Foundation Classes provide a framework for a basic Windows application. Most of this would be useless if you couldn't use OOP and C++ as a way to extend and reuse this code. However, by using object-oriented programming, the MFC can provide a fully functional skeleton application that you can extend in a natural manner to provide a complete Windows application. This has two benefits for you, as a programmer. First, it saves you a lot of time, because you don't have to reinvent the code required to create and manage a standard Windows display. Second, it gives you a large body of code that you can use for guidance on techniques and functions that you need to implement in your own code. When you program using the MFC, you get the benefit of the talent and experience of

Microsoft's engineering staff, who have designed the classes and created the code to implement the tools that help you use them.

Don't think that this is all one-sided, however. Both users and Microsoft benefit from having applications built with MFC. Users benefit because the resulting application will have a standard, familiar Windows interface, which means that they will be productive with the application immediately. For Microsoft, it means that new applications will support all the standard Windows features, even many of the advanced features, immediately and in a common, well-defined manner. Using MFC is a win-win proposition for everyone concerned.

This section of the chapter gives you an overview of how the MFC classes are arranged. There are two purposes in this. The first purpose is to allow you to understand how an application built with MFC looks at the world. The second is to allow you to understand how to select and restructure your application to take maximum use of the MFC classes.

The Framework Architecture

Your MFC application follows a standard architecture that helps ensure that the entire application works the way you would expect. The entire collection of the Microsoft Foundation Class Library (to give it its full name) makes up the framework from which your application is derived. As you have seen with ErectorSet, the framework provides the skeleton for your application and defines the basic set of Windows user interface implementations that your application will require. AppWizard selects the classes that are required to build the skeleton application according to the parameters that you specify. This skeleton is the "framework application" that you have been—and will continue to be—reading about.

How the Application Framework Works

By deriving your application from the MFC, you delegate a substantial amount of processing to the code provided by the application framework. That means that the application framework does most work and provides most of the flow control within your application. Remember that Windows is routing messages to your application. These messages are intercepted by and very often handled by the application framework. You have the opportunity, by overriding framework functions, to respond to any external messages that you want, but any messages that you don't explicitly handle are taken care of by the framework—even if it only ignores the message.

There are two points to note about this process. First of all, you and your application are not in control of the sequence or processing requirements for the messages. The messages are generated in an external environment by the user, and the processing control is handled in the framework itself. This is classic *event-driven* programming. Second, the framework is perfectly capable of handling all these messages itself. Go back to the first compilation of the ErectorSet application. This version didn't do anything. For example, you couldn't draw in the document windows. However, it also didn't crash. If the user selected a window, or opened a new document, or did any one of a hundred standard actions, the application processed those messages successfully. In some cases, like clicking the mouse in a document, it simply ignored the message, but whatever the message routed to the application by Windows, it continued to run. This may not seem earth-shattering to you at first, but this type of robust behavior caused beginning Windows programmers many days and weeks of coding and debugging before MFC was available.

What the Framework Application Provides

The basic application, derived from the framework classes, inherits much of its behavior from the class CWinApp. This class provides most of the basic functions required by any Windows application. The main functions of the application as provided by CWinApp are initialization of the application, running the application, and termination of the application. Let's look at each of these in turn.

The application is initialized when the CWinApp functions `InitApplication` and `InitInstance` are called. `InitApplication` is generally handled directly in CWinApp, but your application class must override `InitInstance`. AppWizard takes care of supplying your application class with the following standard items:

- A message map that describes how to route messages in the application. This is also accessed and used by ClassWizard to implement standard message processing.
- An empty class constructor.
- A variable that declares and holds the only object of your application class, `theApp`.
- A standard implementation of the `InitInstance` function that overrides the function in CWinApp. This standard implementation performs four essential tasks:

1. It loads the standard options from an .INI file, including the names of the most recently opened documents.

2. It initializes and registers the document template(s). This is probably the most important task undertaken in the function.

3. It creates a main frame window, if this is an MDI application. For an SDI application, since there is only one document that can be open at a time, the document template's frame window will also be the application frame window.

4. It opens a file if requested—usually by the user double-clicking on one of your application's documents or dragging a document onto your application's icon. If no file is requested, it opens a new document with the default name.

Basic Class Structure

Certain basic elements are part of every framework application. You need to understand how they are related and something about what they provide. Here is a list of the most important classes in the MFC and a short description of what each provides to the application.

CObject

The CObject class is the base for most other MFC classes. This class provides some common overhead functions that are required by all objects. It is designed with execution efficiency in mind, since it provides inherited behavior for all other objects. CObject provides the following important services: object diagnostics, run-time class information, and object persistence.

To make use of some of these services, you must use specific macros when you create your classes. For example, to make use of the serialization functions in a class, you must derive that class from CObject and use the DECLARE_SER-IAL and IMPLEMENT_SERIAL macros in your class. CErectorBeam is a good examples of this.

CCmdTarget

This serves as the base class for all classes that can receive and process messages.

CWinApp

Each application consists of one—and only one—application object, which must be an instance of a class derived from CWinApp.

CDocument

This class is itself derived from the appropriate DocTemplate class. It is the base class for the application's data handling class or classes.

CWnd

This is the base class for all windows. It provides functions to handle most windows operations. Normally, you will use a class derived from this class, or, more likely, derived one of its derived classes, such as CFrameWnd, CMDIChildWnd, and so on.

CView

This class and its derived classes represent child windows of a CWnd object. They all point to the client area of some frame window. The view implements the display and handling of the document's data.

WORKING WITH THE MFC

You have acquired a lot of information about classes and MFC organization, but so far it's been fairly theoretical. In this section of the chapter, you can use all this information in a very concrete way: by adding message processing to ErectorSet that provides feedback to the user when drawing a beam. This is a practical example of how you use the information about classes and messages and translate that into useful features in your applications.

Adding Movement Message Processing to ErectorSet

As it functions right now, ErectorSet allows the user to draw a beam by clicking the left mouse button and dragging the mouse to a new position, where the mouse button is released. This defines the rectangle that makes up the beam.

However, this isn't very useful at the moment. The user has no way to see the size of the rectangle that is being created. A better approach would be to show some feedback that lets the user decide whether the rectangle is correct or not before it's drawn. A typical way to do this is to display the rectangle that will be drawn as a dotted outline. This section of the chapter adds such a display to ErectorSet.

Let's think about the processing logic that is required to implement this. What you want is to draw a dotted rectangle from the point where the user pressed the mouse button down to the current mouse position, as long as the mouse button is down and as long as the mouse is in the view—in other words, as long as the mouse button is down and the mouse is moving.

In a way, this is just like drawing the beam itself, except that the rectangle display is different. Like drawing the beam, this involves three points: capturing a mouse message that defines the movement rectangle, altering the CErectorView class to display the movement rectangle, and enhancing the CErectorBeam class to calculate the movement rectangle. Let's take each of these in turn and see what you have to do:

1. You have to capture the mouse position as it moves with the left button held down. This position will be the ending point of the movement rectangle. The starting point is the position of the left button when down. To do this, you need to capture the mouse message WM_MOUSEMOVE, which will return the point where the mouse is currently.

2. You have to draw a dotted rectangle from the starting position—where the left mouse button went down—to the current mouse position. To do this, you need to know the rectangle, and you need to set a pen width and brush color that will draw a dotted rectangle.

3. You have to add processing to the beam class to derive the movement rectangle. Only the beam class remembers the starting point of the current beam, so only the beam class can tell you what the movement rectangle should be.

Capturing the Mouse Position

As you might expect, capturing the mouse position involves setting up a message link between your application's view and Windows, using ClassWizard to make the connection as you have before.

Open ClassWizard by pressing **Ctrl+W**, selecting **ClassWizard** from the View menu, or clicking on the **ClassWizard** toolbar button. Select **CErectorView** as the Class name to display and scroll down the Messages to the WM_MOUSEMOVE message. At this point, your screen should look like Figure 6.11.

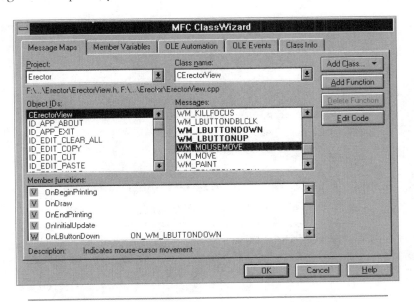

FIGURE 6.11 USE THE CLASSWIZARD TO ADD MOUSE MOVEMENT MESSAGE PROCESSING TO YOUR ERECTORSET APPLICATION.

Double-click on the message or use the **Add Function** button to add this function skeleton to the CErectorView class. The ClassWizard adds a new function with the name OnMouseMove to the Member functions list. Now double-click on the function name or use the **Edit Code** button to go to the new skeleton function.

As usual, ClassWizard adds the code at the end of your class. Since this code logically comes after the mouse button goes down, but before it goes up, I moved the function between OnLButtonDown and OnLButtonUp. I also added a comment to the front of the file saying what changes were made. Make these changes if you want, and then you are ready to add the processing code to display the movement rectangle.

Adding the Movement Rectangle to CErectorView

Most of what you need to do to display the movement rectangle is exactly what you've done before to display the beam itself in the DrawBeam function. The major exceptions are that you need to erase the previous rectangle each time you go to draw a new one—remember that nothing gets removed from the display unless you erase it—and that you are doing this drawing directly in the CErectorView class, so you need an additional function in CErectorBeam that will tell you what rectangle to draw. Listing 6.7 shows the new OnMouseMove function fully operational, along with the header comment.

Listing 6.7

```
// This function handles MouseMove up messages.
//  NOTE that this does _not_ call inherited behavior.
void CErectorView::OnMouseMove(UINT /* nFlags */, CPoint point)
{
    // Mouse button up is notable only if the user is currently drawing
    //    a new beam by dragging the mouse.
    //    In that case, we need to capture the mouse position.
    if ( GetCapture() != this )
        return;          // If this view didn't capture the mouse,
                         //    the user isn't drawing in our window.

    // Display movement rectangle in DC as a dotted rectangle
    //    to show where user is at all times.
    CRect rectDraw;

    // Setup the movement rectangle based on the beam starting point.
    //    TO DO: Add test for SetupRect error.
    m_pBeamCur->SetupRect(rectDraw, point);

    // Now draw the movement rectangle.
    //    First, set the device context to this view...
    CClientDC dc( this );
    //    TODO: Add error handling in case we can't get a DC.
    //    then set the pen and brush for the movement rectangle...
    CPen penStroke;
    CBrush brushFill;
    //          create the pen and brush for the movement rectangle
```

```
if( !penStroke.CreatePen( PS_DOT, 1, RGB(0,0,0) ) )
    return;
if( !brushFill.CreateSolidBrush( RGB(255,255,255) ) )
    return;
//    and paint the movement rectangle.
//        save the old pen and brush and set the new ones
CPen* pOldPen = dc.SelectObject( &penStroke );
CBrush* pOldBrush = dc.SelectObject( &brushFill );
//        erase the old rectangle by painting with the white brush
dc.FrameRect( &m_rectPrev, &brushFill );

//        then draw the new movement rectangle
dc.Rectangle( &rectDraw );
//        and restore the old brush and pen
dc.SelectObject( pOldBrush );
dc.SelectObject( pOldPen );

// Save the rectangle to erase it the next time.
m_rectPrev = rectDraw;

return;
}



// This function handles LeftMouseButton up messages.
//   NOTE that this does _not_ call inherited behavior.
void CErectorView::OnLButtonUp(UINT /* nFlags */, CPoint point)
{
    // Mouse button up is notable only if the user is currently drawing
    //   a new beam by dragging the mouse.
    //   In that case, we need to capture the mouse position.
    if ( GetCapture() != this )
        return;            // If this view didn't capture the mouse,
                           //   the user isn't drawing in our window.


    // End the current beam.
```

```
    m_pBeamCur->EndBeam( point );


    // Now ask the beam to draw itself.
    //    First, set the device context to this view...
    CClientDC dc( this );
    //    TODO: Add error handling in case we can't get a DC.
    CDC* pDC = (CDC*)&dc;
    m_pBeamCur->DrawBeam( pDC );


    ReleaseCapture();              // Release the mouse capture established
earlier
    m_rectPrev.SetRectEmpty();   // Clean up the movement rectangle


    return;
}
```

The function you have here looks very much like the DrawBeam function in CErectorBeam. You begin by testing that this view has the mouse capture. Then you define a CRect object to hold the movement rectangle and call a new CErectorBeam function, SetupRect, which takes the current point and returns a rectangle. This rectangle is calculated from the starting point of the current beam. Next, you perform the required steps to define the desired pen and brush qualities. Here, you set the pen to a dotted line by using the predefined constant, PS_DOT, 1 pixel width, and a black color; and you set the brush color to white by using the RGB macro, setting each color to its maximum, 255.

The next step is to erase the previous rectangle that you drew. This requires you to create a new member variable, m_rectPrev, which saves the previous rectangle. Once you have that, you can erase it by painting the border of the rectangle with the current (white) brush using the FrameRect function. Finally, you draw the beam in the current device context using the Rectangle function. When that's done, you restore the original pen and brush and save the current movement rectangle as m_rectPrev for erasure on the next pass.

The addition of the new member variable requires two additional changes. First, you must clean the rectangle up when you no longer need it. Specifically, you need to set it to Empty once the beam is created. The single line of code added to the end of OnLButtonUp in Figure 6.7 shows you how to do that.

Second, you must define the member variable in the header file. Select the CErectorView class in the Class View pane and use the **Add Variable...** menu item in the pop-up menu to add the new variable, using these settings: CRect for Variable Type; m_rectPrev for Variable Declaration; and select the **Protected** radio button. As usual, I have moved the resulting code in the header and added a comment. Listing 6.8 shows the changes.

Listing 6.8

```
////////////////////////////////////////////////////////////////////
// ErectorView.h : interface of the CErectorView class
//
//
// Created by AppWizard 11 December 1995 11:39:42
// Modifications:
//   16 Dec 95   DH   Add base class operations to generated code:
//                        message handling; drawing.
//   18 Dec 95   DH   Add movement rectangle processing to show
//                        current mouse position
////////////////////////////////////////////////////////////////////

class CErectorView : public CScrollView
{
protected: // create from serialization only
    CErectorView();
    DECLARE_DYNCREATE(CErectorView)

// Attributes
public:
    CErectorDoc* GetDocument();

// Operations
public:

// Overrides
```

```
    // ClassWizard generated virtual function overrides
    //{{AFX_VIRTUAL(CErectorView)
    public:
    virtual void OnDraw(CDC* pDC);   // overridden to draw this view
    virtual BOOL PreCreateWindow(CREATESTRUCT& cs);
    protected:
    virtual void OnInitialUpdate(); // called first time after construct
    virtual BOOL OnPreparePrinting(CPrintInfo* pInfo);
    virtual void OnBeginPrinting(CDC* pDC, CPrintInfo* pInfo);
    virtual void OnEndPrinting(CDC* pDC, CPrintInfo* pInfo);
    virtual void OnUpdate(CView* pSender, LPARAM lHint, CObject* pHint);
    virtual void OnPrint(CDC* pDC, CPrintInfo* pInfo);
    //}}AFX_VIRTUAL

// Implementation
public:
    virtual ~CErectorView();
#ifdef _DEBUG
    virtual void AssertValid() const;
    virtual void Dump(CDumpContext& dc) const;
#endif

protected:
    CErectorBeam* m_pBeamCur;         // pointer to current beam
    CRect m_rectPrev;                 // previous movement rectangle

// Generated message map functions
protected:
    //{{AFX_MSG(CErectorView)
    afx_msg void OnLButtonDown(UINT nFlags, CPoint point);
    afx_msg void OnLButtonUp(UINT nFlags, CPoint point);
    afx_msg void OnMouseMove(UINT nFlags, CPoint point);
    //}}AFX_MSG
    DECLARE_MESSAGE_MAP()
};
```

```
#ifndef _DEBUG  // debug version in ErectorView.cpp
inline CErectorDoc* CErectorView::GetDocument()
    { return (CErectorDoc*)m_pDocument; }
#endif
```

`/////////////////////////////////////////////////////////////////////////////`

This finishes the code changes to the CErectorView class.

Adding an Auxiliary Function to CErectorBeam

You have used a new auxiliary function, SetupRect, in CErectorBeam, and now you have to add that function to the class. The basic calling structure is laid out where you call this function in OnMouseMove. SetupRect takes two parameters: a rectangle object and a point object. It calculates the rectangle from the starting point of the current mouse movement to the point passed in as a parameter and fills in the coordinates for the rectangle into the rectangle object passed in as a parameter.

This is interesting because it is very similar to the calculations that EndBeam currently performs, with the difference that EndBeam simply stores the resulting rectangle in the member variable, m_rectBeam, which is later used for drawing the beam. This suggests two things: first, that you can reuse most of the code in EndBeam for the new SetupRect function and, second, that you can restructure EndBeam to use the new function to perform most of the work.

Add the new function by selecting CErectorBeam in the Class view and choosing the **Add Function...** menu item in the pop-up menu. Then define the new function with the following settings: BOOL for Function Type; SetupRect(CRect& rectBeam, CPoint& ptCurrent) for Function Declaration, and select the **Public** radio button.

Listing 6.9 shows the new and changed code in the CErectorBeam class.

Listing 6.9

```
// This function finishes a beam by calculating the rectangle
//   required for the beam, using the starting and ending points.
void CErectorBeam::EndBeam(CPoint ptStop)
{
    // Regularize the ending point to derive the beam rectangle
```

```
        SetupRect( m_rectBeam, ptStop );
        return;
}



// This function calculates the drawing rectangle
//  from the starting point to the supplied point and returns it.
BOOL CErectorBeam::SetupRect(CRect& rectBeam, CPoint& ptCurrent)
{
    // TO DO: Add error checking code to ensure that
    //    ptCurrent and ptStart are not too close to one another.

    // Set top and bottom
    if ( ptCurrent.y > m_ptStart.y )
    {
        rectBeam.top = ptCurrent.y;
        rectBeam.bottom = m_ptStart.y;
    }
    else
    {
        rectBeam.top = m_ptStart.y;
        rectBeam.bottom = ptCurrent.y;
    }


    // Set left and right
    if ( ptCurrent.x < m_ptStart.x )
    {
        rectBeam.left = ptCurrent.x;
        rectBeam.right = m_ptStart.x;
    }
    else
    {
        rectBeam.left = m_ptStart.x;
        rectBeam.right = ptCurrent.x;
    }
```

```
        return TRUE;
    }
```

All of the existing code for EndBeam is gone and replaced with a single call to the new SetupRect function, using the member variable m_rectBeam as the rectangle object where SetupRect will store the rectangle information. The new SetupRect code mirrors the old EndBeam code, with only the names changed to match the new requirements.

C++

If you're a C programmer, you're probably wondering about the parameters used in the call to SetupRect: CRect& and CPoint&. Traditionally, in C, the & is placed in front of a data item to take the address of that item; obviously, that isn't what's happening here.

This is an example of a new feature in C++ called a *reference variable*. A reference is an alias for another variable. In this, the reference is similar to a pointer, but it does not require the * operator to dereference the pointer to get to the actual variable itself. Using a reference in a function parameter allows you to pass variables that represent structures—as class objects, such as CRect and CPoint do—without the overhead of actually copying the structures, and without the nuisance of using pointers that have to be "dereferenced" throughout the function code. References are one of the nifty new features of C++.

Testing the New ErectorSet Application

At this point, you have added all the code required to display a dotted rectangle to show mouse movement. Now you need to rebuild the ErectorSet application and test your changes.

To do this, return to the Developer Studio and choose **Build Erector.exe** from the Build menu (or press **Shift+F8**). This will recompile all of the modules you have changed and relink the new modules into your ErectorSet application. Figure 6.12 shows you how the new application displays the movement rectangle.

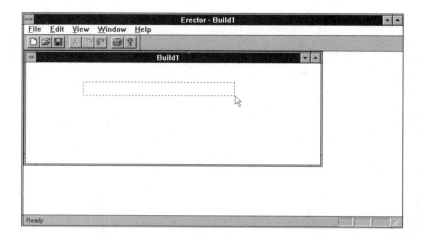

FIGURE 6.12 THE ERECTORSET APPLICATION NOW PROVIDES VISUAL FEEDBACK ABOUT NEW BEAMS.

This is just what you wanted: a display of the beam that will be created by a dotted rectangle. So far, so good.

There is one problem, however, which is illustrated by the finished set of beams that you see in Figure 6.13.

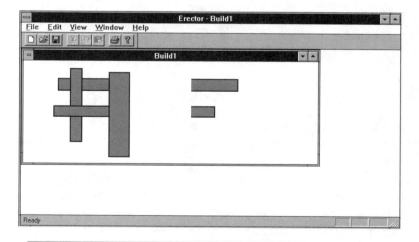

FIGURE 6.13 THE MOVEMENT RECTANGLE ERASES PARTS OF EXISTING BEAMS, LEAVING THE SCREEN IN AN UNFINISHED STATE.

The problem here, as you can see, is that the dotted rectangles are erasing parts of the existing beams while you are drawing them, and the erased parts don't come back when the new beam is finished. This is clearly not acceptable. However, if you do anything at all to the Build1 window, like move it or resize it, all the beams are drawn again correctly, as shown in Figure 6.14.

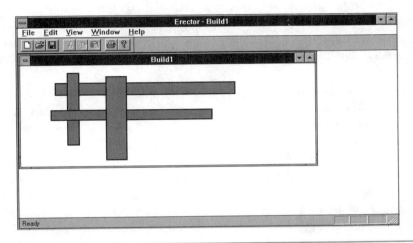

FIGURE 6.14 THE MISSING PARTS OF THE BEAMS GET REDRAWN WHEN THE WINDOW MOVES OR IS RESIZED.

What this tells you is that the problem is not with the beams themselves, but with the way that the view itself is updated. What you need to do is redraw the beams that get erased after every movement of the mouse. This leads you into the world of views and documents, which is the subject of the next chapter.

SUMMARY

In this chapter, you have learned about two important subjects that will help you with your Windows programming. The first is OOP, or object-oriented programming. The second is the MFC, which forms the basis for your Visual C++ Windows applications.

OOP is important for two reasons. First, OOP is a significant step forward in programming techniques. It speeds up development and allows you to reuse code in a safe and efficient way. You also learned about the important issues of classes and the class hierarchy. Once you understand the class structure used in

OOP generally and C++ specifically, you will understand how to add classes and how to modify class behavior. You also read about message processing and how the class message concept is related to Windows event processing. As an example of this, you extended the ErectorSet application by adding a new **Clear All** menu item and processing it.

The Microsoft Foundation Class Library is built in C++ and follows the object-oriented model. You learned in this chapter how the MFC are used by AppWizard to generate the type of Windows application that you want. You also learned how the MFC structure works and how the basic classes interact to make your application.

The chapter finished with a fairly long example and exercise. This section showed you how to integrate all this material into your ErectorSet application. You learned how to add a dotted rectangle to your document display to provide user feedback on the size and position of the beam currently being drawn. You learned how to capture the mouse movement message from Windows and how to use that information to develop the movement rectangle. Even so, testing your revised application showed that you need to investigate further how to handle drawing and the interaction between views and document. This is the subject of the next chapter.

CHAPTER 7

VIEWS AND DOCUMENTS

Most Visual C++ programming is centered around views and documents. You have been informally introduced to these concepts in the preceding chapters as you built the demonstration application. Now you will find out how these important concepts work and how they are implemented in the Microsoft Foundation Classes (MFC). This chapter will describe how views and documents interact and how you can modify each layer of your application to get the functionality you want. Important topics in this chapter include:

- How documents are used in an application
- Similarities and differences in views and windows
- Relationships between views, documents, and your application
- How to draw efficiently in your view
- How to create and use scrolling in your view

DOCUMENTS

Documents are the basic elements that are created and manipulated by your application. Windows provides a graphic interface that gives a user a natural, intuitive way to use your application. To implement this interface, you have to provide a way to see and interact with the information your application creates and uses. You do this by establishing one or more types of documents. Each type of document handles a single type of information that can be processed by your application.

For many purposes, the natural idea of a document as a piece of paper or a collection of pieces of paper is a good metaphor for what your application works on. For example, for word processing, drawing or illustration, or page layout applications, this idea of a document is a natural way to think of and organize what you're doing. However, for some types of applications, such as process control and games, the concept of a document seems out of place, and some developers, fooled by the commonplace meaning of document, try to bypass the MFC document architecture because they feel that "documents" don't fit their requirements. Don't let the label confuse you. A *document* is simply a place to collect common data elements that form the processing unit for your application. For ErectorSet, the idea of a document as a piece of paper is quite appropriate, so you can just think of your documents as sheets of drawing or layout paper.

I don't want you to focus on this analogy too much, however. As you will read in this section, the concept of a document is much more powerful than that, and as is always true of analogies, there are significant and subtle differences.

Relationship of Documents and the Application

Your application class uses documents as a way to organize and present information to your user. Each application derived from the MFC defines at least one type of document that is a part of the application. The type of document and the number of documents that your application uses are defined in the code in your application class, CErectorApp.

Two types of applications are supported by the MFC. The most common are applications that allow you to have multiple documents open at the same time.

This is called an *MDI* (for *Multiple Document Interface*) application. Any standard word processing package, such as Microsoft Word, is a good example of an MDI application. In Word, for example, you can open a number of text files for editing at once; each represents one document. You switch between the documents by using the Windows menu to select the view that should be on top of the display—this is the *active* window. Note that in MDI you can have the same document open in more than one view. Figure 7.1 shows ErectorSet, a typical MDI application, with several documents open.

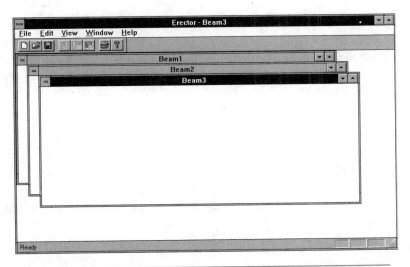

FIGURE 7.1 AN MDI APPLICATION SUCH AS ERECTORSET CAN HAVE SEVERAL DOCUMENTS OPEN AT THE SAME TIME.

The other type of application is an *SDI* (for *Single Document Interface*) application, where there can only be one document open at a time. The Windows accessory program Write is a good example of this type of application. Although Write is also a word processing program, when using it you must close one document before you can open another. Because there is only one document—and hence one view—there is no Window menu and no need for the application to keep track of multiple views. This is a simpler, but generally less useful, type of application. Figure 7.2 shows Microsoft Windows Write, one of the accessories that ships with Windows, which is a typical SDI application.

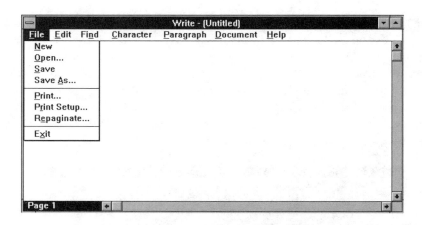

FIGURE 7.2 MICROSOFT WINDOWS WRITE IS A TYPICAL SDI APPLICATION, WHICH ONLY
ALLOWS ONE DOCUMENT OPEN AT A TIME.

Note that an SDI application does not have a Window menu, and the File menu, does not have a **Close** option. Because only one document can be open at a time, opening a document automatically closes the current document. These are two common characteristics of an SDI application.

Luckily, you don't need to worry much about these issues. You only need to make a single choice: whether your application will handle multiple documents or only a single document at a time. When you create your application in AppWizard, you choose whether your application will support MDI or SDI. AppWizard automatically derives your skeleton application from the correct classes to support the type of document interface that you require, including menu items and the required supporting code.

Although SDI applications have a place in Windows programming, you won't deal with them in this book. Because most common Windows applications are MDI applications, the ErectorSet application is an MDI application, and you'll use that to explore all the issues regarding applications, documents, and views.

What Documents Do

The fundamental responsibility of the document is to store all the elements that constitute an application unit. In ErectorSet, for example, each document consists of a series of beams. Every application will have some type of data that it creates, displays, manipulates, and stores. This collection of data is what constitutes the application's document.

NOTE

An application may support more than one type of document; for example, you might have ErectorSet support documents that contained beams and related building materials and have another type of document that contained only text and numbers to display, for example, costs and schedules of a project using the beams and other materials. However, that would naturally require some very basic types of changes to the application. The MFC normally generates an application that has a single type of document. For the purposes of this book, you will use only one type of document with ErectorSet.

One of the difficult tasks in designing an MFC program is defining exactly what information belongs in your document. For ErectorSet, for example, the document naturally needs to include all the beams that are part of it. It does this by keeping a list of beams created in its views. However, the beam list isn't all that the document stores; for example, in CErectorDoc, you also store the default values for the beam color and outline width. Once the beam is drawn, of course, you store the information about color and outline width with the beam itself. After all, the beam color and outline are part of the beam itself, and they should only change, once the beam is drawn, in response to a specific command by the user. The default values, on the other hand, might be changed at any time, so this default information is maintained at the document level because you want all the views of this document to use the same default values. This is why you should think of the document as a storage point for all the data required by a unit of your application, whatever that may be. That includes all important data elements that need to be kept at the document level, even though they may not be directly connected to the displayed contents of the document. As the application designer, it's your responsibility to decide what information is stored at the document level and what can and should be stored in the other derived classes.

The document also controls all the views associated with the document. As the user opens and manipulates windows on the screen, he or she is creating views and associating a document with each view. The document is responsible for controlling and updating the elements within a given view. As you saw in the earlier chapters, the view may either request the document to draw its components or directly request the components to draw themselves; it also must provide a device context where the drawing occurs. All elements of a document must be able to display themselves correctly upon request.

VIEWS

The view is the user's way of seeing what's in a document and of interacting with the document. Each active document will have one or more views available on the display. Generally, each view is displayed in a single window. When you're using any standard Windows application, which is what you get when you work with the MFC, the Window menu allows you to move among the various windows so you can switch among different documents or views, depending on what you have open. In this way, the view is directly connected to both the document it is displaying and the window that contains it. In this section of the chapter, you will learn more about understanding and using views in your application.

What Views Do

The view gives your document a place to display information. It is the intermediary between the document, which contains information, and the user. The view organizes and displays the document information onto the screen or printer and takes in user input as information or operations on the document.

In essence, the view is the active area of your document. Figure 7.3 shows you one way to visualize the relationship among the document, view, and the window that holds the view, called the *frame window*.

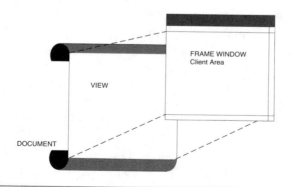

FIGURE 7.3 THE VIEW IS THE ACTIVE AREA OF THE DOCUMENT AND IS DISPLAYED IN ITS FRAME WINDOW'S CLIENT AREA.

Notice that the view is doing two separate, but related, functions. It is the display area for the document data, and it is the input area where the user interacts with the document, normally providing additional commands or data for the document to process. All of this passes through the view before reaching the document. Thus CErectorView handled the mouse messages in functions such as OnLButtonDown. It received the messages, translated the information into an appropriate form if necessary, and then called the required document functions to process the mouse commands.

Although a view is responsible for displaying the document and its information, you may choose to do this in one of two ways. First, you can let the view directly access the document's data elements. Alternatively, you could create a document function that handled access to the appropriate data elements. Either approach is correct; you must decide which is best based on your application.

NOTE As mentioned in Chapter 5, where to control drawing is not a trivial issue. In ErectorSet, for example, you moved responsibility for drawing in the view by including the controlling code in CErectorView's OnDraw function . As an alternative, however, you could chose to have the controlling code in CErectorDoc by creating a new function, say DrawAll, that performs the same processing, and then having OnDraw call DrawAll with the current device context as a parameter. Either solution has advantages and drawbacks.

The choice of doing the drawing directly in the view has two advantages. First, it is the responsibility of the view to handle document display, so having the code there is both clear and appropriate. Second, placing the code in the view keeps all the code regarding the device context in the view where it seems natural.

On the other hand, allowing the view to have direct access to the document data is a bit troublesome because it requires the view to know about the document's contents. In the case of ErectorSet, for example, what happens if you want to add a different type of object, say gears, to the document? As the view is structured, you would have to change the code in the view to process these as well as beams. If you simply asked the document to process the information, the document could worry about what types of object were included in it, which is properly the document's responsibility.

Although a view is tied to a single document, a document may have multiple views. You can create two similar views of the same document by opening another window on the document. You can also present alternative ways to look at the same information by implementing different types of views for the document. For example, ErectorSet documents contain a series of beams. At present, the CErectorView displays these as visual components, that is, as gray rectangles. However, suppose you wanted to display the beams, not as simple rectangles but as outlines with dimensions and weights. To do this, you would implement another view for the CErectorDoc class that used the beam information to display the beams in the way you wanted—most probably, you would also implement several new functions in the beam class to calculate and display the necessary information. We aren't going to do anything that fancy here. The point that I want to make is that you can change how the same information is displayed in your document by adding a different view.

In the sample application here I have opted for simplicity by keeping the drawing code in the view so that the document doesn't need to understand and process graphic information, such as the device context. On the other hand, if you added other types of document data, such as gears and connectors, you might want to think about where you do the drawing again. The nice thing about object-oriented programming is that you can make changes like this to your code without having too much impact on the other elements, which helps keep errors out and encourages experimentation.

There are two important points to note here. The first is that, ultimately, the drawing is done by the document elements—in this case, the beams—which can display themselves correctly whenever requested to do so no matter who asks. The second point is that when you make these choices, you need to think about the overall flow and structure of your application and not simply do one or the other because you did it that way before.

Relationship of Views and Documents

Five key objects work together in your application to allow your user to create and manipulate data. These are created and maintained by the MFC as a part of the process of generating your application. Although you never need to see some of these objects, you should know that they are there, and what they do, so that you can understand exactly how your application works. As you would expect, each object is represented by a specific class in the MFC. Table 7.1 lists the object and its class, and presents a brief discussion of each object.

TABLE 7.1 FIVE KEY MFC OBJECTS

Object	Description
The application (CErectorApp)	There is only one application object. This is derived from the MFC class CWinApp. The application class controls all of the other objects listed here and also provides global application functions, such as initialization or destruction of global data. In particular, the application object is responsible for creating and managing all document types by creating a document template for each type of document that is supported by the application.
The document template (CDocTemplate)	The document template is an abstract base class for document object. It defines the basic functions that a document can handle. The document template creates the documents that are used in your application, and it creates the document frame windows that support the documents. It also keeps pointers to the document, frame window, and view classes. The document template is the manager that links these three important objects together in your application. It also stores information about the overall class of document that it supports, like the file extension for these documents (.set in ErectorSet) and the name on the frame windows for the documents (Build in ErectorSet). Documents are derived from CDocTemplate by using the CMultiDocTemplate class for MDI applications and the CSingleDocTemplate class for SDI applications.

C++

Remember that a base class is a class from which some other class inherits behavior and data; for example, CDocument is a base class for CErectorDoc. An *abstract base class* is a base class that exists only to have other classes derived from it. No actual instance of the abstract base class ever exists in any program, although one or more classes derived from it exist. In ErectorSet, for example, you never have an object of the class CDocTemplate, but you do have a CDocument object (your CErectorDoc object) that inherits behavior from CDocTemplate.

TABLE 7.1 FIVE KEY MFC OBJECTS (CONTINUED)

Object	Description
The frame windows (CMDIFrameWnd, CMDIChildWnd)	Since this is an MDI application, there are two types of frame windows used in the application: document frame windows. (CMDIChildWnd), which display the views that you create, and a main frame window (CMDIFrameWnd), which holds the document frame windows. Views are displayed in the client area of document frame windows. The main frame window for a MDI application also holds the menu bar, status bar, tool bar, and so on.
The document(s) (CErectorDoc)	The document class holds the data for your application. You read about the document class earlier in the chapter.
The view(s) (CErectorView)	The view class is the place where the user interacts with the data. You read about views earlier in the chapter.

The application creates a document template when it is initialized. Listing 7.1 shows you the code in your CErectorApp class that initializes the document template.

Listing 7.1

```
BOOL CErectorApp::InitInstance()
{
    // Standard initialization
    //   ... some initialization code here

    // Register the application's document templates.  Document templates
    //  serve as the connection between documents, frame windows and views.

    CMultiDocTemplate* pDocTemplate;
    pDocTemplate = new CMultiDocTemplate(
        IDR_BEAMTYPE,
        RUNTIME_CLASS(CErectorDoc),
        RUNTIME_CLASS(CChildFrame),        // custom MDI child frame
        RUNTIME_CLASS(CErectorView));
    AddDocTemplate(pDocTemplate);

    //     ... more initialization code here

    return TRUE;
}
```

(Note that this code is already generated for you; there is nothing here that you need to enter.) As Listing 7.1 shows, the application has an `InitInstance` function that is called when the application is first created. This executes the `AddDocTemplate` function, which is inherited from the CWinApp base class. This function creates and stores a document template in the application.

As you can see, the `AddDocTemplate` function itself requires a pointer to a document template. This is provided by the call to new `CMultiDocTemplate`, which creates a new document template object.

The new document template requires four parameters. First, you have to give it the resource ID for the resources used with this document type. This ID points to a string resource that provides up to seven items required for display or use of this type of document; most important are the document name—Build in ErectorSet—and the file extension that goes with the document—`.set` in

ErectorSet. It also points to an icon used for the these documents when they are stored and points to the menu that you see when there is an open document in ErectorSet. The resource ID is simply a number which is defined in your resource.h file; the name follows a standard naming convention, with an IDR_ prefix to show that this is a resource ID, followed by the document name—BUILD—and the suffix TYPE to show that these items refer to the document type. Remember that you saw this used when you added the Clear All message to the Edit menu.

NOTE Resources, such as menus, are an important part of Windows applications. All of these resources are automatically generated by AppWizard when you created your skeleton application. As you recall, at that time you provided this document information to AppWizard. For now, you just need to know that this ID exists, and what it is used for. We will discuss resources in detail in Chapter 9 when you learn about using the Resource Editor.

In addition to the resource ID, the CMultiDocTemplate creator requires three pointers, one to each class that it ties together: the document class, here, CErectorDoc; the document's frame window class, here, the class CChildFrame; and the view class, here, CErectorView. This is where the document template ties together these three important elements.

Since this is all generated for you by AppWizard, this may seem like a lot of information that isn't directly relevant to building an application. However, there are two important points that you need to get out of this discussion:

- The resource ID that is used here—IDR_BUILDTYPE for ErectorSet—links several types of document-related resources. This is important when you are working with resources.
- The document types used in your application are generated and controlled from this block of code in your application class.

Most MDI applications, like ErectorSet, use only one document type and one view per open document, although they may have multiple documents open at any given time. If you need multiple document types, you have to do two things.

First, create a new class, perhaps CAnotherDoc, for your additional document type. Derive this class from CDocument by using ClassWizard. Then fill in the data handling functions as you did for CErectorDoc. Second, add another call to AddDocTemplate, using the appropriate parameters. Use the call to the first document type as an example of how to make the call.

When you choose **New** from the File menu to create a document in an MFC application that supports multiple document types, you get a dialog box that asks you to choose which type of document you want to create from a list of supported documents. When you pick one type, the framework automatically generates a document, window, and view for that type. You can tell what type of document is in a view by the title of the document's frame window.

Multiple Views

There may be multiple views for a single document at any given time. You create a new view for a document by opening a new window on the document in your application, using the **New Window** command in the Window menu. This will give you two windows, and hence, two views, of your document, as shown in Figure 7.4.

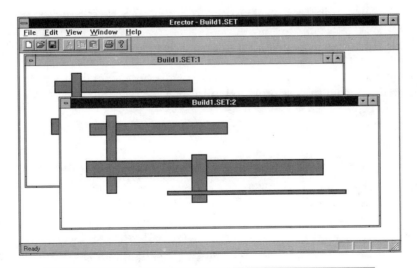

FIGURE 7.4 YOU CAN CREATE MORE THAN ONE VIEW OF THE SAME DOCUMENT.

Notice that MFC provides some automatic features that inform the user about what has happened. Figure 7.4 shows the document Build1.SET—the suffix indicates that this document was read from a saved file. The first view window simply had the title of the document on it. When you open a second view, however, both views are automatically titled with the name of the document, followed by a colon and a number indicating the number of the view, as you see.

Selecting the Active View

Although two views are open on the same document, notice that only one can be active at any time. This is called having the *focus*. The view with the focus is normally in the top window on your display, and can be identified by the fact that its title bar is colored. In Figure 7.4, the view entitled Build1.SET:2 (the second view of document Build1.SET) has the focus, as you can tell by the fact that the window is on top and, most importantly, that the title is colored in.

Each view can show different parts of your document. The second view shown in Figure 7.4 has been resized to take up a larger part of the frame window than the first view; as a result, it shows more of the document than the first view. Later in this chapter, after you add scrolling to the views, you will be able to scroll two views of the same document to different places.

There are two important points here. The first is that you can see different parts of the same document in different views. Once you have scrolling, you can easily move views to different parts of the same document. The second point is that only one view is active, that is, has the focus, at any time. All other views are inactive until you activate them by clicking the mouse in their window or by choosing them from the list provided in the Windows menu item.

Updating Multiple Views

Let's take an example of having two views of one document. Figure 7.5 shows you such an example, with a new twist.

This is clearly a bit disconcerting. Although both of these are views of the same document, the one on the bottom—which is inactive—does not show the new beam that was added in the active top view. This is downright incorrect, and it is a problem.

The problem is that any inactive views are not being updated with the latest information from the document. They don't know that there is a new beam yet, because they are inactive. If you activate the view by resizing it, then the new beam will appear in both windows, as shown in Figure 7.6.

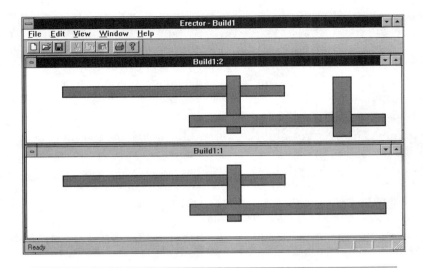

FIGURE 7.5 WHEN YOU CREATE A BEAM IN THE SECOND VIEW, IT DOESN'T SHOW IN THE FIRST VIEW AUTOMATICALLY.

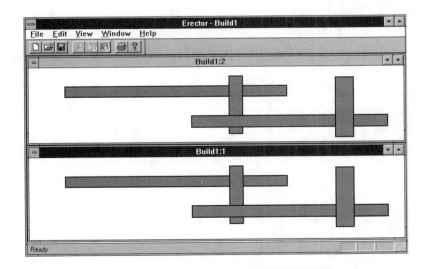

FIGURE 7.6 THE VIEW THAT WAS INACTIVE IS REDRAWN ONLY WHEN IT GETS UPDATED.

There are several points to notice here. First is that the view that was inactive is not updated—and therefore not redrawn—simply by being activated. Nor is it updated simply by moving it. If you resize the view window, however, or if you switch out of ErectorSet to another application and then back in, the view will be updated and redrawn. As you can see, the entire subject of when a view gets updated is fairly complex; in fact, it is sufficiently complex that we will devote an entire section to the problem later in this chapter.

For now, however, we can solve this problem with the information that you have already: the problem is that the inactive views need to be updated when you draw a new beam. So the obvious idea is that there should be functions available that allow you to tell all the views for a document that the view needs to be updated. Sure enough, if you look up the CDocument class reference using the InfoViewer, either by using the on-line index or by choosing **Search** from the Help menu, under CDocument, you will find an `UpdateAllViews` function. The on-line reference for this function is shown in Figure 7.7.

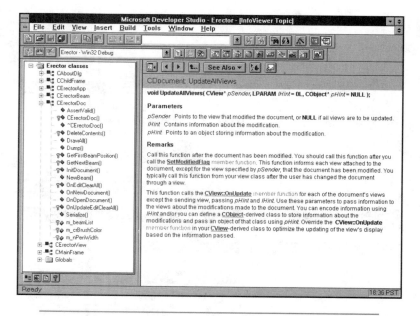

FIGURE 7.7 THE INFOVIEWER WILL SHOW YOU EXACTLY HOW TO USE ANY SPECIFIC FUNCTION THAT YOU NEED.

This gives you the necessary information about how to use the `UpdateAllViews` function. Now all you have to do is figure out where to call it.

Since this is a CDocument function, your first thought might naturally be to put it somewhere in your document class, CErectorDoc. However, let's think about where you need this information. By looking at the problem, you know that you need to perform the update when the beam is drawn. The currently active view is getting updated correctly, but the inactive ones aren't. This suggests that the correct place to put the call to `UpdateAllViews` is in the function that draws the beam, and that's OnLButtonUp in CErectorView. Basically, you want to update the views as soon as the beam is drawn in the current view. The necessary code is shown in Listing 7.2.

Listing 7.2

```
// This function handles LeftMouseButton up messages.
// NOTE that this does _not_ call inherited behavior.
void CErectorView::OnLButtonUp(UINT /* nFlags */, CPoint point)
{
    // Mouse button up is notable only if the user is currently drawing
    // a new beam by dragging the mouse.
    // In that case, we need to capture the mouse position.
    if ( GetCapture() != this )
        return;              // If this view didn't capture the mouse,
                             // the user isn't drawing in our window.


    // End the current beam.
    m_pBeamCur->EndBeam( point );


    // Now draw the beam.
    // First, set the device context to this view...
    CClientDC dc( this );
    //    TODO: Add error handling in case we can't get a DC.
    CDC* pDC = (CDC*)&dc;
    //    then ask beam to draw itself.
    m_pBeamCur->DrawBeam( pDC );
```

```
// Now tell any other views that we have added a beam to the drawing
CErectorDoc* pDoc = GetDocument();
ASSERT_VALID(pDoc);
pDoc->UpdateAllViews( this, 0L, NULL );

ReleaseCapture();        // Release the mouse capture established earlier
m_rectPrev.SetRectEmpty(); // Clean up the movement rectangle

return;
}
```

Since UpdateAllViews is a document function, you need to get a pointer to the document before you can execute it. The CView function GetDocument returns a pointer to the document that owns this view. As good programming practice, you next validate that the document that is pointed to is, in fact, a valid CErectorDoc. You do this using the ASSERT_VALID macro, which will post an Assert dialog box if the document is not valid. (Note that, like all forms of the ASSERT macro, this only works in the debug version of your application; in the release version, the ASSERT_VALID does nothing.) Once you have the pointer to a valid document, you simply call UpdateAllViews with three parameters: this, which is a pointer to the current object—in this case, the current view; and two default parameters, 0L and NULL. In the next section of this chapter, you'll see how to use these two parameters, but for now, the defaults work fine. The first parameter points to the current view; this prevents the update message from being sent to this view, which would be redundant and could cause a loop.

Now rebuild Erector.exe and run it. You will see that, even if you have several views, they all show new beams as soon as the beams are drawn. This is what you want—coordination of all the views for a document.

N O T E   One of the constant problems for MFC programmers is to remember how to access other objects in the application in order to use functions that belong to that object. The problem of accessing the UAV function in the document from the view is a perfect example of this problem. Table 7.2 shows how to reach various objects from each basic element in the application.

TABLE 7.2 ACCESSING ONE TYPE OF OBJECT IN THE APPLICATION FROM ANOTHER

From this object	to access this object	use the function(s)
Document	View	`GetFirstViewPosition` to get the first view position and then `GetNextView` with the position to get that view and subsequent views.
Document	DocTemplate	`GetDocTemplate`
View	Document	`GetDocument`
View	Document FrameWindow	`GetParentFrame`
Document FrameWindow	View	`GetActiveView` to return the currently active view.
MDI Application	Child Window	`MDIGetActive` to return the Frame Window currently active CMDIChildWnd.

C++

Remember that the application frame window and the document frame window are identical in SDI applications. For an SDI application, treat the main application window as a document frame window. Also remember that the views for a document are in an object list; the view order depends on the order that you created the views, and not on whether the view is active or not. The first view that you get is the one with the lowest number in the title bar.

ENHANCING THE VIEW

Since you need to draw in a view, you need to think about how to make drawing fast and efficient. As you can already see, in the Windows environment you may need to draw and redraw your view many times.

Updating Views

All this takes us back to where the last chapter ended: what about the problem of erasing part of the existing beams as you draw a new one? You will recall that the dotted movement rectangles that you drew to let the user know what the new beam would look like were erasing parts of the existing beams, but if you resized the window, then all the beams displayed correctly. This section of the chapter deals with why those beams disappear and how you get them back again. Once you understand that, you can easily fix the problem of the disappearing beams or any similar problem that you happen to encounter.

As you might expect, the problem lies in updating the view. The first thing you need to know is: when does a view get updated? Rather than simply tell you, let's look at some situations where the view does—and doesn't—get updated, as shown by the redrawing of portions of beams that were erased by the movement rectangle in the view.

Figure 7.8 repeats what you saw earlier: that the movement rectangle erases parts of existing beams and those beams don't reappear, even after the new beam is drawn.

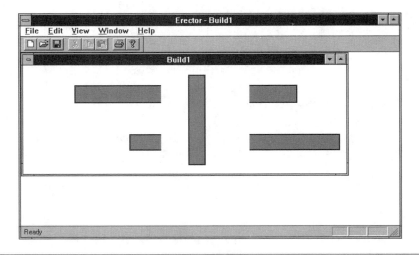

FIGURE 7.8 THE MOVEMENT RECTANGLE CAN ERASE PARTS OF EXISTING BEAMS THAT ARE NOT REPAINTED.

So far, this is exactly what you have seen before.

As a first test, use the **Ctrl+Esc** keys to switch to the main Program Manager window, then use it to switch back to Erector. The result will be as shown in Figure 7.9.

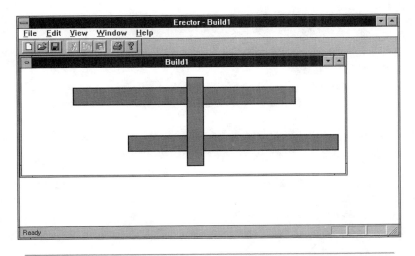

FIGURE 7.9 COVERING AND THEN UNCOVERING THE ERECTOR APPLICATION WILL CAUSE A COMPLETE UPDATE IN THE VIEW.

OK, that makes sense, because the entire screen had to be redrawn, so naturally the view had to be redrawn and so the beams reappear in the view.

Now do this again and click on the **Maximize** button at the top left of the frame window—that's the window labeled Erector - Build1. In this case, the frame window expands to fill your screen, as shown in Figure 7.10, but the missing sections of the beams are not filled in.

Even though the frame grows to its maximum size, the child window inside it, which holds the Build1 view, doesn't have to change size, so it isn't redrawn. In fact, even if you select the Build1 window and move it around the frame, as shown in Figure 7.11, you won't cause the window to be redrawn.

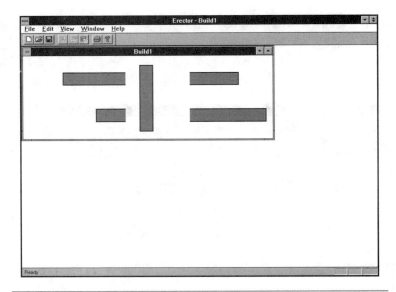

FIGURE 7.10 EVEN THOUGH YOU HAVE MAXIMIZED THE APPLICATION FRAME WINDOW, THE BUILD1 VIEW DOESN'T GET REDRAWN.

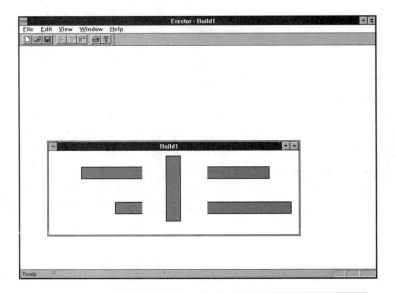

FIGURE 7.11 MOVING THE CHILD WINDOW DOESN'T CAUSE IT TO GET REDRAWN.

However, if you click on the view's maximize button, the beams get redrawn, since the view itself grows to fit the screen, as shown in Figure 7.12.

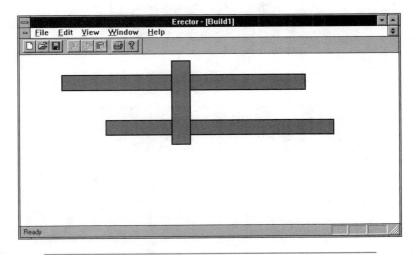

FIGURE 7.12 ANY OPERATION THAT CAUSES THE VIEW ITSELF TO BE RESIZED, LIKE MAXIMIZING IT, WILL AUTOMATICALLY REDRAW THE VIEW.

Here's one last, and very interesting, example. Open two views of the same document and tile them, so that they don't overlap one another, and then make a new beam in the active view, causing some parts of the existing beams to be erased. When you're done, the active view won't have its missing beams replaced, but the inactive view will, as shown in Figure 7.13.

Note that the tiling is an important part of this test: if you cascade the views, so that one of them covers the other, when you switch between views the newly uncovered view is redrawn, so it won't show this effect. In fact, simply switching view causes both views to be redrawn, so that this effect will disappear.

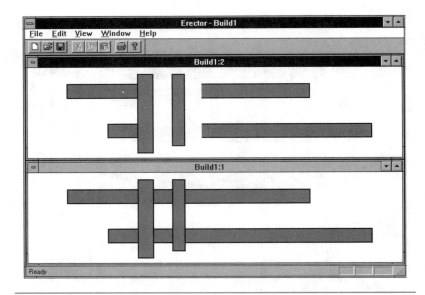

FIGURE 7.13 WITH TWO VIEWS, THE ACTIVE VIEW IS NOW THE ONE THAT IS MISSING AN UPDATE, WHILE THE INACTIVE VIEW IS DRAWN CORRECTLY.

So now you have seen several situations where the view is and is not redrawn. Let's just recapitulate these:

- If the application is covered and then uncovered, the view is redrawn.
- If the application frame window is resized, the view is not redrawn.
- If the document view window is resized, the view is redrawn.
- If the document view window is simply moved, the view is not redrawn.
- If the document has two non-overlapping views, the active view is not redrawn, but the inactive one is.
- If the document has two views, switching from one to another causes both to be redrawn.

What can you conclude from these experiments? The first point to notice is that any time part of the view is obscured and then revealed, the view gets redrawn. This seems simple enough. The part of the screen that isn't currently visible must be reconstructed, that is, redrawn, whenever it becomes visible again. Although these windows appear to overlap, in reality there is only one screen, and one set of pixels that can be used for display, so your application has to redraw anything that appears hidden on the screen when it becomes visible.

The last example is particularly instructive about how the view is updated. Here, both views are visible, but the inactive view gets redrawn while the active one doesn't. What's the difference between these two views? Simply that you recently—in the preceding section, as a matter of fact—added a specific command, `UpdateAllViews`, to force all inactive views to update.

 Remember the `this` parameter in the function call for `UpdateAllViews` was used specifically to avoid updating the active view, which is where you are drawing, because otherwise you would N O T E   enter into a loop.

This gives you two situations where the view is redrawn: first, when all or part of the view is covered up or otherwise altered; second, when you specifically asked for the views to be updated, using the `UpdateAllViews` function.

Let's examine the first situation. As you already know, the views are managed by Windows. When a view is uncovered, Windows sends a message to the view telling it to redraw itself. This message is called `WM_PAINT`. The `WM_PAINT` message is how Windows notifies a given window that all or part of its area needs to be redrawn. You need only be concerned about the client area of the window; Windows handles redrawing any nonclient displays, such as the menu bar.

If Windows covers or uncovers portions of the display, resizes, or otherwise alters the appearance of your display, then one or more windows may be affected. Windows notes the area changed by the operation and then sends a `WM_PAINT` message on the next opportunity to the window(s) that have been affected. The affected window must redraw at least the affected area to redisplay it.

This `WM_PAINT` message is the key to understanding this issue of drawing in the window. For example, when you simply moved the document view window, Windows didn't need to redraw the view, because no part of the view actually changed. Windows simply copied the view window from one position to another on your screen. However, when any part of the view was covered, Windows sent a WM_PAINT message to the view window to force it to redraw.

As you read in the last chapter, this Windows message is translated by the Message Map into a specific function call; following the standard MFC naming conventions, this function is called OnPaint. The default OnPaint is located in the CView class, so it is inherited by your CErectorView. The default OnPaint is shown in Listing 7.3.

Listing 7.3

```
//////////////////////////////////////////////////////////////////////////
// CView drawing support

void CView::OnPaint()
{
    // standard paint routine
    CPaintDC dc(this);
    OnPrepareDC(&dc);
    OnDraw(&dc);
}
```

This is simple code, but it may not be entirely clear as yet because it does some tasks that you weren't aware of. It begins by creating a CPaintDC object from the current window—this. CPaintDC is a special class derived from the standard device context class, CDC. It exists to encapsulate the work that needs to be done to prepare the window for painting and to clean up after painting. It also generates a special PAINTSTRUCT public data member that you can use when required. Next, it executes a special OnPrepareDC function. This function is typically used when printing; when you are displaying data on the screen, it does nothing unless you override it in your view class. Then the function simply passes the device context onto your OnDraw function. So, effectively, the WM_PAINT command calls your OnDraw function.

This leaves the processing that happens when you use UpdateAllViews, but to understand that, you need to know a little more about how to handle drawing in the view.

Using the Invalid Area in Drawing

Given the potential size of a window, which might be the whole screen, Windows would be pretty slow if it needed to redraw all of the window every time any little piece changed. For example, think what would happen if the Program Manager had to redraw the entire screen every time you moved a program group icon. Clearly, that would be unacceptable.

When you receive a WM_PAINT message, the device context that is associated with that message contains a rectangle that specifies the area of the view that has been uncovered or modified and needs to be repainted. This is called the *invalid area*. The invalid area is the part of the client area of the window that needs to be repainted. As you read earlier, Windows calculates this value and passes it on when it sends the WM_PAINT message.

How Areas of the View Get Invalidated

There are two ways that areas of the view get invalidated. The first occurs when a portion of the view is displayed or redisplayed by Windows. Figures 7.14 and 7.15 represent the before and after to show you the invalid area for a simple case of this type.

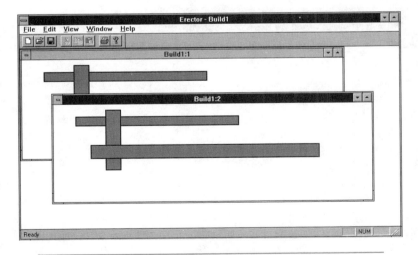

FIGURE 7.14 PART OF THE SECOND VIEW OVERLAPS AND OBSCURES THE FIRST VIEW.

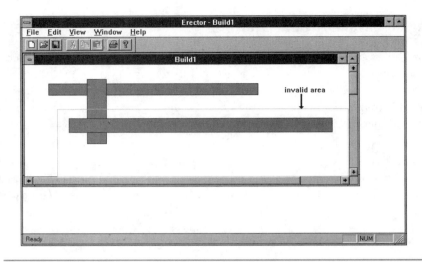

FIGURE 7.15 THE DOTTED RECTANGLE REPRESENTS THE PART OF THE FIRST VIEW THAT WAS PREVIOUSLY COVERED BY THE SECOND VIEW; THIS IS THE INVALID AREA WHEN THE SECOND VIEW IS REMOVED.

This is the area that is automatically invalidated by Windows. You can also set an area as invalid. To do so, you use one of these functions: `InvalidateRect` invalidates a rectangular area in your view; `InvalidateRgn` invalidates any arbitrary area; and `Invalidate` invalidates the entire client area. All of these are public functions in CWnd, so they are available in your view class, CErectorView.

Here is how Windows goes about processing a paint message for your application. If the user displays a part of a window that was not visible previously, Windows calculates the invalid area for the affected windows. It stores this as the update area for each of the windows affected. If the user continues to move, resize, or otherwise change the display, Windows accumulates all the invalid areas together to determine the total invalid area. If you send one of the messages that invalidates some or all of a window, Windows adds that into the update region that it has prepared. On the next available opportunity, it posts a `WM_PAINT` message into the message queue. In this way, it is possible to accumulate a set of changes to be handled at one time, rather than doing the redrawing in a piecemeal fashion. When the `WM_PAINT` message gets to the top of the message queue, it is dispatched to the affected window. As you read earlier, in the MFC, this message is transformed into an `OnDraw` command and executed.

Notice that there are two steps here. First, all or some portion of the view is made invalid. Second, a WM_PAINT message is issued to tell the view to redraw itself. Both of these must be present to cause the view to redraw; for example, if there is no invalid region in the view, then even though a WM_PAINT message is processed, it won't cause the view to redraw. This is the most efficient way to handle drawing, and it helps keep Windows running at a reasonable speed.

Now you're ready to analyze exactly what happens when you call the UpdateAllViews function. It calls the OnUpdate member function in every view except the one represented by the parameter, pSender—in other words, the current view. The default version of OnUpdate (in CView) simply invalidates the entire client area of the view using Invalidate. The next time a WM_PAINT occurs, the entire view is redrawn.

Using the Invalid Area in the View

With this knowledge, you can now fix the problem of the erased bars in your view. The answer is to invalidate the area that you have just erased and then force an update. And, in fact, those are the only two lines of code that you have to add to your CErectorView function OnMouseMove, as you can see in Listing 7.4.

Listing 7.4

```
// This function handles MouseMove up messages.
//    NOTE that this does _not_ call inherited behavior.
void CErectorView::OnMouseMove(UINT /* nFlags */, CPoint point)
{
     // Mouse button up is notable only if the user is currently drawing
     //    a new beam by dragging the mouse.
     //    In that case, we need to capture the mouse position.
     if ( GetCapture() != this )
          return;            // If this view didn't capture the mouse,
                             //    the user isn't drawing in our window.


     // Display movement rectangle in DC as a dotted rectangle
     //    to show where user is at all times.
     CRect rectDraw;
```

```
// Setup the movement rectangle based on the beam starting point.
//    TODO: Test for SetupRect error.
m_pBeamCur->SetupRect( rectDraw, point );


// Now draw the movement rectangle.
//    First, set the device context to this view...
CClientDC dc( this );
//    TODO: Add error handling in case we can't get a DC.
CDC* pDC = (CDC*)&dc;
//    set the pen and brush for the movement rectangle...
CPen penStroke;
CBrush brushFill;
//        create the pen and brush for the movement rectangle
if( !penStroke.CreatePen( PS_DOT, 1, RGB(0,0,0) ) )
    return;
if( !brushFill.CreateSolidBrush( RGB(255,255,255) ) )
    return;
//    and paint the movement rectangle.
//        save the old pen and brush and set the new ones
CPen* pOldPen = dc.SelectObject( &penStroke );
CBrush* pOldBrush = dc.SelectObject( &brushFill );
//        erase the old rectangle by painting with the white brush
dc.FrameRect( &m_rectPrev, &brushFill );
//        redraw the beams in this view
InvalidateRect( m_rectPrev, FALSE );
UpdateWindow();
//        then draw the new movement rectangle
dc.Rectangle( &rectDraw );
//        and restore the old brush and pen
dc.SelectObject( pOldBrush );
dc.SelectObject( pOldPen );


// Save the rectangle to erase it the next time.
m_rectPrev = rectDraw;
```

```
        return;
    }
```

The obvious question here is: how do you know where to insert the new code? Well, you certainly don't want to update the views before you erase the old dotted movement rectangle, since that's what is causing the erasure on the screen. What may be less obvious is that you also don't want to wait to update the views until after you have drawn the new movement rectangle. If you do that, the old beams will be drawn over the movement rectangle, which won't look right—try it and see. So the correct place for this code is between erasing the old movement rectangle and drawing the new one.

Now rebuild ErectorSet and you will see that your beams reappear as soon as you move the mouse, which is what you want.

N O T E

The UpdateWindow function that you use here is a special case of the update process. This updates the client area of the window immediately, without putting the WM_PAINT message into the message queue. In this way, you get the immediate drawing that you need to keep your view up-to-date while the user is still moving the mouse.

Improving ErectorSet Drawing

You can use the same techniques to improve your drawing process as well. Right now, you are redrawing all the beams in a view every time you have to draw any one of them—that is, every time your OnDraw function is called, you draw all the beams whether or not they are inside the invalid area.

You can fix this problem and speed up your display by checking each beam before drawing it to see if it falls within the invalid area. If it does, then all or some of it needs to be redrawn. If it doesn't, you can leave it out of the drawing process. Obviously, this is more efficient than drawing every beam in the view.

Testing Your Beam Objects against the Invalid Area Extents

With the tools at your disposal now, testing your beams to see if they need to be redrawn is quite easy to implement. Listing 7.5 shows you the complete code to make this work.

Listing 7.5

```
/////////////////////////////////////////////////////////////////////
// CErectorView drawing

void CErectorView::OnDraw(CDC* pDC)
{
    CErectorDoc* pDoc = GetDocument();
    ASSERT_VALID(pDoc);

    // Get invalid rect for checking whether beam should be drawn
    CRect rectClip;
    pDC->GetClipBox( &rectClip );

    // The view requests each beam draw itself
    //     by called CErectorBeam::DrawBeam()
    CRect rectBeam;
    for( POSITION pos = pDoc->GetFirstBeamPosition(); pos != NULL; )
    {
        CErectorBeam* pBeam = pDoc->GetNextBeam( pos );
        // Check to see if beam falls inside invalid rect
        rectBeam = pBeam->GetCurrentBeam();
        if( rectBeam.IntersectRect( &rectBeam, &rectClip ) )
        //         and only draw it if it does.
            pBeam->DrawBeam( pDC );
    }

    return;
}
```

There are three parts to this code. First, you retrieve the invalid region by getting the clipping area from the current device context. This isn't quite obvious, so some explanation is in order. What happens is that Windows automatically sets the clipping area—that's the area where you are allowed to draw in the window—to the update or invalid region for this command. Therefore, by retrieving the clipping region for the device context, you get the area where you want to draw; in fact, any attempt to draw outside this area is futile anyway, since it doesn't show.

N O T E More precisely, Windows ignores (clips) any Graphic Device Interface (GDI) calls for any graphic that extends outside of the clipping region. In effect, Windows limits you to drawing in the update area whether you like it or not. For this reason, drawing any information outside the update region is a complete waste of application processing time. If you try it, Windows actually ignores your code, even though it executes it. Thus you save a lot of processing time by checking yourself before making the GDI calls and not doing the drawing at all for items outside the clipping area, since Windows will ignore them anyway.

Once you have retrieved the clipping area, you change the drawing processing loop slightly. First of all, you define a new constant, `rectBeam`, to hold the rectangle for the current beam, and you use the inline function `GetCurrentBeam` in CErectorBeam to return the rectangle for the current beam.

Now you're ready for the actual test. The `if` statement shows you what you need to do. You use the CRect function `IntersectRect` to see if the beam to be drawn actually intersects with the invalid area at all. If it does, then you redraw the beam; if it doesn't, you move on to the next beam.

Passing Hints for Drawing in CErectorView

This handles the `OnDraw` portion of the processing all right. This will be fine when Windows is calculating the values for the update region, since Windows won't invalidate any more of the display than is required. However, the `UpdateAllViews` function calls CView `OnUpdate` function, which by default invalidates all of the client area of the view. Now you know that you would prefer to simply mark the section of the view that needs to be redrawn, instead of redrawing the entire view.

There are two places in your present application code where you call `UpdateAllViews`. (Remember, you can find out how many places a function is used by checking the Browser Definitions and References.) The first is in CErectorDoc, in the `OnEditClearAll` function. In this case, the entire view needs to be redrawn, since you have just deleted every beam in the document, so the default behavior is what you want. The second is in CErectorView, in the

OnLButtonUp function, where you notify any other views that a new beam has been added to the current view. In this case, you don't need to redraw every beam; instead, only the new beam needs to be redrawn.

There is (didn't you just know it?) one catch to this. You can't simply invalidate the area that you want to redraw in CErectorView. You have already drawn the new beam in this instance of the view; the problem is to tell other views what area you need to handle. Remember that the UpdateAllViews function has the following calling sequence:

```
void UpdateAllViews( CView* pSender, LPARAM lHint, CObject* pHint);
```

The last two parameters here, lHint and pHint, are your tools to notify other views of what area you want to handle—in this case, what area of the view should be invalidated. In the current code in OnLButtonUp, these two parameters are unused and set to their default values of 0L and NULL; now you want to use them. Similarly, in the current default OnUpdate in CView, these two hints are ignored no matter what information they have. So you have to pass the hint in OnLButtonUp and override the default OnUpdate to catch the hint.

Since the new beam is the only change in the view, it makes sense to use the third parameter, pHint, which is a pointer to any CObject. If you pass a pointer to your new beam as pHint, then the other views can use it in their OnUpdate function to set the invalid area of the view and ensure that only the changed items get redrawn.

So there are two changes that you need to make to the code:

- Add the required hint to OnLButtonUp to pass the beam to the other views.
- Add an OnUpdate function to CErectorView so that the other views can use the hint.

Listing 7.6 shows these two changes to your CErectorView class.

Listing 7.6

```
// after the function, OnInitialUpdate...

// This function handles Update messages for the view.
```

```
//    When the document notifies the view of a change,
//    we need to re-draw the view.
void CErectorView::OnUpdate(CView* /* pSender */, LPARAM /* lHint */,
CObject* pHint)
{
    // The document tells the view that it needs to be re-drawn...
    //    First, check to see if we have a hint...
    if( pHint != NULL )
    {
        // we have a hint... is it a beam object?
        if( pHint->IsKindOf( RUNTIME_CLASS(CErectorBeam) ) )
        {
            // for a beam object, only re-paint the beam area.
            CErectorBeam* pBeam = (CErectorBeam*)pHint;
            CRect rectBeam = pBeam->GetCurrentBeam();
            InvalidateRect( &rectBeam );
            return;
        }
    }
    //    If no hint, or the hint isn't a beam,
    //          then just invalidate everything.
    Invalidate();

    return;
}


//////////////////////////////////////////////////////////////////////////
// CErectorView printing


// and, make one changesin the OnLButtonUp function...

// This function handles LeftMouseButton up messages.
//    NOTE that this does _not_ call inherited behavior.
void CErectorView::OnLButtonUp(UINT /* nFlags */, CPoint point)
```

```
{
        // Mouse button up is notable only if the user is currently drawing
        //    a new beam by dragging the mouse.
        //    In that case, we need to capture the mouse position.
        if ( GetCapture() != this )
            return;            // If this view didn't capture the mouse,
                               //    the user isn't drawing in our window.

        // End the current beam.
        m_pBeamCur->EndBeam( point );

        // Now draw the beam.
        //    First, set the device context to this view...
        CClientDC dc( this );
        //    TODO: Add error handling in case we can't get a DC.
        CDC* pDC = (CDC*)&dc;
        //    then ask beam to draw itself.
        m_pBeamCur->DrawBeam( pDC );

        // Now tell any other views that we have added a beam to the drawing
        CErectorDoc* pDoc = GetDocument();
        ASSERT_VALID(pDoc);
        pDoc->UpdateAllViews( this, 0L, m_pBeamCur );

        ReleaseCapture();      // Release the mouse capture established earlier
        m_rectPrev.SetRectEmpty(); // Clean up the movement rectangle

        return;
}
```

The hint code is quite simple. You simply pass a pointer to your beam object as the third parameter in the call to UpdateAllViews. The OnUpdate processing is equally straightforward. First you test to see if you have a hint by testing to see if the pHint is NULL; if it isn't, then you test it again to see if it is, in fact, the hint you're looking for by testing to see if it is a type of CErectorBeam object. You do that by using the IsKindOf function which is available for every class derived from CObject, along with the RUNTIME_CLASS macro. This function returns TRUE if the class of pHint matches the class CErectorBeam. If it is an erector beam, then you use the beam to get the beam rectangle and you use the InvalidateRect function to invalidate that part of the view. If either test fails, you don't have a hint that you can use, so you fall back on the default behavior of invalidating the entire client area.

Since you didn't have an OnUpdate function in CErectorView before, you need to add the function. You can do that by displaying the CErectorView class in the editor window. This will show CErectorView in the WizardBar's Object IDs list. Then choose **OnUpdate** from the Messages list. The ClassWizard will see that the Update message isn't currently handled, and ask you if you want to add new code to handle it. Choose **Yes**, which will add the new function to your class. This automatically adds the function prototype to the class header file, ErectorView.h.

Note that you don't need to do any additional processing at drawing time. Once you have set the invalid area for your view, your current drawing code automatically takes that into account and optimizes the drawing.

That's all there is to improving the processing of your data. This basic principle works for all types of data and all views: test the update region to see if you need to draw all the information in your view.

SCROLLING VIEWS

Up to this point, your view has always shown a fixed area, which limits your document to a fixed size. As you know from working with typical Windows applications, this is not the way that applications usually work. Instead, most applications allow you to create documents that are larger than the view and then scroll the view around the document to view different parts of the document. In this section of the chapter, you will see how to create and use a scrolling view for your documents.

What the Framework Provides for Scrolling

If you've only dealt with scrolling as a user, you probably don't realize how complex this process is. There are actually several elements that must be coordinated to make a scrolling view: the document display, the scroll bar itself, and the various parts that are essential in the scroll bar. First of all, of course, the document must move correctly when the user scrolls the window. In addition, the scroll bar elements must be moved to match the position of the document display. For example, suppose in a word processing application that the user hits the **End** key to move to the bottom of the document. At the same time that you move the display, you must move the thumb on the vertical scroll bar to the bottom of the bar to give the user correct feedback on the current location in the document. Conversely, if the user moves the thumb to the bottom of the bar, you need to move the view to display the end of the document. And if the window that displays the view is resized, you need to reposition the scroll bar elements to correctly match the visual feedback to the document display.

Once again, the MFC provide most of the tools and code to make this quite easy to implement in your application. In addition to providing code to manage your scroll bar and the scrolling action in your document, it calls on Windows to actually draw the bar and its associated elements—arrows, thumb, and so on—and keep them correctly tied to your view. In this way the scroll bars in your application will look and function just like those in all other Windows applications, without too much work or worry on your part.

Scroll Bar Terminology

There are normally two scroll bars in a window: the horizontal scroll bar, which allows you to move left and right across the document; and the vertical scroll bar, which allows you to move up and down. Scroll bars have arrows on each end of the bar and a "thumb" or "scroll box" that indicates the approximate current position of the scroll view relative to the entire document. Figure 7.16 shows you a typical scroll view.

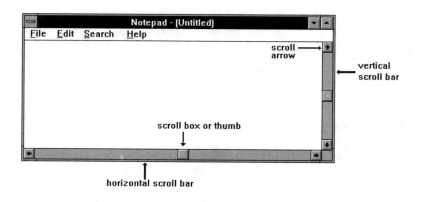

FIGURE 7.16 THIS NOTEPAD WINDOW SHOWS THE TYPICAL FEATURES OF A SCROLLING VIEW.

You can click the mouse on the scroll arrows at either end to move the view in the direction of the arrow by a small amount—for a word processing application, for example, this would normally be one line. If you click and hold the mouse button down on one of the scroll arrows, then the view moves continuously in the direction of the arrow. If you click on the scroll bar in the area between the scroll arrow and the thumb, the view move by a larger amount in the direction of the arrow—typically, by a page or a full screen. Finally, you can click and drag the thumb to move the view in the same direction that you move the thumb.

When you set up the scroll view, you establish for your application what scrolling one line and one page means; that is, you set the exact amount of distance that the view will move when the user clicks on the scroll arrows—to move one line—or in the area between the thumb and the arrow—to move one page. In this way, you determine just what "one page" and "one line" mean on the display for your documents.

Note that the default scroll bars require a mouse for movement. There is no keyboard interface for the standard scroll bars, although you can provide it yourself if you want.

Setting Up a Scrolling View

A scroll bar has two important variables: range and position. The range is a pair of integer variables that specify the minimum and maximum values of the scroll position. When the thumb is at the top or left of the scroll bar, it is at the position corresponding to the minimum value of the range. When the thumb is at the bottom or right of the scroll bar, it is at the position corresponding to the maximum value.

The position is an integer that specifies the relative location of the thumb between the minimum and maximum positions. For example, if the range of a vertical scroll bar were defined as 0 to 2, then 0 would position the thumb at the top of the bar; 1 would put it in the middle of the bar; and 2 would put it at the bottom of the bar. Of course, most ranges are much larger than this, although you can use any integer values that you want for the ranges, typically you will use some values that are related to the overall size of the document.

Windows actually provides much of the functionality of the scroll bars and scrolling views for your application, and MFC provides even more. So the responsibility for handling scroll bars in your application is divided among Windows, MFC, and your application code. Windows itself performs the following functions:

- Draws and maintains the scroll bars in the specified window
- Handles all mouse commands within the scroll bar
- Flashes the view when the user clicks in the scroll bar
- Provides a dimmed "ghost" image of the thumb during scrolling
- Sends scroll messages to the window procedure for the window containing the scroll bar

MFC provides the following functions:

- Enables you to initialize the range of the scroll bar.
- Processes scroll bar messages and scrolls the document accordingly
- Manages window and view sizing
- Adjusts the position and status of scroll bars to match the position of the document

Your application is responsible for the following actions:

- Deriving your views from the CScrollView class to implement the MFC functions (this was done by AppWizard when you created your application)
- Specifying range and position settings
- Providing document size
- Coordinating between document position and screen coordinates

Of all of these, only the last one is somewhat complex; and, as you might expect, there are a number of tools that help you make this connection.

The CScrollView Class

The basic tool for doing all this work for you is the CScrollView class, which is class is a derivative of the standard CView class. Since it is derived from CView, CScrollView does everything that CView does and adds some additional functions specifically to support scrolling. Most of these functions allow you to retrieve or set various size or position values. In addition, CScrollView supports automatic resizing of the view to the parent window. In this situation, the view will have no scroll bars and its is contents are stretched or shrunk to fit the client area of the enclosing window.

Scrolling Windows and Views

Up until now you probably haven't considered where you are in the view. Now this issue becomes very important when handling scrolling views because one of the application's responsibilities is to keep track of the relationship between the document elements and the view.

In your code so far, you really haven't had to pay much attention to where you are in the view. You've simply used the various points and rectangles and so on without any further concern. You have assumed—correctly, up to now—that you could take the point of a mouse click, for example, and use it as the basis for drawing a beam on the screen and for storing that beam and redrawing it later.

Once you get into views that scroll, however, this becomes more of a problem. Since the document can be larger than the view, where is the point that is scrolled off of the view? What position can you associate with it? Remember that the coordinate system in the client area has its origin (0, 0) at the upper-left corner of the client area, with positive x coordinates going to the right and positive y coordinates pointing down the display. In this world, every beam starts its life as a rectangle that is defined by four positive coordinates: the top, left, bottom, and right corners of the rectangle. This was fine as long as the document fit inside a single view, so the coordinates were always the same for both the document and the screen. Now, however, you can scroll a beam out of the view but you must keep track of where it is in the document, so you need a new set of coordinates.

Device Coordinates and Logical Coordinates

What you need to do is keep two distinct sets of coordinates: one set for the device—in this case, your display screen—and one set for the document. The coordinates that you use for your document are called *logical coordinates*, while the coordinates used on the screen are called, reasonably enough, *device coordinates*.

Figure 7.17 illustrates how this works.

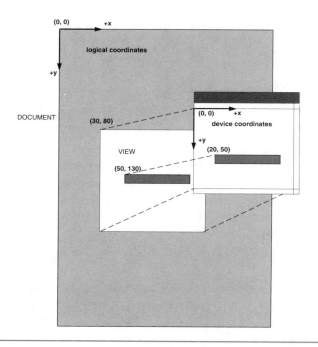

FIGURE 7.17 THE DATA IN THE DOCUMENT ARE STORED IN LOGICAL COORDINATES, BUT THEY ARE DISPLAYED IN THE VIEW'S CLIENT AREA IN DEVICE COORDINATES.

You keep the document data, like the beam shown in the view, in logical coordinates. For example, this beam's top corner is the point (50, 130) in the document's logical coordinates. However, when you display the beam, you use the client area's device coordinates, which place the top corner at the point (20, 50). Translation from one to the other is quite simple; once you know that the view's origin in logical coordinates is (30, 80), you can easily calculate one set of coordinates for the beam from the other.

For now, both sets of coordinates are using the same unit of measure: one unit is one device pixel. As you can imagine, the device coordinates are always in pixels, but logical coordinates may be kept in any units that you want. Later, in Chapter 12, you will learn about other measurement systems that you can use and how they work; for now, keeping the same units in both logical and device coordinates make the job here a bit simpler.

Conversion between Device Coordinates and Logical Coordinates

The next obvious question is who has to do this conversion from device to logical coordinates and back? In fact, everyone contributes a little bit. Windows supplies functions that will do the conversion and keep track of the origin of the view and other issues that need to be handled to make this translation. However, you have to ask Windows to do the translation when required, by using MFC functions that are available in the device context class, CDC. So, you need two know two things:

- Which functions require device coordinates for correct display
- Which functions return device coordinates when you request a position

This actually turns out to be fairly easy, but a bit confusing. Windows provides conversion from logical or document coordinates to device or screen coordinates whenever you are using functions that work with the device context. These functions are called Graphic Device Interface (GDI) functions. So, for example, when you use the `FillRect` function from the CDC class, you will supply the rectangle to be filled in logical coordinates. When you ask for the update region with the `GetClipBox` function, the update rectangle will be returned in logical coordinates. For most other functions, however, you need to use device coordinates: for example, the point where the mouse is clicked will be reported by `OnLButtonDown` in device coordinates, because this is a function in the CWnd class, and not in the CDC class. So this is easy, because you can expect that CDC functions will use logical coordinates—I will note explicitly in the text the few CDC functions that do not; but it is confusing, because the functions that draw and print and so on, which might seem to be the very functions where you need to use device-specific information, are the functions where Windows does the work for you; therefore, they use logical coordinates instead.

Adding Scrolling to ErectorSet

Let's see how you can add scrolling to your ErectorSet application. Here are the steps you need to take:

1. Set the document size in CErectorDoc.
2. Edit the function `OnInitialUpdate` in CErectorView to use the correct size for the view.

3. Modify CErectorView to change from device coordinates to logical coordinates when creating the beams.

4. Modify CErectorView to change from logical coordinates to device coordinates when displaying the beams.

N O T E

Remember that, when you created the ErectorSet application, you set CErectorView to be derived from CScrollView, rather than the default CView. This is an essential part of getting MFC to help you create a scrolling view for your documents. If you don't make that change and want to have a scrolling view, then you would need to make more extensive changes to your CErectorView class to derive it from CScrollView now and to add the necessary interface functions, such as `OnInitialUpdate`, so that scrolling will work.

Setting the Document Size

First, you need to set the document size. You will do this in two steps: first, calculate and store a document size in your document class, CErectorDoc, in a member variable and then provide a function to allow other classes to access the document size. For now, the size of the document can be a fixed amount.

Use the pop-up menu—displayed by pressing the right mouse button—to first add a new member variable to the CErectorDoc class with the following specifications: Variable Type, CSize; Variable Declaration, m_sizeDoc; Protected. The new data member is a CSize object, which is simply a special class, similar to the CRect class, that handle Windows SIZE objects. SIZE objects define a rectangle by storing its width and height. (Remember, you can easily find out all about any MFC class, like CSize, by using the on-line help facility.)

Now you have to change the document header, `erectdoc.h`, to add an access function so that other classes, like CErectorView, can retrieve the document size. Listing 7.7 shows you the required changes to handle that, along with the new variable that was added earlier.

Listing 7.7

```
/////////////////////////////////////////////////////////////////////////
// ErectorDoc.h : interface of the CErectorDoc class
```

```
//
//
// Created by AppWizard 11 December 1995 11:39:42
// Modifiications:
//    12 Dec 95   DH    Add OnOpenDocument to generated code,
//                           along with new common InitDocument().
//    12 Dec 95   DH    Add CErectorBeam class to generated code:
//                           initialization; serialization; contents
//    15 Dec 95   DH    Add menu item Edit>>Clear All with new function,
//                           OnEditClearAll, and aux function, DeleteContents.
//    18 Dec 95   DH    Add SetupRect to support movement rectangle display
//                           and modify EndBeam to use it.
//    19 Dec 95   DH    Add document size member variable, m_sizeDoc,
//                           and new function GetDocSize to access it.
/////////////////////////////////////////////////////////////////////////

// Forward declaration of the data structure class, CErectorBeam
class CErectorBeam;


class CErectorDoc : public CDocument
{
protected: // create from serialization only
    CErectorDoc();
    DECLARE_DYNCREATE(CErectorDoc)

// Attributes
protected:
    CTypedPtrList<CObList, CErectorBeam*> m_beamList;
                                    // each list element is a beam object
    CSize       m_sizeDoc;          // the document size

    // We track the beam color or pattern and outline width
    //    at the document level for all views. This allows
    //    the user to choose a new beam style for all the views
```

```
//     together, rather than one at a time.
COLORREF    m_crBrushColor;       // the brush color
UINT        m_nPenWidth;          // the border width

public:
    POSITION GetFirstBeamPosition();
    CErectorBeam* GetNextBeam( POSITION& pos);
    CSize GetDocSize() { return m_sizeDoc; }


// Operations
```

This is quite simple. You added the new data member, m_sizeDoc, which is a
CSize object, and you now add the new inline function, GetDocSize, which
returns the protected m_sizeDoc when requested.

NOTE You could use the **Add Function...** entry in the pop-up menu to add
this function, but you cannot enter an inline definition like this using
that menu; you can only add a function prototype. In this case, the
function is so short and simple that it's easier to put all the code here,
in the header as an inline definition, instead of splitting the code and
the prototype.

Finally, you need to initialize the variable when the class is set up. Listing 7.8
shows you the new code in the function InitDocument to handle that.

Listing 7.8

```
// This function uses current pen width to create a pen object
//    and a brush for drawing. This must be done whenever
//    a document is created Uses the CPen class.
void CErectorDoc::InitDocument()
{
    // the default pen is 2 pixels wide
    m_nPenWidth = 2;
    // the default brush is solid 50% gray
    m_crBrushColor = RGB(128, 128, 128);
```

```
// default document size is 850 by 1100 pixels
m_sizeDoc = CSize(850, 1100);


return;
}
```

This is simply a single line of code to set the new member variable, m_sizeDoc, to a fixed value of 850 by 1100 pixels

Now you have to use this information when you are setting up the scroll view. You do that by modifying the function, OnInitialUpdate, in the CErectorView class. If you look at the current definition of this function in CErectorView, you will see that it uses a function, SetScrollSizes that uses a CSize element. All you need to do is to replace the existing code with the new code, shown in Listing 7.9, which replaces the existing sizeTotal variable with your document's size information.

Listing 7.9

```
// This function handles the first update message for the view.
//    It sets the document size for scrolling by asking the document
//    to tell its current size.
void CErectorView::OnInitialUpdate()
{
        CScrollView::OnInitialUpdate();


        SetScrollSizes(MM_TEXT, GetDocument()->GetDocSize() );
}
```

As the name implies, the OnInitialUpdate function is called when the first update message is sent to the view, immediately after it is created. The new code consists of one line, which calls the SetScrollSizes function in the base CScrollView class. This function establishes the relationship between the logical coordinates used in the document and the device coordinates that are used for display. It also sets the amount of movement that will happen when the user clicks on the scroll arrows or in the scroll bar.

SetScrollSizes requires two parameters: the size of the document, which you get from the document's GetDocSize function, and a mapping mode, MM_TEXT. The *mapping mode* determines the logical coordinate structure of the document. In this case, you are using a logical coordinate structure where each unit of the coordinates corresponds to one pixel—the same measure that is used in the device coordinates. In Chapter 10, you will read about other types of coordinate structures; for now, however, you should use this approach which is the simplest to work with. The function also has two additional optional parameters which specify the amount of movement that happens when the user scrolls a page or a line. By default, the page scroll distance is 1/10th of the total size of the document, while the line scroll distance is 1/10th of the page scroll distance. For now, you can use these default values.

Converting the Coordinates for Scrolling

All that's left is to transform the coordinates from the screen pixel values to the logical values that you want to use for storing and working with the beams. You need to do this in two places. First, when you get the information from the screen, you have to convert the coordinates to logical form for defining and storing the beam. Then, when you go to display the beams on the screen, you need to convert the logical coordinates in the beam into display coordinates.

As you read earlier, these conversions are mostly handled by Windows. In the MFC, you access these Windows functions by using two functions in the CDC class: DPtoLP to convert from device to logical coordinates, and LPtoDP to convert in the reverse direction, from logical to device coordinates.

Let's begin by converting the mouse coordinates, which you get from the display, into logical coordinates for use in the beams. Listing 7.10 shows you the changes required in CErectorView to handle this.

Listing 7.10

```
//////////////////////////////////////////////////////////////////////
// CErectorView message handlers

// This function handles LeftMouseButton down messages.
//    NOTE that this does _not_ call inherited behavior.
void CErectorView::OnLButtonDown(UINT /* nFlags */, CPoint point)
{
    // CScrollView returns view coordinates, which are device coordinates.
    //    They must be converted to logical coordinates before use.
```

```
//      First, get the device context for this view...
CClientDC dc( this );
//      TODO: Add error handling in case we can't get a DC.
CDC* pDC = (CDC*)&dc;
OnPrepareDC( pDC );
dc.DPtoLP( &point );


    // When the mouse button is down, the user may be starting a new beam,
    //     or selecting or de-selecting an existing beam.
    //     However, for now just create a new beam.
    //     TODO: Add beam selection feature.
    m_pBeamCur = GetDocument()->NewBeam();


    // Insert our point as the starting point of the new beam.
    m_pBeamCur->BeginBeam( point );


    SetCapture();           // Establish mouse capture.


    return;
}




// This function handles MouseMove up messages.
//     NOTE that this does _not_ call inherited behavior.
void CErectorView::OnMouseMove(UINT /* nFlags */, CPoint point)
{
    // Mouse button up is notable only if the user is currently drawing
    //     a new beam by dragging the mouse.
    //     In that case, we need to capture the mouse position.
    if ( GetCapture() != this )
        return;             // If this view didn't capture the mouse,
                            //     the user isn't drawing in our window.


    //      First, set the device context to this view...
    CClientDC dc( this );
```

```
//   TODO: Add error handling in case we can't get a DC.
CDC* pDC = (CDC*)&dc;
// CScrollView returns view coordinates, which are device coordinates.
//   They must be converted to logical coordinates before use.
OnPrepareDC( pDC );
dc.DPtoLP( &point );


// Display movement rectangle in DC as a dotted rectangle
//   to show where user is at all times.
CRect rectDraw;


// Setup the movement rectangle based on the beam starting point.
//   TODO: Test for SetupRect error.
m_pBeamCur->SetupRect( rectDraw, point );


// Now draw the movement rectangle.
//   set the pen and brush for the movement rectangle...
CPen penStroke;
CBrush brushFill;
//        create the pen and brush for the movement rectangle
if( !penStroke.CreatePen( PS_DOT, 1, RGB(0,0,0) ) )
    return;
if( !brushFill.CreateSolidBrush( RGB(255,255,255) ) )
    return;
//   and paint the movement rectangle.
//        save the old pen and brush and set the new ones
CPen* pOldPen = dc.SelectObject( &penStroke );
CBrush* pOldBrush = dc.SelectObject( &brushFill );
//        erase the old rectangle by painting with the white brush
dc.FrameRect( &m_rectPrev, &brushFill );
//        redraw the beams in this view
InvalidateRect( m_rectPrev, FALSE );
UpdateWindow();
//        then draw the new movement rectangle
dc.Rectangle( &rectDraw );
```

```
//          and restore the old brush and pen
dc.SelectObject( pOldBrush );
dc.SelectObject( pOldPen );

// Save the rectangle to erase it the next time.
m_rectPrev = rectDraw;

return;
}


// This function handles LeftMouseButton up messages.
//    NOTE that this does _not_ call inherited behavior.
void CErectorView::OnLButtonUp(UINT /* nFlags */, CPoint point)
{
    // Mouse button up is notable only if the user is currently drawing
    //    a new beam by dragging the mouse.
    //    In that case, we need to capture the mouse position.
    if ( GetCapture() != this )
        return;              // If this view didn't capture the mouse,
                             //    the user isn't drawing in our window.

    //    First, set the device context to this view...
    CClientDC dc( this );
    //    TODO: Add error handling in case we can't get a DC.
    CDC* pDC = (CDC*)&dc;
    // CScrollView returns view coordinates, which are device coordinates.
    //    They must be converted to logical coordinates before use.
    OnPrepareDC( pDC );
    dc.DPtoLP( &point );

    // End the current beam.
    m_pBeamCur->EndBeam( point );

    // Now ask the beam to draw itself.
```

```
        m_pBeamCur->DrawBeam( pDC );

        // Now tell any other views that we have added a beam to the drawing
        CErectorDoc* pDoc = GetDocument();
        ASSERT_VALID(pDoc);
        pDoc->UpdateAllViews( this, 0L, m_pBeamCur );

        ReleaseCapture();                   // Release the mouse capture estab-
lished earlier
        m_rectPrev.SetRectEmpty();  // Clean up the movement rectangle

        return;
    }
```

Since DPtoLP is a CDC function, you first need to get the device context for the
view, if you don't already have it. Next, call OnPrepareDC to set the transformation from the logical origin to the device origin for this view. Finally, pass in
the point (or other coordinate structure) that you want converted. The DPtoLP
function changes the given point from device coordinates to logical coordinates
using the transformation set up in the OnPrepareDC function. This takes care
of one direction of the conversion.

In the functions OnMouseMove and OnLButtonUp, you were already using
the device context for drawing. Notice that the coordinate conversion requires
that you move the call to the device context up a few lines of code, so that you
have it before you make the conversion.

N O T E

The code was written so that each of the three functions could use
identical code to reference the device context and convert the coordinates. Since two of the functions use the device context twice—
once for coordinate conversion and once for drawing—the code gets
the device context, creates a pointer to the context, and then calls the
appropriate function. If you wanted, you could simplify the call in
OnLButtonDown by removing the line of code that creates a pointer
to the device context and change the function call to use the device
context address. The revised code would look like this:

```
CClientDC dc( this );
OnPrepareDC( &dc );
dc.DPtoLP( &point );
```

As far as I can tell, this isn't any more or less efficient than the code shown in the example, but you may prefer it as being more readable when you don't otherwise have to use the device context in your current function. See Listing 7.11 for an example of this use of the device context.

The final requirement is to reverse the coordinate transformation when you compute the invalid rectangle in OnUpdate. Listing 7.11 shows the required changes.

Listing 7.11

```
void CErectorView::OnUpdate(CView* /* pSender */, LPARAM /* lHint */,
CObject* pHint)
{
    // The document tells the view that it needs to be re-drawn...
    //    First, check to see if we have a hint...
    if( pHint != NULL )
    {
        // we have a hint... is it a beam object?
        if( pHint->IsKindOf( RUNTIME_CLASS(CErectorBeam) ) )
        {
            // The current beam is stored in document or logical coordinates
            //    which must be converted to device coordinates before use
            //    by the view as an invalid rectangle.
            CClientDC dc( this );
            //    TODO: Add error handling in case we can't get a DC.
            OnPrepareDC( &dc );

            // for a beam object, only re-paint the beam area.
            CErectorBeam* pBeam = (CErectorBeam*)pHint;
            CRect rectBeam = pBeam->GetCurrentBeam();
            dc.LPtoDP( &rectBeam );
```

```
        InvalidateRect( &rectBeam );
        return;
    }
}
//    If no hint, or the hint isn't a beam,
//        then just invalidate everything.
Invalidate();

    return;
}
```

There are two points to notice here. First of all, you will note that this code does not convert the device context into a pointer before using it in OnPrepareDC; instead, it simply uses the address of the device context directly. Secondly, you see that the LPtoDP function—the inverse of DPtoLP that you used before—is taking a rectangle as its argument, rather than a point. In fact, this pair of functions will take either a rectangle, a single point, or an array of points, for conversion.

The most interesting point here, however, is not in the modifications to this OnUpdate function, but in the fact that you do not have to modify the OnDraw function. On the face of it, you might suppose that you need to add the same code or something similar to OnDraw to get the beams to display correctly. You don't have to do that. All the functions used in OnDraw, and in the actual drawing function in CErectorBeam, DrawBeam, are using GDI functions, like GetClipBox and Rectangle, to work with the beam coordinates. As you already read earlier, GDI functions generally use logical coordinates for their work, performing the necessary conversions internally. So the OnDraw function still works just as it did before.

One step needs to be done before you can use the GDI functions correctly. The origin of the view needs to be positioned relative to the document's origin. This is done by the MFC CScrollView class in its OnPrepareDC function—remember that you called OnPrepareDC in your other functions prior to converting the coordinates. You don't even need to take that step explicitly here, because the CScrollView class does this for you automatically before calling OnDraw. As a result, your OnDraw function doesn't need any changes to work correctly with scrolling views.

At this point, you should rebuild ErectorSet to be sure that you have made all these changes correctly. Figure 7.18 shows how the ErectorSet application looks now.

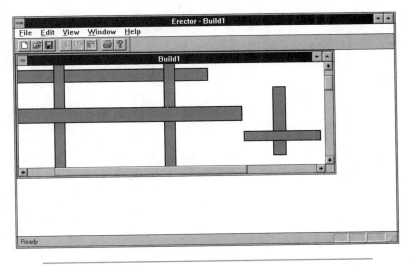

FIGURE 7.18 THIS VERSION OF ERECTORSET SUPPORTS SCROLLING DOCUMENTS.

SUMMARY

At this point, you are beginning to have a fully operational Windows application. As you have learned in this chapter, an important part of working in Windows is understanding the uses of documents and views. You have learned about how documents work and what they are intended to do: hold your application data in a useful and effective way. You have also learned about views and how the view works with the document to display data. As you saw, drawing a document's data in a view can be a time-consuming process, but there are ways to improve this. You learned how to use the invalid area in the view to speed up display, and you learned how to set the invalid rectangle to ensure that your views get updated properly.

Once you understand views and documents, you are ready to enhance your views with scrolling. You saw in this chapter how to add scrolling to your document's views and how to create documents that are larger than the view itself.

As a part of that, you also learned about coordinate systems: the logical coordinates that are used in the document and in Windows GDI functions, and the device coordinates that are used for display and for non-GDI functions.

However, as the application code gets more robust and complex, there is also a greater chance for problems and errors. This means that you now need to know about how to avoid problems in your code, and how to find and fix them when they occur. The next chapter tells you about these issues and will help you build an even more robust application.

CHAPTER 8

EXCEPTIONS AND DEBUGGING

So far—unless you made a typing mistake—all of the code that you have entered has compiled and executed correctly. In real life, however, your code may have errors of one sort or another that you have to discover and fix. This chapter will discuss in detail how to identify and correct problems in a Visual C++ application using the Developer Workbench.

There are two approaches to handling problems in your application: prevention and cure. Just as you would prefer to stay healthy rather than be cured after you're sick, avoiding errors and problems in your application is the best strategy. A large portion of this chapter is devoted to discovering and handling problem situations before they become errors. With the best efforts, however, there will still be times when you need to fix your application. This chapter will show you some of the techniques that you can use to identify problems in your application and how to use the tools in the Developer Studio to implement these techniques.

Important topics in this chapter include:

- Identifying and handling exceptional conditions
- Setting up the Developer Studio debugger
- Using breakpoints and instruction-stepping to debug code
- Using the ASSERT macro and related tools to identify problems
- Using the TRACE facilities to monitor program operation

USING EXCEPTION HANDLING

You have certainly noticed throughout the code that you have entered into ErectorSet so far repeated notes to add code to identify and handle potential problems. Most often, these have been TODO notes that identify certain places in your code where some specific action needs to be taken to avoid the problem. These are typical of a class of coding problem that you need to handle. An *exception* is a situation that may occur that would cause an error when running the application.

Typically, an exception represents some external failure that will prevent your application from executing correctly. Many of the TODO comments in your code, for example, note that the Windows operating system may not return a device context when you request one. This is a good example of an exception. This isn't exactly your problem—there isn't any action that you can take in your code to avoid it, and normally you didn't do anything to cause it—but if it happens, your application will not work correctly and will probably fail. This is disconcerting to the user and certainly not good programming.

Ideally, you should notice that you have not gotten the device context and take some corrective action. Since this is a Windows issue, you could, for example, notify the user that they have too many applications open and ask them to close some. Alternatively, you could notify the user of the problem and simply terminate the application in the normal way, allowing the user to save any open documents. In either case, you are taking some action that will allow the user to handle the error in an understandable way, rather than simply having the application crash and burn.

Normal Execution Processing

When you call a function when writing a program, one of three things may happen:

- The function may execute normally and return correctly.
- An error may occur in calling or using the function.
- An abnormal situation may develop that prevents correct execution.

Let's look at each of these in turn and see how you might ideally handle each one.

The first situation is one that you should always handle in your code. This is the most common occurrence, where the function that you call operates within the parameters set out for it. Notice that this covers all situations where the function executes normally, including those where it returns an exit code that indicates a problem. For example, the function SetupRect in CErectorBeam is designed to return a Boolean value that indicates whether the rectangle could be set correctly, that is, whether the rectangle coordinates are valid or not. Both TRUE, which says that SetupRect worked correctly, and FALSE, which tells you that it failed, are normal results that you should handle in your code.

This point may seem difficult to understand the first time you think about it. Let's look at SetupRect as an example of how this should be handled. Up to this point, SetupRect has simply had a TODO comment at the beginning of the function that indicates that you need to check the rectangle for valid coordinates. This is based on the documentation for the Rectangle function in the CDC class, which is used to draw the beam. This specifies that a rectangle used by the function must have both a width and a height greater than 2 units and less than 32767 units. Listing 8.1 shows the new code in SetupRect that handles this.

Listing 8.1

```
// This function calculates the drawing rectangle
//    from the starting point to the supplied point and returns it.
BOOL CErectorBeam::SetupRect(CRect& rectBeam, CPoint& ptCurrent)
{
    // Error checking code to ensure that
    //    ptStart and ptCurrent are not too close to one another...
    if( (abs(m_ptStart.x - ptCurrent.x) < 2) ||
        (abs(m_ptStart.y - ptCurrent.y) < 2) )
        return FALSE;
    //    and are not too far apart, either.
    if( (abs(m_ptStart.x - ptCurrent.x) > 32767) ||
        (abs(m_ptStart.y - ptCurrent.y) > 32767) )
        return FALSE;

    // Set top and bottom
    if ( ptCurrent.y < m_ptStart.y )
    {
```

```
            rectBeam.top = ptCurrent.y;
            rectBeam.bottom = m_ptStart.y;
      }
      else
      {
            rectBeam.top = m_ptStart.y;
            rectBeam.bottom = ptCurrent.y;
      }

      // Set left and right
      if ( ptCurrent.x < m_ptStart.x )
      {
            rectBeam.left = ptCurrent.x;
            rectBeam.right = m_ptStart.x;
      }
      else
      {
            rectBeam.left = m_ptStart.x;
            rectBeam.right = ptCurrent.x;
      }

      return TRUE;
}
```

This code simply tests the absolute value of the difference between the starting x coordinates and the starting y coordinates to see that both fall within the required parameters; if not, the function returns FALSE.

Now look at Listing 8.2. It shows how the function EndBeam, which calls SetupRect, now handles the return values.

Listing 8.2

```
// This function finishes a beam by calculating the rectangle
//    required for the beam, using the starting and ending points.
void CErectorBeam::EndBeam(CPoint ptStop)
{
```

```
                 // Regularize the ending point to derive the beam rectangle
                 if( !SetupRect( m_rectBeam, ptStop ) )
                     m_rectBeam = CRect( m_ptStart, CSize(2,3) );


                 return;
        }
```

Previously, this function simply assumed that SetupRect worked correctly and did nothing about a possible error, which was fine, since SetupRect itself didn't do any error checking. Now EndBeam tests for a return value. If the return is TRUE, there is no problem, since m_rectBeam is now set correctly. However, if the return is FALSE, m_rectBeam is forced to a valid size. In fact, it is set to be a small rectangle with the upper-left corner at the starting point, a width of 2 units, and a height of 3 units. This keeps the beam rectangle within acceptable bounds and therefore handles both return values as part of normal processing.

N O T E   While this works fine for values that would produce a rectangle that was too small, you may worry that it doesn't work as well if the error is caused by a rectangle that is too large. That's true, but the chances of getting a rectangle that exceeds 32767 units is very small, since the average screen is, at most, less than 1200 pixels wide. (Remember that our coordinate values are in pixels.) On the other hand, getting a rectangle that is too small is quite easy: the user simply has to accidentally click twice on the same point, or very close to it. For this reason, EndBeam automatically makes the default beam very small. Under other circumstances, where both outcomes were equally possible, you might choose to display an error dialog box or use some other method of handling the problem.

The important point here is that both possible outcomes are handled as a part of normal processing. Neither is considered either an error or an exception.

SetupRect is also called from the OnMouseMove function in CErectorView. This is the point where you are creating the movement rectangle for display. Here, too, you need to handle both possible return values: TRUE and FALSE. However, the processing is a bit simpler. If SetupRect gets an invalid rectangle, you simply don't want to draw the movement rectangle; you don't need to do anything else. Listing 8.3 shows you the single line change to OnMouseMove that solves this problem.

Listing 8.3

```
// This function handles MouseMove up messages.
//   NOTE that this does _not_ call inherited behavior.
void CErectorView::OnMouseMove(UINT /* nFlags */, CPoint point)
{
    // Mouse button up is notable only if the user is currently drawing
    //   a new beam by dragging the mouse.
    //   In that case, we need to capture the mouse position.
    if ( GetCapture() != this )
        return;            // If this view didn't capture the mouse,
                           //   the user isn't drawing in our window.


    // ... some other code here...


    // Display movement rectangle in DC as a dotted rectangle
    //   to show where user is at all times.
    CRect rectDraw;


    // Setup the movement rectangle based on the beam starting point.
    if( !m_pBeamCur->SetupRect(rectDraw, point) )
        return;


    // Now draw the movement rectangle.
    //   set the pen and brush for the movement rectangle...


    // ... and so on...
```

This is a simple change. All you do is exit the function if SetupRect is not satisfied with the point provided.

Note that you must provide some error checking here. Previously, OnMouseMove simply went ahead with the processing when the rectangle was incorrect. However, now that SetupRect is checking the coordinates, that simple strategy will no longer work because SetupRect itself now returns immediately if there is an error rather than set an incorrect rectangle. Therefore, if you allow the OnMouseMove function to continue processing now when SetupRect returns FALSE, you will most likely have a large, positive rectangle—based on whatever values happen to be in memory at the location allocated for rectDraw. This will then be propagated to m_rectPrev, where it will cause large areas in your view to be erased as you move your cursor. This would be clearly incorrect.

The important point to notice here is that, once you have added error checking to SetupRect, you must provide handling for both possible return values everywhere that you use the function. You can't simply handle the returns in one place and not in the other without having some additional problems crop up.

The second situation that is described earlier is an error condition: what happens in the program if a function is called incorrectly? Ideally, errors should be found and fixed before the application is sent to users. To do that, you will need both testing and validation techniques that you can use before shipping a program to ensure that it is as free from errors as possible. For this reason, error handling generally involves debugging issues, which you will read about in the next section of the chapter.

This leaves us with the issue of abnormal conditions that may arise when you call a function. These are exceptions because they occur under exceptional conditions. Generally, like the processing in SetupRect that leads to a FALSE return value, they are problems that are out of your control in the sense that they are caused by some external event, such as a user action or a problem within Windows. Unlike the processing in SetupRect, however, they are not a part of normal processing expectations. They present a distinct class of programming problem that you need to solve.

Processing Exceptions

Exceptions are particularly likely to happen in an environment such as Windows, where your application is not in complete control of either the computer or the operating system. As you have already learned, one major difference between Windows and the older DOS operating system is that Windows applications are driven by external events, that is, they must respond to user's requests and Windows messages at any time. In such an environment, more things can go wrong than in a simpler system where your application can more or less control what's happening.

The problem with acquiring a device context from Windows is a good example of this type of problem. Windows provides only five free device contexts for use by all applications. Therefore, under some unusual circumstances, it may happen that when you request a device context from Windows, it informs you that there are no more available contexts. This is an exceptional condition, since five contexts is usually enough for most users in most combinations of hardware and applications; it's also an external event to your program, since you cannot control when or if this will happen. However, if it happens, you won't be able to display your information on the screen and your application will either hang or terminate unexpectedly, depending on what else you try to do after you fail to get the context.

Handling exceptions well is one feature that distinguishes professional-quality code. Code that is intended for commercial applications needs to respond to a wide variety of conditions and possibilities, many of which may result in exceptions. The MFC provide an excellent basic structure for handling exceptions, but you need to use it to make your code as robust as possible. In that way, you will satisfy your users, who, reasonably enough, don't want to use an application that stops working in an unpredictable fashion and possibly brings their systems down at the same time.

Traditional Exception Processing

One traditional way of handling this type of problem was to use standard function return values as an indication of an error. For example, the Windows function GetDC, which is the function that MFC uses to get the client-area device context, returns a handle—a type of pointer—to the device context if it works correctly and returns a NULL pointer if it fails. So the MFC code must test for a NULL pointer on the return from GetDC to tell whether the Windows function was successful or not. This is one traditional method of indicating and handling an exception.

NOTE   The return value of GetDC has a type of CDC*, which means that if it succeeds, it returns a pointer to an object of class CDC. This class encapsulates the functionality of a Windows device context handle. CDC is often referred to as a *wrapper*, just as CWnd is a wrapper around a handle to a window and CSize is a wrapper around a SIZE structure. By returning a CDC*, MFC is actually providing access to a device context.

> As for handles, a *handle* is just Window's way of keeping track of a resource. You can think of a handle as being similar to a pointer, but there is a fundamental difference: A *pointer* contains an actual, physical address, whereas a handle is an index into a table kept by Windows. For now, however, you don't need to worry about the difference between pointers and handles. Just use the MFC classes provided for you.

This type of exception indication presents two problems. First, it means that you need to test for, and handle, the possible null pointer everywhere in your code. This leads to a lot of redundant if...else testing in your code. There is also the problem of what action to take once you discover the error—essentially, how do you get back to the original calling function safely. Second, there is no equivalent of a null pointer as an object of a class, so that it would require some additional handling to pass this indicator down to the working function that is using the device context.

The C language traditionally very often handled this type of problem by using the setjmp(), longjmp() pair of library functions. These allow a function to exit directly back to a calling function without trying to reset or exit in a normal fashion. However, using setjmp() and longjmp() successfully in an application always requires a lot of planning and, even more difficult, comprehensive testing to ensure that you don't cause a worse error than you started with. In any case, for a variety of technical reasons that are outside the scope of our discussion here, these functions are incompatible with C++.

Using C++ Exception Handling

The Developer Studio C++ compiler implements the new standard C++ exception handling by using the exception keywords, try, catch, and throw and a related special MFC exception class, CException. The process works as follows. When a function discovers an exceptional situation, it signals an exception—this is called "throwing" the exception and is done using the keyword throw. The original calling function must use the try and catch keywords together to provide processing for the exception. If the calling function doesn't handle the exception, the exception is propagated up the calling chain until the exception is handled. In this, exceptions work very much like other messages.

The code guarded by the `try` keyword is called the *try-block*. Similarly, the *catch-block* is the code executed by the `catch` keyword. Whenever an exception occurs during execution of code in a try-block, even if the exception occurs inside another function that is called from within the try-block, the exception is handled by the catch-block.

The best thing about using the C++ exception handlers is that they will automatically destroy any local objects that were automatically allocated in the try-block. This ensures that, even if you have allocated additional objects in memory, your application will clean them up correctly if you encounter a problem. This is one of the most difficult situations for a programmer to handle in ordinary code environments. This ability is one important reason to use the C++ `try-catch` exception mechanism.

N O T E

In the previous version of Microsoft's Visual C++ development environment, this exception process was handled in a slightly different way, by using TRY, CATCH, and other supporting macros that performed exception handling. These macros still exist in MFC 4.0 and work correctly. However, with the advent of Visual C++ 4.0, with its support for the new C++ exception handlers, these macros are no longer the best method for handling exceptions. Instead, you should use the native C++ exception handlers demonstrated here, which are very similar to the previous macro implementation but are more robust and transportable.

If you have code using the older macro exception handlers, you can easily convert this code to use the new mechanisms. Look in the on-line documentation, in the section Exceptions: Converting from MFC Exception Macros in the book *Programming with MFC: Encyclopedia*.

MFC Exceptions

In fact, only a limited number of exceptional conditions will arise during execution of your application. The MFC has a special class, CException, that is the basis for all the types of exceptions that it can handle. Table 8.1 lists these exceptions and gives a short summary of what causes them.

TABLE 8.1 EXCEPTIONS IMPLEMENTED BY MFC

Exception Class	Description
CMemoryException	Your application has directly or indirectly requested a block of memory that is larger than what is currently available.
CFileException	A file object has thrown an exception. The exact cause of the exception is defined by the m_cause data member of the CFileException class. Typical causes are file was not available, file name or path invalid, disk is full, and so on.
CArchiveException	An exception has been thrown during saving or restoring information in the serialization processing in your application.
CResourceException	Your application has requested a Windows resource that is not found or not available. For example, you have requested a device context from Windows and one is not available.
COleException	An exceptional condition relating to an Object Linking and Embedding (OLE) operation has occurred. The exact cause of the exception is defined as the m_status data member of the COleException class. Typical causes are format error, network error, OLE server errors, and so on.
CUserException	This is an exception that is thrown in response to something that the user of the application has done.
CNotSupportedException	This is an exception that is thrown in response to a request from your application for an unsupported feature.

Each of the exceptions listed in Table 8.1 has a specific meaning and requires specific handling. So, in addition to handling an exception, you need to check and be sure that you're handling the one that you want. All of this is part of using exception handling correctly.

One major difference between the previous MFC exception macros and the native C++ exception handling keywords is that the C++ keywords can throw and catch exceptions with many different types of parameters, including C++ objects, while the MFC macros only used parameters of the special CException class. Although you can throw and catch exceptions with different parameter types, I think it is best and easiest to continue using the MFC CException class for your work.

Adding Exception Handling to Your Application

There are several places in the ErectorSet application where you should add exception processing. The most notable, of course, is when retrieving a device context, the example that you have been reading about in most of this chapter so far. However, I'm not trying to actually create a full-blown, professional application here. Instead, the intention is to provide clear and understandable examples for your own work. To learn about exceptions, then, you will work with exceptions that are caused in another common part of your program: serialization.

You probably haven't given the serialization process another thought since you first added the serialization code in Chapter 5. And this pretty much works, since you haven't really changed the specifications of your saved documents up to now. However, with the addition of scrolling, your documents now have one additional item of information that should be saved with them: the document size.

N O T E   Since all your documents are one size, it isn't mandatory that you save the size with the documents at this point. And, in fact, you can save and reload a document from ErectorSet now with no trouble, even though it can be larger than the view. However, in most scrolling applications, your documents will be different sizes; in that case, the present code would have an internal error—displaying a document of the wrong size—if you tried to save and restore a document that is not the default size. The code here handles that situation and prevents that error.

Default Exception Handling

The first step in this process is to save and restore the document size when you are serializing the document. Listing 8.4 shows the new code to do that.

Listing 8.4

```
////////////////////////////////////////////////////////////////////////
// CErectorDoc serialization

// This function saves and restores the document to an external file
//    using the class CArchive.
void CErectorDoc::Serialize(CArchive& ar)
{
    if (ar.IsStoring())
    {
        // first store document size
        ar << m_sizeDoc;
    }
    else
    {
        // first retrieve document size
        ar >> m_sizeDoc;
    }

    // now ask our data members to serialize themselves
    m_beamList.Serialize( ar );
}
```

This simply stores the document size as the first element in the saved document date and retrieves it again when you load the saved document.

For testing purposes, rebuild ErectorSet now. Once it is rebuilt, create a document that is larger than the view, using the scrolling feature to move around the document, and then save the document as Serial1.set. You will use this in the next part of the chapter.

However, you have now changed the format of your saved documents. Any document that you saved previously can no longer be restored directly, since it doesn't start with the document size. To reflect that fact, you need to make one other change, as shown in Listing 8.5.

Listing 8.5

```
//////////////////////////////////////////////////////////////////////
// CErectorBeam


IMPLEMENT_SERIAL(CErectorBeam, CObject, 1)


//////////////////////////////////////////////////////////////////////
// CErectorBeam construction/destruction
```

In this case, all you have to do is change the schema number in the IMPLE-MENT_SERIAL macro from 0 to 1, indicating that all documents saved with this schema use the new format, which includes the document size, and previous formats don't. If you don't change the schema number, a user may try to open a file that was created without the document size. If they do that, they will simply get a blank document—since the document isn't in the correct format, none of the beam information loads properly. This is a particularly bad bug, since the hapless user has no way of finding out why the document no longer opens properly.

When you change the schema number, however, the MFC will automatically prevent this problem. Once the schema number is changed, any attempt to read an older version of an ErectorSet file results in the error dialog box shown in Figure 8.1. To test this, simply rebuild Erector and then open Serial1.set with the new version.

FIGURE 8.1 THE MFC AUTOMATICALLY PREVENT THE USER FROM ERRONEOUSLY OPENING AN OLDER VERSION OF AN ERECTORSET DOCUMENT BY DISPLAYING THIS DIALOG BOX.

Here's how it works. The MFC CArchive class tests the schema number as it begins to load a file. If the schema number is less than the current version, CArchive throws a CArchiveException and terminates the load process. The MFC application skeleton code in CDocument traps this exception and displays the dialog box you see in Figure 8.1.

Notice that this depends entirely on the schema number for validation. That's why I asked you to save Serial1.set from this version of ErectorSet. Since you had already added the document size before you saved Serial1.set, this document actually contains all the necessary information for display. However, you can't get it to display, because the schema number on the document is different than that in the current version of the application. The point here is that there isn't necessarily any problem with the document that causes the error; it's the schema number alone that causes the exception to be thrown.

Improving catch Processing

This is certainly an improvement over the alternative of simply displaying an empty document, but it doesn't really give the user much information. "Unexpected file format" tells you exactly what the problem is, in a way that no one will understand unless they already know what the problem is likely to be. In programming circles, this is called CIPU—pronounced "keypoo"—"Clear If Previously Understood."

You can use the try-catch combination to improve on this display. If you use the try macro around the serialization code, you can then use the catch macro to trap the exception in your own code and put up a dialog box that gives a more informative message. This will give you some experience with try and catch.

Listing 8.6 shows the new code using try and catch.

Listing 8.6

```
/////////////////////////////////////////////////////////////////////////
// CErectorDoc serialization

// This function saves and restores the document to an external file
//     using the class CArchive.
void CErectorDoc::Serialize(CArchive& ar)
{
    try
    {
```

```
        if (ar.IsStoring())
        {
            // first store document size
            ar << m_sizeDoc;
        }
        else
        {
            // first retrieve document size
            ar >> m_sizeDoc;
        }

        // now ask our data members to serialize themselves
        m_beamList.Serialize( ar );
    }
    catch(CArchiveException* pEx)
    {
        // If we get here, we have a serialization error...
        // Test for type of error.
        if( pEx->m_cause == CArchiveException::badSchema )
        {
            CString strError;
            strError = "The selected file was created by an earlier"
                        "version of ErectorSet. If cannot be opened"
                        "by the current version.";
            AfxMessageBox(strError, MB_OK | MB_ICONSTOP);
            pEx->Delete();
            AfxThrowUserException();
        }
        else
        {
            throw;
        }
    }
    return;
}
```

The try keyword is quite simple, as you can see. You simply place the previous code within the keyword's braces. This sets up the try to allow you to catch the error.

The catch processing is more complex. As you see, the catch macro takes one function-like parameter. The first information is the type of exception that you want to catch: in this case, a CArchiveException. (The exception type listed here may be any one of the types listed in Table 8.1, or you can use CException to catch all exceptions indiscriminately.) The parameter itself is a variable that will point to the exception object inside your catch code block. In this case, I simply called it pEx, since it's a pointer to an exception object. These two parameters guarantee that any exception that executes the catch code block is a CArchiveException.

Once you're inside the catch code block, you first test the exception to see if the reason for the exception is a bad schema number. You do that by checking that the pEx m_cause member is equal to CArchiveException's badSchema. Every object of CArchiveException type has a data member called m_cause, which is an integer value that is set equal to a defined exception cause. For your purposes here, you only want to handle badSchema exceptions.

C++

Notice how you reference the CArchiveException enumerated type, badSchema. Since this class—CErectorDoc—is not derived from CArchiveException, you need to completely qualify the reference. You do that by prefixing the type name by the class name, followed by two colons. This is standard C++ notation.

If the problem is a badSchema, then you use the MFC global function, AfxMessageBox to display a warning dialog box. If the problem isn't a badSchema, then you use the throw keyword to send the exception on to the next level of exception handling, where it will cause the dialog box shown in Figure 8.1 to display.

The AfxMessageBox function takes three parameters: a string to display; an optional type variable that specifies the number of buttons in the message box, the mode of the message box, and the icon used in the message box; and an optional pointer to help information for the box. In this case, you are using a simple OK button—designated by the constant MB_OK—and a stop icon—designated by the constant MB_ICONSTOP. The default application mode is used for the box. (For a complete list of box type variables, see the documentation on the `AfxMessageBox` function.) The third parameter is optional; it can be used to provide a help ID for the box. You will see in Chapter 13 how to add help information to your application. Since `AfxMessageBox` requires a string to display, you first create a CString object and set it to the desired warning string. This handles all the required parameters for `AfxMessageBox`.

NOTE

For convenience in printing the message text, I have split it into three lines. This isn't necessary, but you may find it convenient to do, so that you can see the entire message at one time. Note that you can't simply place a carriage return inside the text. That will generate an error, since the return character is invalid within the string, just as it is in standard C language code.

After the message has been displayed to the user, you still need to abort the processing so that you don't get an empty document displayed again. As the comments in the file note, you could do this with the `throw` macro, which you use if the current exception is not caused by a schema error. However, if you use `throw`, you will still get the standard error dialog box shown in Figure 8.1 as well as your new dialog box. This is a bit like overkill and will probably annoy your users. As a result, you use the MFC global function `AfxThrowUserException` to continue exception processing without displaying the additional dialog box. Using `AfxThrowUserException` does two things. First, it changes the type of the exception, so that the next level of exception processing will not handle this as an archive exception. Second, by transforming the exception into a user exception, you will generally suppress all further user notification in any case. This happens because objects of the class CUserException are expected to provide notification at the time the exception is thrown, rather than later. Therefore, the MFC default processing for CUserException objects will terminate the current processing without any additional user notification, which is just what you want.

Now rebuild ErectorSet and run it again, opening Serial1.set once more. This time you should see the new dialog box shown in Figure 8.2 that lets you know a bit more clearly what the problem is in opening this file.

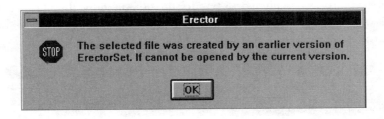

FIGURE 8.2 THE NEW DIALOG BOX GIVES THE USER CLEARER FEEDBACK ON THE PROBLEM WITH

OLDER FILE VERSIONS.

USING THE VISUAL C++ DEBUGGER

The Developer Studio provides an excellent debugger program that is integrated into the development environment. With the debugger, you can trace problems, see how your code works, and even change information in the midst of an operation. This type of tool is essential to seeing exactly what is happening in your program and fixing any problems that you find.

There are a number of things that you can set and control about debugging your application. Luckily, most of these are entirely optional. The standard defaults in the Developer Studio will provide you with most of the debugging that you need. Since debugging is a skill that everyone needs and since the default values for debugging are fine for most purposes, let's start by doing some debugging in ErectorSet. After the basic debugging is finished, you can read about how to set the options for the debugger.

Debugging During Execution

To motivate this process, let's look at the output of ErectorSet once more. In the preceding exercises, you updated the ErectorSet application to display a movement rectangle. Later, when you saw that the rectangle erased parts of the old display, you modified the OnMouseMove function that draws the movement rectangles to update the view so that the movement rectangle doesn't erase parts of existing beams.

Although this processing works fine for the default view, if you move around in the view you will see that the erasing still happens for the portion of the view that is scrolled. Figure 8.3 shows you a simple example.

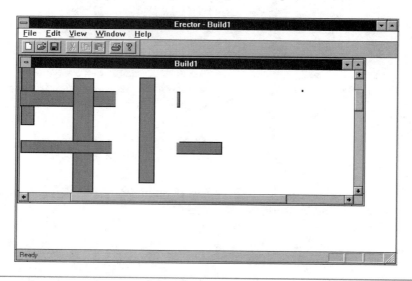

FIGURE 8.3 A SCROLLED VIEW IS STILL ERASED WHEN THE MOVEMENT RECTANGLE OBSCURES THE EXISTING BEAMS.

By the nature of this error, you can immediately tell two things. First, this is similar to the previous error, which was caused by some problems in redrawing the old beams after the movement rectangle was erased. Second, this is probably happening the OnMouseMove function in CErectorView, since this is the function that draws the movement rectangle.

Setting Breakpoints

Since the problem seems to be in OnMouseMove, the obvious way to determine the exact nature of the problem is to watch that function execute and see why it's having a problem. To do this, you can use the debug functions provided in the Developer Studio. All of the debugging tools in the Developer Studio are accessible from the Debug menu, and most of them are available by using keyboard shortcuts as well.

Begin by opening the OnMouseMove function in CErectorView. When you had this problem before, it was caused by a failure to update the views properly. Since you suspect that this might be the problem here, you want to see how the UpdateWindow function is operating. To do that, you want to set a breakpoint just before executing UpdateWindow.

A *breakpoint* is a line in your code where the debugger will stop before executing the line. This is a good way to see what is happening at that point in the code and what might need to be changed to allow your processing to continue correctly.

To set a breakpoint, follow these steps:

1. Scroll to the line where you want the breakpoint and place the cursor in the desired line. In this case, use the line immediately before the UpdateWindow function, as shown in Figure 8.4.

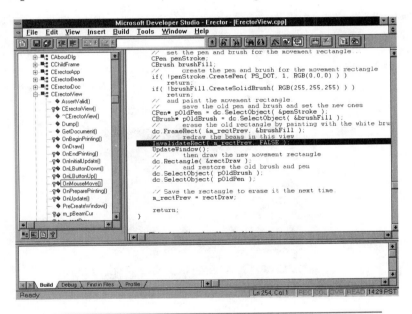

FIGURE 8.4 SELECT THE LINE OF CODE WHERE YOU WANT TO PLACE THE BREAKPOINT.

2. Select **Breakpoints** from the Edit menu, or press **Ctrl+B**. This displays the Breakpoints dialog box. Press the arrow next to the Break at text box to display the current line number, as shown in Figure 8.5. Note that the line of code that you selected is already inserted in this box.

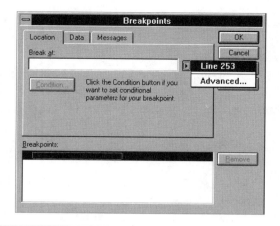

FIGURE 8.5 THE BREAKPOINTS DIALOG BOX ALLOWS YOU TO SET A BREAKPOINT AT ANY EXECUTABLE LINE IN YOUR CODE.

3. Click on the line number to add a breakpoint at the selected line of code. The Breakpoints list box now shows you the new breakpoint that you have added, as shown in Figure 8.6.

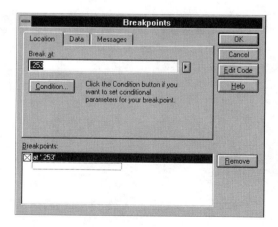

FIGURE 8.6 YOU CAN SEE ALL YOUR CURRENT BREAKPOINTS IN THE BREAKPOINTS DIALOG BOX.

4. Press **OK** to end setting breakpoints.

The checkbox next to the breakpoint is checked if the breakpoint is enabled, empty if the breakpoint is not currently enabled, and contains an asterisk (*) if the breakpoint is not supported on your currently selected configuration or platform.

When you return to your code in the Edit window, you will see that the selected line is has a small dot in front of it in a contrasting color—maroon on my monitor. This tells you that there is a breakpoint at this line of code.

SHORTCUT

To set a simple breakpoint like this one, you can simply press F9. This sets or removes a breakpoint in the current line of code without ever going to the dialog box. The breakpoint that it sets is always a simple, Break at Location type. Another easy way to set a simple breakpoint is by using the right mouse button's pop-up menu, which contains an Insert/Remove Breakpoint item.

You have just set the simplest type of breakpoint, where the program halts temporarily whenever the selected line of code is about to be executed. There are other types of breakpoints as well, which make working with code easier.

As you can see on the Breakpoint dialog box, you can set three types of breakpoints. Each is represented by a specific tab: Location, Data, and Messages. The Location breakpoints are based on a specific line in your code. The Data breakpoints are based on a specific data item in your code. The Messages breakpoints are the most complex and are based on messages sent to or from a traditional "window procedure" or **WndProc**. Generally, you don't need to worry about this when you are developing a simple MFC application, such as ErectorSet.

In addition, you can add a condition to a Location breakpoint so that the program only stops at that location when a specific condition occurs. You do this by clicking the **Condition...** button. This displays the Breakpoint Condition dialog box shown in Figure 8.7.

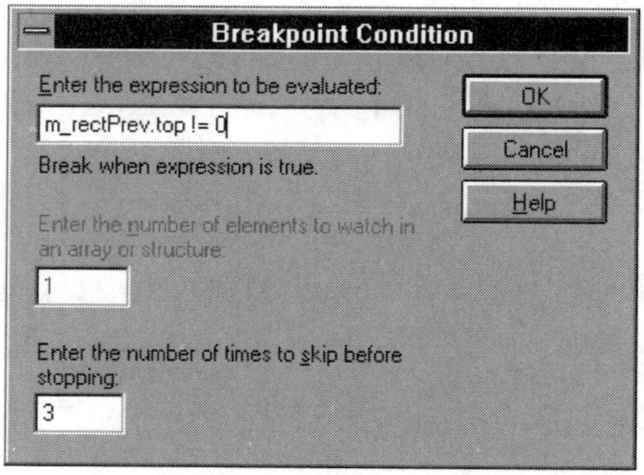

FIGURE 8.7 THE BREAKPOINT CONDITION DIALOG BOX ALLOWS YOU TO SET A VARIETY OF CONDITIONS THAT AFFECT YOUR BREAKPOINT LOCATION.

Enter the expression to be evaluated in the Enter text box. If you enter an expression that evaluates to a Boolean (TRUE or FALSE), the program will stop at the breakpoint location when the condition is TRUE. If you enter an expression that does not evaluate to a Boolean, the program will stop at the location if the expression has changed since the last time through the location. Note that the legend underneath the text box changes according to the expression to remind you what type of evaluation will be performed.

If you enter a Boolean expression or if you enter no expression, you can allow the program to execute a given number of times before executing the break by entering a value in the Skip text box. If the expression is an array or structure, you can enter the exact element to watch in the Number text box.

This set of choices is actually similar to the Data breakpoint, but here the conditional expression is tested only when the specified location in your code is executed. In the Data breakpoint, the data element or expression is tested as each line of code executes.

All of these types of breakpoints have a useful place when you're debugging, but the most common breakpoints are the two types of Location breakpoints: setting an absolute breakpoint at a specific location and setting a conditional breakpoint at a specific location.

N O T E

There are reasons why some of these breakpoint options are used less frequently than others. The problem with Data breakpoints generally is that Visual C++ must actually perform an evaluation of the expression after each line of code. In some cases, the data can be placed in a special *debug register*, which allows the application to run at a reasonable speed even while performing the evaluation. However, very often the data must be accessed from memory on each execution cycle for evaluation. If you set such a breakpoint and run your application, the application may run so slowly that you think that it has crashed or has some grievous internal problem. On the other hand, if you attach the condition to a specific location, then Visual C++ only has to perform the test when that line is executed, and you probably won't experience any slowness from that. Data breakpoints may still be useful; you just need to understand that they will probably slow the processing down enormously.

Tracking Execution

Now that you have set a breakpoint, let's use it to see what's happening in the OnMouseMove function. Go to the Build menu and select **Debug**. Then select **Go** or press **F5**. Both of these start the ErectorSet application, Erector.exe, using the debugger. You should see the application start in the normal way; since you placed a breakpoint in the OnMouseMove function, there is as yet no reason for the breakpoint to be activated (you haven't used the mouse).

Now click the mouse and start to draw a beam. As soon as you do, you execute the OnMouseMove function, and you trip the breakpoint. The debugger immediately stops your application's execution and returns you to the Developer Studio's debug display, with a yellow arrow pointing to the line that contains the breakpoint, as shown in Figure 8.8.

Let's take a moment to look at how the standard debug display works. As you can see, the top pane of the screen is the standard edit pane, now expanded to the full width of the screen, which displays the function that you are currently executing. The bottom of the screen is divided into two panes: a Variables pane, which displays the currently active variables in your function, along with the current execution context for them; and a Watch pane, which shows any variables that you have specifically requested for display. At present, nothing is shown here because you haven't asked for anything to be watched. Finally, there is a small Debug toolbar displayed to the right of the screen. Except the edit pane, all of these panes are dockable, so you can move them around and resize them as you wish.

FIGURE 8.8 WHEN YOUR APPLICATION STARTS TO EXECUTE A LINE OF CODE WITH A BREAKPOINT, YOU ARE RETURNED TO THE DEVELOPER STUDIO IN DEBUG MODE.

In addition to the two panes that are displayed by default, there are four buttons in the Debug toolbar that you can use to display other types of information. These are:

- *Registers* displays a pane that shows the current values in the internal registers.

- *Memory* displays a pane that shows the contents of memory at a given location.

- *Call Stack* displays a pane that shows the call stack. The call stack is the list of all the functions that are currently being executed that lead up to the point where your program is at the time of the break.

- *Disassembly* changes the edit pane to show the current code as assembly language, with the C++ code as comments.

You can now step, line by line, through your application's code, either by using the Debug menu selections or by pressing the appropriate button on the toolbar. Once you have stopped your application at a breakpoint, you can use any one of the commands shown in Table 8.2 to continue processing.

TABLE 8.2 OPTIONS FOR MOVING THROUGH CODE

Command	Shortcut Key	Purpose
Go	F5	Resumes execution of the application. The execution will stop at the next breakpoint, if any is encountered.
Stop Debugging	Alt+F5	Terminates execution immediately in a normal fashion.
Restart	Shift+F5	Terminates execution immediately and then restarts the application.
Step Into	F8	Steps into the next function that will execute, even if the next line of code is in another module.
Step Over	F10	Executes the current line of code and stops at the next line of code in your current function.
Step Out	Shift+F7	Executes all of the code in your current function and stops at the first line of code outside the function.
Run to Cursor	F7	Executes up to the line of code where you have positioned the cursor. This effectively sets a temporary breakpoint at the line where the cursor is located.

The yellow arrow will move as you step through your code, showing the next line to be executed. Whenever the arrow stops, the program also stops.

WARNING

There is one case where this isn't true: when you continue running the program by pressing F5 or by hitting the Go button on the Debug toolbar. In that case, the program takes off, executing at normal speed, but the arrow remains at the line where it was when you resumed execution. This is a little disconcerting until you get used to it. (Personally, I consider this a bug in the Developer Studio—I think the arrow should be hidden whenever your program is running normally—but obviously Microsoft doesn't agree with me, since this has been happening for the last several releases of Visual C++. I don't think it will change any time soon.)

Watching Variables

Before proceeding, however, you need to see what information is presently being used in the function. Some information is automatically displayed in the Variables pane; if what you need is shown there, you don't need to do anything. However, if you want to see other information, you can use the Debug menu command **QuickWatch** (or press **Shift+F9**) to display any current variables.

N O T E

The Variables pane can display several types of information. Notice that there are three tabs at the bottom of the pane. The Auto tab—the default—displays variables used in the current line of code and in the previous line. The Locals tab displays information about variables that are local to the function. The "this" tab displays information about the current object—which, you remember, is referred to by the keyword this in your code.

To use QuickWatch, highlight the variable that you want to see. In this case, for example, you certainly want to see the values in m_rectPrev and rectDraw to verify that everything is working at this point. m_rectPrev is already displayed in the Variables pane, but rectDraw isn't. Highlight rectDraw and press **Shift+F9** to display the QuickWatch dialog box shown in Figure 8.9.

There are several points to note about this dialog box. First, notice that the data element that you selected, rectDraw, appears in the dialog box with a minus sign in front of it, while underneath is another entry, tagRect, which has a plus sign in front of it. The minus sign indicates that the named variable is fully displayed. The plus sign indicates that there is more information that you can display if you want. This is the same display method used for showing the class information, and it works the same way: click on the plus to display additional information and on the minus to collapse the display.

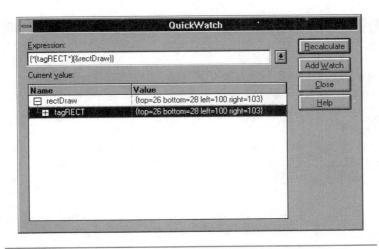

FIGURE 8.9 THE QUICKWATCH DIALOG BOX ALLOWS YOU TO TAKE A QUICK LOOK AT ANY CURRENTLY DEFINED AND AVAILABLE VARIABLE IN YOUR PROGRAM.

Notice that if you select a simple data element—an integer, for example, such as one of the data elements that make up the `tagRect`—it has no parts to be displayed, so it doesn't have a plus or minus in front of it: what you see is what you get. Also, because it is a simple data item, you can now change the value of the selected item by typing a new value over the old one in the display.

SHORTCUT

If all you want is to see the value of a data item, you can simply place your cursor over the data item in the edit window. After a moment, this will automatically trigger a display of the item's value in a contrasting color on the edit pane, similar to the information displayed on the top line of the QuickWatch dialog box. Of course, you can't change values or control the display when you use this method, but it's a quick and easy way to check data information when you're working on a complex problem.

In this case, *rectDraw* looks reasonable, and the values for m_rectPrev are not yet set, since this is the first time that you are executing this function. (This suggests that you may want to initialize m_rectPrev in your constructor at some future time.) To continue processing, press **F5**.

When you do that, you will briefly see the ErectorSet application, and then you will be back at the breakpoint. Once you think about this, it makes perfect sense. You execute OnMouseMove every time the mouse moves in the document view. Naturally, the moment you get back to the view and start to move the mouse, you will cause another break, since you'll execute OnMouseMove again.

Use QuickWatch to display the rectDraw again. Once again, you see coordinate values that appear valid for your rectangle, and m_rectPrev now has the values you saw previously in rectDraw. So far, so good.

However, you want to watch these two rectangles, as one of them is the probable culprit in the problem that you have. You can do this most easily by adding the rectDraw variable to the permanent Watch window. This saves you having to select and QuickWatch the same variable repeatedly.

To move the current QuickWatch variable to the Watch list, simply press the **Add Watch** button. This moves the display to the permanent Watch window, as shown in Figure 8.10.

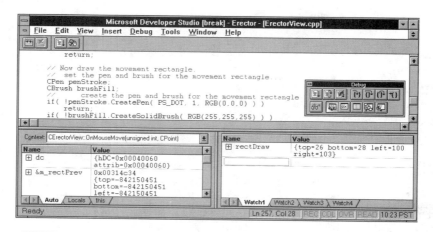

FIGURE 8.10 YOU CAN USE THE WATCH WINDOW TO DISPLAY ANY SELECTED SET OF VARIABLES ON A PERMANENT BASIS.

Of course, the beams don't fail until you scroll the view to another part of the document. How are you ever going to do that, when you keep stopping every time you simply move the mouse? One answer, of course, would be to remove the breakpoint, called *clearing* it, and then do some work and reinstate the breakpoint later, when you expect the error to occur. This works, but it is a bit cumbersome. Luckily the Developer Studio has a special provision that helps speed up this process.

Open the Breakpoints dialog box again by pressing **Ctrl+B**. Highlight the current breakpoint in the Breakpoints list as shown in Figure 8.11.

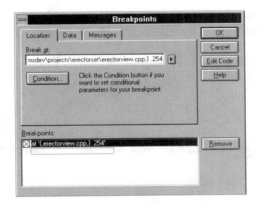

FIGURE 8.11 YOU CAN ALSO USE THE BREAKPOINTS DIALOG BOX TO ENABLE AND DISABLE BREAKPOINTS TEMPORARILY.

Notice that the box in front of the breakpoint is checked; this indicates that the breakpoint is currently active. Now click once on the checkbox to clear it. This removes the check in the box, indicating that the breakpoint is temporarily disabled. It also changes the dot displayed in front of your line of code to an empty circle. By disabling the breakpoint, you allow the application to run normally without losing the breakpoint itself.

SHORTCUT

You can enable and disable breakpoints by placing your cursor on the line of code with the breakpoint in the edit window and pressing F9. This toggles the breakpoint: if it was active, it becomes disabled, and vice versa. Also, if you put your cursor on a line without a breakpoint, pressing F9 will set one at that line.

Now close the Breakpoints dialog box and press **F5** to run the application. Scroll down and to the right and draw a beam. Now use Window's task switching to return to Visual C++ and the Workbench. Once there, use the Breakpoints dialog box again and enable your breakpoint. Then, since ErectorSet is still running, use task switching to return to it and begin to draw another beam in the scrolled area.

As soon as you move the mouse, the program encounters the newly enabled breakpoint and is stopped. At that time, the Watch window display is updated with the current values of m_rectPrev and rectDraw. Now the points in m_rectPrev are all zero because the last action that you took was to draw a beam and that automatically sets m_rectPrev to the empty rectangle, that is, all the coordinates are set to zero.

Press **F5** to continue processing. Again, as soon as you move the mouse, the application trips the breakpoint and stops, and the Watch is updated with the new values. Figure 8.12 shows you what my values were; yours, of course, will be somewhat different.

FIGURE 8.12 THE WATCH WINDOW'S DISPLAY GIVES YOU A CLUE ABOUT WHAT THE PROBLEM IS IN ERECTORSET.

These values are clearly too large; the entire screen is only 640 pixels wide and 480 pixels high. The points shown here can barely be on the screen at all!

And, of course, they're not—they're document coordinates, not screen coordinates. This is a simple, but common, error. Early in the OnMouseMove function, you convert the mouse point coordinates from device coordinates to the logical coordinates used in the beams. This is essential as you need to calculate and draw the movement rectangle based on the beam coordinates. In the same way, the FrameRect function requires the previous rectangle to be in logical coordinates for erasing. However, as you saw in the earlier drawing code, the InvalidateRect function requires device coordinates, not logical ones, since it is not a GDI function—that is, it doesn't reference the device context.

So the problem here is quite simple. You need to convert the logical coordinates in m_rectPrev into device coordinates before you use it in InvalidateRect.

Terminate your debugging session by choosing **Stop Debugging** from the Debug menu or pressing **Alt+F5**. Then add the line of code to your OnMouseMove function shown in Listing 8.7.

Listing 8.7

```
// This function handles MouseMove up messages.
//    NOTE that this does _not_ call inherited behavior.
void CErectorView::OnMouseMove(UINT /* nFlags */, CPoint point)
{
    // Mouse button up is notable only if the user is currently drawing
    //    a new beam by dragging the mouse.
    //    In that case, we need to capture the mouse position.
    if ( GetCapture() != this )
        return;           // If this view didn't capture the mouse,
                          //    the user isn't drawing in our window.


    //   ...lots of code left out...


    //          erase the old rectangle by painting with the white brush
    dc.FrameRect( &m_rectPrev, &brushFill );
    //          redraw the beams in this view
    dc.LPtoDP( &m_rectPrev );
```

```
InvalidateRect( m_rectPrev, FALSE );
UpdateWindow();
//          then draw the new movement rectangle


//   ... and so on...
```

Once you convert the rectangle's coordinates to device coordinates, you will find that the problem of the erased beams disappears throughout your document.

Checking Program Operation

The Developer Studio debugger is tremendously useful in helping you find problems once you notice that they exist. However, the ideal is to avoid having problems in the first place.

I know that sounds like being for motherhood and apple pie. I've never met a programmer who deliberately tried to introduce bugs into his or her code, I never expect to meet one, and I bet you haven't met one either. So what exactly does "avoid having problems" mean in real life?

Basically, it means constructing code that tries to discover problems before they occur and lets you know what the problem is in a clear and useful way. We all recognize that any piece of complex code will have some unusual outcomes—problems or bugs, however you want to look at them. The idea is to add code to our basic processing that checks for errors and anomalous conditions internally. Such code represents a constant guard that can alert you to problems before they become major errors and before they pass into the code you give to your users.

The only problem with this, of course, is that any additional code that you add to your application inevitably takes computer cycles to process and that slows down the actual work that your application is doing. So it appears that you have an unpleasant trade-off: slow code that is self-checking and safe or fast code that is unreliable.

Actually, there is a good solution to this problem. This is the _DEBUG mode for compilation and processing. The MFC defines a preprocessor variable, called _DEBUG, that is set to indicate whether the current code is being created for debugging or for release. When _DEBUG is defined, the MFC performs additional tests in the code to check for correct operation; when _DEBUG is not defined, the code reverts to the fastest mode.

A perfect example of this approach is provided in the CErectorView class. Remember that the AppWizard generated a lot of the basic code for you. As part of this code, AppWizard inserted some debugging code. Listing 8.8 shows you the code that is included in the CErectorView class in ErectorView.cpp purely for debugging.

Listing 8.8

```
//    ...in ErectorView.cpp...


/////////////////////////////////////////////////////////////////////////
// CErectorView diagnostics

#ifdef _DEBUG
void CErectorView::AssertValid() const
{
     CScrollView::AssertValid();
}


void CErectorView::Dump(CDumpContext& dc) const
{
     CScrollView::Dump(dc);
}


CErectorDoc* CErectorView::GetDocument() // non-debug version is inline
{
     ASSERT(m_pDocument->IsKindOf(RUNTIME_CLASS(CErectorDoc)));
     return (CErectorDoc*)m_pDocument;
}
#endif //_DEBUG
```

As you can see, this code is enclosed in a pair of preprocessor directives, #ifdef and #endif. These two directives bracket the code that is used only when _DEBUG is on—that is, when it is defined. If _DEBUG is not defined, then the code shown here is not compiled and is removed from the working application.

Listing 8.9 shows the matching code in ErectorView.h that fills in a non-debug version of the GetDocument function.

Listing 8.9

```
//   ...in ErectorView.h...


#ifndef _DEBUG  // debug version in ErectorView.cpp
inline CErectorDoc* CErectorView::GetDocument()
   { return (CErectorDoc*)m_pDocument; }
#endif
```

Notice that these two pieces of code are exactly complementary: if one is included, the other one is not.

ASSERT *Macro Processing*

The debug version of `GetDocument` provides some additional insight to useful methods for insuring that your code works correctly. In this code, if the _DEBUG preprocessor variable is defined, the new version of `GetDocument` checks to be sure that the available document pointer belongs to the document type, CErectorDoc. This ensures that the remainder of the code, and indeed any subsequent processing that expects to use the returned pointer, can rely on the fact that the pointer being returned actually points to an object of type CErectorDoc.

It does that by using the `ASSERT` macro. The `ASSERT` macro takes a Boolean expression as an argument and tests it. If the argument evaluates to `TRUE` (nonzero), processing continues in the normal sequence. If the argument evaluates to `FALSE` (zero), the macro prints a diagnostic message and terminates the program. For example, if this assertion failed, you would see a dialog box as shown in Figure 8.13.

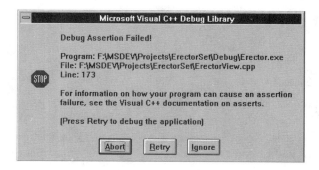

FIGURE 8.13 WHEN AN ASSERTION FAILS IN YOUR DEBUG CODE, YOU WILL SEE A DIALOG BOX LIKE THIS.

As the dialog box states, you can move from here directly into the debugger at the specified location by pressing the **Retry** button. This works even if you are not executing in the debugger at the moment. Alternatively, you can **abort** the execution at this point, or you can ignore the assertion and continue processing.

In fact, the ASSERT macro is used in many places as a way to validate function arguments and other vital information. The important point when using ASSERT is to remember that it takes any expression that will resolve into a Boolean value. If the Boolean is TRUE, the ASSERT macro does nothing; if it is FALSE, it displays a warning message.

NOTE

Remember that the ASSERT macro as defined in the MFC is only operative in the debug version of the classes, that is, when the _DEBUG flag is defined. In the release version of the application, the ASSERT macro does nothing. If you need to test something that must always be executed, you can use the VERIFY macro. This macro performs just like ASSERT in the debug versions, by evaluating its argument and posting a message if the test fails. In the release version, VERIFY still evaluates the argument, but it will never generate a message. This differs from ASSERT, which doesn't even evaluate the argument in the release version.

Object Checking with ASSERT_VALID

Sometimes, particularly in object-oriented programming, you would like to do more than simply test an expression. When you are handling objects that are created from classes, you would often like to ensure that the objects themselves are uncorrupted.

You can do this by using the special macro, ASSERT_VALID. The ASSERT_VALID macro takes a single argument, which is any object derived from CObject, and performs a series of tests to validate the object. If the object fails any of these tests, ASSERT_VALID behaves just like ASSERT and displays a warning dialog box.

ASSERT_VALID performs three tests. First, it tests the pointer to the given object to ensure that the pointer is not NULL. Second, it tests the pointer to ensure that it is a valid pointer. Third, and most importantly, it calls the object's AssertValid function. When you are writing your classes, you can override

AssertValid and test to be sure that all elements required by your class are present in the object.

If you look back at Listing 8.8, you will see that the AssertValid function is automatically overridden in the debug version of your classes by a simple AssertValid function that just calls AssertValid in its base class. If you want to use ASSERT_VALID, you should add your own testing code to the AssertValid function in your classes, placing your tests after the call to the base class. Typically, you would test for the variables and other data that are required by your class, using the ASSERT macro to validate them.

When Not to Use Assertions

From what you have read so far, I think you can easily see that there are two cases where you don't want to use the ASSERT macro or its cousin, VERIFY. First, you don't want to use ASSERT for normal processing. For example, you should never use an assertion for the processing in SetupRect. Although SetupRect returns a Boolean value that notifies the calling function of success or failure, both outcomes are part of normal processing that you should handle in a normal fashion, as you saw earlier.

Second, you don't want to use ASSERT for handling exceptions. As you already know, exceptions are events that happen outside of your own code; they are or may be problems, but they don't represent something that should never happen. Use the ASSERT macro to test for situations that are within your program's control and that should never happen if the program functions correctly. The test for a valid CErectorDoc member is a good example.

Setting up for Debugging

Since all of this extra processing only happens in the debug version of the MFC, the obvious question is how to enable and disable the debug version. First of all, since all of these methods work in your current application, you already understand that any Visual C++ project is normally set up to start immediately using debugging. This is certainly what you want, since most projects start in the building and testing phase and only later move to a release form. Naturally, it is important for you to understand how to enable and disable debug processing in your application.

Essentially there are two steps that you need to take to get debugging in your application. First, you need to set the _DEBUG symbol on so that all of your

#ifdefs work correctly. Second, you need to add specific debugging information to your application so that the Developer Studio debugger can identify the current position in your code and tie it back to the code modules you are using. This type of symbol information must be included in the object modules when you compile them for the debugger to work correctly. Naturally, the Developer Studio makes all of this quite easy for you.

Build Requirements

To set the debugging features on or off, simply choose the correct Default Project Configuration. There are two ways to do this. First, you can choose **Set Default Configuration...** from the Build menu to display the Default Project Configuration dialog box shown in Figure 8.14.

FIGURE 8.14 THE DEFAULT PROJECT CONFIGURATION DIALOG BOX ALLOWS YOU TO SWITCH BETWEEN DEBUG AND RELEASE VERSIONS WITH A CLICK.

As you can see, this dialog box lists the currently available configurations for your project. In this case, you have two: one for Win32Debug and one for Win32Release. When you select one or the other of these, you automatically set your project to use the debug settings for everything or not, as the choice may be. To switch from debug to release is just as simple as clicking on the desired configuration in this dialog and then choosing **OK**.

SHORTCUT

An easier way to make this change is to use the Project toolbar. The default Project toolbar has a list box that displays the currently selected project configuration, and the arrow button next to the list box displays a drop-down list of all the currently available configurations. To change the default, simply select another configuration from the list. That's all there is to it.

An obvious question is how to add and remove configurations from this list. All versions of Visual C++ allow you to create both Win32Debug and Win32Release versions of applications. As a default, all projects created with the Developer Studio have release and debug versions defined, and the debug version is automatically selected as the Default Project Configuration, as you read earlier. You can create and remove project configurations by using the Configurations dialog box, displayed by choosing **Configurations** from the Build menu. The available configurations depend on what you have installed with Visual C++. For example, if you have the Macintosh Cross-Development edition included with your Visual C++, you can set project configurations to create Macintosh applications. You will see how to do this in Chapter 14, when you read about using the Cross-Development edition.

When you choose one of these configurations, you are actually affecting settings in the other parts of the Project Options. So you understand what's happening, let's look at them briefly.

The first set are the compiler options. To inspect them, choose **Settings...** from the Build menu to display the Project Settings dialog box and click on the **C/C++** tab. This displays the general compiler options and specific settings for debugging, as shown in Figure 8.15.

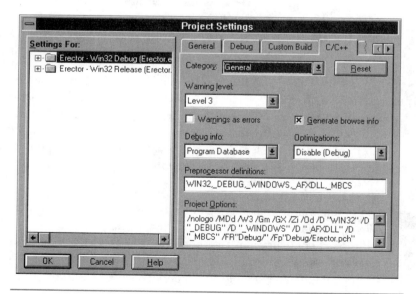

FIGURE 8.15 THE C/C++ TAB OF THE PROJECT SETTINGS DIALOG BOX ALLOWS YOU TO SET THE DEBUG FLAG GLOBALLY FOR YOUR APPLICATION.

Note the Settings for list on the left of the dialog box. You can use this list to choose specific project configurations or even specific files within the project. The settings displayed in the dialog box are the settings for the item(s) you choose here; and any changes you make are used for the item(s) you choose. As you can see, here I have selected the Win32Debug configuration from the list, so all the items displayed are for this project configuration.

The Preprocessor directives text box displayed in Figure 8.15 shows the actual options that are sent to the compiler when you compile any of the modules in this configuration of your application. Notice that the string "_DEBUG" is defined here. In special situations you may find that you will want to modify the preprocessor directives in some ways. If you need to do so, here it is where to do it.

In addition to the compiler options, you also may need to set some linker options. If you press the **Link** tab, the display changes and you will again find one of the debugging options, as shown in Figure 8.16.

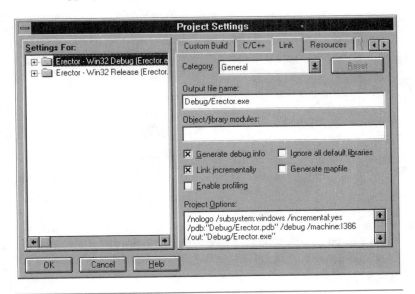

FIGURE 8.16 THE GENERATE DEBUG INFO CHECKBOX IN THE LINK TAB ALSO MUST BE CHECKED TO USE THE DEBUGGER WITH YOUR APPLICATION.

This is a simple checkbox that determines whether the linker creates debugging information or not. Again, this is set automatically by choosing the

Win32Debug project configuration, so you don't need to set it here under ordinary circumstances.

Finally, you can use the Resources tab to set information for the Resource Compiler. Press the **Resources** tab to display the Resources settings shown in Figure 8.17.

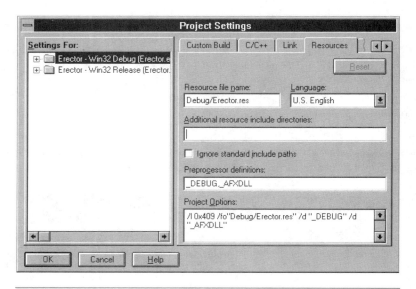

FIGURE 8.17 THE RESOURCE TAB ALLOWS YOU TO DEFINE OTHER SYMBOLS TO BE USED WHEN COMPILING THE RESOURCES FOR YOUR PROJECT.

Again, the Preprocessor definitions section of this dialog box allows you to set strings that will be defined for the selected configuration(s) of your project. Any symbols that you type into this box will be defined for your project's resources automatically. Notice that the _DEBUG symbol is placed here. In this way, you can enter your own symbols that can also be used when working with resources for a selected project configuration.

These are the options that must be set to use debugging in your application. Luckily, the Developer Studio makes it easy for you to set them consistently and correctly.

TRACKING APPLICATION PROCESSING

There is one more tool in the debugging arsenal that is most important and useful. This is the ability to send little messages and notifications to yourself throughout a program. This facility is called *tracing* a program and it is implemented in the MFC by using the special TRACE macro and its relatives.

A *trace* is code in your application that displays a message, and sometimes displays variables to tell you the current state of the program. Although tracing can be useful under many circumstances, there are two times when it is almost the only way—certainly the only simple way—to tell what's happening in your program.

First of all, you need tracing when breakpoints in the debugger can't show you what is happening in your program. This may occur, for example, because the breakpoints interfere with the problem symptoms. One such situation was the problem of erasing the beams. Remember that when you set a breakpoint to monitor what's happening to the beams, when you return to the application the beams will be redrawn. This happens because the debugger switches to the Developer Studio display when it hits the breakpoint, thus covering the application window. When you return to the application, Windows automatically generates an Update message that causes the beams to be redrawn. In the actual code, you were able to debug this problem without returning to the application simply by looking at the variables. However, if you had needed to return to the ErectorSet window to see what the problem was, the tell-tale traces would have been gone when you got there.

The second situation where you need to trace execution is where there is too much going on. A good example of this is something that only fails occasionally. In this case, it's impossible to use the debugger and breakpoints to step through the code for a whole series of times. It's much easier and better to insert a trace and simply display some information about the problem. Often, if you do that, you will find out at least enough to insert a breakpoint with a condition, so that you only stop when the exact problem occurs.

Using Tracing in Your Application

In most programming languages, you have some simple method for displaying a single string of output. In C, for example, you can use the printf or fprintf library functions to display formatted strings and data. Programmers often use these tools to implement tracing in their applications.

Unfortunately, such a simple approach doesn't work in Windows. Since Windows displays everything in a window, there is a fair amount of overhead necessary to create, manage, and display even a single line of text in a window. For this reason, the MFC and Visual C++ don't support functions like `printf`.

But tracing is such a useful idea that the MFC have a special macro, appropriately called `TRACE`, that implements this feature within your MFC application. Using `TRACE` isn't quite as simple as presenting it with a string, but it's almost that easy. Let's see an example of how you might use tracing in your application.

To do this, let me pose a question: how do you know that the hint processing that you installed for displaying beams in the view works? To refresh your memory, here's the situation. You have added code to CErectorView's `OnLButtonUp` function to pass the current beam rectangle as a hint to other views. This hint is then retrieved in the `OnUpdate` function and used to invalidate only the beam rectangle. Finally, the `OnDraw` function uses the invalid rectangle to determine whether to actually redraw a given beam. The idea is that, if the beam wasn't affected by the new beam, it doesn't need to be redrawn. Listing 8.10 shows you the relevant code in `OnDraw`.

Listing 8.10

```
//////////////////////////////////////////////////////////////////////////
// CErectorView drawing

void CErectorView::OnDraw(CDC* pDC)
{
    CErectorDoc* pDoc = GetDocument();
    ASSERT_VALID(pDoc);

    // Get invalid rect for checking whether beam should be drawn
    CRect rectClip;
    pDC->GetClipBox( &rectClip );

    // The view requests each beam draw itself
    //    by called CErectorBeam::DrawBeam()
    CRect rectBeam;
```

```
    for( POSITION pos = pDoc->GetFirstBeamPosition(); pos != NULL; )
{
        CErectorBeam* pBeam = pDoc->GetNextBeam( pos );
        // Check to see if beam falls inside invalid rect
        rectBeam = pBeam->GetCurrentBeam();
        if( rectBeam.IntersectRect( &rectBeam, &rectClip ) )
        //          and only draw it if it does.
            pBeam->DrawBeam( pDC );
}


    return;
}
```

The question is, how do you know that you're not actually drawing all the beams every time or, more precisely, how do you know that the `if` test with `IntersectRect` works?

This is a problem that falls into one of the two categories that I mentioned before. Your first thought might be to simply step through the code and see whether the if function executes every time. Unfortunately, you can't do that because the very fact that you hit the breakpoint will automatically change the invalid rectangle into the entire client area for ErectorSet. So every time you try to track the processing, you will go through the loop for every beam.

This is a job for TRACE! What you want to do here is simply count the number of beams and put out a short message telling what the number of the beam being drawn is when you draw it. If the hint is working correctly, then you should see only some of the beams being drawn; if it isn't, then you will see all of the beam numbers being drawn every time.

It's only the work of a moment to add this simple code to the `OnDraw` function. Listing 8.11 shows you the new, tracing version of `OnDraw`.

Listing 8.11

```
/////////////////////////////////////////////////////////////////////////
// CErectorView drawing

void CErectorView::OnDraw(CDC* pDC)
{
```

```
        CErectorDoc* pDoc = GetDocument();
        ASSERT_VALID(pDoc);

        // Get invalid rect for checking whether beam should be drawn
        CRect rectClip;
        pDC->GetClipBox( &rectClip );

        // The view requests each beam draw itself
        //     by called CErectorBeam::DrawBeam()
        int i = 0;
        CRect rectBeam;
        for( POSITION pos = pDoc->GetFirstBeamPosition(); pos != NULL; )
        {
            i += 1;
            CErectorBeam* pBeam = pDoc->GetNextBeam( pos );
            // Check to see if beam falls inside invalid rect
            rectBeam = pBeam->GetCurrentBeam();
            if( rectBeam.IntersectRect( &rectBeam, &rectClip ) )
            //            and only draw it if it does.
            {
                TRACE("Drawing beam %d\n", i);
                pBeam->DrawBeam( pDC );
            }
        }

        return;
    }
```

This is mostly simple code. You establish your counter, i, outside the beam loop and increment it immediately inside the loop. Then you use the TRACE macro to display the beam number just before you draw the beam.

If you've ever used printf, this will be very familiar territory. TRACE uses the same mechanisms for displaying data as printf. TRACE takes a single argument, which is a string plus an optional series of variables. You display the variables in the string by using format codes. The variables are converted for printing using the format codes specified in the string. Each format code is preceded by the character %. Listing 8.11 illustrates a typical use of the format code: the string to be displayed contains a format code, %d, which specifies that the integer variable, i, is to be converted and inserted at that point in the string. If you want to print additional variables, you would list them after one another, separated by commas. They must be in the same sequence as the format codes in the string to be displayed. Table 8.4 lists the most common format codes and what type of data they convert.

TABLE 8.4 COMMON FORMAT CODES USED IN TRACE

Code Character	Type of Argument
d, i	Decimal number
x, X	Unsigned hexadecimal number
u	Unsigned decimal number
c	Single character
s	String
f	Floating-point number
g, G	Floating-point number using exponential notation
%	A double %% in the string prints as a single %

There are more options than these, but generally you won't need any more for TRACE processing.

At this point, you could recompile ErectorSet and begin to use the trace output. However, there are one or two points that you need to understand before running TRACE. Here are the steps that you need to take to make TRACE work.

1. Add the TRACE code to your application.
2. Rebuild the application with the TRACE code.
3. Use the MFC Tracer application to turn tracing on.
4. Run the application using the debugger to get the TRACE information listed in the Output pane of Developers Studio.

With your code now updated with the TRACE, you need to rebuild the application. Be sure that your project is still in Debug mode—TRACE, like other debugging macros, won't work if the project is in Release mode.

Using the MFC Tracer Application

Just because you have put a TRACE macro into your code doesn't mean that you will see any trace output. To see your trace output, two additional steps have to be taken. First, you have to enable tracing in the application. Second, you have to provide somewhere for the trace output to go.

The first step is to turn tracing on in your application. To do this, you have to set the afxTraceEnabled flag to 1 and enable the trace options that you want by setting the afxTraceFlags to appropriate values. There are, in fact, several ways to do this: you can actually set the flag(s) in your code; you can set it with the debugger while you're running; or you can let it be set from the afx.ini file in your Windows directory.

It turns out that the last option is, in fact, by far the easiest to use, because Visual C++ comes with a useful little utility program called MFC Tracer that manages this for you. MFC Tracer both turns on tracing and sets the trace flags to the appropriate values by the use of a simple dialog box and checkboxes. This is much easier to use than any alternative since it allows you to set the flags and turn tracing off and on in a natural way.

For your purposes here, you will use Tracer to turn tracing on in your application. Simply select **MFC Tracer** from the Tools menu. This launches this program that will display the MFC Trace Options dialog box shown in Figure 8.18.

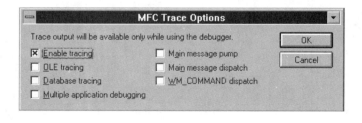

FIGURE 8.18 THE MFC TRACE OPTIONS DIALOG BOX PROVIDES A CONVENIENT WAY TO ENABLE TRACING AND SET TRACE OPTION FOR YOUR APPLICATION.

The first checkbox, **Enable tracing**, sets the TraceEnabled flag in afx.ini to 1. This turns on tracing in your application, since the afxTraceEnabled global flag is set from the `afx.ini` file. The remaining boxes in MFC Trace Options determine what types of tracing are done within the application. As you can see, you can get automatic traces for a variety of Windows messages. This can be very useful if you are having trouble with your application and can't tell where the failure is happening. By enabling message tracing in one of these forms, you can see exactly what messages your application is receiving. Once you see what messages are being sent, you can add your own tracing to your code to see what happens when they are processed. This is a powerful tracking and debugging facility.

However, for now, you only need to review this information. Generally, as shown here, tracing is enabled for your application by default. If it happens to be off, click on the **Enable Tracing** checkbox to turn it on and then click **OK**. Once this box is checked, you can see your TRACE output.

Viewing Your TRACE Information

The last step that you have to take is provide a place for the TRACE messages to be displayed. The way to do this is to run your application using the standard debugger. This allows messages from TRACE to be sent to the Output window.

WARNING

You have to be careful when you have enabled tracing in your application. If you are not running in the debugger and do not have a Debug window open, you may experience problems when running your application. By default, TRACE looks for a debug window to display its output; if it doesn't find one, it will route its messages and output to the AUX port. (This is to allow you to run and debug your application on a different machine than the one you use for development.) This can cause several problems, including hanging your Window system for up to several minutes, or possibly causing the application to crash as TRACE tries to find a way to send the messages somewhere.

N O T E

In previous versions of Visual C++, you could create a special Debug window using the DebugWin application and display the messages there. This was the preferred option for most developers. That's all history now, so you have to run the debugger to see trace messages in Visual C++ 4.0.

Now that you have all this information, you naturally would like to see the TRACE output. Now execute your application by selecting **Debug** and then **Go** from the Build menu to run your application from the debugger.

Since you want to verify that you are not redrawing every beam, use the following steps to draw beams:

1. Draw two horizontal beams in your document. These will be beams numbered 1 and 2. Neither should generate any TRACE output since neither has to be redrawn.

2. Draw a single vertical beam from the bottom to the top of the view, crossing the second beam first. This is beam 3, and it should generate a message that beam 2 is being redrawn and then that beam 1 is being redrawn.

3. Draw a fourth horizontal beam beneath the first two beams that does not cross any other beam. This is beam 4, and again, it should not generate any redrawing messages since it doesn't cross any other beam.

4. Finally, draw a vertical beam that crosses the second and fourth beams but no others. This is beam 5, and it should generate messages that beams 2 and 4 are being redrawn but no others. Figure 8.19 shows you the final result of all this drawing.

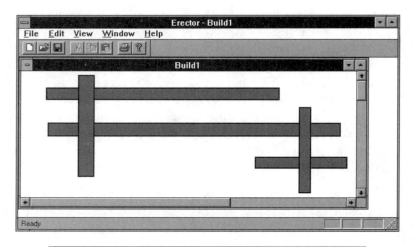

FIGURE 8.19 THIS IS THE DOCUMENT IN ERECTORSET THAT YOU ARE TRACING.

5. Quit the application without saving the document.

The results of the TRACE will be displayed in the Output pane under the Debug tab. The trace messages in mine are shown in Figure 8.20.

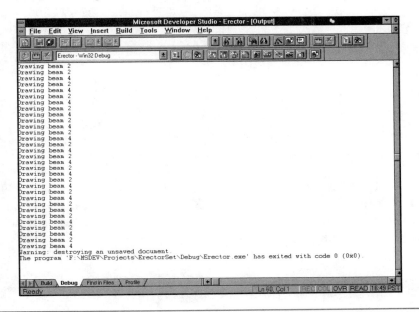

FIGURE 8.20 THE OUTPUT PANE'S DEBUG TAB SHOWS THE TRACE MESSAGES THAT YOU HAVE GENERATED DURING DRAWING THE BEAMS IN YOUR DOCUMENT.

As you can see, the messages are pretty much what you expected. For example, there is no message about drawing beam 3 since it never needed to be redrawn. (The multiple messages about some beams—mostly beams 2 and 4 in my listing—are caused by the update messages generated as the movement rectangle cuts across a beam. There may be any number of these, depending on how quickly you move the mouse.) In any case, this clearly shows you that the hinting mechanism that you set up is working properly.

Alternatives to TRACE

The MFC provide several alternatives to the simple TRACE macro. These are special versions of TRACE that automatically allocate memory for the trace string in a code segment of the application instead of placing it into the default data segment (DGROUP) of the application. This will save DGROUP space and may be significant if you are using a lot of data elements in the application.

There are four variants of the TRACE macro that provide this service. Because these macros have to allocate space for the message string in a code segment, there is one form of the macro for each number of arguments that you will use. The four variants are as follows:

- TRACE0 takes a simple message string with no variable data.
- TRACE1 takes a message string and one data variable.
- TRACE2 takes a message string and two data variables.
- TRACE3 takes a message string and three data variables.

Generally, I only use these versions of TRACE if I have some reason to believe that I need to save data space—if I have a lot of table data, for example. Otherwise, using the simple TRACE is easiest because you can use any number of variables for display.

SUMMARY

I know that this has been a long and complicated chapter, but I think that you will agree that it was worth it. In this chapter, you have learned how to use the tools provided by the MFC and by the Developer Studio to debug your application. This has been done by actually going through the application and cleaning up some important points that have remained problems. This practical, hands-on experience will be very useful for you as your proceed with your own projects.

You have also learned something about how to track and avoid potential problems in your code. The old adage that "an ounce of prevention is worth a pound of cure" is as true in programming as in the rest of life; maybe more so. As you have seen, by using the tools available you can insert a lot of serious testing and debugging code that will not encumber the release version of your application. The benefits are many and immediate, and the cost is only that you take the time to put the code in place to make the tests, and—easy to say but much harder to do—that you put in the intellectual effort to find out where you need to make such tests. In the long run, using these techniques will make your work more reliable and more professional.

CHAPTER 9

USING RESOURCES

This chapter deals with adding resources to your application. Resources represent a part of a Windows application that is generally devoted to the user interface and has special characteristics. Resources are an important part of Windows programming and the Developers Studio makes it easy for you to add, edit, and control the resources in your application.

Earlier versions of Visual C++ added resources by linking to a separate application. Visual C++ 4.0, however, has completely integrated resource editing and handling into the Developers Studio. In this way, you are easily able to work with the resources that you need.

Important features of this chapter are:

- Understanding and using resources
- Editing existing resources
- Adding new resources

RESOURCES AND WINDOWS PROGRAMS

By this point in this book, you have seen that Windows programming is quite different from programming for most other environments, whether personal computers, workstations, or mainframes. If you have had any experience with those environments, some of the features of Windows programming have certainly caused a change in work habits and design methods for you. Indeed, one of the great advantages of using the MFC is that the skeleton application generated by the MFC helps you deal with many of these issues in a simple, coherent, and, above all, consistent fashion.

One of the features that distinguishes Windows programming is its use of resources. Resources enable you to encapsulate all of the user-interface items in your application into one place, so they can be changed without directly affecting any of your application code. This single feature makes using and understanding resources an important part of being a Windows programmer. In this section of the chapter, you will begin to see how these resources integrate into your project and your application and why they are so important to you.

What are Resources?

Resources are an important part of your Windows application. Every Windows application has a series of user-interface items, such as menus, icons, dialog boxes, and so on, that are used to work with the user to display and interpret information from your application. All of these items are examples of a general category in Windows applications called *resources*.

Why Resources are Useful

Many of the items that make up the category of resources are fairly static, that is, they do not change as often as the processing code in your application. For example, once you set up your menu items, you typically won't change them, even when the actual processing for a specific item changes. On the other hand, these items also encapsulate what your user sees on the screen, so they may need to be changed independently of the application's processing code. In either case, having these items segregated in your application improves processing speed and shortens development time.

Consider this simple illustration. Assume that, having developed your application for an English-speaking audience, you now wish to change all of your menu items and dialog boxes to Spanish. Without resources, you would have to change a certain percentage of your application code to do this. In many cases, you might find that the information that you needed to change was in different parts of your code. If you are a conscientious programmer, all of the required information would be placed in defined constants in your header files. If you were in a hurry or momentarily careless, however, you might find some of this information buried in constants defined within the code itself.

Resources alleviate all of these problems. They are all items that are, or can be, placed into your application's resources. By segregating these items, you can set them up one time and then leave them alone. Also, when you want to change them to support a different type of interface, such as another language, you need to change only the resource items, not the internal processing code in your application. After all, the application doesn't know whether the menu item selected is in English, Spanish, or Swahili; internally, the application uses a number to map the menu selection to the correct block of code. As long as the same items correspond to the same selection numbers, the application will work correctly no matter what language the menus or other user interface items happen to be in.

Types of Resources

You have already learned about windows in your application. Outside of the windows and their components, such as scroll bars, what the user sees on the display can be stored and described using resources. Table 9.1 lists all the types of resources that you can put in your application.

TABLE 9.1 RESOURCES THAT CAN BE USED IN MFC WINDOWS APPLICATIONS

Resource Name	Brief Description
Dialog box	A special form of window that contains control items to allow the user to enter or receive information.
Menu	A list of action choices presented at the top of a window.
String Table	A list of string constants used in your application.
Accelerator key	A key attached to controls or menu items that allow the user to choose that item directly. The resource is stored as a list of these keys.
Cursor	The pointer object that is displayed on the screen.
Icon	An object used to denote some feature of an application or the application itself.
Bitmap	A picture used in your application.
Font	A collection of character images, called *glyphs*, that are used to present text information.
Custom	You may define any other type of resource that you want.

The items listed in Table 9.1 are presented in my personal estimate of descending order of importance. Each item has an important place in Windows programming. Unfortunately, we can't present examples of all of them here, but you will learn about and work with the first four, which are the most common and most important of these resources.

The dialog box is probably the most important of these for two reasons. First, it is a very common and useful mechanism for communicating with your user. Second, it contains other elements, such as buttons, lists, edit text boxes, and so on—collectively referred to as *controls*—which you use to display and collect information. Creating and using the dialog box is not an easy task. Therefore, later in the chapter, you will create and use one so you can see first-hand how it all fits together.

Two types of resource may be new to you: the bitmap resource and the custom resource. The bitmap resource is a place to put any graphic elements that you use consistently in the application. For example, you might put a logo that is displayed consistently here. The custom resource is a way to define specialized resources that you will use in your application. The MFC uses this type of resource to define and implement the Toolbar resource that is used in your application. Creation of custom resources is a fairly complex matter and will not be covered here.

The font resource is not one that you will normally use. Most Windows applications use the fonts provided by the Windows operating system. They are still resources, but they aren't directly connected to your application and you don't usually need to be concerned about where they are stored or how they are maintained; that is all handled by Windows itself. However, you can create a private font, store it as a resource in your application, and use it for display if you want.

Accessing Resources

Given that resources are a valuable addition to your application, you need to know how to retrieve them as well as how to create them. Actually, that part is quite simple. Each resource type maintains a list of resources. Each resource within a type has a resource ID number. When you use a resource in your application, you specify the type of the resource and its ID number; Windows then returns a handle (pointer) to the resource that you can use in your application.

MFC uses a simple but elegant mechanism to help you remember these numbers. It defines them as symbolic constants, which are then stored in the `resource.h` header file. This header file is used both by the resource compiler and the application, so you can simply use these symbolic names to refer to your resources.

N O T E It is also possible to use names directly to access resources. However, this method requires Windows to do a name search for the resource. Numbers are much faster. For that reason—and the fact that using symbolic constants gives you most of the benefits of names with the speed advantage of numbers—the MFC uses numbers exclusively for accessing Windows resources.

How Resources are Processed

One big advantage of resources is that they are not always present in the system memory when your application is executing. Instead, the Windows system will only load a resource when it is needed or when you explicitly request it. In this way, Windows saves memory by not keeping information that will be used only occasionally.

Resources are part of your applications data, and they are stored with other application data in the program's .EXE file. However, they are kept in a separate, special data segment. When Windows executes your program, it simply leaves this part of the data on disk until the program requests some element in it; and then only the requested item is loaded. If you have ever watched the disk access light when you are running a Windows application, you may have noticed that, from time to time, the light will go on, indicating that Windows is accessing the disk. Very often, these accesses are to read resources into memory.

Resources are generally read-only data and are marked to be loaded, used, and discarded if necessary. That is, if Windows needs additional memory, it will reuse the memory containing the resources by writing over it. If the resource should be needed again later, Windows simply loads it again from disk.

N O T E This simple statement raises an immediate flag for anyone who is familiar with application loading and processing. If Windows begins to get low on memory, more and more resources and other, similar items get swapped out of memory to allow your application to run. However, if these are items that are needed on a regular basis, they must be re-read frequently. As a result, from the viewpoint of the user, your application begins to run more and more slowly. If the user is not well-informed, he or she may attribute the slow performance to your application or to Windows itself, rather than to the lack of memory.

Resource Definition Files

Since resources are an important part of your application, you may be wondering where they are and how they are defined. The answer is that resources are defined in a special resource language and kept in a separate file, called the *resource script*. The resource script is an ASCII text file—meaning it can be edited and read by any standard text editor—with the special extension .RC to indicate that it is a resource script.

Resources are created from the resource script by compiling them, just as you compile C code. In a similar process, the *resource compiler* (RC.EXE) which is part of your Visual C++ package, converts the resource script into binary form, adds it to your application's executable (.EXE) file, and inserts a *resource table* in the header of the executable file.

Generally, you don't need to worry about any of this. The Developers Studio will handle all of your resources, and it also automatically invokes the resource compiler when required. However, I think that it is worthwhile to take a few minutes to look "behind the scenes," as it were, before proceeding to show you how to use the tools in the Developers Studio, so that you can understand what's going on when you create and access resources in your project.

.RC File Entries

Although you may not know it, the Developers Studio and the MFC together created a resource script for your project. This script contains information about your menus, controls, program and document icons, and so on. It is called `Erector.rc` for the ErectorSet application.

One of these items is the About dialog box that you see if you select **About ERECTOR** from the Help menu. Figure 9.1 shows the box displayed, and Listing 9.1 shows the part of the ErectorSet resource script, `erector.rc`, that defines this dialog box.

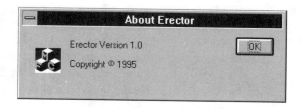

FIGURE 9.1 THE ABOUT BOX IN ERECTORSET IS A TYPICAL SIMPLE DIALOG BOX.

Listing 9.1

```
//////////////////////////////////////////////////////////////////////
//
// Dialog
//

IDD_ABOUTBOX DIALOG DISCARDABLE  0, 0, 217, 55
STYLE DS_MODALFRAME | WS_POPUP | WS_CAPTION | WS_SYSMENU
CAPTION "About Erector"
FONT 8, "MS Sans Serif"
BEGIN
    ICON            IDR_MAINFRAME,IDC_STATIC,11,17,20,20
    LTEXT           "Erector Version 1.0",IDC_STATIC,40,10,119,8,SS_NOPREFIX
    LTEXT           "Copyright © 1995",IDC_STATIC,40,25,119,8
    DEFPUSHBUTTON   "OK",IDOK,178,7,32,14,WS_GROUP
END
```

Like any programming language, some of this looks fairly clear, and some is completely incomprehensible without an explanation. Items such as the CAPTION and the LTEXT entries are clear enough; items such as the STYLE, however, are probably less obvious.

Originally, Windows programmers had to write their own resource scripts, so that knowing how all this fit together was essential. With Visual C++, however, you really don't need to understand all these entries. However, there are a few points that I want to review.

The coordinates used in dialog boxes is one important point. The numbers in the first line of the listing are the location where the dialog window will be displayed on the screen. These are coordinates based on the top-left corner of the main window of your application, but they are not based on display pixels, as the coordinates that you have used for window display have been. These are called *dialog units* and they are a special coordinate system used only in dialog boxes. The units in this system are based on the size of the system font: the x coordinates are 1/4 of an average character width, while the y coordinates are 1/8 of the average character height. Because the characters in a font generally are about twice as tall as they are wide, this gives you units that are about equal for both horizontal and vertical dimensions. All of the coordinates used in the dialog box are based on this coordinate system.

The same coordinate units are used in the ICON item, but in this case—and for all items located within the dialog box itself—the origin of the coordinates is the top-left corner of the dialog box. Thus the icon displayed in the About box is presented at a point that is 11 units horizontally and 17 units vertically from the top-left corner of the dialog box; the following two numbers, 20 and 20, represent width and height values—also in dialog units—that are ignored for an ICON. Using a system like this allows the dialog box to maintain a uniform appearance no matter what type of display is being used.

The ICON definition also demonstrates another point. The first element of the ICON definition, IDR_MAINFRAME, points to an Icon resource. When this dialog box is displayed, the system gets the icon for display at this location by accessing the resources again and loading the referenced Icon resource. This illustrates that you can use resources within other resources, which is an important facility.

Resources and Your Project Files

Resources represent a variety of actual items, such as icons and bitmaps, that may be fairly large. These items are generally created and stored separately from the actual resource script until they are incorporated into the compiled resource file and linked to the application. For example, the icons used for the program and documents in Windows are stored as icon resources in the resource script by simply referencing external files that contain these items.

These files are stored in the res subdirectory of your application. If you look in that directory with File Manager, you will find two icon definitions files, Erector.ico and ErectorDoc.ico, which are simply bitmaps that make up the two icon drawings, and a file, Toolbar.bmp, which is the bitmap that draws the toolbar in your application. If you look in Erector.rc, you will find references to these files in the Icon and Toolbar sections of the script.

The res subdirectory also contains the Erector.rc2 file. This file contains resources that are not accessed or used by the resource editor but are included in your application's resources. At this point, the .RC2 file contains only comments. It is a place where you can define your own resources using the resource script language for manually handled resources that cannot be generated and maintained by the resource editor.

EDITING RESOURCES

A quick look are Listing 9.1, or a more thorough look through the text version of `Erector.rc` will quickly convince you that working directly with the resource script is a difficult task. It requires that you learn what is, in essence, a new programming language—with all its potential problems. In addition, testing the resource script is difficult. As you have seen in the dialog box example, you are specifying locations for items in a set of coordinates that, however useful, are not easy to visualize. Just positioning and checking a simple dialog box might take hours to get right.

The obvious answer to this dilemma for programmers, being who they are, was to create a graphic user interface for generating resource scripts. Ideally, you would like to be able to simply draw the elements that you need on the screen and let some application turn them into a resource script. Since Windows itself is a graphic user interface for information, certainly there should be a graphic method for handling Windows resources.

In the first releases of various Windows development environments, there was no tool that put all of this together. With the Developers Studio, however, you have a complete set of tools that not only allows you to define and edit resources in a graphic interface but tie into your project files and integrate your resources into your application code in a simple and convenient way. This section of the chapter shows you how to use these tools to view and edit your application's resources.

Loading Resources for Editing

The Developers Studio provides you with a set of resource editing tools that allow you to view, edit, create, and delete resources in your application. All the information you see in these editors comes from your application's resource script, and all the changes you make are returned to the resource script where they will be incorporated into your application. By using the integrated resource editors, you can manage the resources in your application with a minimum of problems with language, testing, and so on.

Select the resource to edit by changing into the resource view in your InfoViewer pane. This displays the resources currently in your project. Figure 9.2 shows this display.

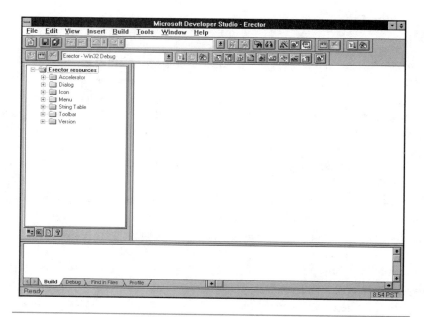

FIGURE 9.2 THE RESOURCE VIEW PANE DISPLAYS THE RESOURCE TYPES CURRENTLY IN THE PROJECT.

This display is virtually identical to the class display you are familiar with and uses the same display conventions of plus and minus signs in front of the resource names to show additional information. As you can see, your application already has a number of resources that were defined for you by AppWizard when you created your project.

You can select any one of these types and click on **OK** to create a new instance of the specific type.

Most of the resource types listed have one or more instances defined in your resource script. For example, click on **Icon** in the list shown in Figure 9.2 to see the IDs of the two icons being currently used in your application, as shown in Figure 9.3.

This shows you two resource items, each defined by a resource ID. These IDs are symbolic names that correspond to an ID number generated by Developers Studio when the resources are created. They are the ID names that you must use to reference the resources within your application, and they are defined for you in the `resource.h` header file. The same header file is also included in the resource script, so that these symbolic references can be used throughout your project.

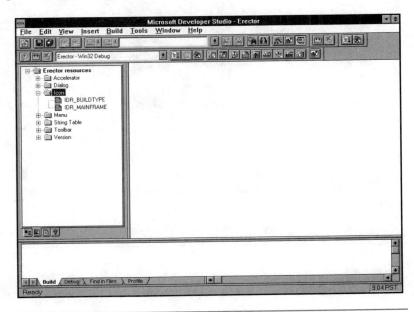

FIGURE 9.3 EXPANDING ONE OF THE RESOURCE TYPES SHOWS THE INSTANCES OF THE RESOURCES CORRESPONDING TO THAT TYPE IN YOUR APPLICATION.

Let's open one of these icons to see what the resource editor can do for you. Select the IDR_MAINFRAME icon and double-click on it. This displays the icon resource editor as shown in Figure 9.4.

As you can see, the icon editor provides a complete set of drawing tools that you can use to create or edit an icon. Since creating or modifying an icon or any other bitmap graphic requires a lot of artistic expertise, I'm not going to try to explain how to use these drawing tools. The Help menu and BooksOnline information tell you everything you need to know.

You read earlier that icons and bitmaps, being graphics, are stored in separate files in your resource script. In fact, Visual C++ finds the correct .ICO file (Erector.ico) and loads it for editing. You can tell which file has been used by using the **Properties** command from the Edit menu. This displays the Icon Properties dialog box shown in Figure 9.5.

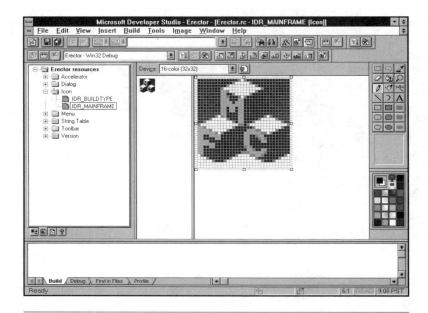

FIGURE 9.4 THE ICON EDITOR DISPLAYS THE SELECTED ICON GRAPHIC AND PROVIDES DRAWING TOOLS FOR EDITING IT.

FIGURE 9.5 THE ICON PROPERTIES DIALOG BOX SHOWS THE RESOURCE ID AND THE FILE NAME OF YOUR ICON.

As you can see, the General tab of this dialog box shows the resource ID number of the icon and the path from your project directory to the file that generated it. When you finish working with this icon and save the resource file—and not before—the resource editor saves the icon file back into the res directory where it found it.

In the same way, if you create a new icon, it will be stored in the correct bitmap format in your `res` directory. However, note that if you delete an icon, the Developers Studio does not delete the matching .ICO file; you must delete it yourself. This prevents any inadvertent loss of a file that may be being used in some other application or in some other way.

This is just one of the variety of resource editors that are now completely incorporated into the Developers Studio. Although each resource editor is different, since each handles a different type of resource, all of them work in much the same way, so you don't need to learn each separately. Once you learn how to work with one editor, you will use the same basic steps with all the others. As you proceed in this chapter you will see how to use these capabilities to create and edit various types of resources.

Editing Resource Information

Now that you've had a chance to get acquainted with one of your resource editors, let's try using it to clean up some loose ends that you have left until now, mostly because they all required editing resource information to make them fully operational.

You need two items to clean up in the current version of ErectorSet. First, you have created a string object in the exception handling section of CErectorDoc to display a warning to the user about opening old files. Second, you have defined an accelerator key (**Del**) for the **Clear All** item in the Edit menu, but it doesn't work. These are both small issues that you can quickly take care of now that you are working with the resources.

Adding a String Resource

One type of resource that you saw in Figure 9.2 is a String Table. This is a table that includes many of the strings used in your application. As you know, strings are an important part of the application; they are used to display information, to provide labels for items, and to give help and feedback during operations.

Resources put all your strings in one place. This has two benefits. First, it allows you to change the wording of messages and other informational items without actually recompiling your program. All you need to do is change the string item in the String Table resource and you have automatically changed the information that is displayed. This is how you can easily make the change from English language displays to Spanish, as you read about earlier.

The second benefit is more subtle but in some ways more important. Remember that when you added the new `try` and `catch` keywords to the serialization section of CErectorDoc, you also used a CString item to display a more informative message to the user. This is a big help because the message is much more informative and is one way that you can improve your application.

There is, however, one drawback to this method. If you review the information under CString, you will see that it creates the actual string data on the memory heap. This means that CString itself might cause an exception to occur.

There is an easy solution to this problem: You can create the string as a resource. In that case, as you read earlier, the memory for the string is preallocated in the resource data segment of the application and is handled by Windows itself. You don't need to worry about cleaning up because Windows will do it for you. Add to this the additional convenience of being able to change the message without recompiling your application, and you see immediately why this is a valuable approach to handling strings.

N O T E In earlier versions of MFC, you would also have needed to explicitly dispose of a CString object before exiting your exception handler if you didn't want to cause a memory leak. As you read earlier, however, MFC now uses C++ exception handing. The standard C++ exception mechanism automatically disposes of any miscellaneous data that has been allocated. So now the data that forms the string in the CString object will be correctly removed from the heap without any additional action on your part. This is a great benefit of the new C++ exception handling mechanism.

Here's how to add this string resource to the existing String Table and use it in ErectorSet. Begin by switching to the Resource View pane (if you're not already in that display) and select the String Table resource. This will display a String Table item. Double-click on it to display all the string resources in your application. You should see a display like Figure 9.6.

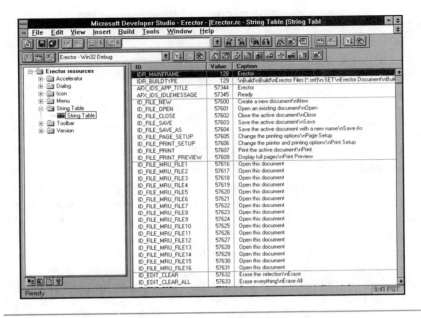

FIGURE 9.6 THE STRING TABLE RESOURCE LISTS ALL OF THE RESOURCE STRINGS BY REFERENCE NUMBER.

The String Table shows all of the strings that will fit on screen, beginning with the one with the lowest ID value. As you can see, most of these strings are part of the help information that is displayed at the bottom of your application in the status bar. For now, you simply want to add one more string to this list. You can add a new entry anywhere, but the easiest place is at the end of the list. This will give your new string an ID number that is one greater than the last string in the list.

Move to the bottom of the list and select the empty string entry outlined there and double-click. (If you wanted to put the string somewhere else in the list, you would simply select the string entry that you want to place the new string after and double-click there.) This displays the String Properties dialog box shown in Figure 9.7.

First of all, enter the caption data as follows: The selected file was created by an older version of ErectorSet. It cannot be opened by the current version. This is the string data that you used earlier to define the CString in your application.

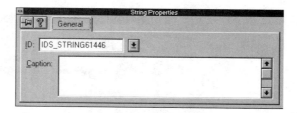

FIGURE 9.7 THE STRING PROPERTIES DIALOG BOX IS WHERE YOU SET THE STRING DATA AND SYMBOLIC CONSTANT.

Next you want to change the ID symbolic constant for this string. As you see, the string editor automatically gives you an ID based on the numeric ID being used for the string—this guarantees that it doesn't conflict with any other symbols, but it isn't very helpful. You want to give it an ID that is both unique and that reminds you of what the string does or says. In this case, I used ERS_IDS_SCHEMA_ERROR. This indicates that it's an application element (the ERS_ at the beginning), that it's a string (the IDS_), and tells something about why the string is used (SCHEMA_ERROR). When you're done, click on the small close box at the top-left corner of the Properties dialog box to close it. This returns you to the String Table display with the new string shown at the bottom, as shown in Figure 9.8.

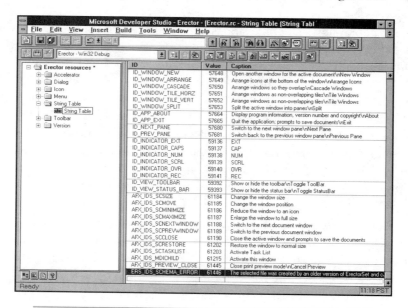

FIGURE 9.8 THE NEW STRING IS NOW INSERTED INTO THE STRING TABLE RESOURCE.

NOTE

When you look at your String Table display, as shown in Figure 9.8, you see that the sets of strings are divided by dark lines. These lines represent the segments of the strings where the strings are stored. Each set of strings within a group marked off by a pair of lines are in a common segment. A segment consists of 16 consecutive string IDs, whether there are strings for all the IDs or not. Therefore the first segment consists of any strings with IDs from 0 to 15, and so on. When Windows loads strings from the String Table, it doesn't load them one at a time; instead, it loads them a segment at a time. For this reason, if you have a group of strings that will be used together, you should put them in the same segment, so that they will be loaded together at one time. As you can see, the new string that you added is in a segment with one other string. This isn't a problem, since no other strings are likely to be used at the same time that the error dialog box is being displayed, which is when this string will be used.

Now that you have added the string to the String Table, you need to save the revised resource script. Choose **Save** from the File menu to do this. You will see the status bar tell you that the resource is being saved. Then choose **Close** from the File menu to close the resource script.

Now return to the Developers Studio. You need to make some small changes to the CErectorDoc serialization code to use the new string resource. Listing 9.2 shows these changes.

Listing 9.2

```
// This function saves and restores the document to an external file
//    using the class CArchive.
void CErectorDoc::Serialize(CArchive& ar)
{
    try
    {
        if (ar.IsStoring())
        {
            // first store document size
            ar << m_sizeDoc;
        }
```

```
        else
        {
            // first retrieve document size
            ar >> m_sizeDoc;
        }

        // now ask our data members to serialize themselves
        m_beamList.Serialize( ar );
    }
    catch(CArchiveException* pEx)
    {
        // If we get here, we have a serialization error...
        // Test for type of error.
        if( pEx->m_cause == CArchiveException::badSchema )
        {
            AfxMessageBox(ERS_IDS_SCHEMA_ERROR, MB_OK | MB_ICONSTOP);
            pEx->Delete();
            AfxThrowUserException();
        }
        else
        {
            throw;
        }
    }
    return;
}
```

As you can see, adding the string resource has actually cleaned up the code quite a bit, since the `AfxMessageBox` function can take the string resource ID directly as a parameter. This is an improvement in creating and using this message box.

Adding an Accelerator Key

Small as that change was, some enhancements don't require any change to your code at all. For example, accelerator keys are used for many common menu items in every Windows application. In fact, the MFC automatically provides a large number of standard accelerator keys for the standard menu items. For example, you can save your file in two ways: by choosing **Save** from the File menu or pressing **Ctrl+S**. Either automatically saves the file. The **Ctrl+S** key combination is an example of an *accelerator key*, which is used to provide shortcuts for common tasks.

The accelerator key for a command is listed immediately after the menu command. In this way, the user can easily determine what keys are used to access any command that they need. Typically, users will choose only the accelerator keys that correspond to commands they use frequently.

When you originally defined the **Clear All** command in Chapter 6, you added an accelerator key listing for that command, the **Del** key. However, up to this point, the **Del** key doesn't actually do anything. Only the **Clear All** menu selection itself actually works. However, you can easily add the accelerator key for **Clear All** using the Accelerator resource.

If you recall, all a menu selection really does is send a command message to your application's document window. To implement an accelerator key, then, all you have to do is send the same command to the window when the desired key combination is pressed as you do when the menu item is chosen. In fact, this is exactly what the Accelerator resource does: it maps keys into commands.

To add the accelerator key for **Clear All** to ErectorSet, begin by switching to the Resource view for your project, then expand the Accelerator types and select the single IDR_MAINFRAME resource. This selects the single list of accelerator keys for your application. Double-click on this to display the current list of accelerator keys. At this point, your screen should look something like Figure 9.9.

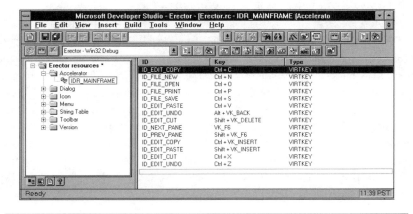

FIGURE **9.9** THE ACCELERATOR RESOURCE IS A LIST THAT MAPS KEY COMBINATIONS TO COMMANDS.

The list of accelerator keys shows three items:

- The ID for the message that the key generates
- The key combination that generates the ID
- The type of key code that is being used (VIRTKEY or ASCII)

Adding a new accelerator key to this list is quite easy. Select the empty key assignment location at the end of the list and double-click. This brings up the Accel Properties dialog box shown in Figure 9.10.

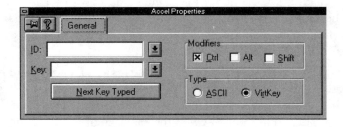

FIGURE 9.10 THE ACCEL PROPERTIES DIALOG BOX ALLOWS YOU TO EDIT OR SET THE ACCELERATOR KEY COMBINATION FOR A GIVEN MESSAGE.

First select the message ID from the drop-down list that is displayed in the ID list box. This shows all the message IDs currently defined in your application. They are the same ones used to map the menu selections to messages, so you know that the one that you want is here. In this case, select the message ID_EDIT_CLEAR_ALL, which is the message that you used in Chapter 6 to map the menu selection to the OnEditClearAll function in CErectorDoc.

Next, you have to set the key combination that will invoke the message. In this case, you have already selected the **Del** key and put that in the menu display. Although you can select a key or set of keys from the drop-down list in the Key list box, the easiest and safest method for adding a key combination is to use the **Next Key Typed** button. When you press this button, the resource editor displays a small dialog box that tells you that it will insert the next key that you press into the Key list box as the accelerator key combination. If you use this approach, all the other settings in this dialog box—Key, Modifiers, and Type—are correctly set for you. This is the best option for setting the key.

Press the **Next Key Typed** button and then press the **Del** key. This inserts the key identification of VK_DELETE into the Key box, turns off all the Modifier flags, and sets type to VirtKey—all exactly what you want. Now close the Properties dialog box. This inserts the new accelerator key definition into the Accelerator resource list in the correct position (the list is in order by the key code).

NOTE

You may be wondering about "virtual keys." In an effort to allow programmers to work with a wide variety of keyboards, Windows translates actual key information provided by the keyboard into a series of standard codes. This is necessary because different keyboards, particularly those designed for use with languages other than English, may use different key codes for some keys. So instead of requiring you to do the translation within your program, Windows does it for you, translating the actual key pressed into a standard code value that you can rely on.

For most things, you want to use these virtual keys rather than the actual key values. However, certain key codes require using the ASCII value for the key rather than the virtual key code. One of the benefits of using the **Next Key Typed** button is that the resource editor automatically determines whether you can use a virtual key or not and sets the Type accordingly.

WARNING

You must keep all your accelerator key combinations unique within an Accelerator resource table. As you can see, all the accelerator key combinations are listed here together, whether they are in the File menu or the Edit menu or whatever. While you can use an *S* to select **Save** from the File menu and use it again to select the Status bar from the Windows menu, you can only use an accelerator key one time— if you use **Ctrl+S** to save a file, you can't use it to select the Status bar.

That's all there is to adding an accelerator key to your application. If you now save your modified resource script and return to the Developers Studio, you can rebuild ErectorSet and test your two new resources. As you will see if you run the test, both the new string resource and the accelerator key work very well.

ADDING RESOURCES

You now know what resources are and how to change them in your application. Since the MFC provide many resources for you, this seemed like a good place to start working with resources. In the long run, however, you will want to add your own resources to the application. In this section of the chapter, you will add a new dialog box that allows your user to control the appearance of the beams in the documents generated in ErectorSet. This will give you a chance to see exactly how you can include additional types of resources in your application.

In addition, this example will show you how to use the various elements that are available in a dialog box. This is important because dialog boxes are probably the most common user interface element that you must design and implement more or less from scratch. Whereas menu items, cursors, and so on, are tied directly into your application in a way that doesn't require much concern about the user, creating a dialog box requires some care and thought to present the required information effectively. The resource editor has excellent tools to allow you to get your dialog box just the way you want it for maximum usefulness with minimum fuss.

Designing a Dialog Box

A *dialog box* is a separate window that allows the user to get and return important information from and to your application. Generally, dialog boxes are displayed when you need to get some information from a user to continue with a requested action. For example, when the user requests that you open a file by choosing **Open** from the File menu, you use a dialog box to allow the user to identify the file to be opened.

There are two types of dialog boxes:

- A *modal* dialog box requires that the user complete working with the dialog box before performing any other task in the application. Basically, the user cannot return to or continue processing in the application until the dialog is finished. The Open File dialog box is a typical example of a modal dialog box; you can't return to the application until you have either selected a file to open or have canceled the request to open a file.

- A *modeless* dialog box allows you to continue processing in the application while it is active. This is useful if the dialog box presents auxiliary information or processing alternatives. The Find dialog box used in many word processing applications and editors is a good example of a modeless dialog box; you can enter a value to be found, find an instance, switch into the application to edit the text, and then switch back to the Find dialog box to continue.

N O T E Modal dialog boxes may be further broken down into *application modal* and *system modal* dialog boxes. As you might guess, an application modal dialog prevents you from continuing with your current application but allows you to switch to another application if you want. A system modal dialog box, on the other hand, prevents you from doing any other task until you respond. For obvious reasons, system modal dialog boxes are restricted to use where continuing with any application might bring down the system or damage an application beyond repair.

The basic issues in laying out a dialog box are what information you need from the user, what information the user needs to understand what you want, and how to present the required information to the user in an effective and useful manner. Over time, some rules have evolved to give you guidelines for doing this.

- Arrange controls in the dialog box that are logically connected in a single row or column.

- Present information in the dialog beginning in the top, left corner and proceed either left-to-right or top-to-bottom. (Of course, if you are creating dialogs in another language or culture, this rule may change; left-to-right and top-to-bottom is the natural order for English speakers.)

- Align selection and data entry items in the dialog box vertically and horizontally so that the cursor moves in a direct line between items.

- Arrange controls in the order users need to complete them, if such an order exists.

- Group related controls and items by using graphic elements, such as group boxes.

- Use clear labels on single controls and groups to describe the purpose of the items.

Elements of a Dialog Box

There are a variety of controls and data fields that you may use in a dialog box. Table 9.2 lists these various elements and gives you a brief description of each.

TABLE 9.2 THE ELEMENTS THAT MAKE UP A DIALOG BOX

Type	Description
Push button	A standard rectangular button to signal some action in the dialog box; typically used to end the dialog or take some action.
Radio button	A round button that is one of a group of items; only one radio button in a group can be selected at a given time.
Check box	A box that can be checked or not; check boxes are used for options that are not exclusive; that is, any given check box may be on or off at a given time.
List box	A box that allows you to enter and edit an item or choose from a given list. The File Name section of the Open dialog box is a good example of a list box.
Combo box	A box that allows you to choose an item from an internal list. Some combo boxes allow you to type in an item in addition to selecting from the list.
Group box	A labeled rectangular area in the dialog box that groups elements. It is not itself a control.
Static graphic	A graphic (bitmap) that is included in the dialog box; it never is selected and does not change.
Static text	A text string that is included in the dialog box. It is never selected and does not change.
Edit box	A box where you can enter text elements—any alphanumeric character—and edit them.
Scroll bar	You may define either horizontal or vertical scroll bars in the dialog box.
User-defined control	If you want, you can define your own type of control object and use it in a dialog box.

If you have used Windows very much, you have probably come across one or more examples of each of these elements in some dialog box or another. The resource editor allows you to insert any of these elements into your dialog box and link them up with your application.

N O T E One element that you may notice is missing from this list is the tab element, which is used in many dialog boxes. This actually is not the same as the elements listed earlier. Creating a tabbed dialog box requires defining property sheets for use with the dialog box, and it requires special handling in your code. You will learn about tabbed dialogs and property sheets in Chapter xx.

Required Information

The first step in creating a dialog box is to determine what information you need from the user. In this case, you will ask the user to determine the color of the beams that are created in ErectorSet and the size of the border that is used for the beams. If you recall, both of these items are currently set to default values without any input from the user. This suggests that you want a dialog with two elements: one to set the beam color and one to set the beam outline width.

Generally, you want to allow the user to control the display as much as possible. If the user doesn't care, there must be default values, which can remain as you have them set now. However, if desired, the user should be able to control, within acceptable limits, the format of the items being displayed—in this case, the beams.

Access to the Dialog Box

The next question is how the user will get access to the dialog box. Basically, there are two methods for accessing a dialog box: it may be called up as part of some general processing or it may be called up specifically by selecting a button, menu item, or some other control. An example of the general access would be if you wanted to display the dialog box every time a new document was created. When the user selects **New** from the File menu, the dialog box would display asking the user to set the correct beam parameters. This is the strategy used by Microsoft Word, for example, when you save a new document that doesn't yet have summary information. In this case, however, it would be best to allow the user to choose when to change the beam attributes by adding a new menu item that allows the user to display the dialog box and change the attributes.

If the item is to be a menu selection, the next decision is whether it should be on an existing menu or on a new one. In this case, none of the existing menus seems to quite fit—you might put it on the Edit menu, for example, but mostly Edit is for handling items after they have been created, not for setting parameters before the beams are drawn. Let's agree then to place this item on its own menu, which will have only the single selection that allows the user to display the dialog box to set the beam features.

Adding a Menu Item

You have already decided that access to the dialog box will be through a menu item. Using the resource editor, you could add the menu item before you create the dialog box or vice versa. I recommend that you create the menu item first for two reasons. First, you already worked with Menu resources when you added the **Clear All** entry in Chapter 6. This is a fairly easy exercise and will refamiliarize you with adding and editing resources. Second, once you add the dialog box, it is best to move directly on to working with the new code to support it. Since this takes you back into the Class Wizard and the Developers Studio, it's easiest to have completed your resource work before moving on, which you will have done if you do the menu item first.

Placement of the New Menu

Let's begin this process, therefore, by adding a new top-level menu item to the existing document menu. Switch to the Resource view, select the Menu resource type and display the Menu items, and then double-click on the IDR_BUILDTYPE menu resource to open it. (Remember that IDR_BUILDTYPE is the menu for the documents, distinguished from IDR_MAINFRAME, which is the menu bar displayed when no document is displayed.) At this point your screen should look something like Figure 9.11.

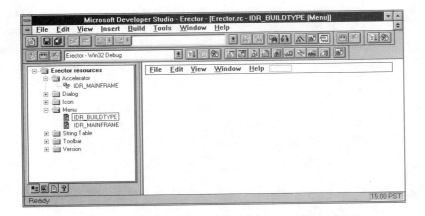

FIGURE 9.11 THIS IS THE DISPLAY OF THE STANDARD DOCUMENT MENU.

Notice that there is an empty entry at the end of the bar. Select this and double-click on it or choose **Properties** from the Edit menu to display the Menu Item Properties dialog box. In this dialog box, enter the caption &Beam. At this point, your screen should look as shown in Figure 9.12.

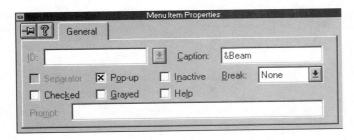

FIGURE 9.12 THE MENU ITEM PROPERTIES DIALOG BOX IS WHERE YOU CAN ENTER YOUR NEW MENU ITEM.

Note that you don't need an ID value for this menu. Since it is a top-level menu that is used only to display menu items underneath it, it doesn't send any command messages itself to the application. When you close this dialog box, the new item appears in the menu bar as Beam, and the first entry under it—which is, of course, empty for now—is automatically selected. Display the Properties dialog box for this item.

This time, all the fields in the dialog box are available. Enter the following values:

- Caption: &Settings
- ID: ID_BEAM_SETTINGS
- Prompt: Change beam settings for outline width and color

Your Properties dialog box should look something like Figure 9.13.

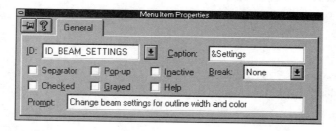

FIGURE 9.13 THESE ARE THE CORRECT SETTINGS FOR THE NEW SETTINGS ITEM IN THE BEAM MENU.

The Caption, of course, is what the user sees when the Beam menu is pulled down. The ID is the message ID for this menu item. The Prompt is the string that is displayed at the bottom of the ErectorSet window in the status bar when the user selects the **Settings** item in the Beam menu. This tells the user what this selection does.

At this point, however, the Beam selection is at the far right end of the menu bar. This really isn't where you want it; you would prefer to have the far-right items always be Windows and Help, as that's the standard display order for most Windows applications. So you need to move Beam to the left—preferably between Edit and View. To do this, simply select the **Beam** item, click on it, and drag it to the left. The displayed cursor changes to an I-beam with an attached icon. You can use this to move the Beam entry to any new position along the menu bar. In this case, simply drag it until the I-beam cursor is between the Edit and View items and then release the mouse button. This moves Beam where you want it.

Linking to the Application

The final step in this process is to use the Class Wizard to generate the skeleton code to handle this menu item. You won't be able to fill in the code until you have the dialog box defined and working, but for now all you need to do is to place the skeleton code into your application.

To do this, select the **Settings** item and choose **ClassWizard** from the View menu. This will display the ClassWizard dialog box with the default Class Name of CErectorView—since you're working with the menu, ClassWizard assumes that you will want to add the new handler to the view. However, in this case you want to save and set the beam parameters in the document itself, not the view. Therefore, change the Class Name to select CErectorDoc.

Select ID_BEAM_SETTINGS from the Object IDs and click on the **COMMAND** entry in the Messages list box. Accept the suggested name of the new function, OnBeamSettings by clicking the **OK** button. At this point, your dialog box should look like Figure 9.14.

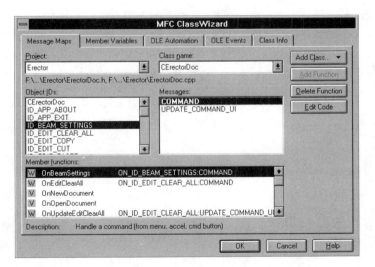

FIGURE 9.14 USE THE CLASSWIZARD TO ADD A SKELETON FUNCTION FOR THE BEAM SETTINGS MENU SELECTION.

For now, that's all that you want to do. This simply adds the OnBeamSettings function skeleton to the CErectorDoc class. In the next chapter, after you have defined the Settings dialog box, you will come back and add the code to process the dialog box to this function. For now, click **OK** to return to the resource editor and close the Menu resource editor to return to the main resource display. This is where you'll start to create your new dialog box item.

Defining the Dialog Box

You have already identified the items that you want in this dialog box: the beam width and a color selection. Let's look at these items in more detail to determine what type of dialog items you can use to get this information from the user.

For the beam width, a simple edit box will be fine. You can display the current width here when the dialog box appears, and allow the user to type any new numeric value into the box. Clearly, for a lot of reasons, you want to limit the width of the beam outline. Let's say that the beam outline, then, will accept any value between 1 and 20.

For the color, things are a bit more difficult. Remember that the color specification in your application sets individual values for red, green, and blue using the RGB macro. Moreover, the values run from 0 to 256. This isn't exactly an intuitive method of specifying colors.

There is also an additional problem that I haven't mentioned up to now: not all values between 0 and 256 make exact colors. The number of colors that can be displayed on your screen is a function of the type of display that you have, the type of display driver that you are using, and the amount of graphic memory in your system. Now, you can access system information about all of these, and adjust your processing accordingly; you can also let Windows handle the problem, but the resulting colors may not look very good. In fact, the whole matter of color settings is so complex that we're not even going to go into it here very far. For our purposes, simplest is best.

So how can you help the user choose a color without overburdening the user, the programmer, or the application? One answer is to present the user with a small set of choices in a drop-down list, called a combo-box. The user can select any one item from this list, and you can transform that into a correct RGB setting within the application to generate the desired color. In this case, let's limit the user to white, black, and two shades of gray: dark gray and light gray. (Dark gray is the color that you've been using so far.) Later, if you want to get more sophisticated, you can expand the list to include as many color choices as you want or you can expand the dialog box to handle a complete range of colors.

There is one more item that you should add to the dialog. Since the user can change these items more or less at will, you should provide a "safe harbor" so that, no matter what happens, the user can always get back to the original settings. The easiest way to do this is to provide a button labeled **Defaults**, which will reset the beams to the original settings no matter what the current settings happen to be.

So the following elements will be in the Settings dialog box:

- An edit box for the width (with limits)
- A combo box with a drop-down list of four available colors
- A **Defaults** push button to return the settings to their original values
- An **OK** push button to accept the new settings
- A **CANCEL** push button to dismiss the dialog box without any changes to the settings

Dialog Box Layout

Now you need to lay out the dialog box, following the guidelines that you read about earlier. Figure 9.15 shows the finished dialog box.

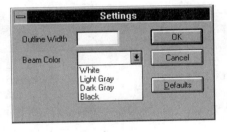

FIGURE 9.15 THIS IS WHAT YOUR FINISHED SETTINGS DIALOG BOX MIGHT LOOK LIKE.

As you can see, this dialog box conforms to the guidelines. The elements are aligned, with the information requested on the left and the buttons on the right. The top button is the default button; **OK** is the most likely to be the desired selection. Also notice that the Beam Color combo box is set up with the four desired colors in a drop-down list.

Creating a New Dialog Box

Now you need to see how to get from the basic resource editor to the dialog box shown in Figure 9.16. Begin by selecting the dialog type in the resource editor and then select **New**. This brings up the dialog editor, which presents you with a basic new dialog box. As shown in Figure 9.16, it has only the two basic **OK** and **Cancel** buttons in it.

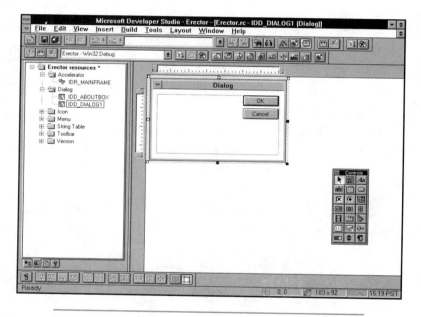

FIGURE 9.16 BEGIN YOUR DIALOG CREATION WITH THIS BASIC DIALOG BOX.

The first step is to set the dialog box's preferences, which include its ID and caption. Select **Preferences** from the Resources menu or simply select the dialog box itself and press **Return**. This will display the Dialog Preference dialog box. Use the following settings for this dialog box:

- ID: IDD_SETTINGS
- Caption: Settings
- X Pos: 35
- Y Pos: 25

This sets the title of the dialog box to Settings and assigns a new symbolic constant, IDD_SETTINGS for referencing the dialog box. It also positions the dialog box at the point (35, 25) from the top-left corner of the main frame window in dialog units. Figure 9.17 shows you the final setting for the Properties dialog box.

FIGURE 9.17 SET THE DIALOG BOX'S OVERALL PROPERTIES AS SHOWN IN THE DIALOG PROPERTIES BOX.

Now you're ready to add the controls to the dialog box. Before you start, notice some points about the dialog editor. First of all, notice that the status bar shows two pairs of numbers in at the right of the status bar: a position number for the top-left corner of the currently selected item and the dimensions of the currently selected item. You will use these to place items in the dialog box as we proceed. Second, notice the controls toolbox shown to the right of the dialog box in Figure 9.16. This toolbox allows you to add every type of control to your dialog box. Figure 9.18 shows you the various elements of this toolbox.

FIGURE 9.18 THE CONTROLS TOOLBOX ALLOWS YOU TO ADD ANY CONTROL TYPES TO THE DIALOG BOX OR TO SELECT THEM FOR EDITING.

To add a control to your dialog box, simply click on the correct tool for the control that you want and move the cursor to the point in the dialog box where you want the top-left corner of the control to be and then click. This will create a control of the type selected; you then use the Properties dialog box to set the correct values for the control. As you enter each control, you will read what settings to make in the Properties dialog box.

First, add the new Defaults button to the dialog box. Choose the push-button tool and place the new button at the point (126, 50). Use the handles on the button to size it to 50 x 14. Then press **Enter** to open the Properties dialog box for the button and make the following settings:

- ID: IDC_SETTINGS_DEFAULTS
- Caption: &Defaults

You can leave all the rest of the items at their default values.

NOTE Using these precise coordinates isn't the important point here. The point is to note exactly where you put the first items so that you can align the other controls on them. The objective is to get the final dialog box to look the way you want.

Next, add the edit box for the pen width for the beam outline. Choose the edit box tool and position the box about the same level as the **OK** button, with a size of 20 x 12. Use the Properties box to set the ID for the edit box to IDC_PEN_WIDTH.

Notice two things here. First, you aren't putting in the captions for these controls as yet. There is a reason you want to put these items into the box in a specific order, as you will read in a moment. The important point here is to do it in this order for now. Second, notice that you don't need to position the box exactly where you will ultimately place it. The dialog editor has tools to align these items so that you don't have to work too hard at placement.

Combo Box Options

The next entry, the combo box, is a little more difficult. This requires some additional settings for the General Preferences and changes in the Style Preferences as well, which is a new area. Let's start by selecting the combo box tool from the toolbox and placing the combo box about underneath the earlier edit box and about at the same level as the **Cancel** button. Make the box have dimensions of 62 x 12. Next, click on the arrow button to the right of the box. This brings down the maximum display area of the box. This is where the list of items that you enter will be displayed for the user. If the list extends beyond the end of the maximum display, there will be scroll bars to allow the user to move around in the list. However, I find it really annoying to have to do much scrolling in dialog boxes, and in this case you will have only four elements. Pull the bottom handle of the box down to give a healthy 62 x 45 dimension to the extended box. This will be enough room to display all the four elements when the list is pulled down.

Now press **Return** to display the Preferences. Notice that these are the General Preferences, as shown by the small drop-down list on the right. First, change the ID to IDC_BEAM_COLOR. Next go the list box titled Enter list choices. Enter the following items, pressing **Ctrl+Enter** to provide a return after each entry (the **Enter** key doesn't work in this box): White, Light Gray, Dark Gray, Black. These are the four choices that the users will see and select from when they pull down the combo box display. Figure 9.19 shows you how the General Preferences should look for the combo box.

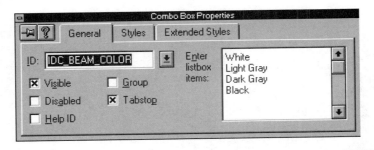

FIGURE **9.19** THE GENERAL TAB IN THE COMBO BOX PREFERENCES INCLUDES ALL THE LIST ENTRIES IN THE BOX.

Now you need to change the Preferences display to the Styles Preferences by selecting **Styles** in the list at the right of the Preferences title. This allows you to customize the style of the control that you are using. Every control has these options, but up to now, you have simply used the defaults. For the combo box, however, there are two forms: one where the user can type information into the box or select from the list and one where the user is constrained to choose only the items in the list. In this case, you want to constrain the user to select only one of the predefined colors. To do this, you must change some settings in the

Styles Preferences. Once the Styles Preferences are displayed, change the Type to **Drop List** and uncheck the **Sort** checkbox. The correct settings are shown in Figure 9.20.

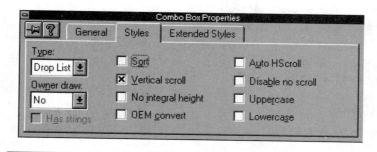

FIGURE 9.20 BESIDES SETTING THE GENERAL PROPERTIES FOR THE COMBO BOX CONTROL, YOU NEED TO SET SPECIFIC STYLE PROPERTIES AS WELL.

This sets your combo box to only allow the user to choose one item out of the list you have already entered. Close the Properties dialog box and return to the dialog editor.

Control Labels

The last thing that you need to do is to make labels for your controls. Select the static text tool and place the text box next to the edit box. Use the Properties to set the caption to `Outline Width`. Close the Properties and select the static text tool again to place another text box with the caption `Beam Color` next to the combo box. Adjust the widths of both boxes to ensure that they don't overlap the controls next to them.

After you have created these, select each one in turn and press **F7** or choose **Size to Content** from the Layout menu to make the item just exactly the right size to hold the text. This is a useful trick to make static text elements, like these, which will never change, take up the least space possible, consistent with showing the required information.

Using the Layout Tools

At this point your dialog box is beginning to take final form, but the various elements in the box are probably wandering around somewhat. You could, of course, painstakingly move each one to align it horizontally and vertically with the other controls in the dialog box. However, the dialog editor provides an easier way.

The Layout menu gives you a series of tools to align all of the elements in your dialog box. Let's align the controls you have defined here.

Begin by aligning the three buttons in the dialog box. Select the pointer tool in the toolbox and use it to select the controls to be aligned. Select the **Defaults** button first, the hold down the **Shift** key and select the **Cancel** button, then continue holding down the **Shift** key and select the **OK** button. At this point, you screen should look something like Figure 9.21.

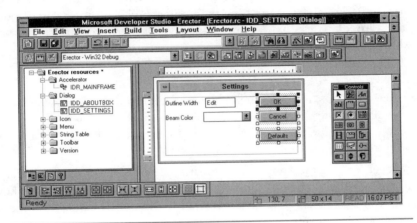

FIGURE 9.21 YOU CAN USE **SHIFT** AND CLICK TO SELECT MULTIPLE ELEMENTS IN YOUR DIALOG BOX.

Notice that all three controls are selected—you can see the handles for each of them—but only the **OK** button, which is the last item selected, shows the handles as solid boxes. This is the *dominant control*. Whenever you are resizing or aligning multiple controls, the dialog editor arranges all the selected controls using the dominant control as a guide.

Now select **Left** from the Align Controls selection in the Layout menu. This aligns all the selected elements on the left side, using the dominant control—in this case, the **OK** button—as the guide. So both the other buttons now line up with **OK** on the left side. If you made the **Defaults** button the size designated earlier, they line up exactly since all the buttons are a standard size.

Move across the dialog box and align the edit box and the combo box—again, on the left. Finally, select the two static text labels and align them on the left as well. This takes care of the horizontal alignment.

To align the items vertically, you don't want to simply align them along the top or bottom edges. Since they aren't all the same size, doing that would cause some irregular visual effects. Instead, do this. Select the static text **Outline Width**, then the edit text box, and then the **OK** button. Notice that this again makes the **OK** button the dominant control. Go to the Layout menu and select **Align Controls** again, but this time select **Vert. Center** from the menu. This aligns all these controls so that their vertical centers are in line. In this way, whatever the size of the control, they look correctly lined up. Do the same thing for the Beam Color static text, the combo box, and the **Cancel** button, using the **Cancel** button as the dominant control. Now your dialog is finally aligned properly.

Setting the Tab Order

There is one last consideration when you are creating a dialog box, which is how the user will navigate through it. Of course, most users will have a mouse and will use it to select the items that they want to change and then use it again to click on the desired button.

However, one of the basic characteristics of Windows programs is that the user should be able to navigate through the entire application using only keys if desired. This allows users to choose whether to move their hands from the keyboard and accommodates users who don't have a mouse. Windows wants to accommodate all these users and so do you, since that gives you the maximum flexibility for your program and the largest audience if you're selling software.

In your dialog box, therefore, you want the user to be able to move around using only the keyboard. By convention, this is done by enabling the **Tab** key to allow the user to move among items in the dialog box. The **Tab** begins at the default item (unless you specify otherwise) which, in this case, is the **OK** button. It move on to other items in the dialog box in the order that they are created. This is called the *tab order* of the dialog box.

Now you understand why you created the controls in the dialog box in the order that you did: the **OK** and **Cancel** buttons are first, created by the dialog editor; then the **Defaults** button, then the two data controls, the edit box first (since it's on top, following our guidelines) and, next, the combo box. Finally, you created the two labels, which don't participate in the tab order because they are not items that can be accessed or changed—remember that these are *static* items. In this way, you have created the dialog box with a tab order that naturally follows the information flow in the dialog itself, just as you want.

However, it certainly happens that you create dialog boxes where you don't know in advance, as you did here, what order you want for your controls. In that case, the dialog editor provides a useful tool for setting the tab order once you have all the items filled into the dialog box. To see how this works, choose **Tab Order** from the Layout menu. This adds a set of numbered superscripts to each field, as shown in Figure 9.22.

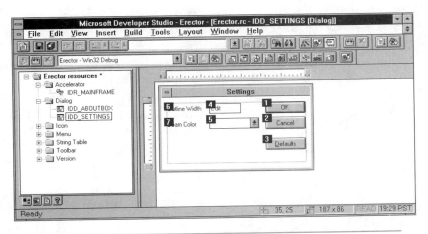

FIGURE 9.22 THE TAB ORDER SELECTION MARKS EACH ITEM WITH ITS CURRENT TAB ORDER.

Once you have this display, you can change the tab order simply by clicking on the item that you want to be first in the tab order. Then click on the item you want to be second, and so on. In each case, the static items will be ignored as the user tabs through the dialog box, so you can place them anywhere in the tab sequence. I generally prefer to place them last, as this makes the ordering a little easier to see. In any case, the current ordering, shown in Figure 9.22, is fine.

Testing the Dialog box

There is only one thing left to do to this dialog box. You would like to know how it looks and how it will work in your application. The display in the dialog editor, while close to the real thing, is still somewhat different than the dialog box will look when it is actually running. However, as always, the dialog editor has a special feature to solve this problem as well.

At the left end of the dialog toolbar, at the bottom of the dialog editor window, is a small icon of a switch. This corresponds to the Test entry in the Layout menu, and it allows you to test the dialog box. If you press this button or select **Test**, you will see the dialog box as it will appear in your application. You can then test the drop-down list, the tab order, any access keys, and any other part of the dialog box that doesn't require actual processing logic. The final result, if you press the drop-down arrow in the combo box to display the list of selections, looks just like the original design that you saw earlier in Figure 9.15. To exit the test display, simply click on the **OK** button in the dialog box.

As a final step, and a precaution, you might now wish to save the resource file by choosing **Save** from the File menu or pressing **Ctrl+S**. This simply ensures that all your hard work doesn't get lost. However, don't exit the resource editor just yet; in the next chapter, you will move from here to adding code, and that's easiest if you go directly from the resource editor into the ClassWizard.

SUMMARY

In this chapter, you have learned about Windows resources. This is an important subject, because it is one of the features that makes Windows programming quite different than most other kinds of programming. You have learned what resources are, how they are used, and how they are accessed from your application. You have also read about how resources are built into your application and how they are incorporated into your project.

That's only the beginning however. Once you understand something about resources, the chapter moves on to allow you to use resources in a practical way to enhance your application. You used resources to handle a display problem. You also added an accelerator key to the application to help the user access a common menu item. But the biggest task in this chapter is to lay out, define, and test a simple but useful dialog box. This resource definition is now done, but the task is really only half finished. In the next chapter, you will learn how to attach your resources to code in your application to support the user interface that you have designed.

CHAPTER 10

CONTROLS AND MESSAGES

In the last chapter, you learned about editing and creating resources. As you saw there, some resources can be easily tied into your application; indeed, adding an accelerator key took no additional code at all. Adding a new dialog box, however, requires a significant amount of new code in your application. To make the dialog box work, you need to bind the controls within it to messages that can be passed to your application. This chapter shows how to use Class Wizard to bind resource controls to processing messages.

Important points in this chapter are:

- Working with controls and messages
- Using Class Wizard to bind messages to application code
- Creating new classes to support resource handling

LINKING RESOURCES TO THE APPLICATION

Now that you have created the dialog box and stored its definition in the resource file, you still need to link it to the ErectorSet application. You need to be able to display the dialog box when the user selects the menu item, and you need to set and retrieve the information that is placed in the dialog box for use in your application. In this chapter, you will see how to link the dialog box that you created in the previous chapter and its internal control items with your application.

Creating a Dialog Box Processing Class

Up to this point, you have been adding new code to your existing classes. However, there isn't a code block in your project yet that will handle the new Settings dialog box. To use the dialog box, you need to create a completely new class and link it to your project. Most development environments require that you do things like this manually, by creating the required files in your editor and then linking them to the project in one way or another. In Visual C++, however, you can do all this by using Class Wizard, which will not only link the new class into your project but will also provide you with a skeleton for the class itself.

Creating a New Class

The important point in all this is to start the process from the resource editor, with the new Settings dialog box open. From there, choose **Class Wizard** from the View menu to launch Class Wizard. This will display the Adding a Class dialog box shown in Figure 10.1.

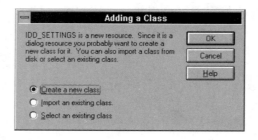

FIGURE 10.1 START THE NEW CLASS FROM THE RESOURCE EDITOR SO THAT CLASS WIZARD
KNOWS THAT THIS IS A NEW RESOURCE.

The dialog box shows that Class Wizard recognizes that this is a new resource and offers you three options for processing data from this resource: create a new class; import an existing class; or select an existing class. For this dialog box, you want to create a new class, which is the default selection, as shown in Figure 10.1. Click **OK** to display the New Class dialog box shown in Figure 10.2.

This is a good example of how all the pieces link together in the Visual C++ environment. By starting Class Wizard from the dialog editor, it understands that you want to build a class to handle dialog box processing, so the new class is automatically derived from CDialog, as you can see, and the Dialog ID that you created for this dialog box is also filled in.

FIGURE 10.2 CLASS WIZARD DISPLAYS THIS DIALOG BOX TO ADD A NEW CLASS TO PROCESS YOUR DIALOG BOX RESOURCE.

Enter CBeamDlg into the Class Name edit box. Class Wizard automatically fills in the other items for you, based on this name. Then remove the check to add this class to the Component Gallery; for now, you don't want to add this to your permanent class collection. Figure 10.3 shows the completed dialog box.

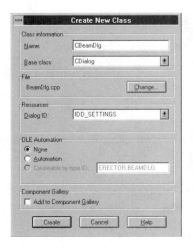

FIGURE 10.3 WHEN YOU ENTER A CLASS NAME, CLASS WIZARD CAN FILL IN THE REST OF THE DIALOG INFORMATION FOR YOU.

Naturally, the File name is simply a recommendation. If your class name was longer and if you're running on a FAT directory system, which doesn't support long names, you might wish to change this name. You use the **Change** button next to the file name to change the names of either or both of the header and implementation file or to choose existing files, if you want to insert the generated code into an existing file. However, unless the new class is very closely tied to an existing class—as the CErectorDoc and CErectorBeam classes are, for example—I recommend that you use new files for each class.

Now click on the **Create** button and Class Wizard creates the new dialog box processing class as you have specified. Once it's created, you are returned to the standard Class Wizard display, shown in Figure 10.4, with the new class selected automatically.

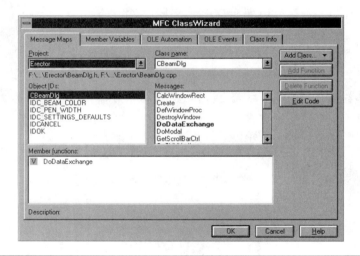

FIGURE 10.4 THE NEW CLASS IS AUTOMATICALLY SELECTED IN YOUR CLASS WIZARD DIALOG BOX.

Notice that the Object IDs list automatically contains all of the symbolic constants for the controls that you have added to the dialog box, as well as the ID for the dialog class itself. All of this automation is based on the connection between Class Wizard and the dialog box that was created when you launched Class Wizard from the dialog editor.

Reviewing the New Dialog Box Class

Before you link the new class and its header with the dialog box controls, let's look at what Class Wizard has generated for you so far. If you want to look at the generated code, you can close the Dialog resource editor, switch into the Class view from the Resource view, and open the new class, CBeamDlg.

Let's look first at the header code that Class Wizard has generated for you. Listing 10.1 shows the code in `BeamDlg.h`.

Listing 10.1

```
///////////////////////////////////////////////////////////////////////
// BeamDlg.h : header file
//
//
// Created by ClassWizard 3 January 1995 08:54:50
// Modifications:
///////////////////////////////////////////////////////////////////////


///////////////////////////////////////////////////////////////////////
// CBeamDlg dialog

class CBeamDlg : public CDialog
{
// Construction
public:
     CBeamDlg(CWnd* pParent = NULL);   // standard constructor

// Dialog Data
     //{{AFX_DATA(CBeamDlg)
     enum { IDD = IDD_SETTINGS };
          // NOTE: the ClassWizard will add data members here
     //}}AFX_DATA
```

```
// Overrides
    // ClassWizard generated virtual function overrides
    //{{AFX_VIRTUAL(CBeamDlg)
    protected:
    virtual void DoDataExchange(CDataExchange* pDX);     // DDX/DDV support
    //}}AFX_VIRTUAL

// Implementation
protected:

    // Generated message map functions
    //{{AFX_MSG(CBeamDlg)
        // NOTE: the ClassWizard will add member functions here
    //}}AFX_MSG
    DECLARE_MESSAGE_MAP()
};
```

As usual, you will note that I have added some comments at the beginning of the code to remind me what state the current code might be in. For now, this simply tells you that this was generated by Class Wizard, and the date and time it was created.

The actual code defines the new class, CBeamDlg, and defines two functions for the class: a constructor function and the function DoDataExchange, which is used to transfer data elements to and from the dialog box.

The most important points are to note that there are two places where Class Wizard can add information to this header. The first one is the AFX_DATA section, which is where Class Wizard will place the data members of your class. Right now, the only thing in this section is a definition mapping the symbolic constant IDD with the ID of your dialog box, IDD_SETTINGS. This is how the class will be linked to your dialog box resource. The second is the AFX_MSG section, which is where the message handling functions of your class will go.

Next, let's look at the implementation code that Class Wizard has generated in the BeamDlg.cpp file, shown in Listing 10.2.

Listing 10.2

```
//////////////////////////////////////////////////////////////////////////
// BeamDlg.cpp : implementation file
//
//
// Created by ClassWizard 3 January 1995 08:54:50
// Modifications:
//////////////////////////////////////////////////////////////////////////


#include "stdafx.h"
#include "Erector.h"
#include "BeamDlg.h"

#ifdef _DEBUG
#define new DEBUG_NEW
#undef THIS_FILE
static char THIS_FILE[] = __FILE__;
#endif


//////////////////////////////////////////////////////////////////////////
// CBeamDlg dialog


CBeamDlg::CBeamDlg(CWnd* pParent /*=NULL*/)
    : CDialog(CBeamDlg::IDD, pParent)
{
    //{{AFX_DATA_INIT(CBeamDlg)
        // NOTE: the ClassWizard will add member initialization here
    //}}AFX_DATA_INIT
}


void CBeamDlg::DoDataExchange(CDataExchange* pDX)
```

```
    {
        CDialog::DoDataExchange(pDX);
        //{{AFX_DATA_MAP(CBeamDlg)
            // NOTE: the ClassWizard will add DDX and DDV calls here
        //}}AFX_DATA_MAP
    }



BEGIN_MESSAGE_MAP(CBeamDlg, CDialog)
    //{{AFX_MSG_MAP(CBeamDlg)
        // NOTE: the ClassWizard will add message map macros here
    //}}AFX_MSG_MAP
END_MESSAGE_MAP()


/////////////////////////////////////////////////////////////////////
// CBeamDlg message handlers
```

Following the header, the class has code supporting two functions. The first is a constructor, CBeamDlg::CBeamDlg. This derives the CBeamDlg class from the CDialog constructor, which takes the symbolic constant, IDD, as a parameter. This directs the constructor to use the dialog box resource that you have created and is the display link between the dialog box resource and this code. The second function is DoDataExchange. Note that, in both cases, Class Wizard has placed special code in the bodies of the functions to allow it to add and remove code elements.

NOTE Class Wizard uses special defined tokens to mark each part of the code that is its responsibility. These blocks of code always begin with //{{AFX_... and end with //}}AFX_... which delimit the area where Class Wizard will modify code. You should never add or remove anything within these delimiters directly; always use Class Wizard to do it.

In addition to these two functions, Class Wizard has also defined an empty message map for the class. Since you have not added any message handling to the class, it doesn't handle any messages yet.

It shouldn't be surprising to you by now that you already have quite a bit of code harnessed in these two files. The MFC and Class Wizard together make a powerful combination.

Linking Buttons

The first work that you want to do is to link the Defaults button in your dialog to the new class. To do this, return to Class Wizard with the resource editor and the CBeamDlg class. If you need to re-open Class Wizard, be sure that the Message Maps tab is selected in the dialog box.

Now select the ID for the Defaults button, IDC_SETTINGS_DEFAULTS in the Object IDs list. When you select this, the Messages list changes to show the two messages that a button can send: BN_CLICKED and BN_DOUBLECLICKED. Select **BN_CLICKED** and click the **Add Function** button. Class Wizard prompts you to add the new member function with a name of OnSettingsDefaults. Accept the name to add the new function to the class.

All this does is add the new skeleton code for the function OnSettingsDefaults to your CBeamDlg class. For now, there is no processing code in the function. You will add that later, after you have linked the other dialog box controls into your class.

Linking Dialog Box Items

Besides linking the button, you still need to create links to the edit box and the combo box controls in your dialog box. As before, Class Wizard provides the tools to do all of this work very easily and confidently.

The process of linking both of these controls is very similar. In essence, you define a new data member for your class matching each control. These items are linked to the dialog box by a *data map*. Look back at Listing 10.2, in the DoDataExchange function, and you will see that the data map is defined there. The Class Wizard uses two standard macros, DDX and DDV, to create the links between the data members in your CBeamDlg class and the dialog box controls.

Because linking the combo box is a little more difficult than linking the edit box, you will start here by linking the edit box. When you have finished that, you will link the combo box. Finally, you will look again at the code that Class Wizard has generated. Notice that all of this work hasn't yet required that you write a single line of code.

Linking the Edit Text Box

Essentially, the process of linking the controls in your dialog box with the CBeamDlg class is one of creating new member variables to handle the control's data values. Class Wizard allows you to create new member variables quite easily. To add a new variable, click on the **Member Variables** tab to bring up the Member Variables display shown in Figure 10.5.

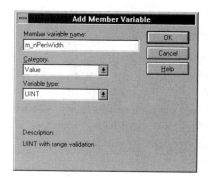

FIGURE 10.5 THE MEMBER VARIABLES DISPLAY ALLOWS YOU TO DEFINE NEW DATA MEMBERS FOR THE CLASS SHOWN IN THE CLASS NAME.

Select **IDC_PEN_WIDTH** from the list of Control IDs to define a new variable to match the edit box—remember, this was the symbolic constant that you defined for the edit box in the dialog editor. Then press the **Add Variable** button to display the Add Member Variable dialog box.

You use this dialog box to name your new data variable. Enter the following in the dialog box:

- Member variable name: m_nPenWidth
- Category: Value
- Variable type: UINT

At this point, your dialog box should look like Figure 10.6.

Notice that you have several choice for how the data in the edit box will be returned. If you expect the user to type alphanumeric information, you can use a CString object to hold the return values. If you expect only numbers, you can use either an int, UINT, or long to hold the return value. In this case, of course, the return value will be a positive integer, so you use UINT.

Press **OK** to return to Class Wizard and the Member Variables display. Now you will see that there is a new addition to the bottom of the display, as shown in Figure 10.7.

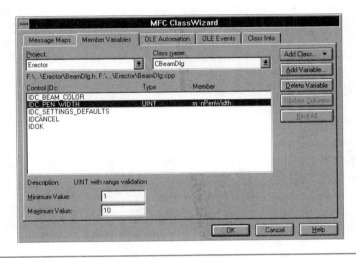

FIGURE 10.6 THE ADD MEMBER VARIABLE DIALOG BOX ALLOWS YOU TO SET THE NAME AND TYPE OF YOUR NEW DATA MEMBER.

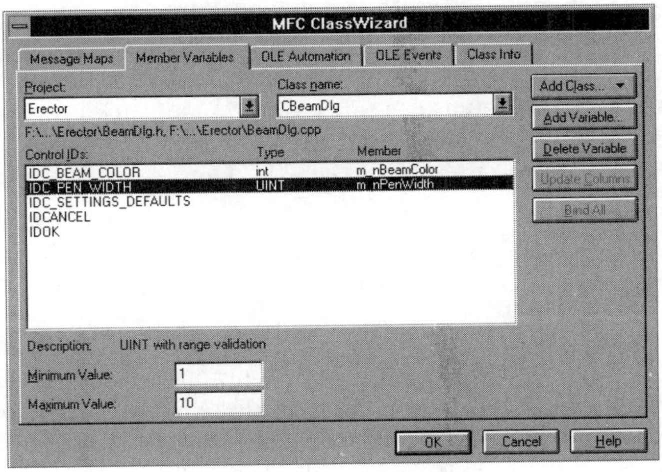

FIGURE 10.7 THE NEW VARIABLE ALLOWS YOU TO ENTER A VALIDATION RANGE.

Since this is the variable for the pen width that will be used for the beam borders, the acceptable range should be from 1 to 10. Figure 10.7 shows these values entered into the Minimum Value and Maximum Value edit boxes.

This is one of the many nice features offered by the MFC. When you create a new data item linked to a dialog control that will contain a number, the MFC will provide automatic validation of the data range for you. If the user attempts to enter a value that is not numeric or outside the range specified here, the application will display a dialog box that tells the user what the legal range of values and that the current value is out of range.

Linking the Combo Box

Now let's proceed to add the combo box data to the map. Select **IDC_BEAM_COLOR** from the list of Control IDs and choose **Add Variable** again. This time, use the following settings for the new variable:

- Member variable name: m_nBeamColor
- Category: Value
- Variable type: int

In this case, there are not so many choices for the Variable type, as you can see. A combo box of the style used here—one that supports only selections from its internal list—can return the selection in only one of two ways: as a CString or as an int. If you use a string, what you get back is the actual string value of the text in the box. In this case, for example, you would get Dark Gray, or Black or whatever was chosen. If you use an int, what you get back is the index of the value selected in the list, beginning with 0. In other words, you will get back 0 if the user chooses **White**, 1 if the user chooses **Light Gray**, and so on.

Of these two, the int is your best selection. You already know that you will have to translate the user's selection into an RGB value. The easiest way to do that is to use a case: statement in your code. For that, an int is perfect.

NOTE

You may wonder why the choice is only an int, and not a UINT. The answer is that, since the index of the list elements ranges from 0 to the number of items in the list, the value -1 is used to set the combo box so that no element in the list is displayed. Since this is clearly a signed number, you can't use a UINT for the return.

Note that, when you return to the Class Wizard Member Variables display, you don't have any range checking since that isn't appropriate for this type of control, even though the return value is a number.

This completes the process of linking the controls in your dialog box with your application. At this point, you are ready to begin to add working code to your new class.

Close the Class Wizard and exit the resource editor. At this point, you have finished using them for now.

Reviewing the Dialog Box Code

Before you add any specific code to the CBeamDlg class, let's look at what the Class Wizard has done so far. This is a good place to look back and compare what you have now with the original listings given in Listings 10.1 and 10.2.

Listing 10.3 shows you the header file, `BeamDlg.h`. In this listing, the highlighted items are not code for you to add. Rather, they represent the new code that has been added by Class Wizard since the previous listing.

Listing 10.3

```
/////////////////////////////////////////////////////////////////////////
// BeamDlg.h : header file
//
//
// Created by ClassWizard 3 January 1995 08:54:50
// Modifications:
/////////////////////////////////////////////////////////////////////////


/////////////////////////////////////////////////////////////////////////
// CBeamDlg dialog

class CBeamDlg : public CDialog
{
// Construction
public:
        CBeamDlg(CWnd* pParent = NULL);    // standard constructor
```

```
// Dialog Data
    //{{AFX_DATA(CBeamDlg)
    enum { IDD = IDD_SETTINGS };
    UINT  m_nPenWidth;
    int   m_nBeamColor;
    //}}AFX_DATA


// Overrides
    // ClassWizard generated virtual function overrides
    //{{AFX_VIRTUAL(CBeamDlg)
    protected:
    virtual void DoDataExchange(CDataExchange* pDX);      // DDX/DDV support
    //}}AFX_VIRTUAL

// Implementation
protected:

    // Generated message map functions
    //{{AFX_MSG(CBeamDlg)
    afx_msg void OnSettingsDefaults();
    //}}AFX_MSG
    DECLARE_MESSAGE_MAP()
};
```

In the data section of the class definition, you now see the two variables that you defined: m_nPenWidth and m_nBeamColor. In the functions that are part of the message map, you also have the new function, OnSettingsDefaults, which responds to the IDC_SETTINGS_DEFAULTS message, which is bound to the **Defaults** button in your dialog box.

In the same way, Listing 10.4 shows you the new code in BeamDlg.cpp.

Listing 10.4

```cpp
///////////////////////////////////////////////////////////////////////
// BeamDlg.cpp : implementation file
//
//
// Created by ClassWizard 3 January 1995 08:54:50
// Modifications:
///////////////////////////////////////////////////////////////////////


#include "stdafx.h"
#include "Erector.h"
#include "BeamDlg.h"

#ifdef _DEBUG
#define new DEBUG_NEW
#undef THIS_FILE
static char THIS_FILE[] = __FILE__;
#endif

///////////////////////////////////////////////////////////////////////
// CBeamDlg dialog


CBeamDlg::CBeamDlg(CWnd* pParent /*=NULL*/)
    : CDialog(CBeamDlg::IDD, pParent)
{
    //{{AFX_DATA_INIT(CBeamDlg)
    m_nPenWidth = 0;
    m_nBeamColor = -1;
    //}}AFX_DATA_INIT
}
```

```
void CBeamDlg::DoDataExchange(CDataExchange* pDX)
{
      CDialog::DoDataExchange(pDX);
      //{{AFX_DATA_MAP(CBeamDlg)
      DDX_Text(pDX, IDC_PEN_WIDTH, m_nPenWidth);
      DDV_MinMaxUInt(pDX, m_nPenWidth, 1, 10);
      DDX_CBIndex(pDX, IDC_BEAM_COLOR, m_nBeamColor);
      //}}AFX_DATA_MAP
}



BEGIN_MESSAGE_MAP(CBeamDlg, CDialog)
      //{{AFX_MSG_MAP(CBeamDlg)
      ON_BN_CLICKED(IDC_SETTINGS_DEFAULTS, OnSettingsDefaults)
      //}}AFX_MSG_MAP
END_MESSAGE_MAP()


///////////////////////////////////////////////////////////////////////
// CBeamDlg message handlers

void CBeamDlg::OnSettingsDefaults()
{
      // TODO: Add your control notification handler code here


}
```

Starting at the bottom, you see that Class Wizard has added an empty function to process the message that results when the Defaults button is pushed. The message map above it (AFX_MSG_MAP) catches the message handling request and routes it to the correct function. Notice that the message map only handles the Defaults button; it routes messages for the **OK** and **Cancel** buttons to the handlers provided by CDialog.

The most interesting part of this code is what is placed into the DoDataExchange function. This adds three lines of code to the data map section of the function: two lines that extract or return data to the dialog box (DDX_ routines) and one that validates the information (DDV_ routine). If you look at it, you can see how the symbolic constant and the variable name are linked here. Also notice that different routines are called depending on the type of control that needs to be handled.

Finally, Class Wizard has placed some data initialization code in the constructor. The new m_nPenWidth is initialized to 0, and m_nBeamColor is initialized to -1. Note that 0 is an invalid value for the pen width, which might cause some problems if you don't correct it before using the dialog box. Also note that the combo box index is set to -1, which will display the box as empty if you leave it like this.

Adding Processing Code

Now that you have used Class Wizard to link your dialog box to the application, you still need to add actual code to set and process the information in it. This actually divides naturally into three sections. First, you need to add the required code to the CBeamDlg class to process the default button and to set default values for your new data members. Second, you need to modify the header for the CBeamDlg class to support color handling. Finally, you need to modify the CErectorDoc class to support the new dialog box.

Working with the Beam Dialog Box Processing

Let's begin by adding the processing for the **Default** button to the CBeamDlg class. The skeleton function, OnSettingsDefault is already in place. All you have to do is set the default values in this function. For convenience, you can simply use the current settings—a pen width of 2 and a dark gray color—as the defaults. Listing 10.5 shows you the complete implementation with this code added.

Listing 10.5

```
///////////////////////////////////////////////////////////////////////
// CBeamDlg message handlers

// This function handles resetting the beam parameters
//    to their default values when the user presses the Defaults button.
void CBeamDlg::OnSettingsDefaults()
{
    m_nPenWidth = 2;
```

```
        m_nBeamColor = DK_GRAY;
        // UpdateData writes data to the dialog box
        //    when the parameter is FALSE
        UpdateData( FALSE );
    }
```

All this does is set the two data members, m_nPenWidth and m_nBeamColor, to their default values. Then it calls the CDialog UpdateData function with FALSE to write the data values back to the dialog box. This resets these values, no matter what else has happened.

Working with the Beam Dialog Box Header

Looking at the code in Listing 10.5, an obvious question is Where is DK_GRAY defined? In fact, it isn't defined yet. You need to define it in the CBeamDlg header.

As you read earlier, the combo box control in the dialog box will return an integer value, indexed from 0, that is the location of the selected item in the list presented to the user. In this case, there are four items for the user to choose from: White, Light Gray, Dark Gray, and Black. The best way to handle this type of information is to make a set of symbolic constants that match the values returned by the dialog box, rather than try to use the actual integer values themselves. And the best way to do that is to use an enum in the header, as shown in Listing 10.6.

Listing 10.6

```
///////////////////////////////////////////////////////////////////////
// BeamDlg.h : header file
//
//
// Created by ClassWizard 3 January 1995 08:54:50
// Modifications:
//      3 Jan 95  DH    Add color enum for use with dialog's combo box.
///////////////////////////////////////////////////////////////////////


///////////////////////////////////////////////////////////////////////
// general constants
enum colors {
    WHITE,
```

```
        LT_GRAY,

        DK_GRAY,

        BLACK

};
```

```
////////////////////////////////////////////////////////////////////
// CBeamDlg dialog


class CBeamDlg : public CDialog

{
```

With this in the header, you can now use these symbolic constants to set and retrieve the color index from the Settings dialog box's combo box.

This is all that you need to do to have a working dialog box class. However, you still have the biggest hurdle—linking all this into your existing application.

Adding Code to the Document Class

Now you need to link all this with your application. Since all of this information is required at the document level, this code will all be placed into CErectorDoc. In fact, you already have the skeleton code for the OnBeamSettings function in CErectorDoc, where you put it when you connected the dialog box in the last chapter.

Basically, you need to do three things. First, you need to revise the processing in the document to take account of the new color and width settings. Second, you need to add code to respond to the menu selection, display the dialog box, and retrieve the new settings. Finally, you will need to revise the header file to handle the new variable information and any new functions that you define.

Let's start by changing the processing in InitDocument, where you are setting the default values for a new document. Listing 10.7 shows you the revised code.

Listing 10.7

```
// This function uses current pen width to create a pen object
//    and a brush for drawing. This must be done whenever
//    a document is created Uses the CPen class.
```

```
void CErectorDoc::InitDocument()
{
    // the default pen is 2 pixels wide
    m_nPenWidth = 2;
    // the default brush is solid 50% gray
    m_nBeamColor = DK_GRAY;
    m_crBrushColor = SetBrushColor(m_nBeamColor);
    // default document size is 850 by 1100 pixels
    m_sizeDoc = CSize(850, 1100);

    return;
}
```

This listing illustrates what is probably the major issue that you need to handle in changing from the previous structure to the new one. Now you are receiving color information as a single integer that maps to a list of colors. This presents two problems: first, how to convert from the color index to an RGB value and, second, how to store that value for future use.

Ideally, you would like to store a single value and use that, simply converting from one to another when necessary. There is a drawback to this approach, however. Keeping the color as a COLORREF, as you have up to this point in the m_crBrushColor variable, is the most efficient method, since this is what the beams actually require to paint. If you simply store the color reference index, you will have to recreate the COLORREF for each beam.

On the other hand, if you store the color as a COLORREF, how will you get back to the index value? There isn't any quick and easy reverse method for decoding the COLORREF value and determining whether it is light or dark gray, for example.

So the answer is a compromise: to keep both values as data members in the class. In this way, there are matching data members in the CErectorDoc class for both the pen width and the beam color, then the beam color index value is turned into a COLORREF value, which is stored and used for painting, as it is now.

The code shown here does two new things. First, it sets a new CErectorDoc member variable, m_nBeamColor, to the default value of DK_GRAY. Second, it uses a new auxiliary function, SetBrushColor, to turn the color index into a COLORREF values.

However, to use the symbolic constants for color, you need to define them where CErectorDoc has access to them. In fact, you will also need to have access to the CBeamDlg class as well, when you go to handle the dialog box. To get access to everything, add an include to the class header file, BeamDlg.h, in the beginning of ErectorDoc.cpp. Listing 10.8 shows you the new header code.

Listing 10.8

```
//////////////////////////////////////////////////////////////////////////
// ErectorDoc.cpp : implementation of the CErectorDoc class
//
//
// Created by AppWizard 11 December 1995 11:39:42
// Modifiications:
//   12 Dec 95   DH   Add OnOpenDocument to generated code,
//                         along with new common InitDocument().
//   12 Dec 95   DH   Add CErectorBeam class to generated code:
//                         initialization; serialization; contents.
//   15 Dec 95   DH   Add menu item Edit>>Clear All with new function,
//                         OnEditClearAll, and aux function, DeleteContents.
//   18 Dec 95   DH   Add SetupRect to support movement rectangle display
//                         and modify EndBeam to use it.
//   20 Dec 95   DH   Add error checking to SetupRect and modify EndBeam to use it.
//   21 Dec 95   DH   Add serialization for document size
//                         and change schema number in CErectorBeam to reflect that.
//   3 Jan 95   DH   Add Beam Settings dialog for setting beam characteristics.
//////////////////////////////////////////////////////////////////////////


#include "stdafx.h"
#include "Erector.h"

#include "ErectorDoc.h"
#include "BeamDlg.h"
```

```
#ifdef _DEBUG
#define new DEBUG_NEW
#undef THIS_FILE
static char THIS_FILE[] = __FILE__;
#endif


/////////////////////////////////////////////////////////////////////////////
// CErectorDoc


IMPLEMENT_DYNCREATE(CErectorDoc, CDocument)
```

Next, let's deal with the auxiliary function. Go back to the Class View and select the **CErectorDoc** class. Then display the right mouse button pop-up menu and select **Add Function...** to display the Add Member Function dialog box. Fill this in as follows:

- Function Type: COLORREF
- Function Declaration: SetBrushColor(int nColor)
- Access: Protected

This adds a skeleton for the new function to your CErectorDoc class. Listing 10.9 shows you the new SetBrushColor function with the required code.

Listing 10.9

```
// ...after InitDocument()...


// This function sets the brush color based on the
//     color reference value passed in as a parameter.
//     At present, only supports shades of gray.
COLORREF CErectorDoc::SetBrushColor(int nColor)
{
        ASSERT( nColor >= WHITE && nColor <= BLACK );
        switch (nColor) {
        case WHITE:
                return( RGB(255, 255, 255) );
        case LT_GRAY:
```

```
                return( RGB(192, 192, 192) );
        case DK_GRAY:
                return( RGB(128, 128, 128) );
        case BLACK:
                return( RGB(0, 0, 0) );
        default:
                return( RGB(0, 0, 0) );
        }
    }
```

This is simple enough. The function takes an index int and returns a COLOR-REF value by using a switch statement. The function has an ASSERT macro at the beginning to assure that the value passed into it is, in fact, a valid color index. The default statement at the end is provided for the compiler, which complains if you don't have it, and as a runtime backup for the actual production program, when the ASSERT macro would be inoperative. During debugging, ASSERT ensures that you won't get an error in this statement.

Next, you have to add the code to activate the dialog box and insert and retrieve data from it. You have already created this as a skeleton function, OnBeamSettings, which the Class Wizard has placed at the end of the ErectorDoc.cpp file. As usual, I moved this code into the body of the CErectorDoc code, inserting it after the OnUpdateEditClearAll and the data management section. Listing 10.10 shows this code.

Listing 10.10

```
// ...after OnUpdateEditClearAll()...



// This function displays the Beam Settings dialog
//     when the user selects Beam>>Settings.
void CErectorDoc::OnBeamSettings()
{
    CBeamDlg dlg;
    // Initialize dialog with current settings
    dlg.m_nPenWidth = m_nPenWidth;
    dlg.m_nBeamColor = m_nBeamColor;
```

```
    // now invoke the dialog itself
    if( IDOK == dlg.DoModal() )
    {
        // get data settings
        m_nPenWidth = dlg.m_nPenWidth;

        m_nBeamColor = dlg.m_nBeamColor;
    }
    // set the brush color from the beam color entry
    m_crBrushColor = SetBrushColor( m_nBeamColor );


}
```

The code begins by declaring a new variable of the class CBeamDlg. This automatically generates the dialog box object and initializes it. Next you set the dialog box object's two data variables to the current values of the document. Notice that, since the names used for the variables in the two classes are identical, this type of equation is really easy to follow in the code. Now you actually display the dialog box, by executing the DoModal function—remember, this is a modal dialog box. This displays the dialog box, with the current values of the variables that you have set previously. It automatically processes all the input from the user, until the **OK** or the **Cancel** button on the dialog box is pushed. When that happens, the processing ends. If the **OK** button was pushed, you retrieve the information from the dialog box into the document's member variables. When that's done, you set the brush color by using the SetBrushColor function using the current value of the color index.

The final step in this process is to add the new member variable, m_nBeamColor to the CErectorDoc class. As before, use the right mouse button pop-up menu, select **Add Variable...**, enter the following in the Add Member Variable dialog box:

- Variable Type: int
- Variable Declaration: m_nBeamColor
- Access: Protected

As you read earlier, using the same variable names in both the document and dialog box classes makes it easy to match them up when it comes to working with the dialog box. Listing 10.11 shows you the changes that have be generated to support what you've done.

Listing 10.11

```
//////////////////////////////////////////////////////////////////////
// ErectorDoc.h : interface of the CErectorDoc class
//
//
// Created by AppWizard 11 December 1995 11:39:42
// Modifiications:
//  12 Dec 95  DH   Add OnOpenDocument to generated code,
//                      along with new common InitDocument().
//  12 Dec 95  DH   Add CErectorBeam class to generated code:
//                      initialization; serialization; contents
//  15 Dec 95  DH   Add menu item Edit>>Clear All with new function,
//                      OnEditClearAll, and aux function, DeleteContents.
//  18 Dec 95  DH   Add SetupRect to support movement rectangle display
//                      and modify EndBeam to use it.
//  19 Dec 95  DH   Add document size member variable, m_sizeDoc,
//                      and new function GetDocSize to access it.
//   3 Jan 95  DH   Add Beam Settings dialog for setting beam characteristics.
//   6 Jan 95  DH   Change beam color handling to use color index
//                      instead of beam color as COLORREF.
//////////////////////////////////////////////////////////////////////


// Forward declaration of the data structure class, CErectorBeam
class CErectorBeam;


class CErectorDoc : public CDocument
{
protected: // create from serialization only
     CErectorDoc();
     DECLARE_DYNCREATE(CErectorDoc)
```

```
// Attributes
protected:
                // each list element is a beam object
      CTypedPtrList<CObList, CErectorBeam*> m_beamList;
      CSize        m_sizeDoc;              // the document size

      // We track the beam color or pattern and outline width
      //    at the document level for all views. This allows
      //    the user to choose a new beam style for all the views
      //    together, rather than one at a time.
      COLORREF        m_crBrushColor         // the brush color
      int             m_nBeamColor;          // the beam color index
      UINT            m_nPenWidth;           // the border width

public:
      POSITION GetFirstBeamPosition();
      CErectorBeam* GetNextBeam( POSITION& pos);
      CSize GetDocSize() { return m_sizeDoc; }

// Operations
public:
      CErectorBeam*    NewBeam();

// Overrides
      // ClassWizard generated virtual function overrides
      //{{AFX_VIRTUAL(CErectorDoc)
      public:
      virtual BOOL OnNewDocument();
      virtual void Serialize(CArchive& ar);
      virtual BOOL OnOpenDocument(LPCTSTR lpszPathName);
      //}}AFX_VIRTUAL

// Implementation
public:
      virtual ~CErectorDoc();
```

```
#ifdef _DEBUG
    virtual void AssertValid() const;
    virtual void Dump(CDumpContext& dc) const;
#endif

protected:
    void InitDocument();
    void DeleteContents();
    COLORREF SetBrushColor(int nColor);

// Generated message map functions
protected:
    //{{AFX_MSG(CErectorDoc)
    afx_msg void OnEditClearAll();
    afx_msg void OnUpdateEditClearAll(CCmdUI* pCmdUI);
    afx_msg void OnBeamSettings();
    //}}AFX_MSG
    DECLARE_MESSAGE_MAP()
};
```

//

As you can see, I have added a new comment to note the changes and have moved the generated items around a bit for ease of reading. That's all there is to it.

Testing the Application

You have finally added all the code required to use the new dialog box. At this point, you can close all the open code modules in the Developers Studio, which ensures that everything is saved, and rebuild the ErectorSet application.

Once you have rebuilt the application, run a short test. Figure 10.8 shows the results of using the new dialog box with several different settings.

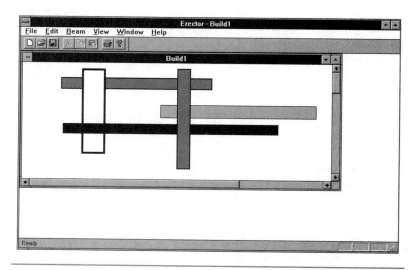

FIGURE 10.8 THE NEW ERECTORSET ALLOWS YOU TO USE THE BEAM SETTINGS DIALOG BOX TO CREATE DIFFERENT TYPES OF BEAMS.

The Settings dialog box should work just as you expect: if you set a value in it, that is the value that will be used to draw the next beam and all subsequent beams in the document until you change the settings again.

SUMMARY

This chapter has concluded the work that you began in the previous chapter. There you laid out and created the Settings dialog box. Here you have linked the box with the code required to invoke it and use the settings provided. As you can see, this type of coding represents a significant effort. As you do more Windows programming, you will discover that a substantial part of your work will be in designing and implementing code to process user interface items, such as dialog boxes.

At this point, the ErectorSet application will let a user draw beams and modify the color and outline width. In the next chapter, you will see how to add some additional processing that will enhance the application even further.

CHAPTER 11

MEASUREMENT AND PRESENTATION

The ErectorSet application now has a user interface and display that are typical of commercial Windows applications. By taking advantage of the MFC and using the Developer Studio tools, you have been introduced to most of the issues that come up when writing an application. However, there are some additional areas that you need to understand for a complete view of how to use and work with Windows and the MFC. This chapter introduces a most important issue: device independence. There are two areas where the present version of ErectorSet has device limitations: in printing and in displaying bitmapped drawings. In this chapter, you will learn about the tools provided by Visual C++ and the Developer Studio for providing device-independent drawing and printing. You will add classes to ErectorSet to change measurement systems to a device-independent mode so that your printed documents come closer to the screen display. You will also learn how to use bitmaps in your drawings, by creating and using a pattern bitmap for the beams. Together, these issues will help you understand how device independence functions in a Windows environment.

Important issues that you will find in this chapter are:

- Printing and print preview functions
- Using device-independent measurements
- Adding new printing functions to ErectorSet
- Creating a pattern bitmap
- Using pattern bitmaps in your application
- Memory handling in MFC applications
- Finding and fixing memory leaks

Printing Enhancements

Up to this point, you have simply used the printing functions that are automatically supplied by the skeleton application. These are actually quite extensive. You can be very happy with the amount and quality of printing support that comes with the skeleton application.

If you have ever created a non-Windows application, you know that providing even the simplest printing support isn't easy. In fact, I knew of a number of commercial DOS applications that did not offer full printing support, being limited to a small subset of printers or other output devices. Windows made all of these issues much easier for the application developer, since Windows actually provides much of the support required by most applications. All you, as a developer, have to do is use the standard Windows printing interface and you can print to any printer that is supported by Windows.

Of course, that simply moves the target for the typical Windows application. In spite of all the work, there are always subtle—and sometimes not-so-subtle—differences between how something looks on screen and how it prints. Now most applications provide a Print Preview function so the user can see the page exactly as it would print before printing. Doing Print Preview is quite a chore, but it's one you don't need to worry much about. Once again, the application that MFC generates for you will provide both Printing and Print Preview as long as you have requested these features when you generated the application skeleton with AppWizard.

The net result of this is that the ErectorSet application provides most of what any user might want in terms of printing and print previewing. The very fact that you have support for both these functions is one of the major strengths of an MFC application.

This support isn't perfect however—or, more precisely, you have not yet adapted ErectorSet to take full advantage of these functions. So far, ErectorSet has been primarily concerned with screen display: first of all, simply drawing the beams on screen; then making the drawing efficient; and finally setting drawing options for the beams. All of this is important, but it has been all focused on the screen display. Now you want to look at how these documents print and preview. This section of the chapter shows you how to create documents that look as good printed as they do on screen.

Measurement Systems

There is a basic problem with the current version of ErectorSet when it comes to printing your documents. This problem is easily illustrated by looking at the screen display for a document and comparing it with the printed version of the same document. Alternatively, you can use the Print Preview, which shows the same problem.

Figure 11.1 shows a typical document that you might create with ErectorSet.

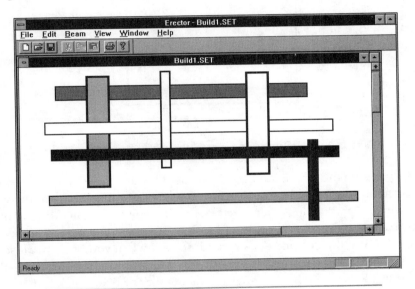

FIGURE 11.1 A TYPICAL ERECTORSET DOCUMENT LOOKS FULL-SIZE ON THE SCREEN.

However, Figure 11.2 shows you the same document if you select **Print Preview** from the File menu.

Although the screen display looks reasonably large, you can hardly see the output in the print preview—and the print preview is a good representation of what you'll get when you print the document. The obvious problem is that the printed output is much smaller than you would have expected, given the screen display. All the elements are there in the right order and position, but the size appears quite different.

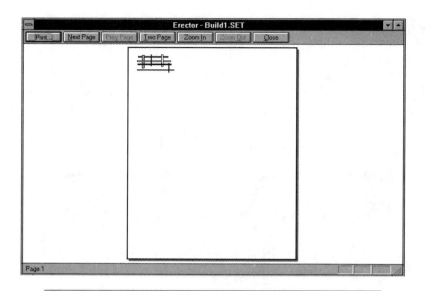

FIGURE 11.2 THE ACTUAL PRINTED OUTPUT, HOWEVER, ISN'T VERY LARGE AT ALL.

Your drawings on the screen look good because they are scaled to match the display you are using. Basically, this is a function of how you measure and lay out the drawings. The drawings that ErectorSet makes now are scaled by the number of pixels on your display; naturally, this looks good when you display the beams. However, this scheme doesn't work so well when you print, because the printer typically has a finer resolution—that is, it has more pixels per inch—than your display. So scaling the drawings by the number of pixels makes them a lot smaller on the printer than they are on the screen.

In Chapter 7 you read about using logical and device coordinates. At that time, you simply used the simplest form of logical coordinates: those that mapped one logical unit into one device pixel. In other words, the mapping from the logical coordinates to the device coordinates was one-to-one. This allowed you to concentrate on this specific issues that were important at that point that is, scrolling views and the concepts of logical coordinates themselves. To print your documents at full size, however, you now need to look further into the varieties of logical coordinates.

Mapping Modes

The basic problem here is that you want to have a standard size unit that you can use on all types of output devices, whether they are standard resolution displays, high resolution displays, or any of the many printers that Windows supports. To do this, you need to have some logical coordinate system where the units are not tied to the number of pixels used by a specific device. Not surprisingly, this problem has been faced and solved before. Windows provides a variety of *mapping modes* that determine how your logical coordinates are converted to device coordinates and vice versa.

Table 11.1 lists all of the mapping modes used in Windows, with a brief explanation of what the mode does.

TABLE 11.1 THE WINDOWS MAPPING MODES

Mapping Mode	Description
MM_TEXT	Maps one logical unit to one device pixel. The positive *y* axis is downward.
MM_LOENGLISH	Maps one logical unit to 0.01 inch. The positive *y* axis is upward.
MM_HIENGLISH	Maps one logical unit to 0.001 inch. The positive *y* axis is upward.
MM_LOMETRIC	Maps one logical unit to 0.1 millimeter. The positive *y* axis is upward.
MM_HIMETRIC	Maps one logical unit to 0.01 millimeter. The positive *y* axis is upward.
MM_TWIPS	Maps one logical unit to 1/1440th of an inch. 1/1440th of an inch is 1/20th of a printer's point (1/72nd of an inch). The positive *y* axis extends upward.
MM_ANISOTROPIC	Maps one logical unit to an arbitrary physical unit. The *x* and *y* axes are scaled independently, so one unit in one axis may not be equal to one unit in the other.
MM_ISOTROPIC	Maps one logical unit to an arbitrary physical unit. The *x* and *y* axes are scaled together, so one unit is the same distance in either axis.

These mapping modes naturally divide into two groups. The first is the mapping modes that provide an arbitrary conversion from logical to physical coordinates: MM_ANISOTROPIC and MM_ISOTROPIC. The second group is all the other modes, which have a fixed relationship between the coordinates and the physical world. Using the arbitrary mapping modes provides a lot of flexibility, but is not too common because of the complications inherent in using them. For our purposes here, you can simply ignore them.

The MM_TWIPS mapping mode may seem peculiar to you if you have never worked in commercial printing or haven't worked with large amounts of commercial printed output. Most printers calculate dimensions in *points*, which are approximately 1/72nd of an inch—in the electronic world, they are exactly 1/72nd of an inch. Most of us are familiar with the term from using type, which is measured in points. So lines of 36-point type are spaced 1/2 inch apart. The MM_TWIPS mapping mode allows you to use points and fractional points in your documents. This can be very useful if you are creating output that will be transferred to a system for commercial printing.

There is one point that you must notice about the fixed mapping modes. In all of these, the *x* axis is positive to the right. However, only MM_TEXT has the *y* axis positive downward. All the other modes—known as *metric* mapping modes because they have specific measurement values associated with them—have the *y* axis positive upwards instead. In all cases, the origin remains at the top, left corner of the document, so that the *y* coordinate values in a document will be negative numbers instead of positive ones if you use one of the metric mapping modes. This has an impact in how you handle the coordinates, as you will see in an example later in this chapter.

So far you have used MM_TEXT as your mapping mode. You set the mapping mode when you used the SetScrollSizes function in your view class. This is what determines how the coordinates that you provide are translated to device coordinates. Because MM_TEXT maps directly into device coordinates, this is the easiest mapping mode to use.

For example, the document size that you have set in CErectorDoc (in the m_sizeDoc member variable) is (850, 1100). Since the mapping mode is MM_TEXT, the document is 850 pixels wide by 1100 pixels high, and the physical size depends on how many pixels per inch are used in the output device. However, if you shift the mapping mode to MM_LOENGLISH, the document size is now 8.5 inches by 11.0 inches—a standard US letter page—no matter what the resolution of the output device may be.

Coordinate Transformations

In some cases, you may want to use alternative coordinate systems. You can do two things to alter the basic logical coordinate system used in your application. First, you can use one of the arbitrary mapping modes to set the coordinate units to anything that you require. For example, you could set them to map one logical unit into 0.01 mile, which might be useful if you are drawing maps; or you could convert into a fraction of a parsec, if you were doing astronomical calculations or displays; and so on. The point is that you can always define your own mapping from logical to device coordinates as you want.

You do this by first using one of the functions provided in the CDC class for setting the mapping mode, then using the function `SetWindowExt` and, if necessary, `SetViewportExt`, to control the mapping from your logical coordinate units into device pixels. You can use these functions to control both the units on each axis and the direction of each axis.

Second, you can also adjust the origin of the view if you want. Moving the origin is called *translating* the origin. You can do this for any of the mapping modes, by using the CDC function, `SetViewportOrg`. However, this only moves the origin and doesn't change the coordinate directions, so if you use it, be sure that you understand where you end up. In my experience, nothing is more frustrating than to get a translation wrong and end up drawing off the screen. This can be an extremely difficult problem to debug.

Changing to Device-Independent Measurements

Let's change the mapping mode so the printed beams become more like the display. To do this, let's use the `MM_LOENGLISH` mapping mode. Yes, you're right. That's why I used 850 and 1100 originally for the document size.

Changing the mapping mode itself is quite simple. You have to change only one line of code, as shown in Listing 11.1.

Listing 11.1

```
// This function handles the first update message for the view.
//    It sets the document size for scrolling by asking the document
//    to tell its current size.
void CErectorView::OnInitialUpdate()
{
```

```
CScrollView::OnInitialUpdate();


SetScrollSizes(MM_LOENGLISH, GetDocument()->GetDocSize() );
}
```

This sets the mapping mode for the document and allows you to use absolute measurements instead of device-dependent ones.

Handling the Reversal of the y Axis

As you read earlier, there is one major difference in use between MM_TEXT and the metric mapping modes such as MM_LOENGLISH: the *y* axis is reversed. Where before the *y* axis was positive down the screen, now it is negative down the screen. As a result, all the logical *y* coordinate values are now negative numbers.

Surprisingly, this doesn't make as much difference as you might expect. If you were to rebuild ErectorSet at this point, with only the single change noted in Listing 11.1, you would find that it does a lot of what it did before. It will still display a movement rectangle, and it will still draw a beam correctly. However, the movement rectangle will erase the existing beam and will not redraw it; if you resize the document window, the beams all disappear.

The reason most of the functions work is that the device context understands how to convert the negative *y* coordinate values into device coordinates correctly. If you recall, when you read about device and logical coordinates earlier, that's one of the benefits of using logical coordinates.

As you might guess from the symptoms I have described, one problem is in setting and using the invalid rectangle. In fact, everything that uses a CRect value needs to be reexamined. This happens because some CRect functions, such as IntersectRect, expect the rectangle to be built in a certain way: with a top coordinate that is less than the bottom one. However, since the *y* axis is reversed, the top coordinate is now actually greater than the bottom—just as -10 is greater than -20. This presents you with a problem: how will you handle these functions?

Most of the drawing and storage functions work just fine. There are really just two places where you have a problem: when you are determining whether a beam needs to be redrawn and when you are setting the invalid rectangle to force the beams to be redrawn. Both of these have difficulties for a simple reason. The device context uses the values of the top and bottom points that correspond to the actual rectangle, so that the top coordinate is, in fact, greater than the bottom.

However, your `SetupRect` function is still forcing the top coordinate to be less than the bottom. In other words, it's setting the real top as the bottom and vice versa. Therefore, when you convert the stored rectangle into device coordinates, you don't get the correct values. In effect, the rectangle is standing on its head.

As it happens, this doesn't matter for drawing functions, such as `Rectangle`, because they don't care whether you draw from top to bottom or bottom to top. But when you start working with the invalid rectangle, and when you are checking whether the beam and the clipping region intersect, this becomes an important point.

The easy answer is to simply convert your beams to follow the actual formation of the rectangles by converting the test to set the top and bottom points in `SetupRect`, as shown in Listing 11.2.

Listing 11.2

```
// This function calculates the drawing rectangle
//    from the starting point to the supplied point and returns it.
BOOL CErectorBeam::SetupRect(CRect& rectBeam, CPoint& ptCurrent)
{
     // Error checking code to ensure that
     //    ptStart and ptCurrent are not too close to one another...
     if( (abs(m_ptStart.x - ptCurrent.x) < 2) ||
         (abs(m_ptStart.y - ptCurrent.y) < 2) )
         return FALSE;
     //    and are not too far apart, either.
     if( (abs(m_ptStart.x - ptCurrent.x) > 32767) ||
         (abs(m_ptStart.y - ptCurrent.y) > 32767) )
         return FALSE;


     // Set top and bottom
     if ( ptCurrent.y > m_ptStart.y )
     {
         rectBeam.top = ptCurrent.y;
         rectBeam.bottom = m_ptStart.y;
     }
     else
```

```
        {
                rectBeam.top = m_ptStart.y;
                rectBeam.bottom = ptCurrent.y;
        }


        // Set left and right
        if ( ptCurrent.x < m_ptStart.x )
        {
                rectBeam.left = ptCurrent.x;
                rectBeam.right = m_ptStart.x;
        }
        else
        {
                rectBeam.left = m_ptStart.x;
                rectBeam.right = ptCurrent.x;
        }


        return TRUE;
}
```

As before, this is just a one-line change in the function, but now the top point really is the top again. This will automatically make the conversion from logical coordinates to device coordinates work again for the invalid rectangle settings in your code, which solves one of your problems.

Now you're ready to handle the problem of redrawing the beams. The issue here is that the OnDraw function checks to see whether the beam to be drawn actually falls within the invalid rectangle—the clipping rectangle—before drawing. Since the IntersectRect function is one of those that requires that the top coordinate be less than the bottom, there is never a hit when you're testing, so none of the beams get redrawn.

The solution is to convert both the clipping rectangle and your beam rectangle into device coordinates before you do the intersection testing. Since the device coordinates are always set up so that the top of a rectangle will be greater than the bottom, this solves the problem. Listing 11.3 shows you the required changes in the OnDraw function.

Listing 11.3

```
void CErectorView::OnDraw(CDC* pDC)
{
        CErectorDoc* pDoc = GetDocument();
        ASSERT_VALID(pDoc);

        // Get invalid rect for checking whether beam should be drawn
        CRect rectClip;
        pDC->GetClipBox( &rectClip );
        pDC->LPtoDP( &rectClip );

        // The view requests each beam draw itself
        //      by called CErectorBeam::DrawBeam()
        CRect rectBeam;
        for( POSITION pos = pDoc->GetFirstBeamPosition(); pos != NULL; )
        {
                CErectorBeam* pBeam = pDoc->GetNextBeam( pos );
                // Check to see if beam falls inside invalid rect
                rectBeam = pBeam->GetCurrentBeam();
                pDC->LPtoDP( &rectBeam );
                if( rectBeam.IntersectRect( &rectBeam, &rectClip ) )
                //          and only draw it if it does.
                        pBeam->DrawBeam( pDC );
        }

        return;
}
```

This converts both the clipping rectangle, which is returned in logical coordinates, and the beam rectangle, which you stored in logical coordinates, to device coordinates. It converts the rectangles so that the top coordinate in both is greater than the bottom, and the IntersectRect function can now correctly interpret whether the beam needs to be redrawn or not.

Erasing the Movement Rectangle

It would seem that this solves the two problems I told you about earlier—and so it does. However, there is still one problem hidden in handling the movement rectangle. Figure 11.3 shows what the display looks like when you draw some beams now.

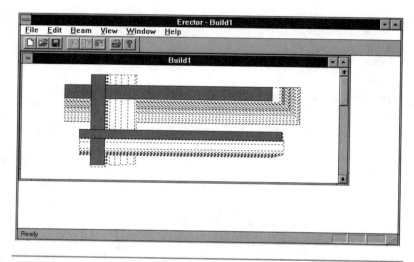

FIGURE 11.3 EVEN WITH THE BEAMS SET CORRECTLY, THE NEW ERECTORSET STILL SHOWS SOME PROBLEMS IN DRAWING.

Figure 11.3 shows that the movement rectangles that you draw are not getting erased correctly. Interestingly, if you resize the document window, the beams are now redrawn correctly, so these leftover traces of movement get erased in that case.

The problem is that the FrameRect function, which is supposed to erase the movement rectangle isn't working. A quick review of the documentation on FrameRect tells you what must be the matter: although FrameRect is a member of the CDC class, it, too, requires that the top coordinate of the rectangle be less than the bottom.

The easy answer to this problem involves a bit more code, but it works consistently. Since Rectangle doesn't have these limitation, you can simply convert the call to FrameRect into a call to Rectangle. Listing 11.4 shows you the required changes.

Listing 11.4

```
// This function handles MouseMove up messages.
//    NOTE that this does _not_ call inherited behavior.
void CErectorView::OnMouseMove(UINT /* nFlags */, CPoint point)
{
     // Mouse button up is notable only if the user is currently drawing
     //    a new beam by dragging the mouse.
     //    In that case, we need to capture the mouse position.
     if ( GetCapture() != this )
          return;              // If this view didn't capture the mouse,
                              //    the user isn't drawing in our window.


     //    First, set the device context to this view...
     CClientDC dc( this );
     //    TODO: Add error handling in case we can't get a DC.
     CDC* pDC = (CDC*)&dc;
     // CScrollView returns view coordinates, which are device coordinates.
     //    They must be converted to logical coordinates before use.
     OnPrepareDC( pDC );
     dc.DPtoLP( &point );


     // Display movement rectangle in DC as a dotted rectangle
     //    to show where user is at all times.
     CRect rectDraw;


     // Setup the movement rectangle based on the beam starting point.
     if( !m_pBeamCur->SetupRect(rectDraw, point) )
          return;


     // Now draw the movement rectangle.
     //    set the pen and brush for the movement rectangle...
     CPen penStroke;
     CPen penErase;
     CBrush brushFill;
     //         create the pen and brush for the movement rectangle
```

```
      if( !penStroke.CreatePen( PS_DOT, 1, RGB(0,0,0) ) )
          return;
      if( !penErase.CreatePen( PS_SOLID, 1, RGB(255,255,255) ) )
          return;
      if( !brushFill.CreateSolidBrush( RGB(255,255,255) ) )
          return;
      //    and paint the movement rectangle.
      //        save the old pen and brush and set the new ones
      CPen* pOldPen = dc.SelectObject( &penErase );
      CBrush* pOldBrush = dc.SelectObject( &brushFill );
      //        erase the old rectangle by painting with the white brush
      dc.Rectangle( &m_rectPrev );
      //        redraw the beams in this view
      dc.LPtoDP( &m_rectPrev );
      InvalidateRect( m_rectPrev, FALSE );
      UpdateWindow();
      //        then draw the new movement rectangle
      dc.SelectObject( &penStroke );
      dc.Rectangle( &rectDraw );
      //        and restore the old brush and pen
      dc.SelectObject( pOldBrush );
      dc.SelectObject( pOldPen );

      // Save the rectangle to erase it the next time.
      m_rectPrev = rectDraw;

      return;
  }
```

The FrameRect function had some advantages over Rectangle. First, it simply redrew the frame around the rectangle, using a given brush. This meant that you could use the white brush, which was already defined, to erase the previous rectangle. Furthermore, it didn't use the current brush or pen settings so you didn't need to define a new pen to erase the old rectangle's border. Finally, it only redrew the border, so you didn't waste any extra effort in erasing the interior of the rectangle, which was already white.

Unfortunately, you now have to give up these small conveniences. You must add a new white pen to the function and you must select it into the device context so that the call to `Rectangle` that erases the previous movement rectangle works correctly.

Given these constraints, the code in Listing 11.4 is quite clear. You define a new `penErase` object and set it to be solid, one pixel, and white. Set this as the first pen to use in the device context, and then use the `Rectangle` function to erase the old rectangle. Then you change the pen in the device context to the `penStroke` for drawing the new rectangle and draw it.

N O T E Given the advantages of using `FrameRect`, you might reasonably wonder if you couldn't simply reverse the coordinates in the rectangle before calling `FrameRect` and get the same results. I thought so, too, but it doesn't work. For some reason, `FrameRect` doesn't seem to be able to precisely erase the border in all cases, so that you get little fragments of a dotted line here and there as you draw. Presumably the conversion from the rectangle to the device coordinates, which must take place somewhere inside the `FrameRect` call, is not working quite right. In any case, the `Rectangle` function works exactly correctly, so that's what I used here.

Updating the Schema

There is one more change that you must make to your application. As you can see, once you think about it, the coordinate changes that you have just made make any documents saved by previous versions of your application no longer useful. The beam coordinates in the old documents are in `MM_TEXT` mapping mode; the new version of the application will assume that these values are in `MM_LOENGLISH` and will therefore try to draw the beams off the screen.

To correct this, you need to change the schema number in you serialization section, as shown in Listing 11.5.

Listing 11.5

```
//////////////////////////////////////////////////////////////////////
// CErectorBeam

IMPLEMENT_SERIAL(CErectorBeam, CObject, 3)
```

Even though you haven't changed the data elements that make up the serialized document, you have changed what they represent. This requires that you change the schema so that older documents don't get read into the program inadvertently.

Checking the Print Preview

All of this was to change from `MM_TEXT` to `MM_LOENGLISH` mapping mode so that the printed output would match the display more closely. So now you can rebuild ErectorSet and test the output. Figures 11.4 and 11.5 show you that, indeed, the Print Preview is now substantially larger than before and much more representative of what's on your screen.

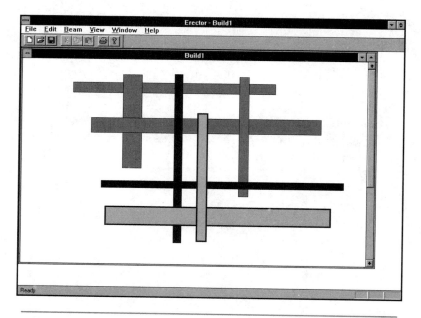

FIGURE 11.4 THE DISPLAY FOR THE NEW ERECTORSET NOW WORKS JUST AS WELL AS IT DID BEFORE YOU CHANGED THE MAPPING MODE.

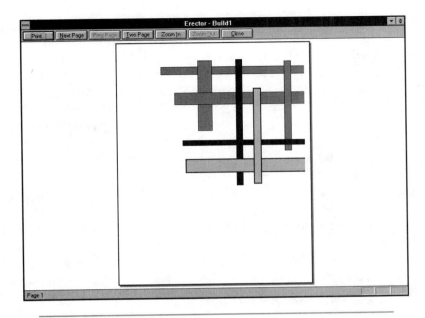

FIGURE 11.5 THE NEW PRINT PREVIEW, HOWEVER, NOW IS MUCH LARGER AND MORE REPRESENTATIVE OF THE SCREEN DISPLAY.

Printing Architecture

The conversion from device-dependent to device-independent measurement is probably the single most important change that you must make to enhance your printing. However, you can do many more things to make your application print better. For example, you can include additional information on your printed documents by using headers and footers, and you can define ways to print documents that are larger than the paper size in your printer. All of these improvements require some help from you to make them work.

To understand what you need to do to make enhancements like these work, you first need to understand the printing architecture—that is, how the skeleton application handles a request to print a document.

How Printing Works

Windows applications print using a technique that is very similar to the way they display data on the screen, by using GDI calls to a device context. You are familiar with the process when you are drawing into the device context for the screen. The OnDraw function requires a pointer to a device context, pDC, as a parameter. This defines where the output will go and how it is transformed from the logical coordinates that you are using to the specific coordinates for the output device. Then, when the window receives a WM_PAINT message, it calls the framework, which sets up a device context for the screen and calls the appropriate view's OnDraw.

Under these circumstances, printing is fairly easy. Windows is designed so that the GDI calls are essentially device-independent. All the application needs to do to support basic printing is to create a device context that matches the printer instead of the display and then use the same GDI calls, such as Rectangle, to draw into the printer's device context. If the device context that is built by the application represents a printer, then the output will be converted and printed appropriately. Now, when the framework receives an ID_FILE_PRINT message, indicating that the user has requested printing the current document, it simply creates a printing device context and the rest of the process is pretty much the same as screen display.

We won't discuss here how Windows handles printing. I assume that you are already familiar with the general Windows printing process: the Page Setup dialog box, the Print dialog box, and so on. The important point here is how to control and use the standard printing process to print your documents.

NOTE

This doesn't mean that an application built with the MFC must simply take the standard process and use it. You have full ability to change the processing as you wish. For example, you can change the contents of the Print dialog box or even replace it with your own. However, the focus here will be on the standard printing process and how you work with it, not on how to modify it for special processing.

The Printing Workflow

As is true for scrolling and many other complex tasks, your view and the skeleton application framework cooperate to perform printing. Here is how the two parts work together. The application framework performs the following functions:

- Display the Print dialog box
- Create a device context (CDC object) that matches the current Windows printer
- Call the StartDoc and EndDoc functions of the CDC object at the appropriate points in the process
- Call the StartPage function at the beginning of each page
- Notify the view of the page number being printed
- Call the EndPage function when the view is done printing the page
- Call the view's overridable functions at the correct points in the process

The view has the following responsibilities:

- Inform the application framework how many pages are in the current document
- Draw the section of the document that corresponds to the required page
- Allocate and deallocate any special GDI resources that are required for printing. Fonts are the most common
- If required, perform any printer-specific functions. For example, if you need to change the orientation of a page during printing, the view must send the required printer codes to make the change. However, the framework and Windows handle setting the standard page orientation selected by the user in the Page Setup dialog box.

The framework also handles display and management of the Page Setup dialog box, which allows the user to select a Windows printer and to set various options for printing, such as the orientation of the page.

Figure 11.6 gives an overview of the standard set of calls used in ErectorSet to print.

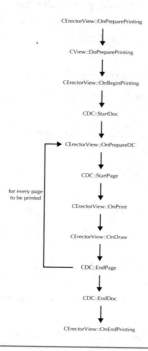

FIGURE 11.6 THE PRINTING LOOP USED IN ERECTORSET IS THE STANDARD ONE USED BY MOST MFC APPLICATIONS.

Printing Setup

Let's look at this printing loop in detail so that you can understand how the parts work together. For convenience, I've used ErectorSet here, so you can actually trace these calls if you want. However, the same basic flow is used in all MFC applications.

The framework begins the printing process by calling the view's OnPreparePrinting function. This is called before the Print dialog box is displayed to the user, so you have the ability in this function to set values to be used in the Print dialog box, such as the number of pages in the document, if you know that.

The OnPreparePrinting function is passed a pointer to the CPrintInfo object that is storing information about the current printing or print preview function. CPrintInfo is an important object when you are printing, as it is passed to most of the printing-specific functions in your view and provides you with the opportunity to find out what's going on and to modify the printing process.

CPrintInfo has important public data members shown in Table 11.2 which you use when printing.

TABLE 11.2 CPrintInfo Data Members

Data Member	Use
m_pPD	A pointer to the current CPrintDialog object. If you want to modify the Print dialog box, you use this object.
m_bDirect	A flag indicating whether the document is being printed without displaying the print dialog box.
m_bPreview	A flag indicating whether the document is being previewed (TRUE) or printed (FALSE).
m_bContinuePrinting	A flag that you can set to tell the application whether to continue printing (TRUE) or to terminate printing (FALSE).
m_nCurPage	The number of the page currently being printed
m_nNumPreviewPages	The number of pages displayed in the preview window; may be either 1 or 2.
m_lpUserData	A pointer to a data structure that you create. This structure is designed to hold printing-specific data that you want to store with the print record, not in your view class. You must create the data structure yourself and then may store the pointer to the structure here.
m_rectDraw	A CRect object giving the current usable drawing area on the page in logical coordinates. The usable drawing area is the area remaining on the page after you print headers, footers, and so on.

TABLE 11.2 CPRINTINFO DATA MEMBERS (CONTINUED)

Data Member	Use
m_strPageDesc	A CString object that defines a format string for the page number display during print preview. The format string is a standard C format string, that uses the usual format conversions. The object is divided into two substrings, each of which must be terminated by a \n. The first substring is used to format page numbers for the single-page display and the second is used for double-page display. The default string is Page %u\nPages %u-%u\n.

It also has some specific functions that you can use to aid in printing as listed in Table 11.3.

TABLE 11.3 CPRINTINFO MEMBER FUNCTIONS

Function	Use
SetMinPage/GetMinPage	Sets or returns the first page number of the document.
SetMaxPage/GetMaxPage	Sets or returns the last page number of the document.
GetFromPage	Returns the number of the first page Requested for printing
GetToPage	Returns the number of the last page Requested for printing

The standard OnPreparePrinting function calls the CView function DoPreparePrinting, which does two things: it displays the Print dialog box and it creates the printer device context. Obviously, if you want to affect the Print dialog display, you need to do that before you call DoPreparePrinting. For example, if you know or can determine the number of pages in your document, you should use the SetMaxPage function to set that information before you call DoPreparePrinting. If you don't know, or don't set this value, the application uses the default values of 1 and 0xFFFF for the first and last pages of the document, respectively.

By the same token, if you want to get information from the Print dialog box, you need to do it after you have called DoPreparePrinting, either in this function or in one of the subsequent functions. DoPreparePrinting captures the information from the dialog box and stores it into the CPrintInfo object, so you can retrieve it at any time after the Print dialog box has been dismissed by the user.

The next function called is your view's OnBeginPrinting. This is the place where you should allocate GDI resources, like setting fonts. Once this has been finished, the StartDoc function for the CDC class (the device context) is called. This function's main purpose is to notify the device context that you are beginning to print a document and that all subsequent calls to StartPage and EndPage should be sent handled as part of the same job. This guarantees that all pages of your document will come out together.

Printing Loop for Each Page

Now you begin the printing loop itself. The loop is repeated for each page that the user wishes to print, up to the maximum number of pages in the document. The first function called is OnPrepareDC. If you remember, this is the function that you call to adjust the coordinates of the device context for the logical coordinates being used. For printing, this function is called with two parameters, a pointer to the device context as pDC and a pointer to the CPrintInfo object as pInfo. The CPrintInfo object has the current page being printed at this time as the public member variable, m_nCurPage. If you need to terminate printing at this point, you set the member variable m_bContinuePrinting in the CPrintInfo object to FALSE. The important point here is that this is your real opportunity to control some of the variables that affect printing the page, rather than the entire document.

One important point to note about OnPrepareDC for printing is that, if the length of the document has not been set, using SetMaxPage, the default version of OnPrepareDC assumes that you only wish to print one page. If you have not set the length of the document, the print loop will terminate after printing one page.

When you have finished `OnPrepareDC`, the framework calls the CDC function `StartPage`. This function prepares the printer driver that has been selected to receive data. Once that's done, your view's `OnPrint` function is called. You may override this function to provide for multipage documents or to handle headers and footers in your document. If the document is more than one page, you will need to adjust the viewport so that `OnDraw` renders only the correct portion of the document. You can use elements of the CPrintInfo object that it passes to `OnPrint` as a parameter to find out what page is to be printed, what the printable area is for the current page in logical units and other useful information. The default implementation of `OnPrint` simply calls `OnDraw` and passes it the printing device context.

Once `OnDraw` is finished, the processing for this page is terminated by a call to the CDC function, `EndPage`. This function notifies the printer driver that the current page is finished, allowing the driver to perform whatever action is required to advance to the next page. At this point, the framework determines whether there are more pages to print or not. If there are, the process repeats from the `OnPrepareDC`; if not, the cleanup processing is started.

Printing Cleanup Processing

The cleanup process for printing begins with the CDC function `EndDoc`. This function ends a print job that was begun by the call to `StartDoc`. It also handles response to a canceled print operation or one that encountered errors. You should not attempt to handle such conditions yourself. For example, you should not use `OnPrepareDC` to handle a request by the user to cancel the print job. That will be done automatically by `EndDoc`, which returns an integer value that tells you whether the print operation was successful or not. Remember however, that this is for information only. `EndDoc` has already handled the error condition itself.

As the last step in the cleanup process, the framework calls your view's OnEndPrinting function. You should use this function to deallocate any GDI resources that you allocated during OnBeginPrinting.

Printing Header Information

One type of information that is always displayed on screen and is missing in your printed document is the name of the document being printed. This is shown in the title bar at the top of the document window, but only the beam information is actually printed by default. You can easily add the document name as a header when you print. This will enhance your printing, and it will also give you an opportunity to see how to work with the standard printing process to make small improvements like this.

Adding Setup Code for Printing

Let's follow this process through the same steps that the printing process itself follows. You can begin, therefore, with the `OnPreparePrinting` and `OnBeginPrinting` functions shown in Listing 11.6.

Listing 11.6

```
///////////////////////////////////////////////////////////////////////
// CErectorView printing

// This function calls DoPreparePrinting to set up the printing DC
//    and display the Print dialog.
BOOL CErectorView::OnPreparePrinting(CPrintInfo* pInfo)
{
    // set the number of pages - for ErectorSet, it's always 1
    pInfo->SetMaxPage(1);
    // default preparation
    return DoPreparePrinting(pInfo);
}


// This function creates any resources that are required for printing.
void CErectorView::OnBeginPrinting(CDC* pDC, CPrintInfo* pInfo)
{
    // Prepare a font for use when printing
    if( !m_fntTitle.CreateFont( 20, 0, 0, 0, FW_NORMAL, FALSE, FALSE, 0,
        ANSI_CHARSET, OUT_DEFAULT_PRECIS, CLIP_DEFAULT_PRECIS,
DEFAULT_QUALITY,
        DEFAULT_PITCH || FF_SWISS, "Arial" ) )
    {
        m_fntTitle.CreateStockObject( DEVICE_DEFAULT_FONT );
    }
}
```

`OnPreparePrinting` is fairly simple. The only thing to set here is the maximum number of pages. For ErectorSet, the documents are fixed to U.S. letter size, and there is only one page per document. This is mostly placed here to show you how the `SetMaxPage` function is used.

`OnBeginPrinting` is a little more complex. Remember that this is where you should set your GDI resources, such as fonts, that are not used in the screen display. In this case, ErectorSet doesn't display any text, and yet you want to print the document name at the top of the page. To do that, you will have to use a font. You could, of course, use the default font provided by the GDI. Actually, that works fine. In this case, however, I want you to see how to create, select, and destroy a font as an example. Therefore, the `OnBeginPrinting` function first creates a new font. Notice that it is using a member variable, `m_fntTitle` that you haven't defined yet. You have to use a member variable because you want to create the font in one function and use it in another function—in this case, in `OnPrint`.

Creating the font is quite simple, in spite of the long list of parameters. Most are simply the default values that are used with a font. The two important values, from your point of view, are the first and last parameters. The first parameter, 20, specifies the height of the font in logical units. Since the mapping mode for ErectorSet is `MM_LOENGLISH`, each unit is 0.01 inch, so 20 units is about 0.2 inch, which about the size of a 15 point font. (You can see here why you might want to use the `MM_TWIPS` mapping mode. If you have much text work to do, `MM_TWIPS` allows you to work directly in points, since one unit is 1/20th of a point.) The last parameter specifies the Arial TrueType font. By specifying a TrueType font, you will get the best possible output, no matter what type of output device you use. Arial is one of the fonts that is standard in all Windows systems, so it's a safe bet. The remainder of the parameters are standard defaults, chosen from the list given for `CreateFont`.

It is possible that you can't create the font, so the `CreateFont` here is enclosed in an `if` statement. If the `CreateFont` fails for any reason, you set the font to be the default font for the device and take your chances. (Well, it's better than nothing.) That's all that you have to do for the setup.

Adding Header Code to the Printing Loop

Now you're ready to add the actual header code itself. As you read earlier, this is best added to the `OnPrint` function, which should be placed in CErectorView. This is an entirely new function that you have to add to your CErectorView class.

It responds to the WM_PRINT message and overrides the default OnPrint function provided by CView to do the header for your document.

Since this is a response to a message, you can use the WizardBar to add the function and its skeleton code to CErectorView. You should have CErectorView already open in your edit pane from adding the code shown in Listing 11.6. Use the Messages drop-down list in the WizardBar to add the new OnPrint function to your CErectorView class.

Listing 11.7 shows you the completed OnPrint function code in CErectorView. I moved the skeleton code and placed the completed function between the OnBeginPrinting and OnEndPrinting functions, which is where it comes in the printing loop.

Listing 11.7

```
// This function prints a page in the document as specified by
//    the CPrintInfo object
void CErectorView::OnPrint(CDC* pDC, CPrintInfo* pInfo)
{
    // First get the document name
    CString strTitle = GetDocument()->GetTitle();
    //    and then print the header.
    PrintPageHeader( pDC, pInfo, strTitle );
    // The PrintPageHeader function reduces m_rectDraw in pInfo
    //    by the amount of the header, so we need to reset the
    //    display window to account for this.
    pDC->SetWindowOrg( pInfo->m_rectDraw.left, -pInfo->m_rectDraw.top );
    // now print the page, using the base class OnPrint function
    CScrollView::OnPrint(pDC, pInfo);
}
```

The function itself does three things. It gets the name of the document and places it in a string variable. Then it passes the hard part off to a new function called PrintPageHeader. When that's complete, it adjusts the window origin in the device context to account for the header that PrintPageHeader has printed. When it's done processing, it uses the base class OnPrint to finish printing.

The only part of this that you may question is how the header is accounted for. The PrintPageHeader function has printed some information at the top of the page—the header—and adjusts the member variable m_rectDraw in the CPrintInfo object to take this into account. This tells you that the drawing origin for the document data must now be moved down to below the header. By doing that, the document data will be displayed correctly on the page.

This only leaves the important new function, PrintPageHeader, to be added to the loop processing. Since this function does not respond to a message, you should add it to CErectorView by using the right mouse button menu selection **Add Function...** to create a skeleton function with the following properties: Function Type void; Function Declaration PrintPageHeader(CDC* pDC, CPrintInfo* pInfo, CString& strTitle); Access Protected. Listing 11.8 shows you this function, which I placed after the other printing functions.

Listing 11.8

```
// This function prints the CString parameter as a header on the document
void CErectorView::PrintPageHeader(CDC* pDC, CPrintInfo* pInfo, CString& strTitle)
{
    // First, set the font
    CFont* pOldFont = pDC->SelectObject( &m_fntTitle );
    // Print a page header consisting of a title string
    pDC->TextOut( 20, -25, strTitle );
    //    and a single horizontal rule across the page.
    // Get the font metrics to set line position
    TEXTMETRIC tmFontTitle;
    pDC->GetTextMetrics( &tmFontTitle );
    //    and position the line .1 inch below the text.
    int y = -35 - tmFontTitle.tmHeight;
    pDC->MoveTo( 0, y );
    pDC->LineTo( pInfo->m_rectDraw.right, y );
    // Now account for the header by adjusting the drawing rectangle.
    y -= 25;
    pInfo->m_rectDraw.top += y;       // Adds a negative number
    // And restore the old font.
    if( pOldFont != NULL )
        pDC->SelectObject(pOldFont);
}
```

The `PrintPageHeader` function does two things. It prints the title information, which is passed to it as a parameter, using the member variable `m_fntTitle` which you set in `OnBeginPrinting`. As you saw earlier with the pen and brush, you want to save the old font when you set the new one and restore it at the end of your work, if it was previously set.

Next, print the title text string. This uses the `TextOut` function to print the string at a point (20, 25) logical units on the page, which comes out to 0.2 inches from the left margin and 0.25 inches from the top margin.

The next part is a little more complex. You create a TEXTMETRIC structure and fill it in with the metrics for the current font. You use the text height from that structure, plus 0.35 inches, which is the distance you moved for the text display plus 0.1 inch, as a coordinate on the y axis. Then you move to the point (0, y) and draw a line from that point to the left margin.

Next you need to account for the amount of room that you have used for printing the header, plus a 0.25 inch margin. You add this value to the current value for the top of the printing area, which is stored in the `m_rectDraw` member variable of the CPrintInfo object. Finally, you restore the original font if it was set.

Adding Cleanup Code for Printing

The only thing that you have to do for cleanup is to remove the font that you allocated in `OnBeginPrinting`. Listing 11.9 shows you the code to do that, which you should put in the `OnEndPrinting` function.

Listing 11.9

```
// This function releases any resources that were allocated
//    in OnBeginPrinting.
void CErectorView::OnEndPrinting(CDC* /*pDC*/, CPrintInfo* /*pInfo*/)
{
    // Cleanup after printing.
    m_fntTitle.DeleteObject();
}
```

You remove the font by simply calling the `DeleteObject` function, which is common to all objects derived from CGDIObject.

Changes to the Class Definition Header

The only thing that you still have to do is to add the new member variable m_fntTitle to the class header. As before, use the right mouse button menu command **Add Variable...** to add a new member variable with the following properties: Variable Type CFont; Variable Declaration m_fntTitle; Protected.

In addition, I added a header comment and rearranged the new items, which isn't necessary but does keep the listing tidy. Listing 11.10 shows you these changes.

Listing 11.10

```
/////////////////////////////////////////////////////////////////////////////
// ErectorView.h : interface of the CErectorView class
//
//
// Created by AppWizard 11 December 1995 11:39:42
// Modifications:
//    16 Dec 95   DH    Add base class operations to generated code:
//                              message handling; drawing.
//    18 Dec 95   DH    Add movement rectangle processing to show
//                              current mouse position
//    20 Dec 95   DH    Added OnUpdate function to allow
//                              use of hints for view updating.
//     5 Jan 95   DH    Added PrintPageHeader function
//                              and new member variable m_fntTitle.
/////////////////////////////////////////////////////////////////////////////

class CErectorView : public CScrollView
{
protected: // create from serialization only
     CErectorView();
     DECLARE_DYNCREATE(CErectorView)

// Attributes
public:
     CErectorDoc* GetDocument();
```

```
// Operations
public:

// Overrides
    // ClassWizard generated virtual function overrides
    //{{AFX_VIRTUAL(CErectorView)
    public:
    virtual void OnDraw(CDC* pDC);   // overridden to draw this view
    virtual BOOL PreCreateWindow(CREATESTRUCT& cs);
    protected:
    virtual void OnInitialUpdate(); // called first time after construct
    virtual BOOL OnPreparePrinting(CPrintInfo* pInfo);
    virtual void OnBeginPrinting(CDC* pDC, CPrintInfo* pInfo);
    virtual void OnEndPrinting(CDC* pDC, CPrintInfo* pInfo);
    virtual void OnUpdate(CView* pSender, LPARAM lHint, CObject* pHint);
    virtual void OnPrint(CDC* pDC, CPrintInfo* pInfo);
    //}}AFX_VIRTUAL

// Implementation
public:
    virtual ~CErectorView();
#ifdef _DEBUG
    virtual void AssertValid() const;
    virtual void Dump(CDumpContext& dc) const;
#endif

protected:
    CErectorBeam* m_pBeamCur;    // pointer to current beam
    CRect m_rectPrev;            // previous movement rectangle
    CFont m_fntTitle;            // title font for use in header

// Helper function
protected:
    void PrintPageHeader(CDC* pDC, CPrintInfo* pInfo, CString& strTitle);

// Generated message map functions
```

```
protected:
    //{{AFX_MSG(CErectorView)
    afx_msg void OnLButtonDown(UINT nFlags, CPoint point);
    afx_msg void OnLButtonUp(UINT nFlags, CPoint point);
    afx_msg void OnMouseMove(UINT nFlags, CPoint point);
    //}}AFX_MSG
    DECLARE_MESSAGE_MAP()
};


#ifndef _DEBUG  // debug version in ErectorView.cpp
inline CErectorDoc* CErectorView::GetDocument()
    { return (CErectorDoc*)m_pDocument; }
#endif
```

//

Testing the Print Header

That's all that you need to do to add the print header. Figure 11.7 shows you the Print Preview of the new page, with a header clearly displayed.

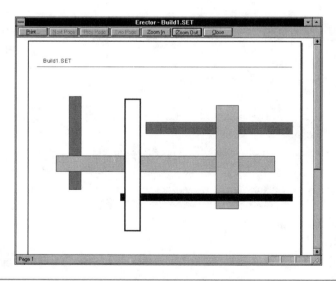

FIGURE 11.7 THE NEW HEADER INFORMATION IS SHOWN AT THE TOP OF THE PRINT PREVIEW WINDOW.

DRAWING BITMAPS

The Windows environment is built around graphics. It uses graphics for controls, such as buttons and toolbars, for icons, for display, and for many other purposes. So far, you have only created graphics for ErectorSet using drawing functions for standard shapes. These are called *vector graphics* because the graphics that they draw are composed of lines. Once the graphic is created with lines, it can be either stroked along the line, filled in inside the lines, both.

Most Windows graphics, however, are actually small pictures. Rather than being made up of lines, they are composed by coloring individual pixels to make the desired picture. Such graphics are called *bitmaps*. Windows uses bitmaps in a wide variety of ways, from the controls and icons mentioned earlier to patterns and cursors. The MFC will support all of these types.

This section of the chapter provides you with a brief introduction to bitmaps and how to use them. The issues in handling bitmaps are quite extensive, and you can use many techniques to accomplish various types of bitmap display. This section covers the simplest type of bitmap, a bitmap pattern, and shows how you can define and use a pattern in your application.

Types of Bitmaps

The very definition of a bitmap—a small picture made up by coloring individual pixels—tells you that there is an immediate problem in handling bitmaps. Because bitmaps deal with pixels, they must be handled with some care. As you saw earlier in this chapter, using a pixel measurement system can make your drawing and display functions depend on the resolution of the device that is displaying them. For this reason, you need to understand the different types of bitmaps that are used in a Windows program.

GDI Bitmaps

The basic type of bitmap that is used in Windows is a GDI bitmap. This is a device-dependent bitmap format. The bitmap object has an associated BITMAP data structure in the Windows environment that defines the bitmap. The application can access these bitmaps and use them quite conveniently, but the internal structure makes it impossible to use these outside of the environment where they were created. They are inevitably linked to the display hardware that they were built for.

A GDI bitmap is simply one more GDI object, such as a pen or brush. In an MFC application, you can access and use GDI bitmaps through the CBitmap class. You use the CBitmap functions to create or load a GDI bitmap, possibly converting it from a device-independent format. Once loaded, select it into an appropriate device-context and then use standard device context functions to work with it. Like all other GDI objects, when you're done with it, you must deselect it and dispose of it.

Device-Independent Bitmaps (DIBs)

The DIB format is an alternative to the GDI format that solves many of the problems generated by the device-dependencies inherent in the GDI bitmap. All Windows applications can use DIBs with any type of output hardware, making these suitable for transferring bitmap data from one Windows system to another. A DIB bitmap is usually stored in an external file, with a file extension of .BMP (for *BitMaP*). The .BMP file format is understood and used by most Windows graphics programs. In particular, the Windows paint program PaintBrush can read and create .BMP files. The resource editor also uses .BMP files to store external images such as the toolbar, icons, and other applicable paint data.

Generally, you will use the DIB format for external use, such as files, and the GDI format for internal processing. However, you should know that there are functions available, such as the Windows function `CreateDIBitmap`, that allow you to directly access and manipulate DIB bitmaps when that's required.

Advantages and Drawbacks of Bitmaps

As is true of most things in programming, there are advantages and drawbacks in using bitmaps in your programs. The advantages generally outweigh the drawbacks—that's why so many bitmaps are used in applications—but you should be aware of both sides of the coin.

The major advantage of using bitmaps is speed of processing, pure and simple. When you're drawing on a display device, the user must wait for you to finish before moving forward. Since you can format bitmaps to match the output characteristics of the system where you are executing, you can use bitmaps to display high-quality graphic information quickly enough that the user doesn't become impatient or dissatisfied. Although this requires some care and feeding in your bitmap handling, the resulting speed improvements over redrawing every item is significant. I don't think it's too strong to say that without bitmaps, graphic user interfaces, such as Windows, wouldn't be worth using.

However, bitmaps have two disadvantages. First, all bitmaps, even the DIB format, cannot be used on all types of devices independently. To give an example, all bitmaps are defined with certain dimensions. Although you can stretch or shrink them, if you do so they are likely to look very bad, perhaps even be indistinguishable, if the conversion required is very drastic. This is always true since stretching or shrinking must mean that you add or remove data from the bitmap, which may result in the problems mentioned. In a similar way, color bitmaps that are displayed on a monochrome output device will often display very poorly, losing essential elements that were coded in the colors being used.

The second drawback to bitmaps is their size. Since a bitmap stores one bit (at least) of data for each pixel, a lot of data is required to make up a full bitmapped image. For example, suppose you want to store a standard letter page of monochrome data using a 300 dots-per-inch bitmap. This comes out to a mere 8.5 times 300 times 11 times 300 bits, or more than 1 million bytes (1,051,875 bytes to be exact). If you throw in color, the numbers can quickly become astronomical. Even in these days of 500 MB drives and 32 MB memory, these are daunting figures—in fact, bitmapped image handling is one of the major features driving the increases in disk and memory size.

Adding a Pattern-Fill Bitmap

To see how these two types of bitmap interact, let's create a pattern to use for drawing the beams in ErectorSet. This is easily done by using the resource editor, which creates the pattern as a device-independent bitmap and stores it as a .BMP file. Then you can create a GDI bitmap object of the class CBitmap in your application, initialize it with the pattern bitmap, and then use it as a form of brush to fill the beam objects that you create.

To keep this in the processing flow that is already established, you can add one more item to the Beam menu in ErectorSet: **Pattern**. This will allow the user to select a pattern fill from the menu as well as the various solid color fills that you already have. This is a good example of how existing programs are extended.

Creating a Pattern in the Resource Editor

Begin by switching to the Resource View pane within the Developer Studio. Now choose **Resource** from the Insert menu to display the Insert Resource dialog box and choose **Bitmap** to create a new Bitmap object. Alternatively, you can press **Ctrl+5** or use the New Bitmap button on the Project toolbar to open a new

Bitmap object. In any event, once the new bitmap is displayed in the Bitmap editor, select the edit pane and choose **Properties** from the Edit menu to display the Bitmap Properties dialog box. Fill in the Properties dialog box with the following items:

- ID: IDB_BEAM_FILL
- Width: 8
- Height: 8

Leave the colors set to 16 colors, and let the bitmap editor fill in the file name. The final version of the Properties dialog box should look like Figure 11.8.

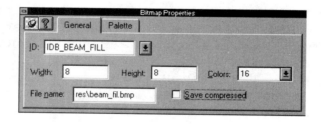

FIGURE 11.8 THESE ARE THE SETTINGS FOR YOUR NEW PATTERN FILL BITMAP.

The height and width are set to 8 bits each because all pattern bitmaps must be 8 pixels by 8 pixels.

Now you need to draw the new pattern. Figure 11.9 shows the one that I used.

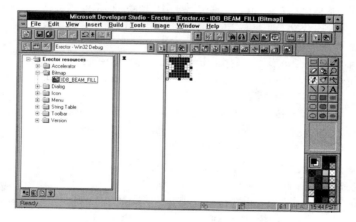

FIGURE 11.9 THIS IS THE NEW PATTERN BITMAP.

As you can see, this begins to look like a small section of an erector beam.

When you are done drawing, close the bitmap editor and save the resource. Then return to the main resource list.

Adding the Pattern Selection to the Beam Menu

Since you want the user to be able to select the pattern from the Settings dialog box, select the Dialog Type, choose IDD_SETTINGS in the Resources list, and open the Settings dialog box.

What you need to do is add one more item to the Beam Color list. To do that, select the Beam Color combo box and open the Properties dialog box for it. Go into Enter list choices and add Pattern to the bottom of the list, as shown in Figure 11.10.

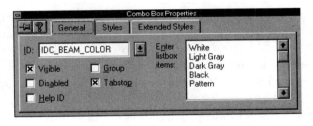

FIGURE 11.10 YOU CAN EASILY ADD A NEW ELEMENT TO THE BEAM COLOR COMBO BOX TO HANDLE THE NEW PATTERN.

After you have added the new list entry, check the extended view of the list to be sure that all the elements still display when the list is dropped down. If not, pull down the bottom of the extended view to allow all five list items to show at once. When you're done, test the dialog box to be sure it works the way you want it to work, then close the Dialog resource editor. At this point, you're done with the resource editor, so close it and return to the Developer Studio.

Restructuring ErectorSet to Handle Patterns

At this point, we need to review how CErectorDoc and CErectorBeam work together to set a beam color. If you remember, CErectorDoc maintains the beam color as both a color selection integer—essentially the index of the color entry in the Settings dialog box—and as a COLORREF structure set from that integer. Then, when the beam is created, the COLORREF structure is passed to the beam to tell it what color to use for drawing.

Now that you will be using a pattern to create the brush to fill the beam, you can't pass a COLORREF structure any more. The COLORREF specifically sets a color, not a pattern. Therefore, you need to change the handling of the beams and how you store and set the beam fill brush.

The obvious answer is to eliminate creating the brush before you get ready to draw the beam. Instead of immediately setting the brush color from the color index value and passing the COLORREF structure to CErectorBeam's constructor function, you can simply store and pass the color index value itself and use that when you draw the beam to determine the correct color or pattern. This has the additional virtue of eliminating the member variable m_crBrushColor from the document, which is redundant since m_nBeamColor gives essentially the same information.

N O T E

Obviously, you could have used this technique from the beginning for setting the color for the beam. However, this is actually the way I developed ErectorSet over a period of time. Although I could easily have used this technique for the entire set of examples, I felt that there were good reasons to let you see how this worked out. By seeing how this needs to be changed, I hope you also discover that making changes, even to this extent, aren't too painful when you're working in C++. Also, I always hated it in school when I felt that the examples were being worked "backward," that is, that they were developed by working back from the final, desired result to the initial stages, rather then realistically being created from the beginning to the end. Here you see the actual process as I experienced it.

Let's review what needs to be changed to use the color index throughout the application:

1. The call to CErectorBeam's constructor must be changed to take the color index instead of the current COLORREF structure.

2. The DrawBeam function must be changed to set the color for the beam from the stored color index.

3. All references to setting the beam color must be deleted from the CErectorDoc class.

4. The function SetBrushColor must be moved from CErectorDoc to CErectorBeam to support the new color handling.

5. The class member variable m_crBrushColor can be deleted in both the CErectorDoc and CErectorBeam classes, since the color will now be set at the time the beam is drawn.

6. The CErectorBeam Serialize function must be changed to store the color index instead of the beam color and the schema number must be incremented to account for this.

Notice that none of these changes are directly tied into supporting patterns in the beam. They are simply the changes needed to eliminate the use of the beam color and to change to using the color index.

To make the change process quite clear, let's make these changes first and then make the changes required to support the patterned brush. Listing 11.11 shows you the changes that are required in the entire ErectorDoc.cpp file to support changing to use the color index. Remember that this file encompasses both the CErectorDoc class and the CErectorBeam class.

Listing 11.11

```
///////////////////////////////////////////////////////////////////////
// ErectorDoc.cpp : implementation of the CErectorDoc class
//
//
// Created by AppWizard 11 December 1995 11:39:42
// Modifiications:
//   12 Dec 95   DH Add OnOpenDocument to generated code,
//                      along with new common InitDocument().
//   12 Dec 95   DH Add CErectorBeam class to generated code:
//                      initialization; serialization; contents.
//   15 Dec 95   DH Add menu item Edit>>Clear All with new function,
//                      OnEditClearAll, and aux function, DeleteContents.
//   18 Dec 95   DH Add SetupRect to support movement rectangle display
//                      and modify EndBeam to use it.
//   20 Dec 95   DH Add error checking to SetupRect and modify EndBeam to use it.
//   21 Dec 95   DH Add serialization for document size
//                      and change schema number in CErectorBeam to reflect that.
```

```
//   3 Jan 95   DH Add Beam Settings dialog for setting beam characteristics.
//   6 Jan 95   DH Change beam color handling to use color index instead of
//                  beam color as COLORREF.
////////////////////////////////////////////////////////////////////////////


#include "stdafx.h"
#include "Erector.h"

#include "ErectorDoc.h"
#include "BeamDlg.h"

#ifdef _DEBUG
#define new DEBUG_NEW
#undef THIS_FILE
static char THIS_FILE[] = __FILE__;
#endif


////////////////////////////////////////////////////////////////////////////
// CErectorDoc

IMPLEMENT_DYNCREATE(CErectorDoc, CDocument)

BEGIN_MESSAGE_MAP(CErectorDoc, CDocument)
    //{{AFX_MSG_MAP(CErectorDoc)
    ON_COMMAND(ID_EDIT_CLEAR_ALL, OnEditClearAll)
    ON_UPDATE_COMMAND_UI(ID_EDIT_CLEAR_ALL, OnUpdateEditClearAll)
    ON_COMMAND(ID_BEAM_SETTINGS, OnBeamSettings)
    //}}AFX_MSG_MAP
END_MESSAGE_MAP()


////////////////////////////////////////////////////////////////////////////
// CErectorDoc construction/destruction

CErectorDoc::CErectorDoc()
```

```
{
     // TODO: add one-time construction code here

}


CErectorDoc::~CErectorDoc()
{
}



// Move the function SetBrushColor to the CErectorBeam class



// This function uses current pen width to create a pen object
//     and a brush for drawing. This must be done whenever
//     a document is created Uses the CPen class.
void CErectorDoc::InitDocument()
{
     // the default pen is 2 pixels wide
     m_nPenWidth = 2;
     // the default brush is solid 50% gray
     m_nBeamColor = DK_GRAY;
     // remove call to set beam color
     // default document size is 850 by 1100 pixels
     m_sizeDoc = CSize(850, 1100);

     return;
}



// This function clears the current drawing in response to
//     the Edit>>Clear All or any equivalent user action.
void CErectorDoc::OnEditClearAll()
{
     DeleteContents();                      // delete the beam list data
```

```
        SetModifiedFlag( TRUE );        // mark the document as dirty
        UpdateAllViews( NULL );         // re-draw all the views


}



// This function updates the user interface to allow the user
//    to select the Edit menu item, Clear All.
void CErectorDoc::OnUpdateEditClearAll(CCmdUI* pCmdUI)
{
        // If the document is not empty (i.e., has at least one beam)
        //    enable Edit>>Clear All; otherwise, disable it.
        pCmdUI->Enable( !m_beamList.IsEmpty() );


}



// This function displays the Beam Settings dialog
//    when the user selects Beam>>Settings.
void CErectorDoc::OnBeamSettings()
{
        CBeamDlg dlg;
        // Initialize dialog with current settings
     dlg.m_nPenWidth = m_nPenWidth;
     dlg.m_nBeamColor = m_nBeamColor;

        // now invoke the dialog itself
        if( IDOK == dlg.DoModal() )
        {
            // get data settings
            m_nPenWidth = dlg.m_nPenWidth;
            m_nBeamColor = dlg.m_nBeamColor;
        }
        // remove call to set beam color


}
```

```
///////////////////////////////////////////////////////////////////////////
// CErectorDoc data management

// This functino creates a new beam object
//    and initializes it with the document default settings
//    for pen width and beam color.
CErectorBeam* CErectorDoc::NewBeam()
{
     // create a new beam object using our pre-set width and color
     CErectorBeam* pBeam = new CErectorBeam( m_nPenWidth, m_nBeamColor );
     // insert the beam into the list of beam objects
     m_beamList.AddTail( pBeam );
     // and mark the document as modified to avoid accidental close without save
     SetModifiedFlag();
     return pBeam;
}



// This function returns the position of the first beam in the list
POSITION CErectorDoc::GetFirstBeamPosition()
{
     return m_beamList.GetHeadPosition();
}



// This function retrieves from the list the beam at the given position
//    and updates the POSITION to point to the next beam in the list.
CErectorBeam* CErectorDoc::GetNextBeam( POSITION& pos)
{
     return m_beamList.GetNext( pos );
}



// This function provides a way to destroy the document's data
//    when you wish to save the document itself. The function iterates
//    through the data list and deletes the beam objects. It also
```

```
//    clears the pointers to the beam in the beam list.
void CErectorDoc::DeleteContents()
{
        while( !m_beamList.IsEmpty() )
        {
            delete m_beamList.RemoveHead();
        }

        return;
}


/////////////////////////////////////////////////////////////////////////
// CErectorDoc serialization

// This function saves and restores the document to an external file
//    using the class CArchive.
void CErectorDoc::Serialize(CArchive& ar)
{
    try
    {
        if (ar.IsStoring())
        {
            // first store document size
            ar << m_sizeDoc;
        }
        else
        {
            // first retrieve document size
            ar >> m_sizeDoc;
        }

        // now ask our data members to serialize themselves
        m_beamList.Serialize( ar );
    }
    catch(CArchiveException* pEx)
```

```
        {
                // If we get here, we have a serialization error...
                // Test for type of error.
                if( pEx->m_cause == CArchiveException::badSchema )
                {
                        AfxMessageBox(ERS_IDS_SCHEMA_ERROR, MB_OK | MB_ICONSTOP);
                        pEx->Delete();
                        AfxThrowUserException();
                }
                else
                {
                        throw;
                }
        }
        return;
}


/////////////////////////////////////////////////////////////////////////////
// CErectorDoc diagnostics

#ifdef _DEBUG
void CErectorDoc::AssertValid() const
{
        CDocument::AssertValid();
}


void CErectorDoc::Dump(CDumpContext& dc) const
{
        CDocument::Dump(dc);
}
#endif //_DEBUG


/////////////////////////////////////////////////////////////////////////////
// CErectorDoc commands


// This function sets up and initializes a new document,
```

```
//    generally in response to user choosing File>>New from the menu.
BOOL CErectorDoc::OnNewDocument()
{
    if (!CDocument::OnNewDocument())
        return FALSE;

    // initialize document parameters
    InitDocument();

    return TRUE;
}



// This function opens and initializes an existing document,
//    generally in response to user choosing File>>Open from the menu.
BOOL CErectorDoc::OnOpenDocument(LPCTSTR lpszPathName)
{
    if (!CDocument::OnOpenDocument(lpszPathName))
        return FALSE;

    // initialize document parameters
    InitDocument();

    return TRUE;
}


//////////////////////////////////////////////////////////////////////////
// CErectorDoc end


//////////////////////////////////////////////////////////////////////////
// CErectorBeam

IMPLEMENT_SERIAL(CErectorBeam, CObject, 4)
```

```
/////////////////////////////////////////////////////////////////////
// CErectorBeam construction/destruction

// This is an empty constructor required by serialization.
//    It is defined as protected in the header file.
CErectorBeam::CErectorBeam()
{
    // This empty constructor is used by serialization only
}



// This is the standard public constructor.
//    When you invoke this, it initializes the class variables
//    to the requested pen width and brush color, and clears out
//    the rectangle by setting all coordinates to 0.
CErectorBeam::CErectorBeam(UINT nPenWidth, int nBeamColor)
{
    m_nPenWidth = nPenWidth;
    m_nBeamColor = nBeamColor;
    m_rectBeam.SetRectEmpty();
}



// This is the standard public destructor.
CErectorBeam::~CErectorBeam()
{
}


/////////////////////////////////////////////////////////////////////
// CErectorBeam data management

// This function adds the first mouse location to the beam.
//    The coordinates are stored in the class member variable.
void CErectorBeam::BeginBeam(CPoint ptStart)
{
    m_ptStart = ptStart;
```

```
        return;
}



// This function finishes a beam by calculating the rectangle
//    required for the beam, using the starting and ending points.
void CErectorBeam::EndBeam(CPoint ptStop)
{
        // Regularize the ending point to derive the beam rectangle
        if( !SetupRect( m_rectBeam, ptStop ) )
                m_rectBeam = CRect( m_ptStart, CSize(2,3) );

        return;
}



// This function calculates the drawing rectangle
//    from the starting point to the supplied point and returns it.
BOOL CErectorBeam::SetupRect(CRect& rectBeam, CPoint& ptCurrent)
{
        // Error checking code to ensure that
        //    ptStart and ptCurrent are not too close to one another...
        if( (abs(m_ptStart.x - ptCurrent.x) < 2) ||
                (abs(m_ptStart.y - ptCurrent.y) < 2) )
                return FALSE;
        //    and are not too far apart, either.
        if( (abs(m_ptStart.x - ptCurrent.x) > 32767) ||
                (abs(m_ptStart.y - ptCurrent.y) > 32767) )
                return FALSE;

        // Set top and bottom
        if ( ptCurrent.y > m_ptStart.y )
        {
                rectBeam.top = ptCurrent.y;
                rectBeam.bottom = m_ptStart.y;
        }
```

```
        else
        {
            rectBeam.top = m_ptStart.y;
            rectBeam.bottom = ptCurrent.y;
        }

        // Set left and right
        if ( ptCurrent.x < m_ptStart.x )
        {
            rectBeam.left = ptCurrent.x;
            rectBeam.right = m_ptStart.x;
        }
        else
        {
            rectBeam.left = m_ptStart.x;
            rectBeam.right = ptCurrent.x;
        }

        return TRUE;
}


/////////////////////////////////////////////////////////////////////////
// CErectorBeam drawing

// This function draws a beam by drawing the beam rectangle.
//    It requires a Windows device context (DC) to draw in.
BOOL CErectorBeam::DrawBeam(CDC* pDC)
{
    CPen penStroke;
    CBrush brushFill;
    COLORREF crBrushColor;

    // Create the pen and brush values for this beam using
    //    initialized values of width and color.
    if( !penStroke.CreatePen( PS_SOLID, m_nPenWidth, RGB(0, 0, 0)) )
```

```
            return FALSE;

       crBrushColor = SetBrushColor(m_nBeamColor);
       if( !brushFill.CreateSolidBrush( crBrushColor ) )
            return FALSE;


       // Save the old pen and brush values and set the new ones into the DC
       CPen* pOldPen = pDC->SelectObject( &penStroke );
       CBrush* pOldBrush = pDC->SelectObject( &brushFill );


       // Draw the beam
       pDC->Rectangle( m_rectBeam );


       // Restore the old brush and pen
       pDC->SelectObject( pOldBrush );
       pDC->SelectObject( pOldPen );


       return TRUE;
}


// This function sets the brush color based on the
//    color reference value passed in as a parameter.
//    At present, only supports shades of gray.
COLORREF CErectorBeam::SetBrushColor(int nColor)
{
       ASSERT( nColor >= WHITE && nColor <= BLACK );
       switch (nColor) {
       case WHITE:
            return( RGB(255, 255, 255) );
       case LT_GRAY:
            return( RGB(192, 192, 192) );
       case DK_GRAY:
            return( RGB(128, 128, 128) );
       case BLACK:
            return( RGB(0, 0, 0) );
```

```
        default:
            return( RGB(0, 0, 0) );
    }
}



//////////////////////////////////////////////////////////////////////
// CErectorBeam serialization

// This function saves and restores the beam information
//     using the class CArchive.
void CErectorBeam::Serialize(CArchive& ar)
{
    if (ar.IsStoring())
    {
        ar << (WORD)m_nPenWidth;
        ar << (WORD)m_nBeamColor;
        ar << m_rectBeam;
    }
    else
    {
        WORD w1, w2;
        ar >> w1;
        m_nPenWidth = w1;
        ar >> w2;
        m_nBeamColor = w2;
        ar >> m_rectBeam;
    }
}
```

Listing 11.11 shows the entire file for both classes because I want to make two points here. The first is how (relatively) few changes are required to make this work. The second is that you can make changes like this without ever using the Developer Studio tools. Up to this point, you have always let the Developer Studio add classes and member variables for you. Here, however, you see that you can make such changes directly to the code file when that makes sense.

Now look at Listing 11.12, which shows the changes required in the header file, `ErectDoc.h` to support these changes.

Listing 11.12

```
/////////////////////////////////////////////////////////////////////////
// ErectorDoc.h : interface of the CErectorDoc class
//
//
// Created by AppWizard 11 December 1995 11:39:42
// Modifiications:
//      12 Dec 95   DH    Add OnOpenDocument to generated code,
//                           along with new common InitDocument().
//      12 Dec 95   DH    Add CErectorBeam class to generated code:
//                           initialization; serialization; contents
//      15 Dec 95   DH    Add menu item Edit>>Clear All with new function,
//                           OnEditClearAll, and aux function,
DeleteContents.
//      18 Dec 95   DH    Add SetupRect to support movement rectangle display
//                           and modify EndBeam to use it.
//      19 Dec 95   DH    Add document size member variable, m_sizeDoc,
//                           and new function GetDocSize to access it.
//       3 Jan 95   DH    Add Beam Settings dialog for setting beam characteristics.
//       6 Jan 95   DH    Change beam color handling to use color index instead of
//                           beam color as COLORREF.
/////////////////////////////////////////////////////////////////////////


// Forward declaration of the data structure class, CErectorBeam
class CErectorBeam;


class CErectorDoc : public CDocument
{
protected: // create from serialization only
     CErectorDoc();
     DECLARE_DYNCREATE(CErectorDoc)
```

```
// Attributes
protected:
     CTypedPtrList<CObList, CErectorBeam*> m_beamList;
                                     // each list element is a beam object
     CSize      m_sizeDoc;            // the document size


     // We track the beam color or pattern and outline width
     //    at the document level for all views. This allows
     //    the user to choose a new beam style for all the views
     //    together, rather than one at a time.
                                     // remove the brush color
     UINT       m_nPenWidth;          // the border width
     int        m_nBeamColor;         // the beam color index

public:
     POSITION GetFirstBeamPosition();
     CErectorBeam* GetNextBeam( POSITION& pos);
     CSize GetDocSize() { return m_sizeDoc; }


// Operations
public:
     CErectorBeam*    NewBeam();


// Overrides
     // ClassWizard generated virtual function overrides
     //{{AFX_VIRTUAL(CErectorDoc)
     public:
     virtual BOOL OnNewDocument();
     virtual void Serialize(CArchive& ar);
     virtual BOOL OnOpenDocument(LPCTSTR lpszPathName);
     //}}AFX_VIRTUAL


// Implementation
public:
     virtual ~CErectorDoc();
#ifdef _DEBUG
```

```
        virtual void AssertValid() const;
        virtual void Dump(CDumpContext& dc) const;
    #endif

protected:
        void InitDocument();
        void DeleteContents();
        // move SetBrushColor to CErectorBeam class


// Generated message map functions
protected:
        //{{AFX_MSG(CErectorDoc)
        afx_msg void OnEditClearAll();
        afx_msg void OnUpdateEditClearAll(CCmdUI* pCmdUI);
        afx_msg void OnBeamSettings();
        //}}AFX_MSG
        DECLARE_MESSAGE_MAP()
};



//////////////////////////////////////////////////////////////////////////////
// class CErectorBeam
//
// A beam defines the size and characteristics of a rectangle
//    that is filled to make a beam element of the drawing.
// An erector document may have multiple beams.
//

class CErectorBeam : public CObject
{
public:
        BOOL SetupRect(CRect& rectBeam, CPoint& ptCurrent);
        CErectorBeam(UINT nPenWidth, int nBeamColor);

protected:
        CErectorBeam();                         // required for serialization
```

```
      DECLARE_SERIAL(CErectorBeam)

// Attributes
protected:
      CRect       m_rectBeam;         // the beam rectangle
      CPoint      m_ptStart;          // the beam starting point
      int         m_nBeamColor;       // the beam color index
                                      // remove the color for the rectangle
      UINT        m_nPenWidth;        // the rectangle border size

public:
      virtual ~CErectorBeam();
      // This is both prototype and inline definition
      CRect* GetCurrentBeam() { return &m_rectBeam; };

// Operations
public:
      void BeginBeam(CPoint pt);
      void EndBeam(CPoint pt);
      BOOL DrawBeam(CDC* pDC);

// Helper Functions
public:
      virtual void Serialize(CArchive& ar);
protected:
      COLORREF SetBrushColor(int nColor);


};
```

//

This mostly consists of removing the two member variables for beam color, changing the calling sequence for CErectorBeam's constructor, and moving the SetBrushColor function. Again, notice that you can simply make these changes by editing the file when that's the easiest way to accomplish what you want. The Developer Studio is a support for your method of working, not a straitjacket.

All in all, this isn't a lot of work to make an architectural change in your application. If you've done much work like this in the past, I think that you will agree that this has been relatively painless.

Drawing with a Pattern Brush

With this change out of the way, you can now move on to use the pattern bitmap that you created earlier. You have already made the modifications to the resource file to include the pattern bitmap and to add a new item to the drop-down list in the Settings dialog box's Beam Color combo box. All you need to do now is take advantage of these features.

To do that, you need to take two steps:

1. Add another entry to the enumerated list of colors in the Setting's dialog box header. This will account for the new item that you've added.
2. Use the new setting value when you go to draw the beam.

Listing 11.13 shows the new entry in the `colors` list in the CBeamDlg header.

Listing 11.13

```
//////////////////////////////////////////////////////////////////////////
// BeamDlg.h : header file
//
//
// Created by ClassWizard 3 January 1995 08:54:50
// Modifications:
//      3 Jan 95   DH     Add color enum for use with dialog's combo box.
//      6 Jan 95   DH     Add pattern selection to color enum.
//////////////////////////////////////////////////////////////////////////


//////////////////////////////////////////////////////////////////////////
// general constants
enum colors {
     WHITE,
     LT_GRAY,
     DK_GRAY,
```

```
        BLACK,

        PATTERN_FILL

    };
```

This simply adds the new symbolic constant, PATTERN_FILL to the end of the list, to match the entry that you added to the combo box earlier.

Listing 11.14 shows the changes to make to the DrawBeam function to use the new value.

Listing 11.14

```
// This function draws a beam by drawing the beam rectangle.
//    It requires a Windows device context (DC) to draw in.
BOOL CErectorBeam::DrawBeam(CDC* pDC)
{
    CPen penStroke;
    CBrush brushFill;
    COLORREF crBrushColor;
    CBitmap bmBrushFill;

    // Create the pen and brush values for this beam using
    //    initialized values of width and color.
    if( !penStroke.CreatePen( PS_SOLID, m_nPenWidth, RGB(0, 0, 0)) )
        return FALSE;
    // the new way...
    if( PATTERN_FILL == m_nBeamColor )
    {
        // Use a pattern brush.
        // First, load the bitmap from the resource...
        if( !bmBrushFill.LoadBitmap( IDB_BEAM_FILL ) )
            return FALSE;
        //    then create the new brush from the bitmap.
        if( !brushFill.CreatePatternBrush( &bmBrushFill ) )
            return FALSE;
    }
    else
```

```
        {
                crBrushColor = SetBrushColor(m_nBeamColor);
                if( !brushFill.CreateSolidBrush( crBrushColor ) )
                        return FALSE;
        }


        // Save the old pen and brush values and set the new ones into the DC
        CPen* pOldPen = pDC->SelectObject( &penStroke );
        CBrush* pOldBrush = pDC->SelectObject( &brushFill );

        // Draw the beam
        pDC->Rectangle( m_rectBeam );

        // Restore the old brush and pen
        pDC->SelectObject( pOldBrush );
        pDC->SelectObject( pOldPen );

        return TRUE;
}
```

Here is where you get to use the new bitmap fill. This is done in several steps. First, you test to see if the color index value requests the PATTERN_FILL or is one of the color values. If it's a color, you can simply use the previous code to set the color as before.

If it's PATTERN_FILL, then you need to retrieve the pattern bitmap from the resource file. You do that by creating a CBitmap object and requesting that it be initialized to the value of the bitmap stored in the resource file. Then you use that bitmap object to create a new, patterned brush and select that into the current device context. Next, you simply use the brush that you created, whether a pattern or a solid color, to paint the beam interior.

The point where you go from DIB to GDI bitmap is truly invisible to you, thanks to the MFC. That happens when you load the CBitmap object, bmBrushFill from the resource. The resource, remember, is stored in a device-independent format, in a .BMP file; bmBrushFill is a GDI object and is loaded with a device-dependent bitmap.

That's really all there is to using bitmaps for patterns. You can now rebuild the ErectorSet application and run it. Now, when you select the Pattern entry for the Beam settings, you will get a display that looks something like Figure 11.11.

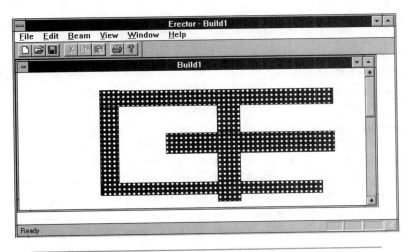

FIGURE 11.11 THE NEW BITMAP PATTERN GIVES A DIFFERENT LOOK TO YOUR BEAMS.

TRACKING MEMORY LEAKS

If you have been reading along and checking the function calls that are used in these classes, you may be wondering why you don't have code to delete the pattern that you load from the bitmap. The CBitmap::LoadBitmap function reference specifically warns you that "an application must call CGdiObject::DeleteObject function to delete any bitmap loaded by LoadBitmap." This might lead to think that you need to delete the bitmap object specifically in your code to avoid a memory leak.

This is a general problem in programming, and one that is rightly considered one of the most serious. A *memory leak* is a situation where you, as the programmer, have allocated memory is some fashion and do not release it when you're done. The problem is that the system will reserve the memory for you, even after your application is done using it unless you tell the system that you are finished and release the memory for reuse. Of course, under Windows the memory will be recovered when your application finishes, but that might be quite some time, if your user loads the application and leaves it running. In the meantime, every time you perform the bad memory allocation, more and more memory is lost to use.

Memory leaks are serious problems for two reasons. First, they will slow down your program and, ultimately, they will cause it to crash. Second, memory leaks are notoriously hard to spot, since the problem symptom occurs long after the leak itself. So you are right to be worried about the problem of handling memory and whether you need to delete your bitmap.

MFC Memory Diagnostics

Because memory handling is so important, the MFC provides good facilities for you to track how memory is used in your program. You can use these functions to check memory use and to display whether there is a problem in handling memory allocation and deallocation.

The basic method for tracking memory in your application is to use the MFC class, CMemoryState. This class has functions for taking a picture of memory at a given moment and comparing two memory pictures to see if there are memory leaks, that is, undeleted objects.

The function that takes the picture of memory at a given moment is called Checkpoint. This function takes a snapshot of memory at the time it is called and stores the snapshot in the associated CMemoryState object. Two functions use this information. The first is DumpAllObjectsSince, which displays a list of all objects allocated since you took the last Checkpoint for this CMemoryState object. The second is Difference, which takes two memory states as parameters and stores the differences between then in a new memory state object. You can then use the DumpStatistics function to report the differences between the first two objects. Together, these functions make a powerful set of tools for finding and solving memory problems.

The Difference function is particularly useful for finding memory leaks. The approach is to take a Checkpoint at one place in your code, before the memory is allocated, and then take another when the memory should be recovered, and do a Difference. If the memory has been allocated and deallocated correctly, then there will be no difference; if not, you can use DumpStatistics to display the objects that have caused the difference and clean them up.

Using Memory Tracking

Now let's check whether you need to delete the CBitmap object or not. The first issue is where to perform the memory checks. Since the concern here is that the bitmap being created in DrawBeam is not deleted, and therefore is leaking, the obvious choice would be to place the checks in the DrawBeam function itself. However, this really won't perform the check that you want, because the C++ compiler cleans up a lot of memory allocations automatically when you exit a function. For that reason, you want to test for leaks outside the function itself, at the point it's called, to allow the compiler to clean up everything that it can before you make the test.

If you use the Browser, you will see that DrawBeam is called from CErectorView in two places: once, when the beam is created and again in the code that redraws the beams when required. The obvious choice here is to place the test around the call when the beam is created; this is the first place the beam is drawn and is one that you know will be executed once for each beam.

Listing 11.15 shows you the new code that you should add to the OnLButtonUp function in CErectorView to check for memory leaks in DrawBeam.

Listing 11.15

```
// This function handles LeftMouseButton up messages.
//    NOTE that this does _not_ call inherited behavior.
void CErectorView::OnLButtonUp(UINT /* nFlags */, CPoint point)
{
    // Mouse button up is notable only if the user is currently drawing
    //    a new beam by dragging the mouse.
    //    In that case, we need to capture the mouse position.
    if ( GetCapture() != this )
        return;          // If this view didn't capture the mouse,
                         //    the user isn't drawing in our window.


    //    First, set the device context to this view...
    CClientDC dc( this );
    //    TODO: Add error handling in case we can't get a DC.
    CDC* pDC = (CDC*)&dc;
    // CScrollView returns view coordinates, which are device coordinates.
```

```
            //    They must be converted to logical coordinates before use.
            OnPrepareDC( pDC );
            dc.DPtoLP( &point );

            // End the current beam.
            m_pBeamCur->EndBeam( point );

    #ifdef _DEBUG
            CMemoryState msOldState, msNewState, msDiffState;
            msOldState.Checkpoint();
    #endif       // DEBUG
            // Now ask the beam to draw itself.
            m_pBeamCur->DrawBeam( pDC );
    #ifdef _DEBUG
            msNewState.Checkpoint();
            if( msDiffState.Difference( msOldState, msNewState ) )
            {
                    TRACE( "Memory Leak!\n" );
                    msDiffState.DumpStatistics();
            }
    #endif       // DEBUG

            // Now tell any other views that we have added a beam to the drawing
            CErectorDoc* pDoc = GetDocument();
            ASSERT_VALID(pDoc);
            pDoc->UpdateAllViews( this, 0L, m_pBeamCur );

            ReleaseCapture();        // Release the mouse capture established earlier
            m_rectPrev.SetRectEmpty();  // Clean up the movement rectangle

            return;
    }
```

Notice that all the code for the memory checking is loaded between #ifdefs. This ensures that this code is only created and used when you are debugging the program.

Other than that, this follows the course of action that you read earlier. First, three CMemoryState objects are allocated. Then one of these, msOldState, is used to take a snapshot before anything else is allocated.

Now you call the function. Immediately after the call you take another snapshot and store it in msNewState. Then you test for differences by using the Difference function. If there is no difference, Difference returns FALSE and you're done—there's no memory leak. However, if the Difference returns TRUE, you display a TRACE message and dump the statistics to tell what the variance is between the two states.

Now rebuild the ErectorSet application. Since the DEBUG flag is set, the code that you have added will be included. Now you have to get ready to test this code.

Testing for a Memory Leak

Now run your new version of ErectorSet in Debug mode to get the TRACE and memory messages. Create several beams, using both patterns and no patterns. Then quit the application without saving your document. The result should be a display in the Output pane that shows no memory leaks.

Causing a Deliberate Leak

However, you may be concerned that your new code didn't work correctly. (And, besides, I want you to see what an error dump looks like.) To do that, you can introduce a deliberate error into your code, as follows. Change the line

```
CBitmap      bmBrushFill;
```

to read

```
CBitmap*    pbmBrushFill = new CBitmap;
```

This directly allocates a new CBitmap object, instead of letting the framework and C++ handle it. I will tell you now that anytime you directly allocate an object using new, you will probably have to directly delete it as well.

Go through the code and change all references to bmBrushFill to use the new pointer, pbmBrushFill. Now rebuild the application and rerun your test. This time, the Output pane should look something like Figure 11.12.

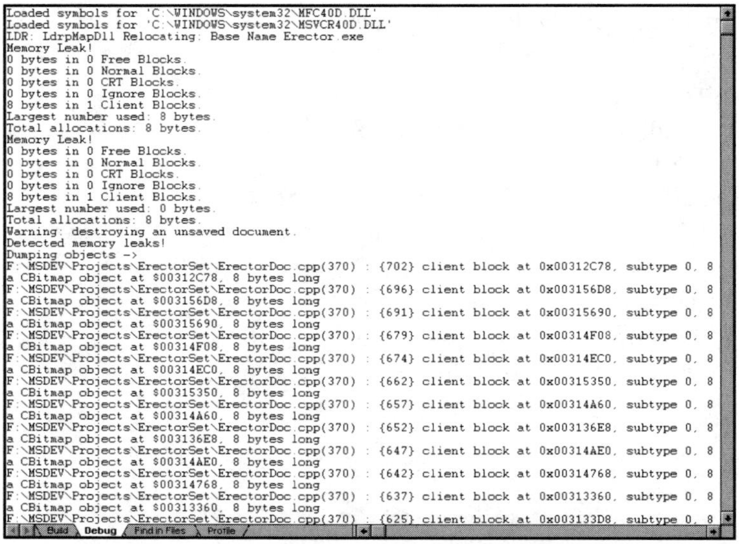

```
Loaded symbols for 'C:\WINDOWS\system32\MFC40D.DLL'
Loaded symbols for 'C:\WINDOWS\system32\MSVCR40D.DLL'
LDR: LdrpMapDll Relocating: Base Name Erector.exe
Memory Leak!
0 bytes in 0 Free Blocks.
0 bytes in 0 Normal Blocks.
0 bytes in 0 CRT Blocks.
0 bytes in 0 Ignore Blocks.
8 bytes in 1 Client Blocks.
Largest number used: 8 bytes.
Total allocations: 8 bytes.
Memory Leak!
0 bytes in 0 Free Blocks.
0 bytes in 0 Normal Blocks.
0 bytes in 0 CRT Blocks.
0 bytes in 0 Ignore Blocks.
8 bytes in 1 Client Blocks.
Largest number used: 0 bytes.
Total allocations: 8 bytes.
Warning: destroying an unsaved document.
Detected memory leaks!
Dumping objects ->
F:\MSDEV\Projects\ErectorSet\ErectorDoc.cpp(370) : {702} client block at 0x00312C78, subtype 0, 8
a CBitmap object at $00312C78, 8 bytes long
F:\MSDEV\Projects\ErectorSet\ErectorDoc.cpp(370) : {696} client block at 0x003156D8, subtype 0, 8
a CBitmap object at $003156D8, 8 bytes long
F:\MSDEV\Projects\ErectorSet\ErectorDoc.cpp(370) : {691} client block at 0x00315690, subtype 0, 8
a CBitmap object at $00315690, 8 bytes long
F:\MSDEV\Projects\ErectorSet\ErectorDoc.cpp(370) : {679} client block at 0x00314F08, subtype 0, 8
a CBitmap object at $00314F08, 8 bytes long
F:\MSDEV\Projects\ErectorSet\ErectorDoc.cpp(370) : {674} client block at 0x00314EC0, subtype 0, 8
a CBitmap object at $00314EC0, 8 bytes long
F:\MSDEV\Projects\ErectorSet\ErectorDoc.cpp(370) : {662} client block at 0x00315350, subtype 0, 8
a CBitmap object at $00315350, 8 bytes long
F:\MSDEV\Projects\ErectorSet\ErectorDoc.cpp(370) : {657} client block at 0x00314A60, subtype 0, 8
a CBitmap object at $00314A60, 8 bytes long
F:\MSDEV\Projects\ErectorSet\ErectorDoc.cpp(370) : {652} client block at 0x003136E8, subtype 0, 8
a CBitmap object at $003136E8, 8 bytes long
F:\MSDEV\Projects\ErectorSet\ErectorDoc.cpp(370) : {647} client block at 0x00314AE0, subtype 0, 8
a CBitmap object at $00314AE0, 8 bytes long
F:\MSDEV\Projects\ErectorSet\ErectorDoc.cpp(370) : {642} client block at 0x00314768, subtype 0, 8
a CBitmap object at $00314768, 8 bytes long
F:\MSDEV\Projects\ErectorSet\ErectorDoc.cpp(370) : {637} client block at 0x00313360, subtype 0, 8
a CBitmap object at $00313360, 8 bytes long
F:\MSDEV\Projects\ErectorSet\ErectorDoc.cpp(370) : {625} client block at 0x003133D8, subtype 0, 8
```


FIGURE 11.12 WHEN YOU ALLOCATE AN OBJECT DIRECTLY AND DON'T DELETE IT, YOU DEFINITELY GET A MEMORY LEAK.

I created two separate beams for this test, one with the pattern and one without. Then I destroyed the document without saving the information. All of this is reflected in the display that you see in Figure 11.12.

There are two important points that I want you to notice about this display. First, each time you run the DrawBeam function the `TRACE` output and the difference display show that there is an object, derived from CObject, that is not destroyed. This information, in itself, tells you that you have a memory leak.

Standard Memory Diagnostics

The more interesting point, however, is the display that you see after the message concerning destroying an unsaved document. The unsaved document message is generated at the end of the test, just before you terminate the program. Yet there is a very useful display after that that provides a lot of memory information.

This display is generated by the a set of functions that are enabled by default in the debug versions of the MFC. These are collectively called the *diagnostic memory allocator*. As you see, when enabled, these functions keep track of all memory that is allocated and deallocated in your application. The tracking process adds some overhead to your memory handling, so it is not used when you create a production application, but for diagnostic and debugging purposes, it is invaluable.

You can see from the display that the diagnostics tell you that a number of objects of the CBitmap type were not deallocated and have remained in memory at the termination of the program; there are memory leaks. This does two things. First, it tells you a lot about the memory problem. Second, since there all these objects where created at the same point in your program—at line 370 in ErectorDoc.cpp—you also know that the rest of your program is handling memory correctly.

The global diagnostic dump is very useful for helping track memory problems. The diagnostic message shows the exact line where the memory was allocated; in this case, that's the line that created the new CBitmap object. With this information, you can get a good start on figuring out where the leak occurred in your program. Once you know that, you can add the memory checkpoint and difference functions to isolate the specific errors. Believe me, these are great tools for a Windows programmer!

SUMMARY

In this chapter, you have learned about several important issues. First, you learned how to change the coordinate system in your application so that your printed output looks more like your screen display. Then you read how to add header information to the printed output to match the title that you see on the document window. It also gave you an opportunity to read a little about fonts and text handling in your application.

Next you learned about bitmaps, which are an important component of the Windows GDI. You learned about the two important types of bitmaps: device-dependent bitmaps, stored in GDI bitmap format; and device-independent bitmaps (DIB), stored in .BMP files. You created a DIB bitmap using the resource editor and then used it to fill in your beams with a pattern.

To do that in the same way that the rest of the beam settings are done, you had to do two things to your application. First, you added a new entry to the Settings dialog box to allow you to set the beam pattern as one of the colors.

Then you restructured the CErectorBeam and CErectorDoc classes to pass only the color index rather than the color value for new beams. This is a serious change, but you were able to do it quite easily using Visual C++.

The last part of the chapter focused on memory problems. This is an important issue when you are programming, so you need to understand how it works. You learned about the MFC tools that allow you to check memory use to ensure that you are handling it properly Then you put this into practice by using these tools in the DrawBeam function and you saw what information is presented to show memory problems. Together, these tools are an important part of avoiding memory problems when you are programming for Windows.

CHAPTER 12

ENHANCING YOUR APPLICATION

There is much that you can do to make even a simple application such as ErectorSet more valuable to users. In general, the application should be as easy to use and practical as possible. For example, most Windows applications retain information from one use to the next. Additional features common to high-quality Windows applications are support for multiple panes in windows and a status bar display. You may have noticed that ErectorSet has some of these qualities: It retains a list of files that you have opened, and it has a simple status bar display. With a little work, your MFC application can enhance these features and add support for multiple pane display. This chapter shows how to support and use these features.

Important topics in this chapter include:

- Creating persistent information
- Split windows
- Using optional MFC classes
- Status bar processing

CREATING PERSISTENT INFORMATION

The version of ErectorSet that you created in Chapter 10 allows a user to set beam outline width and color within any document. However, if the user opens a new document, the beam settings return to the default values. It would be preferable if the user could set these values once for all documents created subsequently. Even better would be the capability to save these settings from one execution of ErectorSet to the next. That way, the user wouldn't have to reset these settings every time the program was used.

This is a common issue in Windows programs: most programs need to store information from one execution to the next. Windows provides a standard method for handling such information, and MFC provides easy access to these methods. In this section, you will see how to save and reuse information from one document and one execution to the next.

Saving Information in a File

If all you want is to save the settings from one document to another, there are several techniques you could use. For example, you could move the settings values from the document class to the application. This follows the same logic as that used when you decided where to place the information initially. If you want all the beams in a document to use the same settings, then the settings must be stored at the document level, because the document creates the beams. By the same token, if you want all the documents to use the same settings, then you must store the information at the application level, because the application creates the documents.

However, neither approach would save information from one execution of ErectorSet to the next. Each time ErectorSet was launched, it would use the original default settings for beams in any new document. In that case, the beam outline width and color would have to be reset each time ErectorSet were run if the user wished to work with anything other than the default values. It's important to implement the behavior that matches how users will employ these settings.

How you save the settings has to match how you expect your users to employ them. Table 12.1 shows how to match three important issues. The first column gives the pattern that you expect most users to adopt. The second column shows how to save the settings variables to support the pattern of use given in the first column. Finally, the third column describes the preferred storage mechanism to handle the type of behavior for saving the variables shown in the second column.

TABLE 12.1 DETERMINE HOW USERS WILL WANT TO HANDLE THE BEAM COLOR AND OUTLINE SETTINGS AND THEN IMPLEMENT THAT BEHAVIOR.

Expected Pattern of Use	How Settings are Saved	Implementation of User Settings
Set once for most work; change occasionally	Save user settings between executions	Preferences dialog box
Usually use default settings on restart; use other settings temporarily for set of documents	Save user settings between documents; save default settings between executions	Application level
Change settings only for one document	Save default settings between documents	Document level
Change settings regularly and need most recently changed settings	Save user settings between executions	Application level

The Application Profile and Windows

The obvious solution to the problem of saving information between executions of an application is to save the desired information in a file. Windows provides a standard file for saving this kind of information and standard functions for handling this file.

The file is called the *application profile* or the application *initialization file*. It is stored in the Windows directory on your system and has the name of your application with a file extension of .INI. The profile for ErectorSet is called `Erector.ini`. The application profile is a place to store all types of information about your application that you wish to save.

You are probably aware of this type of file from your use of Windows. Windows itself has a profile file, called `win.ini`, which is an important part of using and controlling Windows. Windows uses several types of profile files, all with the same extension, to support all its functions.

Windows supports two ways to save application-level data. One is to read and write your own profile information in the application profile. The other is to store information for your application in the Windows profile itself. There are two drawbacks to using the Windows profile. First, Windows must open and analyze this file every time it runs; the more information in the file, the longer it will take Windows to open. If you write application-specific data in the Windows profile, this is excess information that Windows must read and skip when using its own profile data. Second, any time you change `win.ini`, you run the risk of causing problems to the user's Windows system. I don't recommend using the Windows profile as a place to store application-specific data.

Windows provides system calls to read and write both the Windows profile and an application profile. For convenience, MFC provides functions that access and use Windows calls to read and write the application profile; following the reasoning presented earlier, these functions do not directly support reading and writing the Windows profile.

The Structure of an .INI File

All Windows profile files—the Windows profile and all application profiles—follow a standard format. You are probably familiar with the Windows profile file, `win.ini`. Because the `win.ini` file is fairly complex, let's look at a simpler file to see how such files are constructed: `Erector.ini`.

It may surprise you that you even have an `Erector.ini` file. To see what's in the file, use either Notepad or Write—two accessories that come with Windows—to open the file, which will be located in your Windows directory; normally, this directory is `Windows`. You will see a file that looks something like Figure 12.1.

As you can guess by looking at this file, this is the list of most recently opened files that ErectorSet displays when you pull down the File menu. This list must be saved in a file because it displays files that were created and saved in previous executions of your application. Because this type of information is ideal for storing in the application profile, the MFC skeleton automatically creates an application profile and stores this list in it.

Next, look at the structure of this file. The file consists of a section name, which is enclosed in braces, followed by a list of *keyword entries*, each of which has a specific string value associated with it. In this case, the section name is `[Recent File List]`, and the first entry is `File1`. Each keyword entry is followed by an equals sign and then the value associated with that keyword. Note that there are no spaces separating the keyword entry, the equals sign, and the value. The value assigned to a keyword entry may be one of two types: an integer or a string. If you need a real number—a number with a fractional part— you need to store it as a string and then convert it within your application.

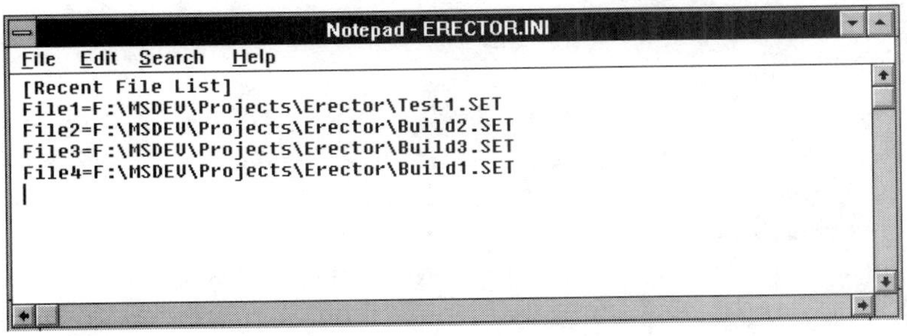

FIGURE 12.1 THE ERECTOR.INI FILE IS A TYPICAL APPLICATION PROFILE.

One additional benefit comes with Windows system calls for these files. The system calls—and the MFC functions that you use to invoke them—automatically provide for the situation in which any part of this structure is missing. When you write a profile entry, if the file is missing, Windows creates it; if the section is missing, Windows creates it; and if the entry is missing, Windows creates it. In a similar way, when you read a profile entry, you must supply a default value that Windows can use. If any of these items is missing—file, section, or entry—the default value will be returned to you. In this way, you don't need to worry about the usual file handling problems, such as what to do if the file isn't there, if an entry is missing, and so on. You can use these functions with full confidence that Windows and MFC will handle all the usual file drudgery.

Using the Application Profile

MFC provides special functions that allow you to read and write your own application's profile. The MFC class CWinApp provides the following functions for reading and writing your application's initialization file: `GetProfileInt`, `SetProfileInt`, `GetProfileString`, and `SetProfileString`. As you can tell from the function names, each pair of functions gets or sets an integer or string to or from the profile.

The standard Windows system calls require information such as the application name and the initialization file name. The MFC calls automatically provide this information so that you need only specify the section name, the entry name, and the value you want to assign to that entry; the MFC functions do all the rest.

Let's use these facilities to store and retrieve the settings data for ErectorSet. Both the outline width and the color are kept as integers—m_nPenWidth and m_nBeamColor. The integer format is directly supported, so you will use that format for this data.

One issue remains to be addressed: What names will you use for the section and entries, and how will these names be stored? The names are an obvious and rather simple issue; you've had to assign many names in the course of these exercises. However, the question of storage may be a surprise. You will be using these names in at least two places: once to set the values and once to retrieve them. When you use names repeatedly, you should set the information in one place and use that place every time. In that way, you don't need to worry about maintaining the names in several places in your code. The idea is to store the names as class variables in a place where you can easily get and use them.

Because this information will be used exclusively in the document class, that's the natural place to put these definitions. If you were writing in C, you would create variables in the class header and preassign them to the string values that you wanted to use for the names, which might look something like this:

```
const char szSectionName[] = "Settings";
```

The problem is that you can't do this in a C++ class definition. C++ does not allow you to define a string with initialization within the class header. The class definition only defines the class; it doesn't allocate any memory for it. Because initializing a string requires memory, it isn't possible to assign a value to a string within the class declaration. The problem, then, is where to assign these values in your class so that they will be immediately available.

The memory for a specific instance of the class isn't allocated until the class is created using its constructor function. That fact gives the answer to the problem: you must declare the name strings in your class header and initialize them in the constructor. The easiest and safest way to do this is to derive these member variables from the CString class. Listing 12.1 shows how this would look.

Listing 12.1

```
/////////////////////////////////////////////////////////////////////////
// ErectorDoc.h : interface of the CErectorDoc class
//
//
// Created by AppWizard 11 December 1995 11:39:42
// Modifiications:
//    12 Dec 95   DH   Add OnOpenDocument to generated code,
//                         along with new common InitDocument().
//    12 Dec 95   DH   Add CErectorBeam class to generated code:
//                         initialization; serialization; contents
//    15 Dec 95   DH   Add menu item Edit>>Clear All with new function,
//                         OnEditClearAll, and aux function, DeleteContents.
//    18 Dec 95   DH   Add SetupRect to support movement rectangle display
//                         and modify EndBeam to use it.
//    19 Dec 95   DH   Add document size member variable, m_sizeDoc,
//                         and new function GetDocSize to access it.
//     3 Jan 95   DH   Add Beam Settings dialog for setting beam characteristics.
//     6 Jan 95   DH   Change beam color handling to use color index instead of
//                         beam color as COLORREF.
//    12 Jan 95   DH   Use Strings to access ERECTOR.INI file.
/////////////////////////////////////////////////////////////////////////


// Forward declaration of the data structure class, CErectorBeam
class CErectorBeam;


class CErectorDoc : public CDocument
{
protected: // create from serialization only
     CErectorDoc();
     DECLARE_DYNCREATE(CErectorDoc)


// Attributes
```

```
protected:
        // each list element is a beam object
    CTypedPtrList<CObList, CErectorBeam*> m_beamList;


    CSize       m_sizeDoc;              // the document size


    // We track the beam color or pattern and outline width
    //    at the document level for all views. This allows
    //    the user to choose a new beam style for all the views
    //    together, rather than one at a time.
    COLORREF    m_crBrushColor          // the brush color
    UINT        m_nPenWidth;            // the border width
    int         m_nBeamColor;           // the beam color index


    //    String constants to define profile sections.
    CString m_szSection;
    CString m_szEntryWidth;
    CString m_szEntryColor;


public:
    POSITION GetFirstBeamPosition();
    CErectorBeam* GetNextBeam( POSITION& pos);
    CSize GetDocSize() { return m_sizeDoc; }


// Operations
public:
    CErectorBeam*   NewBeam();


// Overrides
    // ClassWizard generated virtual function overrides
    //{{AFX_VIRTUAL(CErectorDoc)
    public:
    virtual BOOL OnNewDocument();
    virtual void Serialize(CArchive& ar);
    virtual BOOL OnOpenDocument(LPCTSTR lpszPathName);
```

```
        //}}AFX_VIRTUAL

// Implementation
public:
        virtual ~CErectorDoc();
#ifdef _DEBUG
        virtual void AssertValid() const;
        virtual void Dump(CDumpContext& dc) const;
#endif

protected:
        void InitDocument();
        void DeleteContents();
        COLORREF SetBrushColor(int nBrushColor);

// Generated message map functions
protected:
        //{{AFX_MSG(CErectorDoc)
        afx_msg void OnEditClearAll();
        afx_msg void OnUpdateEditClearAll(CCmdUI* pCmdUI);
        afx_msg void OnBeamSettings();
        //}}AFX_MSG
        DECLARE_MESSAGE_MAP()
};
```

The three strings are named simply, following the conventions you know. Listing 12.1 defines these strings as part of the class; you still have to set them in the class constructor, as shown in Listing 12.2.

Listing 12.2

```
/////////////////////////////////////////////////////////////////////////
// erectdoc.cpp : implementation of the CErectorDoc class
//
//
// Created by AppWizard 11 December 1995 11:39:42
```

```
// Modifiications:
//   12 Dec 95 DH  Add OnOpenDocument to generated code,
//                      along with new common InitDocument().
//   12 Dec 95 DH  Add CErectorBeam class to generated code:
//                      initialization; serialization; contents.
//   15 Dec 95 DH  Add menu item Edit>>Clear All with new function,
//                      OnEditClearAll, and aux function, DeleteContents.
//   18 Dec 95 DH  Add SetupRect to support movement rectangle display
//                      and modify EndBeam to use it.
//   20 Dec 95 DH  Add error checking to SetupRect and modify EndBeam to use it.
//   21 Dec 95 DH  Add serialization for document size
//                      and change schema number in CErectorBeam to reflect that.
//    3 Jan 95 DH  Add Beam Settings dialog for setting beam characteristics.
//    6 Jan 95 DH  Change beam color handling to use color index instead of
//                      beam color as COLORREF.
//   12 Jan 95 DH  Use ERECTOR.INI profile to save and restore
//                      default pen width and beam color.
///////////////////////////////////////////////////////////////////////////

#include "stdafx.h"
#include "erector.h"

#include "erectdoc.h"
#include "beamdlg.h"

#ifdef _DEBUG
#undef THIS_FILE
static char BASED_CODE THIS_FILE[] = __FILE__;
#endif


///////////////////////////////////////////////////////////////////////////
// CErectorDoc

IMPLEMENT_DYNCREATE(CErectorDoc, CDocument)
```

```
BEGIN_MESSAGE_MAP(CErectorDoc, CDocument)
    //{{AFX_MSG_MAP(CErectorDoc)
    ON_COMMAND(ID_EDIT_CLEAR_ALL, OnEditClearAll)
    ON_UPDATE_COMMAND_UI(ID_EDIT_CLEAR_ALL, OnUpdateEditClearAll)
    ON_COMMAND(ID_BEAM_SETTINGS, OnBeamSettings)
    //}}AFX_MSG_MAP
END_MESSAGE_MAP()


/////////////////////////////////////////////////////////////////////
// CErectorDoc construction/destruction

CErectorDoc::CErectorDoc()
{
    m_szSection = "BeamSettings";
    m_szEntryWidth = "PenWidth";
    m_szEntryColor = "Color";
}


CErectorDoc::~CErectorDoc()
{
    m_szSection.Empty();
    m_szEntryWidth.Empty();
    m_szEntryColor.Empty();
}
```

Here, the constructor function assigns the actual string values to the predefined string member variables. Notice that you also have to provide a destructor for the strings. As discussed in Chapter 9, strings are allocated as both C++ objects and the string value. Because the C++ object is allocated when the document is created, it is automatically destroyed and its memory recovered when the document is destroyed. However, this is not true of the string constants used to initialize the CString members. To avoid a memory leak, you must explicitly destroy these in the document destructor function, ~ErectorDoc, as shown here.

You need to save the settings values when you get them from the dialog box and use the saved settings when you create a new document. All documents currently use the InitDocument function to set these default values, and that's where you will use the profile data, as shown in Listing 12.3.

Listing 12.3

```
// This function uses current pen width to create a pen
//    object and a brush for drawing. This must be done
//    whenever a document is created. Uses CPen class.
void CErectorDoc::InitDocument()
{
    CWinApp* pApp;
    pApp = AfxGetApp();
    // get default entries from the .INI file;
    //     default pen is 2 pixels wide if .INI doesn't exist
    m_nPenWidth = pApp->GetProfileInt( m_szSection, m_szEntryWidth, 2 );
    //      and default brush is solid 50% gray
    m_nBeamColor = pApp->GetProfileInt( m_szSection, m_szEntryColor, DK_GRAY );
    m_crBrushColor = SetBrushColor( m_nBeamColor );
    // default document size is 850 by 1000 LO_ENGLISH units (.01")
    m_sizeDoc = CSize( 850, 1100 );
    return;
}
```

Here's how this code works. Because the profile access functions are part of the application class, CWinApp, you first define and then retrieve a pointer to the application object. Next you use the GetProfileInt function to retrieve the m_nPenWidth variable, calling it with the section name m_szSection and the pen width entry name m_szEntryWidth. As in the previous version of this function, the value of 2 pixels is provided as the default value to be returned if the user has not set any saved values in the profile. The same technique is used to return m_nBeamColor.

Notice that this approach doesn't require that anything exist in the initialization file. If the section or entry requested doesn't exist, the default value supplied in the function is returned. The next thing to do is to place the values into the initialization file when the user sets them in the Settings dialog box. Listing 12.4 shows the revised code in the OnBeamSettings function that does this.

Listing 12.4

```
// This function displays the Beam Settings dialog when the user
//   selects Settings from the Beam menu.
void CErectorDoc::OnBeamSettings()
{
    CBeamDlg dlg;
    // Initialize dialog with current settings
    dlg.m_nPenWidth = m_nPenWidth;
    dlg.m_nBeamColor = m_nBeamColor;

    // now invoke the dialog itself
    if( dlg.DoModal() == IDOK )
    {
        // get data settings from the dialog
        m_nPenWidth = dlg.m_nPenWidth;
        m_nBeamColor = dlg.m_nBeamColor;
        // and save these settings in the profile
        CWinApp* pApp;
        pApp = AfxGetApp();
        pApp->WriteProfileInt( m_szSection, m_szEntryWidth, m_nPenWidth );
        pApp->WriteProfileInt( m_szSection, m_szEntryColor, m_nBeamColor );
    }
    // set the brush color from the selected color entry
    m_crBrushColor = SetBrushColor(m_nBeamColor);

}
```

Again, you have to get a pointer to the application object to have access to the required functions. With that, you use the WriteProfileInt function to store the desired information in the profile. Listing 12.5 shows what the initialization file looks like after you have stored some changed values, with the new section highlighted.

Listing 12.5

```
[Recent File List]
File1=C:\MSVC\MFC\SAMPLES\ERECTOR\SERIAL3.SET
File2=C:\MSVC\MFC\SAMPLES\ERECTOR\SERIAL1.SET
File3=C:\MSVC\MFC\SAMPLES\ERECTOR\BUILD1.SET
File4=C:\MSVC\MFC\SAMPLES\ERECTOR\TEST.SET

[BeamSettings]
PenWidth=4
Color=1
```

Now when you run ErectorSet, you will see that any saved settings values will be used for all subsequent executions.

SPLIT WINDOWS

Although a view is tied to a single window, a window is not necessarily limited to showing one view. You can create a window that shows multiple views; such windows are called *splitter windows* because the window is split between two (or more) views.

Splitter windows are particularly valuable in certain types of documents. For example, if you are working on a long text document, you may want to see the document both as a working document and in an outline format. By using a splitter window, you can have one view in the window display the document in standard text format, and the other view display the document in outline format.

You could do this in two separate windows, but that wouldn't be as convenient as splitting the one window into two views, because the two windows would have to be positioned and handled independently to show the desired information. It's much easier to use a splitter window for something like this than to use two windows.

A splitter window adds additional elements to the window to allow the user to control the splitting process. Figure 12.2 shows an example of a splitter window.

Splitter windows must have scrolling. At the top of the vertical scroll bar or at the left of the horizontal scroll bar is a splitter box. Selecting this box with the mouse changes the cursor and allows you to pull down the splitter bar, dividing the window into two sections horizontally or vertically, depending on which splitter box you are using. The splitter bar shows where the views are located within the window.

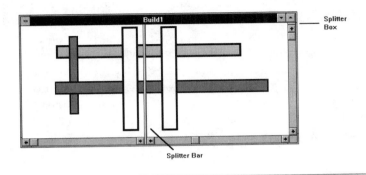

FIGURE 12.2 A SPLITTER WINDOW PROVIDES USER CONTROLS AND FEEDBACK ON HOW THE WINDOW IS SPLIT INTO VIEWS.

Notice two things about the splitter window. First, you can have only two segments for each direction; you may have one of the following: a window with one view—not split at all; two views—split either horizontally or vertically; or four views—split both horizontally and vertically. Second, the scroll bars appear only at the left and bottom of the window, meaning that the two views scroll together in the direction that they are not split. If you split a window vertically, as shown in Figure 12.2, then there are two horizontal scroll bars but only one vertical scroll bar. When you scroll the vertical bar, you move both views at once—both views show the same place in the document vertically.

Splitter Windows and Views

To understand how this works, you need to understand more about how windows and views are related. Recall from the discussion about documents and views in Chapter 7 that the view portion of your document corresponds to the client area of the window. This is where you normally draw and change information.

The Frame Window

There is more to the window than the client area. Around the client area are the scroll bars, the menu and title bars, and the window frame itself. All these elements are part of the window, although they are not part of the client area. This part of the window is called the *frame window*. The frame window creates and manages the view as a part of its responsibilities, which also include handling the scroll bars and other visual components of the window display.

For a multiple document interface (MDI) application such as ErectorSet, this process of creating and handling the frame window is done in the CMDIChildWnd class in MFC. As you will recall from Chapter 7, your application creates a document template that links the document, the frame window, and the view. The document template uses these links to create and display the document's data in the view. The frame window portion of this set is CChildFrame, an object of class CMDIChildWnd. I did not discuss the frame window in Chapter 7 because we were concentrating on the document-view interaction, which is more important. Now, however, you need to learn about handling frame windows.

Defining a Splitter Window

Until now, you have simply let the MFC skeleton application handle drawing and updating the elements in the window, and, generally, that's what you should do. However, to use a splitter window, you need to work with a third element in the frame and view: a splitter window that will work with the frame window and the view(s) to display the document.

The processing flow needs to change slightly to handle this new element. As before, there are three elements that are part of the document template: the document, the view, and the splitter window. The splitter window is derived from the frame window class, so it can perform as a frame window, but it also supports splits as required. In particular, it allows you to have more than one view associated with a document, each in its own pane in the window.

N O T E

This discussion and the following example are predicated on the fact that ErectorSet is an MDI application. If you were creating a splitter window for an SDI application, you would derive your splitter window from the CFrameWnd class instead of from the CMDIChildWnd class. Except for that, most of the information here works fine for an SDI application. Because our example application is an MDI application, I will confine the discussion to MDI applications. If you have questions about how to derive a splitter window for an SDI application, see the on-line reference material.

MFC encapsulates in the CSplitterWnd class all the required functionality for handling a split window with multiple views as panes. This class provides for handling multiple horizontal and vertical *panes*, or views, of the same document. The class handles drawing and controlling the splitter box and the splitter bar for the window, and it also handles scrolling. Using the functions in this class, you can select the size of panes when they are initially displayed; the user can change the size once the panes are opened.

The CSplitterWnd class creates a dynamic splitter window as a default. In a dynamic splitter window, the user can create and destroy additional panes in the window by using the controls provided. A dynamic splitter begins with a single view and two splitter boxes: one for a horizontal split at the top of the vertical scroll bar and one for a vertical split at the left of the horizontal scroll bar. The most important point about a dynamic splitter window is that all the views must be of the same class. Many popular applications, such as Microsoft Word for Windows, use dynamic splitters.

You can also create a static splitter window. In that case, the views may be from different classes. In a static splitter window, as the name implies, the views are created when the window is created and they never change in number, although their size may be changed by the user. The familiar Windows File Manager display, which shows the directory structure on the left and file list on the right, is an example of a static splitter window style. This style of splitter does not display splitter boxes, because views cannot be created or removed.

Following is a brief review of the terms used when discussing a splitter window derived from CSplitterWnd class:

- *Splitter window*: A window that provides multiple panes with controls and scroll bars that are shared between the panes. The panes in a splitter window are numbered by row and column from the upper-left corner, where the first pane is row 0, column 0.

- *Pane*: A child window managed by the splitter window class. This is normally a view for the given document.

- *Splitter box*: The small control at the top or left of the appropriate scroll bar that allows the user to create new rows and columns of panes in the splitter window.

- *Splitter bar*: The control displayed between the rows and columns of panes, which can be used to adjust the size of the panes.

- *Splitter intersection*: The point where vertical and horizontal splitter bars cross. This can be used to resize the panes in the vertical and horizontal directions at once.

Adding splitter windows to ErectorSet

Once you understand how all the pieces work together, adding splitter support to your application is quite easy. In fact, this is such a common option that you can add split window suppoprt with a few keystrokes (or mouse clicks) from the new Component Gallery in Developer Studio.

Let's see how you can use the Component Gallery to add split window support to Erector Set.

N O T E

You could have added splitter windows to your application when you created it if you wished. I didn't suggest this earlier because adding this code simply complicates to basic view-document processing that I wanted to cover first. However, in general, if you want splitter windows in your application, you can add this to the skeleton application by checking the Use split window checkbox in the Window Styles tab of the Advanced Options dialog when you create your new project.

Using the Component Gallery

The first step is to select Component... from the Insert menu. This displays the Component Gallery selection dialog shown in Figure 12.3.

The tabs along the bottom of the dialog allow you to select a variety of projects which have component element available. With some preparation, you can use the Component Gallery to add elements from any other project to your current project and application. For this exercise, however, you will use the Microsoft tab, as shown in Figure 12.3, to display components that Microsoft has pre-built to add additional functionality to your application.

Scroll down the display of icons for the various components to find the one labelled Split Bars and select it, as shown in Figure 12.3.

This component adds split bar processing to your ErectorSet appliction. The dialog shows you a short description of what the selected component does, and the question button next to the description provides a more extensive explanation, usually including specifics of how to use the new code.

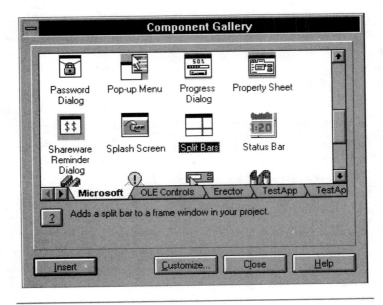

FIGURE 12.3 THE COMPONENT GALLERY ALLOWS YOU TO ADD COMPLETE PROCESSING ELEMENTS TO YOUR MFC APPLICATION.

Once you have selected the Split Bars component, press Insert. This displays the Split Bar dialog shown in Figure 12.4.

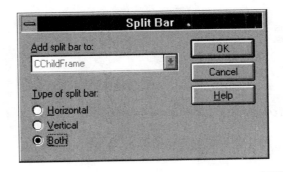

FIGURE 12.4 THE SPLIT BAR DIALOG ALLOWS YOU TO SET OPTIONS FOR YOUR SPLIT BAR PROCESSING.

The only option for you to set here is whether you want only horizontal or vertical splitters, or both. In this case, you will add both, so select that radio button as shown in Figure 12.4. Once you have made your options selection, click the Insert button, and the Component Gallery goes to work and adds all the processing components that you need to display and use split bars in ErectorSet. That's all there is to it.

Reviewing the new frame class

Before you run your newly enhanced ErectorSet, let's look at what the Component Gallery has done for you. From the earlier discussion, you know that the CChildFrame class has to be modified to add splitter boxes and bars to the view. This is where the Component Gallery has inserted the new code.

N O T E One easy way to see the changes that are added by the Component Gallery is to save all your original code—.cpp files, .h files, the .mak file, and any resource files—in a separate directory. Then, after you have done your work with the Component Gallery, you can use the WinDiff application to see any changes that have been made to the code. In this case, if you do that, you will find that the only differences are in childfrm.cpp and childfrm.h, which is what you would expect.

The CChildFrame class is very similar to the CMDIChildWnd class from which it's derived. As a proof of this, let's look at the code generated for the class, including the new additions. Listing 12.6 shows you the header file for the CChildFrame class.

Listing 12.6

```
// ChildFrm.h : interface of the CChildFrame class
//
////////////////////////////////////////////////////////////////////////////

class CChildFrame : public CMDIChildWnd
{
      DECLARE_DYNCREATE(CChildFrame)
public:
      CChildFrame();
```

```
// Attributes
public:

// Operations
public:

// Overrides
    // ClassWizard generated virtual function overrides
    //{{AFX_VIRTUAL(CChildFrame)
    virtual BOOL PreCreateWindow(CREATESTRUCT& cs);
    //}}AFX_VIRTUAL

// Implementation
public:
    virtual ~CChildFrame();
#ifdef _DEBUG
    virtual void AssertValid() const;
    virtual void Dump(CDumpContext& dc) const;
#endif

// Generated message map functions
protected:
    CSplitterWnd m_wndSplitter;
    virtual BOOL OnCreateClient(LPCREATESTRUCT lpcs, CCreateContext* pContext);
    //{{AFX_MSG(CChildFrame)
        // NOTE - the ClassWizard will add and remove member functions here.
        //     DO NOT EDIT what you see in these blocks of generated code!
    //}}AFX_MSG
    DECLARE_MESSAGE_MAP()
};


/////////////////////////////////////////////////////////////////////////////
```

As you can see, most of this is just class overhead: the class definition, the constructor function, and an empty message map. The items of interest are shown in bold in Listing 12.6: the class member variable, m_wndSplitter, and the

OnCreateClient function, which have been added by the Component Gallery. These are the two elements that allow your new application to create and use multiple views for a document.

The implementation code from CChildFrame is shown in Listing 12.7.

Listing 12.7

```
// ChildFrm.cpp : implementation of the CChildFrame class
//

#include "stdafx.h"
#include "Erector.h"

#include "ChildFrm.h"

#ifdef _DEBUG
#define new DEBUG_NEW
#undef THIS_FILE
static char THIS_FILE[] = __FILE__;
#endif


/////////////////////////////////////////////////////////////////////////////
// CChildFrame

IMPLEMENT_DYNCREATE(CChildFrame, CMDIChildWnd)

BEGIN_MESSAGE_MAP(CChildFrame, CMDIChildWnd)
    //{{AFX_MSG_MAP(CChildFrame)
        // NOTE - the ClassWizard will add and remove mapping macros here.
        //    DO NOT EDIT what you see in these blocks of generated code !
    //}}AFX_MSG_MAP
END_MESSAGE_MAP()
```

```
///////////////////////////////////////////////////////////////////////
// CChildFrame construction/destruction

CChildFrame::CChildFrame()
{
    // TODO: add member initialization code here


}


CChildFrame::~CChildFrame()
{
}


BOOL CChildFrame::PreCreateWindow(CREATESTRUCT& cs)
{
    // TODO: Modify the Window class or styles here by modifying
    //  the CREATESTRUCT cs

    return CMDIChildWnd::PreCreateWindow(cs);
}


///////////////////////////////////////////////////////////////////////
// CChildFrame diagnostics

#ifdef _DEBUG
void CChildFrame::AssertValid() const
{
    CMDIChildWnd::AssertValid();
}


void CChildFrame::Dump(CDumpContext& dc) const
{
    CMDIChildWnd::Dump(dc);
}
```

```
#endif //_DEBUG


/////////////////////////////////////////////////////////////////////
// CChildFrame message handlers


BOOL CChildFrame::OnCreateClient(LPCREATESTRUCT lpcs, CCreateContext*
pContext)
{
    // CG: The following block was added by the Split Bars component.
    {

      if (!m_wndSplitter.Create(this,
          2, 2,               // TODO: adjust the number of rows, columns
            CSize(10, 10), // TODO: adjust the minimum pane size
            pContext))
        {
          TRACE0("Failed to create split bar ");
          return FALSE;     // failed to create
        }

        return TRUE;
    }
}
```

The only active element in this class as you see is the OnCreateClient function, which is used to create the splitter window within the frame. The parameters for the Create function, used here, allow you to determine the maximum number of horizontal and vertical panes and the minimum size of a pane. The maximum number of horizontal and vertical panes is each set at 2; this is the maximum value that you can use for these parameters. The minimum size for a pane is set to 10 units in each direction; if any pane is less than that, it will not be displayed. For most processing, the default values used here are quite acceptable.

Using your new Splitter windows

Now that you have reviewed this new code in the CChildFrame class, all that you have to do is to use it in your document template. To do this you simply rebuild your application.

And that's all there is to it. With this change, you have now linked your documents with a frame window that supports splitter windows. When you execute ErectorSet now, the result should display something like Figure 12.2 which you saw earlier.

USING OPTIONAL MFC CLASSES

To this point, you have been working with the classes that are basic to any application derived from MFC: the document, the document's data, and the view of the document. These are the classes you will be working with most of the time as you build a Windows application. However, other classes are available that support and improve your processing. These classes implement useful features of standard processing as class behavior. For example, MFC has a rectangle class, CRect, that you have already used; it's the basis for the data objects in CErectorBeam and for the invalid area of your view. This section introduces other useful classes and shows how to use these classes to display additional information in your application's status bar.

The status bar is one of the useful features that have become expected in Windows applications, even though it is not, strictly speaking, a required part of the Windows user interface. Toolbar processing is another such feature. Both facilities are part of your ErectorSet application, courtesy of MFC, which provides them automatically for any skeleton application if the **Initial Toolbar** option is checked when you create the skeleton with AppWizard.

STATUS BAR PROCESSING

As set up in the skeleton application, the status bar display is simple and doesn't display much. As you build your application, you will want to enable this feature to invoke commands, just as you did for menus. The default status bar is shown in Figure 12.5, with all the available elements filled in.

The default status bar contains four elements. The first, a help display, shows the help string associated with the current menu selection or "Ready" if you are ready to draw or are drawing in the document view. You will remember that you set this string for the **Settings** menu selection when you defined the menu item in Chapter 9. The second, third, and fourth items are indicators that tell you whether the **Num Lock**, **Caps Lock**, or **Scroll Lock** key is currently active. On many keyboards, these keys have indicator lights, but it's often useful to be able to see the current status on-screen without having to look down at the keyboard.

The status bar is similar to the scroll bars displayed in the document windows. The status bar is a control bar displayed as a child window attached to its frame window. The status bar contains a row of text display panes, each of which may be used either to display a message to the user or as an indicator of the current status within the application. Like the indicators in Figure 12.4, indicators are implemented as simple text strings—usually defined as string resources—that are displayed when the condition is true and are blank if the condition is not true.

Status Bar processing

One item that I personally would like in the Status Bar is a display of the current time. This can be very useful if you work for long periods in the same application. So, for this example, let's see how you can add the current time to the Status Bar display. As you think about it, this requires three steps:

1. Redefining the Status Bar to have a place to display the time
2. Getting the current time from the system and formatting it for display.
3. Updating the time display on the Status Bar at regular intervals so that the time shown is correct.

Like the splitter window processing, all of these steps can be handled by one visit to the Component Gallery to add date and time processing to your current status bar.

Using the Component Gallery

Once again, select Component... from the Insert menu to display the Component Gallery selection dialog shown earlier.

This time, scroll down the display of icons for the various components to find the one labelled Status Bar and select it, as shown in Figure 12.6.

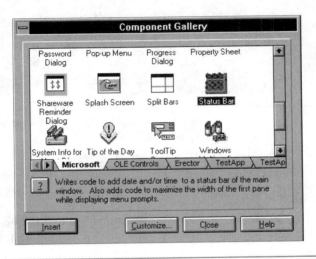

FIGURE 12.6 THE STATUS BAR COMPONENT ALLOWS YOU TO ADD DATE AND/OR TIME DISPLAY TO YOUR STATUS BAR PROCESSING.

As the description shows, this component can be used to add date and/or time display to the status bar already present in your ErectorSet appliction. The dialog shows you a short description of what the selected component does, and the question button next to the description provides a more extensive explanation, usually including specifics of how to use the new code.

Once you have selected the Status Bar component, press Insert. This displays a series of option dialogs that allow you to configure how the date and time will be displayed in the status bar. The first option dialog is shown in Figure 12.7.

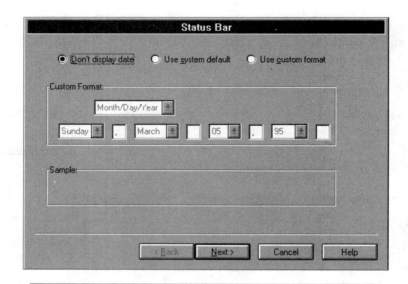

FIGURE 12.7 THE FIRST STATUS BAR DIALOG ALLOWS YOU TO SET OPTIONS FOR DATE
DISPLAY IN THE STATUS BAR.

This dialog allows you to choose whether to display the date in the status bar and how the date should be displayed. Personally, I don't find the date a useful element in the status bar, so I left the radio button selection here at the default value of Don't display date. If you want to display the date, you would change the radio button selection to either use the system standard display (03/01/96 for example) or you can set a custom display using the other elements of the dialog. You'll see how these work in the next section, as you'll use them to display the time component. Press Next to move to the next options display shown in Figure 12.8.

This dialog allows you to set the options for display of the time in the status bar. As you can see, I have used a custom format. To do this, you select the Use custom format radio button. This activates the Custom format group of selections in the dialog. You use these to set how your time display will look in the status bar. I have selected Military Time display, removed any seconds from the display, and changed the string following the time display to say 'PST' rather than 'PM'. Note that the empty text boxes—the ones without arrows next to them—are locations where you can enter any text string. That's how I could change 'PM' to 'PST'. I mention this because the first time you look at these, you might think that these were fixed strings that you can't change.

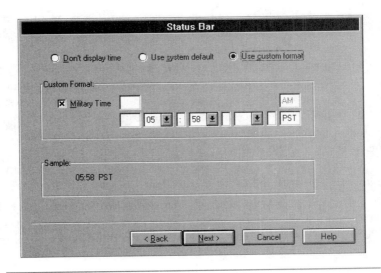

FIGURE 12.8 THE SECOND STATUS BAR OPTION DIALOG ALLOWS YOU TO SET OPTIONS FOR
TIME DISPLAY IN THE STATUS BAR.

As before, make whatever settings you want and press Next to move to the final
option dialog, shown in Figure 12.9.

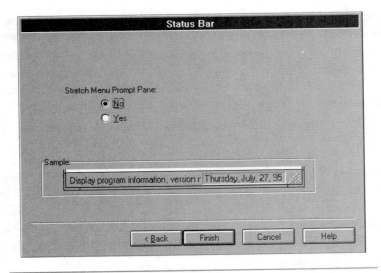

FIGURE 12.9 THE THIRD STATUS BAR OPTION DIALOG ALLOWS YOU TO CHOOSE HOW TO
DISPLAY THE FIRST PANE IN THE STATUS BAR.

This dialog box allows only one option: whether the first pane of your status bar—the one that displays the information about the current selection—will vary in size or whether it will be fixed. Generally, you want it to be fixed to fill the space from the left edge of the status bar to the second pane in the bar. However, sometimes the status bar is so full, or the window is so small, that the entire prompt string cannot be displayed in the first pane. This option allows you to force the first pane to stretch to the size of the string, blotting out other information in the status bar if necessary. The sample at the bottom of the dialog shows you how each of these choices would look. Click on Yes to see the variable pane display, and No to see the fixed pane approach. As you can see in Figure 12.9, I've left it with the default fixed pane approach.

When you've made your choice, press Finish. Now the Component Gallery goes to work and adds all the processing components that you need to display time (and date, if you selected that) in ErectorSet's status bar. That's all there is to it.

Reviewing the new Status Bar code

This time, the Component Gallery works for some time, adding all the necessary items. As before, I think you should always review the changes added by Component Gallery to be sure that you fully understand what has been done for your application.

In order to find the changes in the current definition and processing of the Status Bar, you need to determine where these are. If you go back and look at the display in Figure 12.5, you see that the Status Bar, like the Toolbar, the menu bar, and the window's title bar, is a part of the display outside the normal windows area. This gives you a good clue about where you can find the Status Bar definition code.

As you already know, the windows that display the documents in your application are child windows, inserted within a main window. This organization is what allows you to have multiple document windows open at the same time. These document windows are displayed in the main window's client area, in exactly the same way as the beams are displayed in the document window's client area. In fact, as you might anticipate, the main window has the exact same organization as the document windows that you have been working with.

All of this should suggest to you that the Status Bar, along with the other components of the main window that are displayed outside of the client area, are part of the main frame window, in the same way that the scroll bars and splitter boxes are part of the document frame window. In that case, you should look in the main frame window code for the Status Bar definition code. And, right enough, if you open the main frame window processing code, in the class CMainFrame, you will find the code which defines the Status Bar.

As I mentioned before, the easiest way to find the new code added by Component Gallery is to save all the original code in a temporary directory, then use WinDiff to find all the changes at once. However, this requires space on your hard disk, and some planning. Here I'll simply show you the changes, but for your own work, you will find using WinDiff is easiest.

NOTE

Listing 12.8 shows you the header code for CMainFrame, with the new code added by Component Gallery highlighted.

Listing 12.8

```
// MainFrm.h : interface of the CMainFrame class
//
//////////////////////////////////////////////////////////////////////

class CMainFrame : public CMDIFrameWnd
{
     DECLARE_DYNAMIC(CMainFrame)
public:
     int m_nTimePaneNo;
     CMainFrame();

// Attributes
public:

// Operations
public:

// Overrides
     // ClassWizard generated virtual function overrides
```

```
        //{{AFX_VIRTUAL(CMainFrame)
        virtual BOOL PreCreateWindow(CREATESTRUCT& cs);
        //}}AFX_VIRTUAL

    // Implementation
    public:
        virtual ~CMainFrame();
    #ifdef _DEBUG
        virtual void AssertValid() const;
        virtual void Dump(CDumpContext& dc) const;
    #endif

    protected:  // control bar embedded members
        afx_msg void OnUpdateTime(CCmdUI* pCmdUI);
        CStatusBar  m_wndStatusBar;
        CToolBar    m_wndToolBar;

    // Generated message map functions
    protected:
        //{{AFX_MSG(CMainFrame)
        afx_msg int OnCreate(LPCREATESTRUCT lpCreateStruct);
            // NOTE - the ClassWizard will add and remove member functions here.
            //    DO NOT EDIT what you see in these blocks of generated code!
        //}}AFX_MSG
        DECLARE_MESSAGE_MAP()
    private:
        BOOL InitStatusBar(UINT *pIndicators, int nSize, int nSeconds);
    };

    ////////////////////////////////////////////////////////////////////////
```

As you can see, Component Gallery has added one new class member, m_nTimePaneNo, and two new functions, OnUpdateTime and InitStatusBar. Note that the Status Bar, m_wndStatusBar, was already present.

As its name indicates, m_wndStatusBar is a class member variable. It is defined here as being an instance of the CStatusBar class, which is the class used by the MFC to encapsulate and provide all of the processing for the Status Bar. The new member variable, m_nTimePaneNo, is used to add the time pane to the status bar, as described later.

Creating the new Status Bar

Now let's switch to the processing code for CMainFrame. First. look at the code block shown in Listing 12.9. This includes some new code, added by Component Gallery, and some of the old code, which has an important bearing on how the status bar is processed.

Listing 12.9

```
//////////////////////////////////////////////////////////////////////
// CMainFrame

IMPLEMENT_DYNAMIC(CMainFrame, CMDIFrameWnd)

BEGIN_MESSAGE_MAP(CMainFrame, CMDIFrameWnd)
      ON_UPDATE_COMMAND_UI(ID_INDICATOR_TIME, OnUpdateTime)
      //{{AFX_MSG_MAP(CMainFrame)
            // NOTE - the ClassWizard will add and remove mapping macros here.
            //    DO NOT EDIT what you see in these blocks of generated code !
      ON_WM_CREATE()
      //}}AFX_MSG_MAP
END_MESSAGE_MAP()

static UINT indicators[] =
{
      ID_SEPARATOR,            // status line indicator
      ID_INDICATOR_CAPS,
      ID_INDICATOR_NUM,
      ID_INDICATOR_SCRL,
};
```

```
/////////////////////////////////////////////////////////////////////////
// CMainFrame construction/destruction

CMainFrame::CMainFrame()
{
    // TODO: add member initialization code here

}

CMainFrame::~CMainFrame()
{
}

int CMainFrame::OnCreate(LPCREATESTRUCT lpCreateStruct)
{
    if (CMDIFrameWnd::OnCreate(lpCreateStruct) == -1)
        return -1;

    if (!m_wndToolBar.Create(this) ||
        !m_wndToolBar.LoadToolBar(IDR_MAINFRAME))
    {
        TRACE0("Failed to create toolbar\n");
        return -1;      // fail to create
    }

    if (!m_wndStatusBar.Create(this) ||
        !m_wndStatusBar.SetIndicators(indicators,
          sizeof(indicators)/sizeof(UINT)))
    {
        TRACE0("Failed to create status bar\n");
        return -1;      // fail to create
    }

    // TODO: Remove this if you don't want tool tips or a resizeable toolbar
    m_wndToolBar.SetBarStyle(m_wndToolBar.GetBarStyle() |
        CBRS_TOOLTIPS | CBRS_FLYBY | CBRS_SIZE_DYNAMIC);
```

```
// TODO: Delete these three lines if you don't want the toolbar to
//   be dockable
m_wndToolBar.EnableDocking(CBRS_ALIGN_ANY);
EnableDocking(CBRS_ALIGN_ANY);
DockControlBar(&m_wndToolBar);

// CG: The following block was inserted by 'Status Bar' component.
{
    // Find out the size of the static variable 'indicators' defined
    // by AppWizard and copy it
    int nOrigSize = sizeof(indicators) / sizeof(UINT);

    UINT* pIndicators = new UINT[nOrigSize + 2];
    memcpy(pIndicators, indicators, sizeof(indicators));

    // Call the Status Bar Component's status bar creation function
    if (!InitStatusBar(pIndicators, nOrigSize, 60))
    {
        TRACE0("Failed to initialize Status Bar\n");
        return -1;
    }
    delete[] pIndicators;
}

    return 0;
}
```

First notice that the frame window's message map has been updated to add a new message handler. This calles the new function, OnUpdateTime, to update the status bar's time pane when a new message, designated by ID_INDICATOR_TIME, is passed to the window.

Next, note the code in the if statement that sets up the status bar. This executes two functions in CStatusBar. First it uses the Create function to attach the Status Bar object to the main frame window (this), and then it sets the indicators that are in the status bar using the SetIndicators function. Each of these functions returns a Boolean value which is TRUE if the function worked and FALSE otherwise. As you can see, if either of the functions fail, you get a TRACE message and OnCreate returns a -1 to signal an error.

Like many child windows, the Status Bar is created in two steps. First, the object itself is created using the class standard constructor. Then the Create function is used to attach the new object to a frame window and to define the style of the new window. For most cases, the default style used here, which makes the Status Bar display along the bottom of the frame window, will be correct. The Create function also sets the ID of the new child window, which is used to reference the child window. The default ID is defined as AFX_IDW_STATUS_BAR, which is what is used here. If you wanted to change this, you would insert the new ID that you want to use in this function—you can use the reference entry for CStatusBar::Create to tell you how to do this.

The SetIndicators function is the one that sets up the Status Bar display elements. Listing 12.9 also shows you the indicators array which is an essential element in creating the status bar display.

This indicators array is an array of UINT values. These each define one pane of the Status Bar. If the value is ID_SEPARATOR, the pane is defined as a message line pane and is blank. If the ID is anything else, the pane is defined as an indicator pane and the ID is expected to refer to a string resource that holds the string to be displayed in that pane. As you would expect from the display in Figure 12.5, there are four panes defined by array elements in indicators: a message pane and three indicator panes.

Panes are accessed in the Status Bar by use of their *position index* or their *string ID*. The index is the position of the pane within the Status Bar. The 0 pane is the leftmost pane, pane 1 is immediately to its right, and so on for the number of panes in the bar. The string ID is simply the resource ID of the string used in the indicators array. As you can see, the only way to access a message pane is by its index, since all message panes use the same ID_SEPARATOR as an ID value.

Finally, the size of a message pane defaults to one-quarter of the width of the Status Bar unless you specifically set a different size; the size of an indicator pane is exactly wide enough to hold the indicator string. There is one exception to this rule. By default, the first pane in the Status Bar stretches. All the panes are aligned on the right, and then first pane stretches to fill up the width of the bar.

However, the indicators array doesn't have any place for the time pane, so the new block of code adds the time pane to the status bar. It does this by getting the size of the indicators array, creating a temporary version of that pointed to by pIndicators, and then calling the new function, InitStatusBar, to add the new pane. Listing 12.10 shows you the InitStatusBar code.

Listing 12.10

```
BOOL CMainFrame::InitStatusBar(UINT *pIndicators, int nSize, int nSeconds)
{
    // CG: This function was inserted by 'Status Bar' component.

    // Create an index for the TIME pane
    m_nTimePaneNo = nSize++;
    nSeconds = 10;
    pIndicators[m_nTimePaneNo] = ID_INDICATOR_TIME;

    // TODO: Select an appropriate time interval for updating
    // the status bar when idling.
    m_wndStatusBar.SetTimer(0x1000, nSeconds * 1000, NULL);

    return m_wndStatusBar.SetIndicators(pIndicators, nSize);


}
```

Now that you know how the status bar is accessed, this is fairly straightforward. The function creates a new index value to access the time pane and stores this as the member variable, m_nTimePaneNo. Then it updates the temporary array pointed to by pIndicators with the time pane. Next, it sets the system timer to specify an interrupt time interval using the SetTimer function. This sets how often the time pane will be updated in normal processing. Finally, it sets the new set of indicators into the status bar.

Although the Status Bar is defined in the main frame window's OnCreate function, it obviously isn't updated there. The Status Bar needs to be updated whenever the user presses one of the keys that are linked to the indicator panes, or whenever the user selects a menu item that will display a help prompt in the message pane. In the same way, you will need to display the time repeatedly while ErectorSet is running if you want to display the current time. This use the new auxiliary class, CTime.

Using the CTime Auxiliary Class

Before you start work on the status bar, you should look at how to get and display the time from the system. MFC provides a class, CTime, that gives all the functions you need for getting and displaying time in your MFC application.

An object of the CTime class incorporates the values and functions of the ANSI date and time functions defined in the `time_t` data type and the associated functions defined in `time.h`. The `time_t` data type represents the current calendar time, and the associated functions allow you to create time variables matching any calendar date and time and to manipulate time data in a variety of formats.

The CTime class has functions that allow you to retrieve the current system time—the time shown in your system clock—and to create time objects that are set to any date and time. The time is kept internally as the number of seconds since December 31, 1899, and is based on universal coordinated time (UCT), which is equivalent to Greenwich mean time (GMT). CTime has an associated class, CTimeSpan, that represents the difference between two CTime objects.

You need CTime to do two things for the status bar display: get the current time and convert it to a format that can be displayed. To do this, use the CTime functions `GetCurrentTime` and `Format`. `GetCurrentTime` is straightforward. Call this function to create and return the current system time in a CTime object. Format is almost as easy: It formats a CTime object according to a format string, similar to a `printf` format string, that tells what elements of the CTime object you want to see and how you want them displayed. Table 12.2 shows the complete list of format elements that you can use in Format.

TABLE 12.2 THE FORMAT CODES THAT YOU CAN USE FOR A CTIME OBJECT.

Code   Displayed Value

Code	Displayed Value
%a	Abbreviated weekday name
%A	Full weekday name
%b	Abbreviated month name
%B	Full month name
%c	Date and time display according to the locale setting

TABLE 12.2 THE FORMAT CODES THAT YOU CAN USE FOR A CTIME OBJECT. *(CONTINUED)*

Code   Displayed Value

Code	Displayed Value
%d	Day of the month as a decimal number (01 to 31)
%H	Hour in 24-hour format (00 to 23)
%I	Hour in 12-hour format (01 to 12)
%j	Day of the year as a decimal number (001 to 366)
%m	Month as a decimal number (01 to 12)
%M	Minute as a decimal number (00 to 59)
%p	AM/PM indicator for a 12-hour clock according to the locale setting
%S	Second as a decimal number (00 to 59)
%U	Week of the year as a decimal number (weeks begin on Sunday; 00 to 51)
%w	Weekday as a decimal number (0 to 6; Sunday is 0)
%W	Week of the year as a decimal number, with Monday as first day of the week
%x	Date representation according to the locale setting
%X	Time representation according to the locale setting
%y	Year without the century as a decimal number (00 to 99)
%Y	Year with the century as a decimal number
%z	Time zone name or abbreviation; blank if no time zone is set

Use these format codes in the format string in the same way you would use format codes in a printf function; as with the format strings used for printf, you can insert other text into the format string to help define the display.

WARNING CTime uses the `srtftime` function, which is not supported in Windows DLLs. Therefore, CTime objects can't be used in a Windows DLL. For our work this isn't an issue, because ErectorSet is an independent application program (an EXE rather than a DLL). If you need to create a DLL, be sure not to use CTime objects within the code.

Updating the Status Bar

Let's look at what you need to do to display a CTime element in the status bar. This process is handled by the new function, OnUpdateTime, shown in Listing 12.11.

Listing 12.11

```
CMainFrame::OnUpdateTime(CCmdUI* pCmdUI)
{
    // CG: This function was inserted by 'Status Bar' component.

    // Get current date and format it
    CTime time = CTime::GetCurrentTime();
    CString strTime = time.Format(_T("%H:%M  "));
    strTime =  strTime +_T("PST ");

    // BLOCK: compute the width of the date string
    CSize size;
    {
        HGDIOBJ hOldFont = NULL;
        HFONT hFont = (HFONT)m_wndStatusBar.SendMessage(WM_GETFONT);
        CClientDC dc(NULL);
        if (hFont != NULL)
            hOldFont = dc.SelectObject(hFont);
        size = dc.GetTextExtent(strTime);
        if (hOldFont != NULL)
            dc.SelectObject(hOldFont);
    }

    // Update the pane to reflect the current time
    UINT nID, nStyle;
    int nWidth;
    m_wndStatusBar.GetPaneInfo(m_nTimePaneNo, nID, nStyle, nWidth);
    m_wndStatusBar.SetPaneInfo(m_nTimePaneNo, nID, nStyle, size.cx);
    pCmdUI->SetText(strTime);
    pCmdUI->Enable(TRUE);

}
```

Ignore the comments in this section of code relating to date. These are shown in common code elements used by both the date and time updates to the status bar; in this case, although I didn't add the date, these functions are still needed for processing. As a result, they are added to the code here, and the comments reflect their original purpose, not their current use.

N O T E

This function is called every time the frame window receives an ID_INDICA-TOR_TIME message. The code simply defines a CTime object, time, and sets it to the current time using the CTime function, `GetCurrentTime` which returns a new CTime object that contains the current system time. Once you have the time, then you use the Format function to select the hour (in 24-hour format) and the minute and insert these into a new string object. Finally, you concatenate the formatted string with a new string that contains the text element 'PST' that you added to the dialog box. (Of course, you should use whatever time zone abbreviation is appropriate; I just happen to live in the Pacific time zone.) Now that you know the appropriate format strings for a CTime object, you could also use the %z format string to add the system timezone identifier, if you wanted.

The time zone identifier comes from the TZ environment variable. The default value is PST8PDT, which signifies that the time zone name is PST, which is 8 hours behind UCT, and that daylight savings time is used. This works for me—I live in California—but it may not suit you. If you need to change this, read up on the time environment variable in the discussion of _tzset in the *Run-Time Library Reference* manual in *Books Online*, or do a search on _tzset.

N O T E

As discussed earlier, the default size of this kind of message pane is one-quarter of the width of the status bar—much larger than required for the time display. You need to find out how much space it will take to display the formatted string that contains the time. Once you know that, you can use the `SetPaneInfo` function to set the width of the selected pane—in this case, the time pane. The `SetPaneInfo` function allows you to reset three items for the selected status bar pane: the ID, the pane style, and the pane width. In this case, you are resetting only the pane width. The other two values remain the same as their current values.

To find out the size of a text string, use the `GetTextExtent` function of the DC. This function returns a CSize object that gives you the width and height of the bounding rectangle for the given string. You need only the width, so you call GetTextExtent with two required parameters: the string object itself and the length of the string—the number of characters in the string—and take only the cx component of the returned CSize object.

Once you have set the size of the pane, simply use the `SetText` function to set the same text string for display in the pane. Finally, you enable the pane display by using the UI function `Enable`.

That's all it takes to add the time of day to the status bar. Now rebuild the new version of ErectorSet and see the new time display, as shown in Figure 12.10.

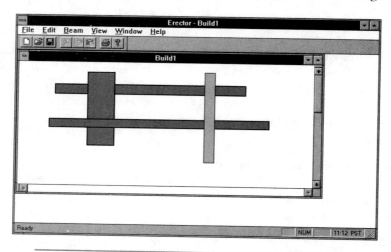

FIGURE 12.10 THE TIME IS NOW DISPLAYED ON THE ERECTORSET STATUS BAR.

SUMMARY

This completes the work of enhancing ErectorSet. This chapter has covered a variety of enhancements: adding persistent data to the application, using split windows, and adding an item to the status bar display. Each improvement is something you might want to do in any Windows application. The idea is to give you an introduction in how to find and use the classes and functions that MFC makes available. It takes time to fully understand the variety of classes in MFC, but there isn't much that you can't do if you put your mind and talent to work on it.

INDEX